SOUTH TO AMERICA

ALSO BY IMANI PERRY

Breathe: A Letter to My Sons

Looking for Lorraine: The Radiant and Radical Life of Lorraine Hansberry

May We Forever Stand: A History of the Black National Anthem

Vexy Thing: On Gender and Liberation

More Beautiful and More Terrible:

The Embrace and Transcendence of Racial Inequality in the United States

Prophets of the Hood: Politics and Poetics in Hip Hop

SOUTH
TO AMERICA

A JOURNEY BELOW *the* MASON-DIXON
to UNDERSTAND *the* SOUL *of a* NATION

IMANI PERRY

An Imprint of HarperCollins*Publishers*

HarperCollins books may be purchased for educational, business, or sales promotional use. For information, please email the Special Markets Department at SPsales@harpercollins.com.

Ecco® and HarperCollins® are trademarks of HarperCollins Publishers.

FIRST EDITION

Designed by Michelle Crowe

Library of Congress Cataloging-in-Publication Data

Names: Perry, Imani, 1972– author.
Title: South to America : a journey below the Mason-Dixon to understand
    the soul of a nation / Imani Perry.
Identifiers: LCCN 2021047476 (print) | LCCN 2021047477 (ebook) |
    ISBN 9780062977403 (hardcover) | ISBN 9780062977380 (ebook)
Subjects: LCSH: Perry, Imani, 1972—Travel—Southern States. | Southern States—
    Description and travel. | Southern States—Social life and Customs—
    21st century. | Southern States—Race relations.
Classification: LCC F216.2 .P47 2022 (print) | LCC F216.2 (ebook) |
    DDC 917.504—dc23
LC record available at https://lccn.loc.gov/2021047476
LC ebook record available at https://lccn.loc.gov/2021047477

23 24 25 26 27 LBC 11 10 9 8 7

For
Easter
Esther
Mary
and
Stace

The dance speaks to everyone. Otherwise, it wouldn't work.

—ALVIN AILEY

CONTENTS

A NOTE FROM THE AUTHOR

I HAVE LONG THOUGHT *BLACK*, in reference to people, should be capitalized. Finally, the style guides agree with me. But I also capitalize *White* in this book. That is less common. I do so because the categories, Black and White, were made together. They are strangely symbiotic, opposing yet intimate. Historically, *White* was a term reserved for those who could possibly be full citizens and members of the country. *Black* was for the "ultimate others" held down or at the margins. I also capitalize Indigenous, a people of many nations, named "Indian" by European error, who were colonized, expelled, robbed, and shuttered from their native lands. Generations have expanded and challenged the meanings of race that were created by colonialism. Nevertheless, in this country's history, *Black* and *White* have never been mere adjectives, and *Indigenous*, a global term, is specific in this nation. These are identity categories that were made by law, custom, policies, protest, economic relations, and perhaps most potently, culture. Politeness, grammar rules, and political pieties aside, this strikes me as a simple truth that ought to be acknowledged. I didn't make the rules. I am trying to tell them to you.

INTRODUCTION

A FRENCH QUADRILLE IS A DANCE of four couples. At certain moments all dancers take the same steps. Other times they pivot and turn against each other. They twist and curtsy in and out of unison. Music tailored to this set dance signals when to be still and when to glide. See how they separate and come back together? Train your eyes on *one* duo. See how they initiate and how they follow? You'll get lost if you try to look everywhere at once. You have to pay attention *somewhere* to understand the dance.

On January 24, 1804, there was a ball in New Orleans to celebrate the purchase of Louisiana. There had already been numerous celebratory balls, and as with the previous ones, some Spaniards came. Some French Creoles, too, White ones. And the Americans. Ladies' gowns were empire-waisted, peach, mango, pale blue, and green. The men's coats were embroidered elaborately. A fight broke out between two of them. Only five weeks into a shared citizenship, and the Americans were already encroaching too much. Yes, there were two French songs played to each English one, but the Americans took too long to finish a turn. Unlike the French quadrilles that started eight dancers at a time, in the American set dances, each couple went one by one. Their procession dragged on, past the length of the music. Someone called for "Another English song!" and a French Creole struck the speaker. An officer grabbed the Creole. The head of the provisional government, William C. C. Claiborne, saw the conflict brewing. He couldn't speak French or Spanish. His words of calm were empty. Several dozen men brawled in the ballroom.

Louisiana had just become part of this nation. And with that, the United States of America had doubled in size. But the local dancers were taking part in a negotiation that had an old root. It was called in some circles the "stately quadrille." As in the dance, the empires circled around each other, entering and exiting alliances, all while vying for control of land that had been conquered and claimed far away from their mother countries. New Orleans was a perfect example. It had been French, then Spanish, then French again, and now American. That night in New Orleans was three centuries after Europeans had arrived in the Americas. Generations into the process of settlement and conquest, slavery and incorporation, it was still contested territory.

The Africans danced quadrilles, too. Out of doors. In Congo Square on Sundays. And they did the calinda, hips shimmying until they touched a partner's, then easing back in unison. They did the bamboula, in a round. The women's head ties were as bright as they could be. Some hawked calas and popcorn. Some brought word of the revolution in Hayti. They were Virginians, Bajans, Bini, Edo, and Kongo. And native Orleanians. They danced to fiddles, on beat. On other days they danced to flogs, jumping away from searing pain. The Americans, White people, stood around the perimeter and watched. And learned.

A flock of black skimmers might have flown over the slave pens that night. Or rested there, callow jailbirds. How could they know their presence taunted, that the people inside wished they could fly? Or that the nights they were up, bodies rubbed with beef tallow, hair painted to gleaming black, faces scrubbed, had the most terrible foreboding? Sale tomorrow.

In 1839, Henry Bibb, with his wife and child, lived in a slave pen. Henry had what was called drapetomania: the psychiatric condition of repeatedly running away to freedom. The Bibbs were brought to New Orleans to be auctioned off. But there wasn't much interest from buyers. The trader, eager to be done with them, gave Henry a decent coat and allowed him to roam the streets, looking for someone to purchase him and his family.

He approached a man and asked, "Do you need a slave?" And mistaking Henry for one of those mixed-race Creoles with a tinge of Blackness but the privilege of property, the man replied, "Do you have one for sale?" Later, though, a better judge of Henry's station asked Henry in response, "Are you for sale?" He and his family made it out of the slave pens, together, and onto a plantation. A marginally better, if still terrible, fate. But a momentary relief turned disastrous. Deemed superior among slaves, Henry was bought to be an arm of the master. And when the master told Henry to rub salt brine into the torn, bleeding back of a whipped woman, she screamed. Henry wept. The point: I wish people wouldn't truncate history into romance. I mean, really, do you think that house slaves lived in ease? Do you think a "kindly master" was anything but an oxymoron? Witness the dance.

In this book about the US South, I can't begin at the beginning because there isn't one beginning to the United States. But it did begin in the South. When John Smith made the first British maps of Virginia, in 1607, aided by the Powhatan people, they were drawn from the perspective of a ship arriving from the Atlantic Ocean, through to the Chesapeake Bay. That was the path to bounty.

There are so many birth dates: 1492, 1520, 1619, 1776, 1804, 1865, 1954, 1964, 1965. The result now, after centuries, is a fractured American people: children of the colonized, colonizers, enslaved, marginal, poor, wealthy, exploitative, White, Black, shades of brown, citizens, and fugitives running from the law. People with jobs but no papers, people with papers but no door or mattress. The American way is what has been bequeathed to us all in unequal measure. The United States is, formally speaking, the child of Great Britain. And we teachers, historians, and patriots all have inherited a British inclination to tell history in a linear forward sequence. But that just won't work for the story of the South. Or the nation.

Quadrilles are rare, novelties these days. But regardless, the metaphor still applies. When it comes to the choreography, most folks are lost. They think they know the South's moves. They believe the region is out of step, off rhythm, lagging behind, stumbling. It is a convenient misunderstanding. This country was made with the shame of slavery, poverty, and White supremacy blazoned across it as a badge of dishonor. To sustain a heroic self-concept, it has inevitably been deemed necessary to distance "America" from the embarrassment over this truth. And so the South, the seat of race in the United States, was turned on, out, and into this country's gully.

An 1860 political cartoon titled "The Political Quadrille: Music by Dred Scott" has Scott, the enslaved Black man who sued for his freedom, and who lost before the Supreme Court, playing the fiddle in the center of four couples. In one corner, John Breckinridge, vice president and soon-to-be Confederate general, and President James Buchanan, a man who sought to keep the sectional peace, are dance partners. Abraham Lincoln is with a grinning Black woman in another, apparently already marked as an abolitionist and a "Negro"-lover despite his ambivalence about slavery and slaves. Stephen Douglas, the "whole hog" Democrat and slaveholder who was defeated by Lincoln, holds the arm of an Irishman. And John Bell, a Tennessean who believed in moderation when it came to national expansion, dances—both hands clasped—with a Native American man. Each image is a somewhat grotesque caricature. And it is funny to think of Dred Scott, who Chief Justice Taney said was not only unfree but had "no rights which a white man was bound to respect," as the composer. But I suppose it made sense to see him, undeniably Black, at the center of the maneuvering.

Race is at the heart of the South, and at the heart of the nation. Like the conquest of Indigenous people, the creation of racial slavery in the colonies was a gateway to habits and dispositions that ultimately became the commonplace ways of doing things in this country. They came to a head at the dawn of the Civil War, only to settle back into the old routines for a hundred years before reaching a fever pitch again before receding.

On January 6, 2021, the Confederate flag was raised aloft in Senate chambers, a potent event. It was a reminder that we live in an ice-cold, ever-chilling civil war. It was a specific horror, but not unprecedented. From the beginning, this nation was experimental and innovative as well as invasive. Resourceful even. But any virtues were distorted by a greater driver: unapologetic greed, which legitimized violent conquest and captivity. This is the American habitus. We are in awe at the sublime natural landscape and then use up its abundance into oblivion. We are primed to be destroyers with a disregard for the moral, human, and environmental costs of it all. We are a nation that stratifies, often putting the people who build and sustain it at the bottom. Among us, there are citizens, second-class citizens, noncitizens, and those who are cast so far beneath every other category that it is as though they are seen as nonpersons. Although these habits are not *all* directly about race, race remains the most dramatic light switch of the country and its sorting. And yet "racism," despite all evidence of its ubiquity, is still commonly described as "belonging" to the South. I don't just mean that other regions ignore their racism and poverty and project them onto the South, although that is certainly true. I also mean that the cruelest labor of sustaining the racial-class order was historically placed upon the South. Its legacy of racism then is of course bloodier than most. But other regions are also bloody in deed. Discrimination is everywhere, but collectively the country has leeched off the racialized exploitation of the South while also denying it.

You've seen the footage, hazy and menacing, of "Colored" and "White" signs on fountains and waiting rooms: they are among the most potent visual symbols of the South. Two statuses, one America—that's how the founders and legislatures and judges crafted this country. And the South totes that water. But the truth is that the South, like every region of the United States, has never been a place where there are only two "races." Others have always been there. Sometimes, with respect to status, they have been cast just below White people. Other times they've been cast alongside Black people. Regardless they've always been precariously situated and expelled from the South by law and policy, and also in memory. Remember, the Deep South was made at a crossroads between the lust for cotton and the theft of Indigenous land. It was a tandem movement. The aftermath is a ghostlike presence: place-names, landmarks, and only tiny communities where numerous nations once belonged. Spanish and French are centuries-old Southern languages, even if their speakers are recent immigrants. Indigenous, European, and African people appear and reappear in different configurations over the past five hundred years. Chinese Mississippians have been making a home in the Deep South for 150 years, and a larger Asian diaspora finds common grounds with Southern ways in setting up corner stores and living on waterfronts as well as in the professions and higher education. The repetition of a cruel "You don't belong" as response resonates back to the legal cases in the early twentieth century. They said South Asians, East Asians, and Middle Eastern Asians could not be classified as White, nor become citizens. Even though anthropologists claimed Whiteness was a bigger category than European, their professional judgment didn't carry much weight. The truth is race is a fiction, and Blackness is at the heart of the making of the South. But it is no privilege. That gift belongs to Whiteness and whoever it chose and chooses to embrace. Whiteness is not only domineering. It has also been fickle.

The consequence of the projection of national sins, and specifically racism, onto one region is a mis-narration of history and American identity. The consequence of truncating the South and relegating it to a backwards corner is a misapprehension of its power in American history. Paying attention to the South—its past, its dance, its present, its threatening future, and most of all how it moves the rest of the country about—allows us to understand much more about our nation, and about how our people, land, and commerce work in relation to one another, often cruelly, and about how our tastes and ways flow from our habits. I try to explain, but I am impious in my movements. I passed over many famous places and lingered in unusual ones. I was fascinated and sometimes furious at the sons of the Confederacy. I love my people without apology. My son Issa has warned me about the danger of making things *look* too beautiful. To *be* beautiful, it must be truthful. And the truth is often ugly. But it's funny, too. And strange. Also morbid. This is a collection, but it is also an excision, a pruning like we might do to a plant in order to extend its life. Most of all, please remember, while this book is not a history, it is a true story.

I

ORIGIN STORIES

AN ERRAND INTO WILDERNESS

Appalachia

THE MAN CALLED THE "EMPEROR OF NEW YORK" was also known as Shields Green. He was born into slavery in South Carolina. As a free adult, he met John Brown at the home of Frederick Douglass in Rochester, New York. Inspired by the firebrand White abolitionist, the Emperor joined Brown's raid at Harper's Ferry, Virginia. On December 16, 1859, like Brown, he was executed as punishment.

There isn't much in the way of documentation of Green's life. For example, we don't know why he was called Emperor, much less of New York. We don't know whether to trust contemporaries who described him as incomprehensible, disagreeable, and "very" illiterate. More certain is the fact that he had "a Congo face," meaning dark skin. He was small of stature and muscular. According to Douglass, he had a speech impediment: "[H]e was a man of few words, and his speech was singularly broken, but his courage and self-respect made him quite a dignified character." We also know that George Washington's great-nephew Lewis was his hostage and found the Emperor's bearing absolutely intolerable for a Black man. The Emperor was tried for treason, an impossible crime for a Black man to commit given that he wasn't a citizen by law. He was executed anyway.

Although Frederick Douglass had introduced Green and Brown, he didn't join the raid. Brown wanted Douglass to agree to be the president of the provisional government he was planning. Douglass declined. He considered Brown's plan a suicide mission. He was right. Harriet Tubman reportedly said no to Brown's invitation because she was ill. That was either a bit of fortuitousness or wisdom. At any rate, the whole group that stormed the arsenal was brought to submission quickly. They succeeded in killing the mayor of Harper's Ferry, but not many more than that. Brown's vision of a mass insurrection of Black people streaming in to join the fight didn't materialize until the Civil War.

Although Green was reported to have had a son in South Carolina, his dead body was not claimed by, nor granted to, family. Instead, he was dissected at Winchester Medical College. The lack of consent from an heir—the fact that he, a freedom fighter, would be put back into physical service for White men after death—was a cruel twist. Unspeakable acts were performed on a personage whose story was left, in the main, unspoken.

What remained intact after the deaths of Brown, Green, and the others were pikes. Brown had had the weapons made for Black people, who, due to prohibitions on their possessing firearms, hadn't learned to shoot. He'd warehoused the pikes in Maryland in preparation for the revolt. They were steel-headed blades fitted onto six-foot ash handles, and soon became collector's items. Several years later, in 1863, actual firearms would be placed in Black people's hands as they saved the Union, served the Union Army, and freed themselves.

There are a few words, however, from John Copeland, the other Black man executed on the same day as Green, a companion in the raid. He was literate and from Oberlin, Ohio. He wrote a prayer to his family "that you may prepare your souls to meet your God that so, in the end, though we meet no more on earth, we shall meet in heaven, where we shall not be parted by the demands of the cruel and unjust monster Slavery."

I decided to go to West Virginia. And I threatened to go a bunch of times before I went. I guess I was scared, and people's reactions to me stating my intentions didn't help any. Eyebrows raised. Eyes got wide. I could see night-riding Klansmen dancing in their minds' eyes. I had been to West Virginia before, but folks warning "Don't go there alone" made me especially nervous in the Trump era.

At any rate, Harpers Ferry seemed like the safest place to begin in mountain country. While West Virginia, which used to be Virginia, and which became West Virginia because it was anti-slavery territory, has succumbed to the worst of Whiteness, according to everyday scuttlebutt and assumption, I imagined Harpers Ferry, scene of Brown's raid, wouldn't be worrisome.

I drove in on a spring day as I was having an argument in my head with the historian Tony Horwitz. I'd read many books about the South, and my direct inspiration for this one from the beginning was Albert Murray's *South to a Very Old Place*, a 1971 travel narrative that captured the changes, consistencies, and sensibilities of the region of our shared birth. I'd also been influenced by non-natives, like V. S. Naipaul, who published *A Turn in the South* in 1989, and descendants of the region like James Baldwin, who described the South as his homeland. But Tony Horwitz left me unsettled. I'd met him once in person when I was inducted to the Society of American Historians and had experienced him as a completely delightful person. But when we met, I hadn't yet read *Confederates in the Attic*. I finally read it when I was starting to work on this book, and found myself unsettled. My chief complaint was that I thought he was too sympathetic with the Confederate reenactors who were his subject. He seemed mostly unfazed by their casual "lost cause" bigotry, and although I understood that was what allowed him to get close to his subjects, I still didn't much like it. And, I noted, the one person who he seemed to actively take issue with was my friend Kindaka's mother, Rose Sanders, a longtime civil rights attorney and organizer in Selma, Alabama, because he found her Black nationalism disconcerting. Horwitz told the story of their argument in detail, and I felt irate for her. How could he, I thought, care so much about understanding what made Confederate reenactors tick and disregard how for the Black Southerner the noose of Whiteness can elicit passionate rage and refusal? It is a wonder that hate isn't what drips from our tongues daily. Our equanimity by most objective accounts would read as foolhardy. Why couldn't he see that, even from his vantage point, embedded with the Confederates? He had died before I had a chance to ask any of it.

I also thought, along my West Virginia drive, that unlike Horwitz, because I'm Black, I would never be able to access the minds of those who hold on to the Confederacy. Like my forebearers, who couldn't enter libraries and had to build bodies of knowledge by hook or by crook, I couldn't get inside the Confederate's head. That was a part of the Southern story I would be prohibited from telling. Even if I tried, I just knew that they'd be steely and resentful of my prodding. But I understood another side of Southern history with ease: resistance to the slave-based society. I would offer another kind of Southern story.

Harpers Ferry is a historical chiasmus. In school, we learn how slavery was heroically defeated. Harpers Ferry was a precipitant. In Harpers Ferry, we learn of a hero's defeat by the forces of a slave society. It is the main event. The flip is all the more pointed because of the political history and public memory of the South. Many in the region haven't ever really accepted the loss of the Civil War, or perhaps more accurately, The South is on a recurring loop of cold Civil War battles that repeatedly bend towards the logic of the slavocracy. Even now, with some Confederate monuments toppled, many—literal and symbolic—remain. They are evident in the crowing about states' rights and gun rights, efforts to disenfranchise

Black voters, and desperate attempts to keep the world's puppet strings in the hands of elite White Americans. Ironically, then, like places throughout the South, Harpers Ferry is a monument to the defeated. Only here the defeated are wild-eyed radical abolitionist John Brown and his companions, and *not* the Confederate dead.

West Virginia seceded from Virginia over the question of slavery. It was foundationally anti-slavery. As the poet Nikki Giovanni once described it in an interview: "I think that when you look at the great history of Appalachia, we know that the Civil War . . . would have been lost if West Virginia had not broken up, then Virginia would have gone over to the Ohio River. It would have changed the war. So in many, many respects, West Virginia saved the nation." So maybe, I speculated, standing on John Brown's side of the dance between Southern defeat and victory was the perfect way to ease into West Virginia and Appalachia, as subject and territory.

Fact and fiction collide at the site because the reenactment and rebuilding are so precise. After parking, I walked up to the pristine train depot entrance and knocked, expecting the man I saw inside to open the window and describe the exhibition to me. He pointed to my right. I then went to the next door and pulled. Inside was just a regular train station with some historic details preserved. Oh. I wandered into town. It was active but not bustling. The place is earth-toned. All over, shades of tan and pine, deepening into mahogany with snatches of pale gray and charcoal. When you face it, shielded by teeming green flora to your back, it looks like what you think of the Old West based upon movie stills. Harpers Ferry is like a campus. On its map, you can trace the course of the raid with a finger. The men overran the arsenal under the cover of night and by morning they were surrounded. Brown went to the gallows first.

"I, John Brown, am now quite certain that the crimes of this guilty land will never be purged away but by blood"—his last words before execution were recorded, and, as has often been noted, they were prophetic. But they were also only partly true. Certain crimes were ceased by the Civil War, but they have not been purged. Not yet.

Harpers Ferry is shaped like a seal head, with the Potomac River above, the Shenandoah below. The tip of the nose is where Maryland, Virginia, and West Virginia meet. At this crossroads, in 1866, fresh from the disaster of the war, Black people came together in homage to Brown and built a one-room schoolhouse for freedpeople, called Storer. It grew into a degree-granting four-year historically Black college. There is a small exhibition about the establishment of Storer College and subsequent events.

In 1906, after the promises of Reconstruction had been denied, and Jim Crow had settled across the South, members of the Niagara movement gathered at Storer College. This was the second meeting of the racial justice organization. Its leaders, W. E. B. Du Bois and William Monroe Trotter, were influential Black intellectuals. But everyone there was in some way distinguished. At the gathering, Bishop Reverdy C. Ransom, a socialist pastor, spoke to the group about the spirit of John Brown, saying:

> He felt the breath of God upon his soul and was strangely moved. He was imbued with the spirit of the Declaration of Independence and clearly saw that slavery was incompatible with a free republic. He could not reconcile the creed of the slaveholder with the word of God.

Ransom went on to indict the nation for failing to meet John Brown's call, even after the devastation of the Civil War: "The Negro regards the Democratic party as his traditional and hereditary foe. Tradition, gratitude and sentiment bind him to the Republican party with an idolatrous allegiance which is as blind as it is unpatriotic and unreasoning. TODAY THERE IS VERY LITTLE DIFFERENCE BETWEEN THE TWO PARTIES AS FAR AS THEIR

ATTITUDE TOWARD THE NEGRO IS CONCERNED." His words about Democrats and Republicans are inverted today, but still commonplace: the Republican is foe to Black people; the Democrats possess Black loyalty notwithstanding their neglect of those most loyal constituents. That we live with that same binary is more than ironic.

John Brown, according to the men gathered at Harpers Ferry in honor of him, was a hero, and he had the kind of imagination that made it possible to envision freedom. Perhaps that had something to do with the landscape. Ransom said, "From a child he loved to dwell beneath the open sky. The many voices of the woods, and fields, and mountains, spoke to him a familiar language. He understood the habits of plants and animals, of birds and trees and flowers . . ." A gentleness of spirit is hard for me to imagine in John Brown given his image as a wildman for freedom. But then again, the beauty might have softened him.

The photographs of the Niagara movement members, in their three-piece suits and mutton-sleeve blouses, looking so genteel, are deceptive. A gathering of this sort was always dangerous. People were lynched for much less. The Niagara movement, though not taking up arms, was radical in its time. As measured and intellectual as their pursuits were, such work was driven by a passion that was more often than not punished.

As with many HBCUs, Storer was once a high school in addition to a college. The first president of postcolonial Nigeria, Nnamdi Azikiwe, completed his high school education at Storer before going on to Howard University. I tried to imagine—with some difficulty—the brilliant and fiery African revolutionary leader up here in the West Virginia mountains. Mostly, I wondered how he experienced this brand of Whiteness that in its speech patterns and sartorial details was not like that of British colonists, yet just as insistent upon superiority. Did he contemplate the trees, just as green as in Nigeria, but full of leaves that spiked out rather than arched? Did he ache with loneliness? Though Azikiwe is mentioned in the Storer College exhibit, there isn't much discussion of his time or reflections about what it meant for a man who became so great out *there* to have been a Black boy *here*.

Maybe I am projecting too much onto the place, keeping myself from seeing it fully. Maybe there is nothing unusual about a leader of African independence studying math, running a pawnshop, and being a coal miner in Appalachia. After all, Martin Delany, one of the fathers of Black nationalism, was himself from West Virginia. He said, "It is only in the mountains that I can fully appreciate my existence as a man in America, and my own native land." "Native land" had by then, even for those who eventually returned to Liberia like Delany, a remote and aspirational quality. But he knew the mountains.

Storer—which, according to the exhibition signage, was one of three historically Black colleges in West Virginia—was closed after the *Brown v. Board of Education* ruling in 1954. Its Blackness violated the prohibition of segregation. The other two are still open today, but have tiny numbers of Black students in attendance. I stood in the room alone. The silence was eerie.

The terseness of history is hard to endure for long. So I took a walk. I stepped along the Shenandoah, under the heavy iron of a bridge. There were outdoor exhibition signs along the way that began to blur for me. Flood, rebuilding, flood again. I grew tired thinking about how that cycle of re-creation and destruction had variations all over the South. Even the gently rushing water wore at me. Wandering more, I made my way to a general store. Inside, the register didn't seem to be in operation. It looked authentic and very old. Dried fish hung from a wire above me, sweet-smelling barrels surrounded us, and glass jars lined the walls. I figured it was an artifactual place. But then I wondered, was this all newly made stuff to make you feel like it was back then, or were these actual artifacts?

"Can I ask you a question?"

"Ask now, 'cause I'm fixing to go to lunch."

That's how my conversation with a real live Confederate reen-actor began. And I realized that in the argument I'd waged in my head, with Horwitz and with history, I was wrong. I could, in fact, talk to a Confederate soldier.

I'll call the Confederate Bob. It was his birthday. Harpers Ferry was where he wanted to spend it. So he took the day off from his job in Washington, DC, as an archivist, work that he described as a "prison sentence," and came to volunteer at Harpers Ferry, some-thing he'd been doing his whole adult life. Hailing from what I have heard Marylanders call "out in the county," Bob was a part of a Maryland regiment. Armed with what Tony Horwitz had written, I asked informed questions about "Farbs," the people who are not authentic reenactors. Bob spoke with proud criticism but also ad-dressed the hardships of authenticity. Take his eyeglasses, for ex-ample: "I was once called out 'cause my glasses weren't authentic. It cost me $400 to get 'em right, and that was way back in the '80s, to get real Civil War–era glasses. They were so thick, you couldn't hardly see out of 'em anyway." His frock coat had cost a pretty penny, too, and though he didn't have it with him, he described it in such detail that I could visualize it. The ground, as I learned from Tony's book, was uncomfortable to sleep on, but the camaraderie and archives of knowledge that it took to get things as close to real as possible were thrilling.

He told me he'd been visiting Harpers Ferry all his life. The ac-cent fell on "all." And as an adult he volunteered all year round, even when the snow was piled up so high you could hardly get in or out. As skeptical as I was of why anyone would want to playact at pre-serving slavery, I was endeared to him. He was friendly. Also, I was intrigued by him: this was a man who had advanced degrees and a job that satisfied his passion for history. But something made him yearn for more. He wanted to live inside history, to know its nooks and crannies, to imagine the everyday. A lot of art comes from rural places, even if that's not where it gets distributed, because it is fertile ground for the imagination. I think maybe reenactment should be described as a performance art, even if I am still uneasy about the pleasure it provides.

We talked for a good hour, as people came in and out, eyeing us curiously. I suppose we made an odd pair. Eventually he really did have to get to lunch. He was getting a free meal for his birthday. Next year, he said, he would turn sixty and expected a ticker tape parade.

I laughed and felt a twinge of sadness. I wondered if his dislike of DC was not really about his work but about it being a chocolate city or the seat of government, or both—basically two faces of disdain that could both be about Blackness, one over demographics and the other over the right-wing commonplace "The government does too much for the Blacks." He'd started out curt with me. But I hadn't really challenged him. I spoke to him earnestly. And I watched him relax. I'd decided to maintain the easy tenor of our conversation out of curiosity but also in an effort to create and keep the peace. I was vaguely ashamed of that. I didn't ask him why he wanted to be a Confederate, even though he was here at Harpers Ferry all the time, the place known for one of the greatest White allies to the cause of Black freedom.

I wondered, did Bob face down Black soldiers on the battlefield? If so, did he see nothing but a blur of Black, no faces, no features? Confederates didn't take Black soldiers prisoner. They killed every one of them they could.

I didn't ask him about being a Confederate because I didn't want to hear what I thought would probably come: talk about Northern aggression and heritage, apologetics for the violence of a slave society, tales of loyal Black people. It wasn't that he wouldn't allow me to dig; it was that my spirit, generations tired, didn't want to. I met a reenactor, and we had a detailed conversation despite my expectation. That was good. And yet I realized I felt something deeper without an agenda, just being alongside mountain folks at stops on the road to and from Harpers Ferry in Gatlinburg, or down in Charleston. It was something less detailed and more impressionistic but ultimately more profound.

Like this: Stop at a Walmart late at night. Sometimes a person jonesing or tweaking looks you dead in your eyes and smiles a little bit with ashamed courteousness if you aren't a reporter asking them to spill their guts. Sometimes you walk behind a man with his hair plastered to the back of his head, dirty blond, and he's fussing with his girlfriend and the cursing sounds more like frustration than anger. Sometimes, a mama saying that the children "ain't getting nothing" is meant to sound disciplinary, but it comes out sad by mistake. Somebody has bad teeth. It's more a sign of social neglect than failed hygiene. You might think about the blood streaming from his mouth, and how the ever-present bad taste and the feeling of bloating around each tooth can make a person especially miserable when there's nothing to do about it. When the dead tooth finally falls out, it might be a relief.

Walking, close to midnight, in the Walmart, with that insistent sickly blue brightness against the dark outside that turns everyone sallow and shows every crevice and caked sore, is a lesson in the loneliness of poverty that was born in the shadow of prosperity. And I, a Black woman witness, am unremarkable in every aisle. No one does a double take. In proximity, though my body is always raced, my presence is not alarming. We are all regular folks in a regular place, presumed to be "scuffling," as my grandmother would say, through life.

I wasn't able to reconcile the distance I felt in conversation and this silent intimacy in proximity. So I went deeper into an archive of historical memory, hoping to sort it out. Admittedly, it proved to be at best an imperfect autopsy.

In 1839, Washington Irving declared his dislike for the name of the nation. "America" was inadequate. Irving, known for classic

American stories "The Legend of Sleepy Hollow" and "Rip Van Winkle," wondered why we should have a country named after an Italian explorer. He wrote:

> I want an appellation that shall tell at once, and in a way not to be mistaken, that I belong to this very portion of America, geographical and political, to which it is my pride and happiness to belong; that I am of the Anglo-Saxon race which founded this Anglo-Saxon empire in the wilderness . . .

The impressive mountain terrain mattered to him as well.

> We have it in our power to furnish ourselves with such a national appellation, from one of the grand and eternal features of our country; from that noble chain of mountains which formed its back-bone, and ran through the "old confederacy," when it first declared our national independence. I allude to the Appalachian or Alleghany mountains. We might do this without any very inconvenient change in our present titles. We might still use the phrase, "The United States," substituting Appalachia or Alleghania, (I should prefer the latter), in place of America . . .

Edgar Allan Poe agreed, in part:

> There should be no hesitation about "Appalachia." In the first place, it is distinctive. "America" is not [a distinctive name] . . . South America is "America," and will insist upon remaining so.

Poe thought claiming the Indigenous name "Appalachia" might be some recompense for Indigenous people who had been "unmer-

cifully despoiled, assassinated and dishonored." But Poe disagreed
that "Alleghania" was preferable:

> The last, and by far the most truly important consideration
> of all, however, is the music of "Appalachia" itself; nothing
> could be more sonorous, more liquid, or of fuller volume,
> while its length is just sufficient for dignity. How the gut-
> tural "Alleghania" could ever have been preferred for a mo-
> ment is difficult to conceive. I yet hope to find "Appalachia"
> assumed.

It is, but not in the way Poe imagined it, not in terms of being
taken on. Assumed in the false security of knowing what happens
down there.

Poe, Massachusetts-born, was adopted and reared by Virginians. More than anywhere, he is associated with Baltimore, that
interstitial space, Southern and yet not. With his attraction to the
gothic and sublime horror, however, he reads as a Southern writer.
It is unsurprising that he found the mountain range that reaches
from up North deep into the US South to be an apt expression of
this country. Appalachia is a vast territory. Its natural resources fueled the nation's growth in the industrial age. Its beauty awed early
settlers. My own ancestors and family in northern Alabama and
northwestern South Carolina were Appalachian geographically. But
"Appalachia," as we use the word, tends to be understood mostly as
a cultural region, centered lower than New York but farther north
than Alabama. This symbolism is both the dream and the evasion.
At once the fantasy and shame of the republic. A South, at least
imagined, without Blackness.

There is a dissonance between the romance Poe and Irving had
for the region, and how it is commonly described. Shame, horror,
and humor are cast upon Appalachia. It is the Whitest region of the
South and among the poorest, plagued by failed American dreams.

Whether or not people use the distasteful pejorative "trash," they often imply and apply it to the people here. But maybe the inconsistency between the romance of the region, heroically rendered by Davy Crockett, and the shaming of lean and stick-straight-haired mountain people can be reconciled with the reality that Americans love underdogs. We like stories about frontierspeople and tough living against the odds. Even under the mocking taunts about inbred cousins, feuds, and rednecks, there lies a fantastical admiration for Appalachia's folk heroes, including miners and subsistence farmers. We have a love affair with the sound of the bluegrass singer yodeling into the night. His voice is labor, faith, and fight. In marvelous contradiction, the mountains represent the heart of American romanticism, that tradition of writing, art, and music in which vast emotions are yoked to awe-inspiring nature, and disaster is the condition of a natural nobility. Heroism becomes a kind of prison.

James Robert Reese, a linguist, argues that Appalachians are thought of not as "actual people who reside in the same world," but as "mythic personages who represent a way of life incompatible with the essential, rational, everyday mode of behavior" that we expect from the American mainstream. Take, for example, the bad multigenerational joke that "inbreeding" is the cause of their spectacular moral failure and grotesqueness, and a reason why Appalachians are "not quite right." There is plenty of genetic research to debunk that pernicious rumor. Still it sticks. The contradiction has everything to do with Whiteness and class. Appalachians, White ones, can be used to tell the story of conquering nature. Armed with only Whiteness, they can be the Americans facing the wild. However, they, Southern and isolated, can also be convenient repositories for shameful Whiteness—virulently racist, backwards, and unsophisticated.

There's a historical event that haunts and shames the region. And shows the machine of power. The story is about a boy named George. George was owned by Lilburn Lewis, the nephew of Thomas Jefferson, in the Kentucky mountains. In 1812, a cherished water pitcher slipped from the fifteen-year-old George's hands, and it shattered. In a drunken rage, Lilburn and his brother tied George to the floor of the kitchen and told the other slaves to build a fire. They did and cowered. The master struck George across the neck with an ax, then commanded one of his fellow slaves to cut him up dead. Bit by bit, George's body was burned in the fireplace. As his body burned and blackened, an earthquake hit in the middle of the night. The chimney collapsed, snuffing the fire.

All through the following day, aftershocks kept coming. Walls cracked; buildings tumbled. They could not keep a fire going long enough to disappear George. Parts of his body remained intact, and so they hastened to bury them. But with the succession of more earthquakes over the coming weeks, the body kept being unearthed. A dog even brought George's skull to the main street.

This drew the attention of townspeople, who soon found out what happened. Disgrace fell on the family. The Lewis brothers, who were supposed to be gentlemen, were revealed to be excessively violent. One died by suicide; the other disappeared. The horror of killing is something the Lewis brothers could live with; the shame of that skull coming back up and up, they could not. They were of the planter class, not commoners. Shame was not supposed to be theirs.

The trill of history: On the surface, Lewises were genteel and grace-filled figures, maybe flawed but noble. Underneath them, the ones who labored were uncouth, rough, maybe only part human or maybe horrifically debased. The myth of surface gentlemanliness was a sly fiction then; it is certainly understood as a loud fiction now. But still, we don't hold it up to the light nearly enough. Gentlemen were not gentlemen at all.

Elites owning enslaved people who performed domestic service was one part of Appalachian history. But industry was the greater part. It was ungentlemanly, too. Or, depending on how you see it, it was a classic structure of how gentlemen ruled. In Appalachian industrial life, the bosses would reap the benefits of coal through the labors of the soot-covered White folks and the unburied Black folks. It sometimes erupted into disaster. That terrible shared heritage, I think, was the source of silences between me and Bob. Start talking too nakedly and all kinds of things have to come up. That's why I chose to be witness more than interlocutor.

Being a Black American requires double consciousness, in the words of W. E. B. Du Bois, the habit of seeing from inside the logic of race and the lives of the racialized, and from the external superego of what it means to be American, with all its archetypes and interests. Inside Harpers Ferry, I experienced a carefully maintained history. It was authentic and yet controlled. But there is a wild haunting just beyond its borders.

History, out of order, is a dizzying assortment of things: chain stores, cheap goods, luxury resorts, hungry suffering people, hardworking people, venomous people and generous ones.

So many people live in the ruins of the American drive for prosperity. The residual mining towns are evidence. If you tell a story about the American worker in the twentieth century, you have to talk about the miner, Appalachia's heroic archetype. Coal was the something indispensable for the industrial revolution. It is one of the most impactful fossil fuels in the history of the world. In the sediment, dark brown or black, rich in carbon, it is unearthed and used up, nonrenewable, and yet this nation won't stop feasting on it.

Coal-mining innovations kept coming over the nineteenth and twentieth centuries. Picks and shovels gave way to wheelbarrows, mules, and oxen. Electricity in the last decade of the nineteenth century displaced animals, and in the twentieth century the work was mechanized: trains, belts, shuttles. But still, with all that, laborers were necessary. And they made their way deep into the earth to feed the nation's desires for comfort.

Coal companies built towns for workers and their families. Theirs was an isolated and organized life. Miners were poor folks who usually stayed poor no matter how hard they worked. The company store kept the books, placing them in crippling debt even though they were the ones whose labor made others rich and gave light and heat to the country.

Mining is disabling. It injures, permanently. Eyes grow rheumy from the lack of light. Bodies are beaten by cramping and lifting and the unrelenting exertion. Today coal mining is a dying industry when it comes to workers. Conservative politicians make promises of revival that simply aren't possible. The tops are blasted off the mountains now without hand-to-rock-wall labor. The jobs have dwindled. And yet miners, historically speaking, continue to be the subject of lore and, presently speaking, are completely neglected by the rest of the nation.

One piece of earned heroism is the miners' place at the center of our history of organized labor. Miners understood their importance to industrialization and would become central figures in the history of unions. One of the most impactful strikes happened at Matewan, West Virginia. In West Virginia the word "Matewan" is written along the highway in white italics over green roadside markers. It is one way West Virginia announces itself. Matewan is a story that has also been recounted repeatedly in history and film, a hero's tale.

In the spring of 1920, the miners in Matewan went on strike to have their union recognized. They'd been inspired by famous organizer Mother Jones, and fueled by being overworked and underpaid. Guards from a private detective agency called Baldwin-Felts, which was working on behalf of Stone Mountain coal company, came to evict the miners from their homes. They did so, with a break for dinner in between the displacements. Done for the day, they went to catch an evening train out of town. But the guards were stopped by the Matewan chief of police, who said he had warrants for the guards' arrest. Chief Hatfield sided with the miners against the bosses. The Baldwin-Felts agents claimed to have a warrant for Hatfield's arrest from the mayor.

As the conflict developed, miners, all of them armed, watched the standoff, surrounding the police and the agents. A gunfight, the details of which are disputed, ensued. It left ten dead, most of them agents of the Baldwin-Felts company.

The governor tried to take control of the town, but the miners were not willing to back down. They went on another strike in July. And all hell broke loose. Explosives were attached to railroad cars; miners were beaten near to death. The company agents came back to kill the chief of police and his deputy. This is but one of many such events in mining history, a face-off between the haves and the laboring have nots. The miners created tent cities and their movement grew. In 1921, these union men battled the bosses from Blair Mountain. Finally, in an event famous in labor history, the miners were quelled by a threat from the federal government, which was planning to bomb them out.

Blackness added another layer to the story. Historically, Black miners were assigned to the edges of town and less lucrative work. Mining work has always been dangerous as well as excessively demanding. Some of the worst industry-related incidents around the globe have been mining disasters. In West Virginia, this includes the one at Hawks Nest. When the conflict didn't get you, the labor would. And Black people were got most.

The year was 1930. Workers were charged with building a three-mile tunnel through Gauley Mountain. The tunnel was planned to divert water to a hydroelectric plant that would produce electricity for metal production. Hundreds of men were recruited for the work. A majority of them were Black.

They drilled and blasted through the mountain, and white dust billowed through the air and into every orifice of the workers' bodies. Their eye sockets went dry, their airways were irritated, and their skin and clothes were covered in chalky white from head to toe. They did not have masks. There was very little air as they worked through the mountain.

Soon the sickness came. The officials called it "tunnelitis." It was, in fact, silicosis. That dust settled in the lungs and strangled. The men simply couldn't work anymore. Many returned to the homes from which they'd migrated, farther south. Upwards of seven hundred men of the nearly three thousand who worked in the tunnel died. That's an estimate. None of the departed were counted, though many, it is speculated, were left to die or died along the way home.

There was no Black cemetery in that mountain town. So the Black dead were buried alongside one another in an open field. There they rested until another building project years into the future meant they would be dug up and interred again elsewhere. Kill them, throw them away, dig them up, repeat. Remember that choreography.

People who live in coal country didn't and don't have to suffer through a disaster like Hawks Nest to experience the ravages of the industry. The whole endeavor is dangerous to the air, the drinking water, everything with a face, and the flora. As Tennessee Ernie Ford sang, "You load sixteen tons, and what do you get? Another day older and deeper in debt. St. Peter, don't you call me 'cause I can't go. I owe my soul to the company store . . ."

The miners who went on strike again and again would insist that the world knew all the innovation and skyscraping wealth of the country rested at least in part on their digging deeper into the earth. These stories of mining, of the arduous work and the struggle for rights, are fascinating in part because law is an unsettled matter in them. Who was in charge, and who should be in charge, was often unclear. Where national solidarity would exist, and with whom, was also a challenge.

The challenges faced by miners are local. But the resistance of miners can be mapped all over the globe. Nnamdi Azikiwe was a miner in West Virginia, and as an activist in Nigeria, he stood with miners against colonial authorities. One of the most important global throughlines of the twentieth century is that of exploited workers demanding their due. Another is, as Du Bois put it, the problem of the color line. In mountain country, these two legacies clashed. Poor and working-class White Americans were taught that if they expressed solidarity with Black people, also exploited, also laboring hard, they'd lose what Du Bois termed "the wages of whiteness," those benefits that went along with not being at the bottom of the social hierarchy. It is well established that poor and working-class White people have hoped to gain something from Whiteness—and yet also have a complaint with the way it excludes them from all the status it promised.

The consequence has been that the moments of class solidarity across the lines of race were fleeting in US history. And now, when politicians use "working class" to mean White people rather than the whole working class, they extend a terrible distortion. But still, what *should* be matters as much as what is. History orients us and magnifies our present circumstance.

The postindustrial United States, in which we have shifted to a service economy in which workers don't produce goods but provide services to others, has been a hard transition for the American working class. I think the commonly reported resentment about American companies outsourcing work to Asia is a result of both frustration and envy. Somewhere else, someone has been given the work of usefulness, of creating things that make the engine of the country possible. Disregarding the horrific terms of that labor— sweatshops and debt—is easy in a place where slaves were once similarly hated competition.

Today, in the absence of mining work, and with limited options besides service jobs, some fugitive labor has come into the picture for mountain folks. Having a hustle outside the law isn't new. Up here is where a lot of the good liquor was first made. Moonshine runners were popular during Prohibition. Long after alcohol was restored to legality, some folks still preferred the taste of illegally produced home brew. Mountain Dew soda, the most excessively sweet drink you can think of, is called that after moonshine, mastered in mountain country. Their first bottles had a picture of a hillbilly on them. You can even watch reality shows these days that show you how people called hillbillies still make moonshine. It has a fresh, brighter, and antiseptic taste compared to manufactured liquors. The scent leaps up sharp and slightly yeasty out of the bottle rather than with a smooth rise. At least that's true of the kind I've had. Even if people didn't prefer the taste, after Prohibition ended, the fact that 'shine is tax-free sells it, too. Also, drinking hooch is a flirtation with danger, and not just because it's illegal but because if the kitchen distiller who makes it doesn't know what they're doing, you could end up dead from partaking. I wonder, can we see that these are Davy Crockett's grandchildren, heirs to the king of the wild frontier who could shoot a gun and split a bullet in half on an ax? They are manifestations of Ralph Waldo Emerson's mandate of self-creation and recognition of the power of experience. Appalachia can also give us an eye towards how the national personality refracts like a diamond into a thousand rays. Playacting and self-made people are country cousins to Horatio Alger. With Southern charm sprinkled on top.

Among the newer hillbilly hustles is ginseng. Ginseng thieves go onto private or state land and forage for it, under threat of surveillance and chase. The kind of ginseng grown in Appalachia is of a particularly good quality for Asian markets. In traditional Chinese medicine, Asian ginseng cools, but North American ginseng warms the body. A fresh pound can go for $200, and dried it can go up to $800 and higher.

This has given rise to legislatures creating newly defined crimes. Keep in mind "crimes" are created. Governments declare actions criminal all the time that don't have to be, like making moonshine or "ginseng larceny." Lest you think this is quaint, please note that ginseng is a billion-dollar industry. The wild growth in the mountains is so fine, not like the mass-produced pesticide-sprayed variety that comes by the regular means.

Now, not all ginseng harvesting is illegal. There are official government seasons for it on public land. But the competition is tight and the profit margin lower when you do it the legal way. And West Virginia and the surrounding mountain country is poor and struggling. Theft makes money sense. The risks now are not collapsed lungs but prison sentences.

Taking up this errand in the wilderness, individual foragers can sell to ginseng companies and stay afloat. Some reality shows have picked up on this practice and depict the drama of gathering ginseng and evading the law. Like a lot of reality television, it comes across as just another example of "those quirky Southerners." But there's something that is of a piece between that fugitive entrepreneurship outside the law and the opioid crisis, which is an awful lot about chasing some sense of peace inside the body.

The methamphetamine and heroin epidemics have increased ginseng poaching's allure. West Virginia and Kentucky have some of the highest rates of opioid overdosing in the country. Ginseng theft is a good way to feed the opioid habit because the turnover is quick. You can have cash in hand the same day.

Foragers steal to provide what will heal others, and that same bounty circulates to palliate their own pains with chemicals that eat away at them. Meth labs and ginseng roots sometimes even share residence in dealers' homes. It's a hardscrabble cycle. A few people make a heap of money from it, while regular mountain folks stay scratching a life from digging into the dirt.

In Harpers Ferry, I saw a cheerful sign and stepped down into the True Treats Historic Candy shop. It bills itself as "the nation's only research-based historic candy store." This little shop is a dream to someone with a sweet tooth and an historian's imagination. The candy is bagged and grouped by historical period and region from the eighteenth century forward. I selected the traditional African American bag for obvious reasons. There was crystallized cane sugar, molasses pulls, and licorice root. The candied rose and violet petals were delicately chalky, and the peanut brittle had a sharp taste. Of course there was crystallized sorghum syrup processed out of the sweetgrass that grows throughout the South.

According to epidemiologists and physicians, Southerners weigh too much, have too much tooth decay, eat too much fat, and drink too much coke. We cushion against the hurt with the abundance of love found in food. And we revel in taking up space with sayings: "Only a dog wants a bone," we say. The constraints are rarely mentioned: overwork, poverty, the convenience of fast food. That's all a part of the story. It really isn't a regional story so much as a national one and a historic one. But the sweetest of the sweet tooths grew down here in part because of how the land was organized by deprivation even when what it yielded was abundant. Slave labor, barely free labor, and the land itself were all worked to their limits. Something sweet gives you a little piece. Or peace.

My grandmother, who we called "Mudear" or "Mudeah," a Southern contraction of "Mother dear," used to repeat the words she learned from her auntie: "You weren't born to live on flowerbeds of ease." From the eighteenth-century pen of the "godfather of English hymnody" Isaac Watts, the phrase made its way to a Southern meditation of, as Gwendolyn Brooks described it, "living in the along" by facing adversity and making do. This sentence that echoed through our lives as a mantra might be a testament to toughness or a simple reckoning that your circumstances simply weren't going to be easy. Sometimes a body is desperate for some relief from the weight of worry and the sadness of feeling trapped. And the nasty trick with opioids is that they ease both physical pain and a hurting heart. Both are in abundance in mountain living. At the same time as we track the beauty, we must witness the trouble. The story of when work disappears isn't just a story for American cities filled with Black people slipping down from working classes to poor. It is also up here, down there.

The tenderness I feel for the descendants of White miners is limited by my own sense of the story of Black folks in Appalachia and how many of their untended dead lie across the landscape. Despite the struggle and the labor movement, Jim Crow existed here, too. I use the word "tenderness" deliberately. I do not simply mean solidarity with their experiences of being exploited, though I do mean that. I also mean a certain heartache.

Moreover, in a rural place, you have intimacies across the color line as well as borders. There are too few people and too much needing of one another to maintain an always strict color line. It falters. Appalachian people deal with dueling afterlives. The afterlife of slavery is a vertical hierarchy, a brutal exploitation even as Black and White people are often closely intertwined. The afterlife of Jim Crow is jobs that go to one group or another, different sides of town, prison and, where the borders aren't respected, violence.

My advisor in graduate school, Henry Louis Gates Jr., known as Skip, wrote about coming of age in a West Virginia mountain town in his memoir, *Colored People*. Like Albert Murray, he is a man whose brilliance stuns and with whom I argue, at least in my mind, on a few political questions. No matter. My heart remains soft for the meticulousness of an erudite Southern gentleman who understands the gutbucket and hustle just as well as the canonical Western literary forms, and all the Black American cultural forms, too. And their confident Black genius set against a White supremacist history has always inspired me. Just like my mother's friend Marva, who grew up in Lynch, Kentucky, and was part of the circle of elders in my midst as I grew up, Skip has a crisp elocution and a penchant for impeccable style, as though accustomed to being defined by oneself instead of one's circumstance of origin.

In *Colored People*, there are two simultaneous and tension-filled motifs: the tight-knit cultural mélange of Black, White, and everything in between, and the forces of segregation in the itty-bitty place. Affrilachians have a broad Southern experience but also a rare one, with a color line, a fragile Jim Crow, a problem with cruel racism and poverty, and the kind of intimacy that comes when you live in small places even if they are unequal. To that point, in Appalachia, there's a long history of what anthropologists call tri-racial isolates: groups of multiracial people who retreated from the American racial matrix to be their own thing. They have varying names: Melungeons, Red Stockings, Brass Ankles, and the like. They kept to themselves historically and had to stay that way to remain ambiguous. Genetic testing, though admittedly unreliable, has disturbed some of the mythologies that held them together. Yet while a few of the myths are exposed (like the ones that say they don't descend from Africans), it is good to remember that all identity is in part myth, the kind that we can use to sort out living, for better or worse, depending upon its uses. Swarthy mountain folks, according to the one-drop rule of the United States, are significantly Black, but in the rules of the local, rural South, they are a people with a persistent but also submerged history of being not quite Black. The Black-White binary of race has never been as permanent or fixed as people like to claim, not when you live up real close. Of course shared ways grew. Take, for example, a few women who sat in different places along the color line, from deep in the Mountain South. Doris Payne, a native of Slab Fork, West Virginia, is a striking and elegant elderly Black woman known as an international jewel thief. As her lore goes, she was a child in a jewelry store, giddy because her father had told her she could purchase a watch as a gift. But then the store owner, seeing White patrons enter, ushered her out rapidly. She left, but not before she had slipped a watch in her pocket. After she was dismissed by the proprietor, the comeuppance was sweet. It would be the driving force in her life. Her skill grew. She remade herself into a lady who lunched, poised and elegant, with the veneer of wealth that she had in theatricality, if not in the bank. Diamond Doris has perfected polish, and she had a heap of social security numbers and names to go with her genteel resistance. With the gestures of a wealthy doyenne, she can slip diamond rings, from one carat to ten, on her long, elegant nutmeg fingers. She is a glorious outlaw; her memoir and a documentary about her life are celebratory rather than ambivalent. We want her to get away with it, to escape the yoke of crime and punishment. Maybe we live vicariously through her, feeding both our fantasy of being Cinderella-ed into a life without cares or debilitating bills, and our desire to stick it to the aristocrats?

Or Dolly Parton, an honest-to-God multimillionaire who grew up a poor mountain woman. She says, "It takes a lot of money to look this cheap," and stays so garishly adorned that she has no trouble going unrecognized when she isn't "dolled" up. She makes me know that the shape-shifting of humble mountain folks is not just a matter of costuming or gesture to get over on the ones with power and wealth, to sneak into their ranks. It's living play. Maybe up and away from the action in the mountains is just the perfect place for dreaming up a self and a story. Dolly's organization Imagination Library, at the request of families, sends every child in Tennessee (and several other locations as well) a collection of books from birth until age five. Maybe play can keep you from getting dried up by the difficulty of making do.

And then there was the infamous "welfare queen" of President Ronald Reagan's agenda against the welfare state. Linda Taylor was from Golddust, Tennessee. Her birth certificate identified her as White. She was raised as Black. In her navigation of the world beyond Appalachia, she was a changeling: White, Black, Latina, Asian, and Jewish. She had a host of aliases and identifications. Taylor ultimately served six years of a two-to-six-year sentence for welfare fraud.

Though cast in a stereotypical image of a Black woman on public assistance, Taylor was like Payne and Parton, unprecedented in her self-creation.

To remake ourselves from our imaginations is a classically American endeavor, and we are charmed by its many forms, whether the work of thieves, entertainers, or presidents.

The civil rights struggle in Appalachia, as elsewhere in the South, was an effort at remaking what it meant to be Americans. The Highlander Folk School is one of the most important institutions in that generations-long endeavor. In 1932, in the Tennessee hills, Highlander was established. Its founder, Myles Horton, was a native of Savannah, Tennessee. Horton grew up poor and critical of the exploitation that was the everyday experience of rural Tennesseans. He traveled far from home, initially for education, ultimately studying under theologian Reinhold Niebuhr at Union Theological Seminary in New York. While in Denmark, Horton had been inspired by the model of the folk school, a place where rural workers learned skills but also developed social and political perspectives out of their collective experiences. Highlander was built on that example, an educational site for ordinary people. Horton also was an organizer, supporting miners in Fentress County in the early 1930s. It was a violent clash. Horton's colleague, the union president Barney Graham, was killed by company bosses. Horton said that event radicalized him.

Highlander was integrated, pro-union, committed to nonviolent resistance, and often accused of being "communist." As time unfolded, the center of gravity of social movement shifted, and Highlander maintained itself as a space that allowed integrated meetings to take place—a rarity in the South—and became a site for developing strategies for the freedom movement.

As with many of the civil rights movement organizers you know of, Rosa Parks attended a workshop at Highlander before the bus boycott. She was already an organizer as an active member of the NAACP. Same as Martin Luther King Jr., who first visited in 1957.

Highlander did not create organizers, but rather facilitated organizing. At Highlander, the citizenship schools, led by Esau Jenkins and Septima Clark, and the debates of the Student Nonviolent Coordinating Committee over whether to engage in direct action or voter registration took place, along with other important strategizing sessions. They plotted collective actions that became real through myriad instances of courage and personal commitments. In an article from the Highlander newsletter, the school was described as ". . . like a mirror, to reflect the community and group it comes into. It helps us see things about ourselves and our condition that are hard to see by ourselves. Like a mirror, by spreading awareness and information about the way things are—and ways they can be changed . . ."

In 1961, the state of Tennessee revoked Highlander's license and seized its property. This wasn't surprising. Berea College, also in the mountains of Kentucky, had been founded as a coeducational integrated college in 1855 and was forced to become White only from 1904 until 1950, by which time its progressive Christian politics were less incendiary, though much of the South remained segregated. Highlander pushed even further against the grain than Berea, and they were punished for it. However, they regrouped and reopened in Knoxville.

Through the movement's heyday, and as the mainstream period of the civil rights era waned, Highlander continued. From the 1970s onward, they organized against strip mining, toxic dumping, and pollution, advocating for workers, including the undocumented. Threats came from the state over the years, but Highlander lived on, even after Horton's death in 1990. A multiracial institution that is networked nationally and internationally and invested in the lives of working people who are the backbone of the world, Highlander belies the mythology of Appalachia. But it also fits directly in the history of organized labor and a history of imagining, in particular imagining a different way of being in the world, together.

In 2019, the Highlander Center's main office building caught fire. This was just a year after another, more publicized fire had raged in Tennessee's mountain range. That was discovered to be an adolescent accident, tragic but largely innocent. This time, in the detritus and ash left after the flames were extinguished, a souvenir remained. It was a White power symbol. The perpetrators have yet to be discovered, and perhaps it doesn't matter if they are. Were legal justice brought to them, their ideas wouldn't be extinguished. John Brown's weren't after he lay moldering in the grave. But nor have Highlander's. As director Ash-Lee Henderson describes it, Highlander is sacred and also resilient. She quoted Myles Horton after the fire: "You can padlock a building, but you can't padlock an idea."

Arson is merely an overt symbol, surface activity on a sea of action. In a profoundly unequal place, Whiteness is supposed to mean something. Whenever that is threatened, a hot resentment bubbles. I cannot help but read the fire-setting that way. It was a way of suffocating the imagination with the bindings of Southern tradition.

Which brings us to my regional designation: an errand in the wilderness. In 1670, Samuel Danforth, a Puritan pastor, preached a sermon called "An Errand into the Wilderness" up in Boston. It detailed Puritans' belief in a covenant with God whereby they had been elected to conquer the New World. It was followed by the philosophy of Manifest Destiny, and then finally the closing of the American frontier. Appalachia, however, began as a different kind of errand in the wilderness, one that I would argue is much more central to who we are as Americans, despite how remote Appalachia is from most of our lives. The gospel was extracting abundance from the wild landscape. Human sacrifice was expected. Suffering death and repetition served the new-world aristocracy of wealth. In Appalachia the errand isn't an end but a repetition. Alliances and affections shift, but the whole cast repeats itself. And the frontier hasn't closed up even now, even where the earth has been sucked dry. People wrestle against the landscape, living on land that only yields a little bit, or on abundant land from which they only have legal right to a little bit, if anything. The song of the Mountain South is that which rings out into open air. It, too, is a way of asserting oneself, as not a cog in the system but a presence. The vibrato, the Southern yodel, cracked grief in wet bluegrass, is a sermon that repeats itself.

And in our lives, an intimate détente remains. A polite tension on top, a flame below. This might sound unfamiliar to you, but if you think for a moment about how conversations about race are approached in your life, the tentativeness and the terror that the conflagration might hit, you'll see it's much the same. Shame and rage collide. You might not understand why that is. The matter isn't simply about anger, resentment, misunderstanding, or saying the wrong or right words. It is earthquake, fire, unmarked graves, and ash. Over and over again. You might think you know, but you probably don't. There's an old joke about an out-of-towner stopping at a filling station. He asked the old man working, "Hey, Grandpa, which way to Hazard?" And the old man responded, "How did you know I was a grandpa?"

"I guessed."

"Well, guess which road takes you to Hazard then."

Acting like you know everything and acting like you don't know how to be respectful will keep you ignorant. Be humble.

MOTHER COUNTRY

Virginia

ON DECEMBER 4, 1619, Captain John Woodlief held a service in honor of the arrival of English settlers: "Wee ordaine that the day of our ships arrival at the place assigned for plantacon in the land of Virginia shall be yearly and perpetually keept holy as a day of thanksgiving to Almighty God . . ."

This first Thanksgiving took place on the Berkeley Hundred: one thousand acres set before the James River. Precisely where a number of the "first families" of Virginia settled. Elites at home, wealthy journeymen here. These were not the persecuted Puritans of farther north.

Virginia has nicknames that are appropriate to its upper-crust origins. One is "Old Dominion" because it was the first permanent British colony in the New World. "En dat Virginia Quintum," read its coat of arms, meaning "Behold Virginia gives the fifth as in fifth domain of the Crown. Ironic, then, perhaps, that at the end of the Revolutionary War, Lord Cornwallis surrendered to Washington in Virginia. Or maybe not. It was actually in the revolutionary period that the nickname really grew in popularity. Virginian elites were disinclined to remain colonial subjects in part because of how well they exercised dominion over land, slave, and society alike.

Patrick Henry shouted "Give me liberty or give me death" from the podium at the Second Virginia Convention in 1775, a call for independence. As a young man, Henry was moved by the First Great Awakening and became a supporter of religious liberty and an orator who understood the value of emotional as well as intellectual impact. A fiddler, a lawyer, and eventually a politician, Henry believed that both slavery and the fact that the Anglican church remained the official church of Virginia were injurious to the development of the colony. He was also a slaveholder. This is what I think of when people say we must have practical politics. Murderous hypocrisy is an old American habit.

"Dominion" in Virginia's history is a word for both freedom and slavery. Disparate historical facts are enlisted when the story of a nation's identity is told. Details add texture to the creation. Virginia is "first" in the history of the settler colony of Great Britain that would become the United States. And the year 1776, the moment of founding, was a culmination. But the process of creation, the imagined community of a nation, begins long before the actual founding. A people add and subtract facts as the mythology of making a nation is turned into official story. Although I know the cultural power of myth, I believe honesty is far more useful if you want to do more than justify a nation. If you want to understand a nation, or have aspirations for it that are decent, myth ought to be resisted. If we tell the story of the nation as it began, in Virginia, with the founding fathers and the bulk of early presidents and the first permanent British settlement, the terms of our nation are clear. Conquest, violence towards the Indigenous, a drive to mastery and master-class abundance reaped from other's labor—those were the terms.

Thomas Jefferson published *Notes on the State of Virginia* in 1781, with subsequent editions in the following years. It is a survey, a philosophical treatise, and thick description filled with grousing in the extreme. His disdain for slavery was mild in comparison with his disdain for the enslaved. He said of Black people:

> Comparing them by their faculties of memory, reason, and imagination, it appears to me, that in memory they are equal to the whites; in reason much inferior, as I think one could scarcely be found capable of tracing and comprehending the investigations of Euclid; and that in imagination they are dull, tasteless, and anomalous.
>
> . . . [N]ever yet could I find that a black had uttered a thought above the level of plain narration; never see even an elementary trait of painting or sculpture. In music they are more generally gifted than the whites with accurate ears for tune and time, and they have been found capable of imagining a small catch . . .
>
> . . . I advance it therefore as a suspicion only, that the blacks, whether originally a distinct race, or made distinct by time and circumstances, are inferior to the whites in the endowments both of body and mind.

I took the DNA test that is marketed on Ancestry.com, and among the details it displayed was that a significant number of my ancestors were Black people in eighteenth-century Virginia. In the previous passages, I was literally reading Jefferson's thoughts on my progenitors. Or at least the Black ones. Like Jefferson, there are White men in my tree with Black issue (in the sense of offspring). Jefferson in his racist generosity allowed that some infusion of European ancestry afforded Africans somewhat greater capacity, but it is quite clear he would have found me, credibly 81 percent African, lacking. I hold instead to what W. E. B. Du Bois said: "I sit with Shakespeare and he winces not. Across the color line I move arm in arm with Balzac and Dumas, where smiling men and welcoming women glide in gilded halls." I was taught to think this way as an assertion of dignity, but I must also express outrage that as an American I am expected to digest the founding fathers' venom casually, as though it is merely a part of the nation's genealogy but not its soul.

The *Notes* were published nine years after the Declaration of Independence, which said nothing about Whiteness but very clearly *meant* Whiteness. Some critics have made a great deal of Jefferson's aversion to slavery. But like Henry's aversion had a limit at his own ambition, Jefferson's had a limit at his own lust. The nascent nation's deeds would be strong evidence that aspiration trumped virtue when it came to Africans. Whatever theological or philosophical questioning they had about owning humans, it was undoubtedly secondary to the drive for power and wealth.

James Madison, another Virginia planter, another future president, was one of the authors of the Federalist Papers, that collection of documents we all read in high school to learn about how the citizens of the thirteen colonies were convinced to ratify the constitution. Madison wrote Federalist no. 54 as a distillation of a basic legal order about race. Altogether, the Federalist Papers are a series of documents, argumentative essays, acts of suasion and assuagement, imagination, reason and passion. No. 54 makes clear that the logic of dominion when it came to Black people and also when it came to Southern gentlemen, implicit but potent, was built into our nation's founding. Published on February 12, 1788, No. 54 covers one aspect of the separation of powers, titled "The Apportionment of Members Among the States."

The enslaved, it explains, were property and people both. The logic that followed was insincere: as people they must have some form of representation. But of course the three-fifths clause was not representation of the enslaved at all. This is what it doesn't say: we believe in amplifying the representation of those who have dominion over other souls, and this is why those individuals must count for more in our government. It is not the case, as some argue, that the clause was a term of art meaning that Black people counted for three-fifths of a person. They did not count at all. Rather slaveholders were made larger people by virtue of holding others as slaves. Sven Beckert described the impact as follows: "Southern slaveholders had enshrined the basis of their power into the Constitution with its three-fifths clause. A whole series of slaveholding presidents, Supreme Court judges, and strong representation in both houses of Congress guaranteed seemingly never ending political support for the institution of slavery."

There are three kinds of apologetics for this disingenuous argument: one, they operated out of political necessity; two, they were men of their time; and three, their aversion to the word "slaves" means that they didn't really like slavery, but they found themselves in a bind. The truth is, values are never necessities. They are priorities, choices, modes of self-creation. Whatever the intentions, this is the world the founders made.

A few years into the future, when *Notes* was in active circulation, Benjamin Banneker, a Black farmer, surveyor, mathematician, and—notably—one of two people who delineated the boundaries of Washington, DC, responded to Jefferson's racism in the now classic text:

I suppose it is a truth too well attested to you, to need a proof here, that we are a race of Beings who have long laboured under the abuse and censure of the world, that we have long been looked upon with an eye of contempt, and that we have long been considered rather as brutish than human, and scarcely capable of mental endowments . . .

Now Sir if this is founded in truth, I apprehend you will readily embrace every opportunity to eradicate that train of absurd and false ideas and opinions which so generally prevails with respect to us, and that your Sentiments are concurrent with mine, which are that one universal Father hath given being to us all, and that he hath not only made us all of one flesh, but that he hath also without partiality afforded us all the Same Sensations, and endued us all with the same faculties, and that however variable we may be in Society or religion, however diversifyed in Situation or colour, we are all of the Same Family, and Stand in the Same relation to him.

Banneker did what we, Black people, are often told we must not do when confronting history. He responded directly to the ugliness of a founding father. Banneker, a man of his time, refused the "Jefferson was a man of his time" argument and challenged Jefferson's bigotry. Jefferson was stingy yet superficially gracious in answering Banneker:

Philadelphia Aug. 30. 1791.

Sir,

I thank you sincerely for your letter of the 19th. instant and for the Almanac it contained. no body wishes more than I do to see such proofs as you exhibit, that nature has given to our black brethren, talents equal to those of the other colours of men, & that the appearance of a want of them is owing merely to the degraded condition of their existence both in Africa & America. I can add with truth that no body wishes more ardently to see a good system commenced for raising the condition both of their body & mind to what it ought to be, as fast as the imbecillity of their present existence, and other circumstance which cannot be neglected, will admit. I have taken the liberty of sending your almanac to Monsieur de Condorcet, Secretary of the Academy of sciences at Paris, and member

of the Philanthropic society because I considered it as
a document to which your whole colour had a right for
their justification against the doubts which have been
entertained of them. I am with great esteem, Sir, Your most
obedt. humble servt. Th. Jefferson

Don't you see he wished, truly, to be proven wrong? (I hope my sarcasm is evident.) Jefferson conceded to Banneker to acknowledge that Banneker's achievement as a blue-black man, as African as he could be, was a sign that perhaps he, Jefferson, was wrong. He would even share Banneker's words with others, he claimed. Though Banneker did not speak this vernacular, I imagine and can hear this phrase echoing in his head: "Tell me anything while I'm looking to you." It's a Southern expression of skepticism directed at those who speak with forked tongues.

Some years later, writing about Banneker, Jefferson was more honest:

Bishop Grégoire . . . wrote to me also on the doubts I had expressed five or six & twenty years ago, in the Notes on Virginia, as to the grade of understanding of the negroes, & he sent me his book on the literature of the negroes. his credulity has made him gather up every story he could find of men of colour (without distinguishing whether black, or of what degree of mixture) however slight the mention, or light the authority on which they are quoted. the whole do not amount in point of evidence, to what we know ourselves of Banneker. we know he had spherical trigonometry enough to make almanacs, but not without the suspicion of aid from Ellicot, who was his neighbor & friend, & never missed an opportunity of puffing him. I have a long letter from Banneker which shews him to have had a mind of very common stature indeed.

"Common" is a Southern insult. I do not know when it became so, broadly speaking, but I know that *here* in this letter is a twinge of evidence of its root. It is a quotidian expression that shows democracy's underside. Why yes, the common good and the commons are virtuous and necessary, but to be common, or to be common and act it, that's a low-status thing. "Common" is a term that communicates the hierarchy in the purported democracy. "Common" was the height of what Black people could be in the White imagination, and also was the low level of the White people who ought to be ruled, but so, too, was the "common" sense of general superiority of White over Black.

Jefferson admittedly gets more scrutiny than some of his peers, like Madison and Washington, when it comes to matters of race and status. This is largely because it is well established that he held his children born to Sally Hemings, his slave who was thirty years his junior, as slaves as well. (And yet there are people who still want to argue that the relationship might have been consensual.) That said, I don't know that Jefferson merits special judgment. Across the board, the founding fathers of the planter elite committed most of the same sins.

Here is a comparison that might crystallize this point. Three of the four presidents on Mount Rushmore, idolatry knifed into the Lakota Sioux's Six Grandfathers holy site, are Southerners. Two— George Washington and Thomas Jefferson—are from Virginia, and the third was the Kentucky-born Abraham Lincoln. There are also three Southerners on the Confederate monument at Stone Mountain in Georgia: two from Virginia, Robert E. Lee and Stonewall Jackson, and the Kentucky-born Jefferson Davis.

Janus-faced history: two monuments, two visions of heroism, one tradition. The tension implied in Stone Mountain, that between the Union and the Confederacy, is deceptive. Let's accept that slavery and its attendant value, racism—though debated—was integral to the founding of the nation. It was a sign of greed that couldn't be released if the national aspirations were maintained.

Once we note that, the seams begin to show. The virtues of republicanism were always unsteady. The plantation ensured an aristocracy of people with amplified citizenship. Slavery ensured a herrenvolk nation, in which all were not treated as having been created equal. Even in the evasiveness of Federalist no. 54, even in the words carefully crafted to not be unseemly, what stitched the nation together was apparent.

Virginia has slogans, like "Virginia is for lovers." In my apartment complex when I was a child, there was a girl named Virginia and she was from Virginia, and she had a little sign with the slogan that hung at the front of her bike. It made me uncomfortable. My own socialization as a Black girl from Alabama had taught me that the word "lovers" was inappropriate for children and polite company. But I learned later that that slogan was an abbreviation of an earlier tourism campaign wherein that statement was followed by a prepositional phrase, as in "Virginia is for . . . lovers of beaches . . . lovers of mountains," and so forth.

And in magazines, back then, Virginia Slims cigarettes had an extremely successful slogan: "You've come a long way, baby." It announced itself a feminist tobacco, a cigarette as skinny as the models and just as pretty. The ads were glamorous, and even though the women in my family were more likely to smoke menthols, I associated that glamour with theirs. Long fingers, squinted eyes, curling smoke. A habit that once upon a time brought prosperity to the colonies and subjugation to our ancestors. History is a funhouse mirror.

At this point in my life, I have been all over the state of Virginia and I have my own notes. I've visited friends in the northern suburbs of DC, where they claim to not really be from Virginia. They say they've come a long way. I've been to Richmond on business, where

Jefferson Davis's white house is now a museum, but I've never gone inside. My leisure visits have been to water cities, Newport News and Norfolk, which have an unusual mix of country and polish. One thing is clear: Virginia is a hard place to rival for telling US history. It has Jamestown, Colonial Williamsburg, Monticello. The variation is dramatic, but there is always a stateliness to it. Virginia is for lovers of history, capital *H*.

Several years ago, I visited Washington and Lee University to speak before the English department faculty and students. It is a beautiful drive. In the Shenandoah Valley, days that start cloudy turn brilliant. Driving you into a bed of leaves, distant from your body but still cozy. There, in the breadbasket of the Confederacy, I delivered a lecture that I hoped was appropriately theoretical and dispassionate, qualities that I not-so-subconsciously associate with being in Virginia.

When I arrived, the day was already darkening. The main drag scared me with its unapologetic Confederateness. There were hotels named after Southern generals, like the university (named for George Washington and Robert E. Lee), and landmarks that lavished praise on the fight to keep the South a slave society. I wished I had arrived in daylight, when I could better see what was going on. I would have felt safer. The next day, at a meal with faculty, I was told about how Robert E. Lee Day and Martin Luther King Day are in fact the same day. And they were anticipating competing demonstrations: one celebrating civil rights and the other lost-cause history. The disinfectant of light, in fact, wasn't comfortable. That said, everyone was gracious even beyond what I am accustomed to in the South. I was treated warmly, and my talk was responded to with polite appreciation. But I still felt . . . strange. That is until I rose very hungry on the third day. I went looking for a place to have breakfast, and window-shopping along the way, I peered into a store that sold crafty things and saw a pillow that read, "Don't act ugly." I chuckled. Yes, there was something I know of the South, where ugly isn't an appearance but rather an attitude, one that is especially unwarranted for (White) ladies and girls who are expected to be gracious and composed even if not smiling, but of course smiling is better. This has a common root with another concept particular to the Black South, "nice nasty," which is at the crossroads of being persnickety and "high siddity," a term that describes a critical cut above being snobbish. It is a way of communicating you are not "common," but doesn't necessarily have anything to do with socio-economic class (except it does) and has everything to do with disposition. Don't be ugly.

At the end of the block there was a diner. I went in and ordered grits and biscuits (with a lot of gluten, I suspected, because they were too heavy to have been made with cake flour). I expected to nestle in comfortably with my comfort food and thoughts about how important it is to not act ugly and how I wished that I had space in my bag to buy that pillow, but since I didn't, I would just post the picture I snapped on Instagram. Again, though, I felt discomfited. It was quiet. I realized that folks had not greeted me or even looked at me. I observed myself as the only Black person in the place. It occurred to me that perhaps I had breached a quiet but firm social norm. Black and White Southerners greet each other, mind you, all over the place. But local people also generally know the places to be and not to be, the unspoken zones of segregation. I think I was caught unawares. I left half my grits on the plate, folded my second biscuit up in a paper napkin that I put in my pocketbook, and left.

Southerners got grits making and eating from the Muscogee people, also called Creek, who lived across the Deep South before being pushed out under threat of death. The Muscogee made them by grinding corn down with a stone mill. Corn has multiple food uses throughout the South: meal for cornbread, hoecakes, johnny-cake, and grits, plus just corn on the cob. I am particular about all of mine. Despite popular perception of a sweet bias, I grew up among Black people who eat both sweet and unsweet cornbread.

Unsweet is better, in my estimation, if you have it with pot liquor, the juice that clings to greens (and mind you, not just collards, but other greens of the South via Africa like turnips and mustard) on the plate. It gets soaked up by the lightness of well-made cornbread. Sweet cornbread is better suited to small simple meals—some beans, some greens, and some cornbread—not Sunday dinner, family gathering, plates piled high. I never heard of sweetened grits, though, until one breakfast in Chicago in the 1980s when I saw kids on the West Side pouring spoonfuls of sugar in theirs at breakfast as I looked on in horror, and later from a few Texans who eat them like that as a matter of course. I've learned not to claim food things as authentically Southern or not based on what I know from *my* people, because there is a lot of variation across the region and its descendants. For example, I don't like grits in South Carolina at all, despite their claims to authenticity. And I've tried them more times than I like to remember. The hominy is grainy and dark, and it tastes too much like it's still a plant to me. I like my grits bleached, only yellowed by butter, milled finely, and cooked all the way down to a delicate creaminess, the way my grandmother always made them. They should have salt, but if the butter is fresh enough, you don't need hardly any salt for them to be good. Anyway, the Shenandoah Valley grits were right to me, but because it seemed I wasn't where I was supposed to be, I didn't bother to finish them. But I did wonder if a Black woman in the back had fixed them. Not that I necessarily suspected it; it just *could* likely have been.

I go to Charlottesville more often than anywhere else in Virginia because work takes me there. Thomas Jefferson's university is an important place for African American studies, having employed a number of important scholars of the field. For obvious reasons, that is an ironic fact.

With the Blue Ridge Mountains as the backdrop, the campus feels like an estate. It is beautiful. But for my taste, it's just too pristine, knowing the blood in the soil. That said, Charlottesville is a picturesque college town, with quaint cosmopolitanism and, yes, Southern hospitality, too. I suppose that is why when the deadly violence happened in Charlottesville, the Southern habit of attributing it to outside agitators fell out of the mouths of locals so quickly. It's true, people did come from all over for the fracas. Just like in the civil rights movement, another time when the term "outside agitator" was thrown around. But there's something to be said about outsiders thinking that your place could be a place for their hate to bloom. Something that they know or feel that ought to be acknowledged. Jefferson would have found the screaming violence common, but he would have had common ground with the sentiment. After all, he was one of the people who couldn't imagine a free Black people alongside White ones. "Send them back to Africa" was his preferred solution. We have heard similar formulations from White supremacists for generations. The terror is, of course, ongoing, even after the heartbreaking tragedy of Heather Heyer's murder and all of the amends making, which included some Confederate flags being taken down in various parts of the South and proclamations from even the most lost-cause-oriented politicians that it was a horrifying event. It was both horrifying and a painfully accurate representation of how destructive the US has been and can be. Charles Lynch, Virginian statesman and planter, son of an indentured laborer from Ireland who became a slaveholder, is thought to be the source of the term "lynching." He punished British loyalists during the Revolutionary War without due process of the law. Lynch law began as a means of wresting power from the dominion of the Crown and continued as a means of exercising dominion over the vulnerable. There are people who continue to believe that a version of lynch law is necessary to claim their territory as Americans. The landscape (and here I don't mean Charlottesville but the United States) is still frightening because one doesn't know what is lurking beneath the professions of equality. I think that's the part that people who defend sites of violence against their tragedies (as in "See, we really aren't like that!") remain deliberately ignorant about. It is a cruel and willful ignorance. They just act like they don't know.

Despite nights of terror, most days, the polished part of the legacy of the South dwells here. With the echo of the founding in the even columns and the spacious library, the Enlightenment casts a shadow over everything. Republicanism, free economic markets, a reconciliation between science and religion, and, of course, reason are found in both the archived documents and the expressed sensibilities.

But the fire-and-brimstone legacy of the religious right is situated in Virginia as well. The founding fathers were champions of the Enlightenment, but the presumptions of Christian faith were never disregarded. And when the racial, gender, and sexual orders were threatened in the mid–twentieth century by civil rights activists and hippies, an old-time religion and ideology flowered on the terms of discontent. In 1979, Jerry Falwell's Moral Majority was born in Virginia. That's not incidental.

The White religious right rest their theology on an ideal of moral "cleanliness" that is, if challenged, to be defended violently. There is nothing new about ugliness in a very dressed-up place. It is endemic in some ways. That is something you must understand. Perhaps you remember from lessons of the civil rights movement that the White citizens' council made up of respectable city leaders was simply the other side of the coin to the Klan? I want to repeat that because if you demur and refuse the reality of a vicious undertow, you can wind up giving some of us a White citizens' council feeling. It's the lesson history has taught us to be watchful for.

"Family values" was a catchphrase of the rise of the religious right. The way they did it was hypocritical at best. The veneration of the fetus and the degradation of the poor baby once born is cruel to the living and the dead. But there is something to be said about the *what* and *how* of the notion of family in the South. People say that family is important in this region. Family, I feel certain, is important everywhere. But the image that comes to mind with the word "family" varies. The Southern ideal of family is distinct from that of the Northeast, and a little word says why. In the Northeast, "we," that two-letter word, provides an alchemy of domestic partnership. It is the word of the married couple, the unit of significance, the collaborative propertied venture: We decided to send our kids to the neighborhood school. We summer in Newport. We bought this house ten years ago, and its value has appreciated dramatically.

In the South you are more likely to hear "me 'n'": Me 'n' yo' mama got to talking, and before you know it, we had talked all night. Me 'n' Buck went down to Wingstop. "'N'em" is a companion orientation: Clara 'n'em lost they home in the storm. I'm going over by Johnny 'n'em's party. The "me 'n'" and "'n'em" give you the flexibility of grouping. They specify, but you know that the intimate relations with parent, child, spouse, cousin elder, are many. This is the language of people who are used to thinking of family as a sprawl.

As much as I like that, and think family is at best more than nuclear, the "me 'n'" isn't necessarily something that is better or more humane. With the responsibility of a larger set of people to whom one is connected comes a way of being than can have you caught by the cruelest members of the sturdy culture of family. I thought about this a lot when the reality program *17 Kids and Counting* first aired. The Duggars are an enormous family of Christian dispensationalists who all got themselves spouses and children, and who follow rules against birth control and expectations of the Rapture. However intolerable a family member found their rigid ways, how could they extricate themselves if such an act required losing not just a parent or two, but one's whole network of affection? The web of relation can be a straight-jacket. When one of the young men in the family was found to have abused his sisters and their friends, he went through a process of religious devotion after which the web remained the same. Those women are not alone in the expectation that they will endure for the sake of the larger unit. What, by analogy, happens to the family of the university, or the town, or the state, or the Old Dominion, or the nation itself, given what has been built into its creation? I am not answering the question, but I am confident it has to be asked. And you ought to think hard about the answer.

The last time I went to Charlottesville, I had a Lyft driver who was from North Carolina. She had very large bangs that kicked up and back, and her hair was long, chestnut, and reached to her waist. She was a hardy woman, with turtle-like features and a natural ruddiness in her cheeks and a light in her eyes. Sometimes I feel, especially when it's a long ride, that the awkwardness of the fact that I am Black and the driver is White creates a nervousness that forces people to act like friends more than just drivers. She was like that. And while I don't care for the nervousness, I like the friendliness.

She started to tell me that once upon a time she had her own business. It was thriving. She was rich. And she had a husband. But all lives have a villain or two, and there was a woman he worked with at his second job with boobs as big as Dolly Parton's. "He looked at them thangs for a good year 'fore he figured he was gon' do something about it." I imagined the other woman, still a Southern belle in bloom. A Jolene, a Daisy Duke, a Jessica Simpson, the source of envy that would one day become the bitter gall of schadenfreude. The driver's back widened towards the bottom, like a sack, embarrassed in the organic devolution that we all undergo. She didn't wear a girdle or a control top. It was there to be seen.

I gave her the sounds that we give to encourage a person to go on, sounds of sympathy, shock, and laughter on time. The end of the marriage, as these things often unravel, was a financial disaster. "I was at my lowest point, nothing to my name, lost every last thing." I knew what was coming. I knew it. "And then I found JESUS." The church gave her a sense of purpose, saved her soul. I didn't guess what was coming next. "And I found I have the power to heal."

She stretched her hands off the wheel for a minute, and I leaned in. "But you know, doctors don't believe in the power of Jesus." She found a way to circumvent that issue. "So I would sneak into hospital rooms back at home." Oh . . . I leaned forward a bit more. "For real?" "Yes, ma'am, I did. One time I went into this black feller's room. And he asked me, 'What the hell are you doing in here?'" We giggled. "And I said, 'Just relax.'" She laid hands on his injured arm, in the sling. And he raised it up, in awe at the miracle. All the pain was gone. "I'm healed!"

The driver reminded me of televangelists I sometimes watched with my grandmother when I was a child. We didn't gravitate towards the faith healers. We preferred *The Hour of Power* hosted by Robert Schuller. But every once in a while, we'd catch one of those other guys: red-faced, hair slicked back, fiery, and just shy of being a snake charmer of the sort one can still find in a few backwoods who performs full-immersion baptisms in a river or creek. One thing about being Black and Catholic in the South, you're always a little bit Protestant, too, even if you've never been inside a Holiness, Southern Baptist, COGIC, or AME Church—but you probably have because people invite you to church as a social as well as spiritual matter. So I wasn't wholly unfamiliar with a story like hers. It was just unfamiliar, for me, coming from a woman and a person in a car rather than a pulpit. Even more so when it entailed illegally sneaking into a hospital and a Black feller who proclaimed himself "HEALED!"

What arrogance, I thought, to presume one self-aggrandized touch could heal the wounds of distance made clear by the lynching tree, that it could level the most rational distrust under the banner of religion. To think it could purify her of an inherited untrustworthiness and, more than that, give her the authority to set the world aright in the personal chamber of an ailing and vulnerable Black man.

"I learned that with Jesus I didn't have to worry about nothing on this earth." I knew this part of the gospel, that there is something greater in the beyond, to not be limited by earthly things, to not place your value in the status you have here but in your spiritual wealth.

"You know Jesus says that when we are saved, we will rule with him like kings and queens in heaven? In our abodes. I looked up the word 'abode' in the dictionary, and it means 'mansion.' So, imagine your perfect house, with everything just like you like it, French doors and a pretty bedroom with ruffles on the bed skirt and everything. And that's where we will be." I've tried since to figure out what parts of the dictionary or Bible she meant. Dictionaries are fickle things. It might have been a sixth or seventh meaning of "abode" where she got her proof. But where did it say such a thing in the Bible? Did she mean 1 Samuel 23:18: "And they two made a covenant before the Lord: and David *abode* in the wood, and Jonathan went to his house"? Or maybe the journey in the book of Numbers in which the children of Israel abode upon the tabernacle? Perhaps it was John 14:15–23: "If ye love me, keep my commandments. And I will pray the Father, and he shall give you another Comforter, that he may abide with you for ever; . . . Jesus answered and said unto him, If a man love me, he will keep my words: and my Father will love him, and we will come unto him, and make our abode with him"—a verse that suggests only an elect few will sit alongside the lord.

But the bigger question for me was this: *Who* did she plan to rule like kings and queens over? Nonbelievers? Sinners? Others? Speakers of different languages, those of different traditions or different bodies or desires? This God of which she spoke, it struck me, was the God of masters. It was the God that dictated that it was righteous to slaughter the Indigenous and enslave the heathens, and then later said that they could only come into his kingdom stripped of all of who they had been and supplicants to a Jesus with unlikely blue eyes and cascading blond hair, though born in

Asia. It was the God of the settlers, whether Anglican, Presbyterian, or Baptist.

Virginia was named for Queen Elizabeth I of England, who was known as the Virgin Queen. Her unwillingness to marry allowed her to consolidate her power. Her virginity protected her from certain humiliations and allowed her to stay atop the pedestals of patriarchy. I wonder what my driver would have thought of that Virginia queen. She wanted to rule. She wanted some revenge, to not be left behind, a loser. She wanted to be something more than "common." All of that, the driver had learned, was elusive, at least until death.

The repository for her despair was the God of Jerry Falwell and the Moral Majority. Homegrown right here in Virginia, this God is reaped with the Christian Coalition and its backlash against hippies and women's libbers and civil rights. This God could look favorably upon Donald Trump no matter how many sins were found on his moral ledger because he hated the right (or rather left) folks. This is the God of televangelists Jim and Tammy Faye Bakker, who with dramatic tears and lashes asked the public to hitch onto their ride to salvation (and pay an ample fare for the honor) until they got unhitched and exposed as sinners like the rest of us. Still the promise has remained alluring enough that all kinds of sins by their own calculus will be forgiven as long as you're a politician or a pastor who will hold this vision aloft even in the moments of deepest shame.

The God I was taught to believe in, a God rendered by the enslaved, was and remains at odds with that God. The God we'd been taught was the God of Exodus, the one who thundered "Let my people go." Our God saw Caesar's way was wrong, not because of who was on top and who was on bottom, but because of the addiction to the idea of top and bottom, and the sin of working people to death, and the crises of vice and viciousness.

My Lyft driver and I came together, and we departed over the same texts. Our ancestors had had a holy battle over those words.

Some kneeled and prayed to the God of Exodus as they were dragged from civil rights marches; some preached fire and brimstone against race mixing and Negro agitation. The colors of the bodies have nonetheless mixed over time. There are Black preachers and parishioners who see owning jets as a sign of God's favor. Theirs is the God of masters, too. There are White ones, a few, who are willing to die for a freedom that stretches across abodes and borders. There are people not attached to any church at all whose whole lives are nonetheless framed by these logics. The American fantasy of fantastic wealth and power lies on one side, and the passionate defense of the ideals of democracy and liberty on the other. This is another Janus face that splits into a thousand variations. Our roots take different routes.

At the end of the ride, she asked if I wanted to pray, and I said yes. We bowed our heads and joined hands. I don't know what she prayed for. But I did know that she was still drinking from the font that delivered her pain, and therefore living in a cycle of contradiction. She had been stricken from her marriage, rendered near penniless by the events, and was now an older and disregarded woman. It's a harrowingly common feeling, even if the details of her experience and solution are particular. We women age, eyes sweep over us in obvious disregard, our moments of confusion are mocked, our knowledge makes us schoolmarms rather than experts, nags rather than wise. She believed in the architecture of her own suffering, but also that faith might grant revenge. It was a coping mechanism. I didn't approve of it, but I understood it. As I was praying, I could not in good faith respond to her with revulsion. I had an ethical obligation to wish her well. And so, as usually is the case, I prayed against the cruel violence of dominion and diminishment. And armed with the belief in things unseen and miracles alike, I prayed she might be swayed to love the God of slaves. That God is far more tender than the one she praises, even to women like her.

ANIMATED ROULETTE

Louisville

KENTUCKY'S EAST IS APPALACHIA. To the west is bluegrass country. Louisville, at the edge, reaches to the tip of what we call the Midwest. It's one of those places, like St. Louis, that reminds you that cultural borders are more porous than maps. It is Louisville's studied elegance, however, that makes it feel Southern despite the fact that its accent is gentler than much of the South and its political sensibilities quite expressly (if not substantively) are moderating among the Southern states.

On Frankfort Avenue in Louisville, just up the street from some apartment complexes, you can peer through the windows of the Heigold House. You will see light shining through blue sky and trees. Step through the door and look out the other way. You will see outside, again, different trees, and also the sky. This facade has no building. As though the emperor is clothed, but he is an invisible man.

Christopher Heigold, a German stonemason, moved to Louisville in 1850 and had this house built. He took up residence among the New Orleanians, Irish people and his fellow Germans, in a neighborhood called the Point, which is a few miles away from the current location of the Heigold facade. He built his home as an homage to becoming American and made it in the nation's image. The facade was adorned by presidents, George Washington's face and events from his life, and James Buchanan, a leader who Heigold loved for his commitment to a strong union and rejection of the anti-immigrant Know Nothing Party. With his patriotic design, Heigold announced himself a member of American gentry, but Louisville's population wasn't so quick to agree. Knowing who was inside, many believed he had no claim to the nation.

Louisville was a large city at the time. Enslaved Africans were sold and transported down to the Deep South via the Ohio River, which joins with the Mississippi at Cairo, Illinois. Some residents were slaveholders; some were abolitionists. The Ohio River was also a waterway for runners on the Underground Railroad. The anti-immigrant Know Nothing Party had grown in popularity in Louisville. Hence the words carved in the house's facade: "Hail to Buchanan, Now and Forever" and "Hail to the Union Forever; Never Dissolve It." Above the entrance, "Hail to the City of Louis-ville" was blazoned. In August of 1855 a mob of American Protes-tants attacked the neighborhood filled with immigrant Catholics. They killed twenty-two people in what came to be known as Bloody Monday. Heigold survived.

Public works did further damage to this upper-crust immigrant community. The city diverted water from Beargrass Creek towards the Point in the late 1850s. Soon, the Point began to flood regularly. That marked the beginning of the slow demise of Heigold's grand home. The lack of municipal support was most pronounced in the wake of the Great Flood of 1937. The Point was devastated by the waters, and the city vowed to stop rebuilding and maintaining mu-nicipal services to the area due to the constant crisis.

By 1953, the city of Louisville began to buy and demolish prop-erties in the Point in order to expand a dump site that had been encroaching on the neighborhood for a few years. The Point had virtually disappeared by then. Buildings were eroded or covered in city waste. But the Heigold House remained, albeit in growing disrepair. In 2007, when a developer bought the land, a hefty seventy thousand pounds of structure had to go. The facade was moved to its current location.

But a century and a half prior, the war came and Heigold's antagonists, the Know Nothings, were divided between pro-Confederate and pro-Union factions. In general, most of the wealthy identified as Confederates, and the middle and working class believed in the Union. Although Kentucky stayed in the Union, it was never a completely Union-identified state. Perhaps the most telling evidence of this detail is that the meaning of the old minstrel song "My Old Kentucky Home, Good-Night" was, from the mid–nineteenth century, disputed. Some, like Frederick Douglass, saw it as an abolitionist tune and others as a sentimental pro-plantation ballad. This tension persisted in Louisville's history. For example, although many in Louisville have cast themselves as always having been the racially egalitarian South, by some accounts the very term "Jim Crow" came from Louisville. As the story goes, an enslaved Black man named Jim Crow worked at a livery stable in the city and danced happily through his labors, thus providing subject matter for a blackface minstrel named Thomas Rice, who sang the song of Jim Crow.

Getting back to history, rather than lore, during the war Louisville was a stronghold of Union troops and a central base of operations. The Ohio River and the railroad made it a target for the Confederacy. They tried to destroy the railroad and capture the city, and failed. Black people escaping slavery flooded into the city. Locally enslaved people freed themselves as well. Slaveholders panicked and grew embittered that their human wealth had taken possession of themselves. This is the source of the quip "Kentucky did not join the Confederacy until after the Civil War." The human coffers were emptied.

After freedom, Louisville became home to what is arguably

the world's most famous horse race, the Kentucky Derby. And the Derby's history is also a story about race, wealth, and region. If you've spent time there, you know that Kentucky is horse country. The science of maintaining horses grew in popularity in the 1830s. With time, the value of horses grew, and they were aboded in architectural sophistication. The barns were called cathedrals and palaces, a sign of the vaunted station of the animals. The earth full of limestone is good for horses, too. They graze, luxuriously, on nutrient-rich bluegrass.

Horse races have always been intriguing to me, mostly because of the stories my parents told me of attending them when I was young. My father, the Brooklynite, would yell and scream; my mother, the Southerner, would be mortified, but still enjoyed it. William Faulkner said about this thrill at the Derby in Louisville: ". . . [I]t is not just betting, the chance to prove with money your luck or what you call your judgment, that draws people to horse races. It is much deeper than that. It is a sublimation, a transference: man, with his admiration for speed and strength, physical power far beyond what he himself is capable of, projects his own desire for physical supremacy, victory onto the agent."

The first Kentucky Derby was held in 1875, the year Churchill Downs was built. At that point, Black jockeys, small of stature and superb athletes, wielded horses. The labor of slavery, which included the tending of horses, had created a font of knowledge among Black people that translated well to racing. And for a time, no one could pretend it was simply the majesty of the horse that allowed them to win. It had to be admitted that there was a human element, an excellence in people who in fact could not be counted as beasts, no matter how much they were treated as such. Like Isaac Burns Murphy, who has a yet-unequaled winning percentage of 44 percent, and who won the Derby three times. The races were interracial affairs. But as Jim Crow settled into the city, the enthusiastic Black fans and the celebrated Black jockeys were increasingly seen as a problem. Progressively, Black jockeys were supplanted. When Isaac Murphy died in 1896, the same year that the Supreme Court decided *Plessy v. Ferguson* and declared racial segregation constitutional, Murphy was interred in an unmarked grave and left there until sometime in the '60s, when he was dug up to be properly buried.

And then there's the drinking. I'd first heard of the Derby's famous Southern drink, the mint julep, when I read *The Great Gatsby* in seventh grade. And it remained polite in my head forever after. By then, the drink was neatly uprooted from Black bartenders who concocted that and other drinks under the yoke of slavery. Skill with spirits got them free, or at least loosened the chains enough to make a difference. Recently, the names of these men have been written down and circulated, such as Jim Cook and John Dabney, whose recipe reportedly was "Crushed ice, as much as you can pack in, and sugar, mint bruised and put in with the ice, then your good whiskey, and the top surmounted by more mint, a strawberry, a cherry, a slice of pineapple . . . or any other fixings you like."

Bruise a mint leaf, and the flavor and fragrance explode onto tongue, hand, and air. Liquor softens ice enough to make it slip and crumble but not immediately fall apart in your hot mouth. If you recall, in American history, whiskey has served as currency, the subject of battle, the basis for legislation, and a darling of the black market. It's also a feature of regional culture. Such luxury, in the nineteenth century, and such abandon were rare. Dabney was also known for making a delicious terrapin stew of rich flesh excavated from a hard shell for wealthy folks in Richmond. This was the world for the word "highfalutin," and while it was wild, it was never a joke. Foghorn Leghorn, the cock of the walk in Looney Tunes cartoons, or Boss Hogg, the corpulent sheriff who wore a white suit and cowboy hat every day in *The Dukes of Hazzard*, might have taught you to laugh at these folks, to find them a bumbling, incompetent elite. But if you are so inclined to this misunderstanding, I encourage you to look at Mitch McConnell's eyes in his gotcha moments. His common playfulness is never stronger than his unrelenting grasp upon power, his insistence on maintaining it. Look harder.

Hunter Thompson's 1970 rendition of the utter bacchanal of the Derby crowd, titled "The Kentucky Derby Is Decadent and Depraved," was a necessary provocation of the Derby image. He depicted a no-holds-barred excess of liquor and sex, the sloppy underside of the planter elite on full display. It was an exposé that reminds me of Roger Khan's description of horse racing as animated roulette. Those at the top of the social hierarchy used the occasion to teeter on the edge, to take risks, to live precariously (if only for a quick moment) like those people whose lives they made vulnerable.

Everybody in the South (I say that with the regional habit of linguistic excess) knows how to get their hands on some good liquor. Everybody knows how to get a hold of a pistol or two. But the reins and the stockpiles, the armory and the yoke, are in the hands of those who would be falling down drunk as the horses they own race. The ones who own the mines. The fact that they get "tore up" (a colloquialism for drunkenness) like the rest of us, and weep, and must rest their eyes, doesn't change that fact. I have never personally had to wash a rich White man's drawers for a living, but it doesn't mean I don't know what is in them.

All of that is to say, the question of the facade, whether it is the front of a building or a grand fascinator hat with a veil covering the face, is not as easy to interpret as we might think. We think to look behind the facade is to get to the truth. But there is instruction in the surface as well, to what we provide as a surface, what they or we choose to present.

Behind and on either side of Churchill Downs there is a neighborhood known as the Backside. It used to be populated by Black folks, and now it is mostly populated by immigrants from Mexico and Central America who train horses for millionaires. Hundreds of stable workers earn as a little as $400 a week and scrounge for a place to sleep and a way to make it here. Paid, but barely, and so vulnerable to the whims of the ones who own the horses and the cathedrals, nevertheless they have begun to politically organize and gain some leverage. That, too, is tradition.

Some years ago, I had some Kentucky liquor. I went on a bourbon tour in Lexington with a group of Black women professors. We were attending a writing retreat. The tour was a welcome respite. Earlier, we'd had some conflict. Together we watched a World Cup match between Ghana and the United States, and our loyalties were divided. Vociferously rooting for Ghana, I was surprised by the patriotism of some of my colleagues. Though I was among the most "homegirl" of the bunch, with country roots in the Deepest South, I was the most passionately disappointed about Ghana's loss.

The conflict cooled during a writing workshop with poet Nikky Finney. Tears flowed; Audrey McFarlane read a soul-shaking story about her Jamaican mother sewing her a pretty pink robe. I remembered the old whirring sound of my mother's machine in rhythm to the pitch of her voice. It was a testimony to the way they took snatches of time from their busy lives to give us comfort, so critical to Black women's histories. I think of that moment often. By the external measure, we were a group of Black women who had scaled heights. But we talked about mothers and grandmothers who had tended to us in the constraints of their lives. Some of us could trace our ancestries back to plantations here, others to plantations in the Caribbean. Others still to lifelines forever altered by colonial authorities. Some came from elite families, most from struggling ones, all from people who eked out from under race and gender rules. The past, for us, was something sorrowful and beautiful at once.

A bourbon tour was our capstone. I loved it. The science, the aging process, the history. The scent was intoxicating. The barrels that deep, oily lush brown. Such tours are detailed but also devoid of history's contextual funk. Distilleries emerged in the antebellum period and, as Professor Erin Wiggins Gilliam began documenting around 2018, depended on enslaved labor. She's found slave-auction documents that advertise distillery skills among the enslaved and the records of human property among whiskey manufacturers.

In retrospect, knowing what I know now, and reflecting on the sensory and social pleasure of that visit, I feel uncomfortable. Shouldn't we always be disturbed by such elegant surfaces, by the tendency to prune? Don't we always need to look round the back to see what made all this happen? Should I have reveled so easily in the bourgeois luxury? Given who I was, who we were, who we are, what we'd been talking about, how was reveling so easy? This is a bit of navel-gazing, but if you gaze anywhere with a critical eye, you do have to look at your own belly, too.

In 2017, Sofia Coppola received a good deal of criticism for removing the Black characters from her Civil War film, *The Beguiled*. At the time she explained she thought the briar patch of race was too complicated to cover. In the upheavals of 2019, she would apologize. It was a short but intense drama. But also, and this is worth noting, the author of the original novel upon which this film and an earlier version were based had also managed to tell a story about the Civil War in which Black people were fairly incidental. Coppola took them out, but they didn't figure centrally before anyway. In various iterations, there was a pretense that the story was about the interior of the slave society, but it wasn't. Now, I'm not interested in re-litigating *The Beguiled*, but I'm thinking about it as a quick example. It was an easy case to judge. But there's an analogy to my own ahistoric frolic on a bourbon tour or at the races. There's a lot of delight in the pomp of the American South, and if you can take the ugliness out of the equation, not just historically but conceptually, there's a lot of fun to be had. Americans are quite good at taking up pleasures of history and leaving its victims to fend for themselves. From *Gone with the Wind* to now, we have so many examples. Sure, today that old film has the specter of shame, with Mammy and all that. But we still have a taste for the facade. Maybe because once you agree to go down the rabbit hole, everything gets messy.

There is a distillery in Louisville owned by Kaveh Zamanian, an Armenian immigrant, that is named Rabbit Hole. Zamanian describes how, upon arriving in the United States, he fell in love with bourbon. He abandoned his career as a psychoanalyst in favor of owning a distillery. Of that affair, he says (or at least the marketing says):

> Bourbon was a revelation. Neglected for decades, undergoing a Renaissance of both quality and vision. The product of Kentucky's corn and pure, iron-free water; aged by the region's hot summers and cold winters in barrels hewn from native oak; Bourbon reclaimed its birthright: American to its core, genuinely ours, unlike anything else in the world, I had to be a part of it.

In 2019, the Rabbit Hole distillery added a new whiskey to its portfolio called the Heigold, after the stonemason whose facade remains. Zamanian says he shares Heigold's passion for America, and therefore the whiskey has been branded in his honor. Heigold is written romantically in the history of Louisville. He is redeemed from the nativist hostility he once experienced. Louisville has changed. But it also hasn't.

I began this chapter when I was still reeling. A grand jury investigation had been completed regarding the death of Breonna Taylor, a Black woman, an essential hospital worker, who was killed by police officers in Louisville while she was in her bed sleeping. There were months of protests locally. Her image covered national magazines. Our hearts broke for Breonna. In the end, the grand jury only charged one of three involved officers—not for killing Breonna Taylor, but for shooting into the home of her White neighbor. That was called wanton endangerment. There were centuries of preparation for this conclusion. There are centuries of such contortions of legal interpretation. Something like justice was a long shot from the outset.

I have wondered about her final seconds. The sputtering metallic sound of a lock breaking that awoke her from her sleep. She was probably disoriented, terrified, couldn't ascertain who was in her home or why. Did she know they were police officers before they executed her? Was there any warning in the starting shot? Was there enough time to speculate on whether this was a miscarriage of justice or a crime? Does it even matter? After all, the lynching already happened. The theft is completed. It will happen again, if history is any indication. Deterrence isn't a theory applied to police officers. They are the crudest enforcement arm of White supremacy. In recent years, we've seen millions take to the streets in protest against police killings of unarmed Black people. I would like to think that on the other side of outrage we will map the relationships that allow the killings to continue. We treat politics like horse stalls, artificially separating our issues we race from here to there wearing blinders. We delight in the prettiest facades without looking around the back to what makes them possible. If we did, we might understand the cruelty of our diversions.

I wonder more. In the coming years, will the people return with their hats and juleps and garden parties, wearing kitten heels that sink into the roots of the bluegrass and laughing tinkling laughs? Will the out-of-towners delight in Southern dress-up? Will the Backsiders be rounded up and sent to detention? Will they revolt? Will the Black folk resist, again, on the grounds of their captivity? I don't know. I know a three-year-old filly owned by J. S. Stables named Breonna was raced at Churchill Downs during Derby Week. She won. The jockey rode her like a beast. They claimed it was a way to "say her name." If I had been there, I suppose I would have been driven to drink myself into a stupor.

MARY'S LAND

Annapolis and the Caves

A FEW YEARS AGO, I began to look at the two census reports where my one known ancestor from Maryland appears every so often: 1870 and 1880. I'm always hoping to discover something I missed. About myself. About my past. Every gaze is a moment of wonder and frustration. There she is, twice. In 1870, she is Easter Lowe. Born in Maryland in 1769, 101 years old, Black. In 1880, she is Esther Watkins, born in Georgia in 1789, 91 years old, widowed, Black. Both improbable and extraordinary. In rare, lighter moments, it makes me think of Mark Twain's humorous story about George Washington's mammy, Joice Heth, who in newspaper report after newspaper report kept getting older until her age rivaled Methuselah's (as we say it). Whereas Twain noted a sentimentalism towards the old plantation darky that verged on the ridiculous, my own ancestor's imprecision is a bitter wound. And I have some awe, too, at what must have been a daunting attempt to name her age. "How to place her in history?" somebody speculated. Most of the time I feel a combination of reverence and sadness. It is unlikely I will ever know what happened or when exactly she was born. I can guess. The ages are probably wrong but could be right. There were some enslaved people who lived to extraordinarily old ages. Perhaps she was sold from Maryland down the river. Maybe from a man named Lowe to a man named Watkins who wanted to settle the Georgia frontier. And later, as Mississippi was carved out of Georgia and South Carolina, and Alabama out of Mississippi, she, a woman who at least by one account was born before the nation was a nation, was still living, an elderly freedwoman in Madison County, Alabama.

Even if I doubt her age, there is the AncestryDNA evidence that says I descend from people who lived in early eighteenth-century Virginia. Inexact borders aside, what holds is this: we came before America was America. This woman who bore the name either of my favorite biblical queen or my favorite holiday was here, not as an accomplice to the settler colony, but as the victim of its displacement and captivity. She was a witness to the very exclusions that laid the foundation for the creation of a national identity. It is a remarkable status.

I wanted to travel to Maryland, to see something about my ancestral beginnings, but I had no idea of where to go. The Mason-Dixon Line sits at the bottom of the state in which I live, Pennsylvania, and at the top of Maryland. It was drawn because of a feud. The Crown had given Pennsylvania to the Quaker Penns and Maryland to the Catholic Calverts. But where each territory stopped and each began was hard to ascertain with just the raw numbers of parallels and degrees. The geometry of sunlight, tracking where it hit when and how it moved, would allow for more precise mapping. So two scientists, Charles Mason and Jeremiah Dixon, were sent to the New World to draw the line. Together, aided by soldiers who beat back, displaced, and killed Indians along the way, and accompanied by dozens of workers, they traced the 233 east-west and 83 north-south miles of borderland between Maryland and Pennsylvania with their newly gleaned knowledge. Stones were placed at every mile along the way. And every fifth mile, a seventy-pound crownstone, imported from England, was placed. Each had an M on the Maryland side and a *P* on the Pennsylvania side. That was how the Mason-Dixon Line was made. It was completed in 1767, which might have been two years before Easter was born. Or more.

I ultimately chose to go to Annapolis, the capital of Maryland. It is a precious town. One that is self-consciously old, like it was manicured that way. I wasn't sure exactly what I was looking for there at first. I just went. Parking was hard to find, but I got a spot close to the Banneker-Douglass Museum. It is a small and beautifully curated place on a cobblestoned street. The significance of Black history of Maryland is captured there with dioramas, warm light, and tempered prose, including the births of Frederick Douglass, Harriet Tubman, and Thurgood Marshall. Key figures of Maryland's civil rights movement and Black leadership class are given tribute as well.

You'd be hard-pressed to find a Deep Southerner who would EVER call Maryland or Washington, DC, the South. Even the storied history of enslaved people from Maryland doesn't keep it from seeming Northern. Not Althea Browning Tanner, an enslaved woman who sold vegetables directly outside of the White House. Not even Frederick Douglass and Harriet Tubman, heroes of history who were both held captive in Maryland. I still am reticent to call the mid-Atlantic South the *South*. And yet I have learned in the course of my travels that there are "Souths," plural as much as singular, despite my Deep South bias. I know that while the South is a determined thing, it is also a shifting and varied one. Re-declared many times as a fact, it echoes far beyond its moving borders. I lived in Maryland, in Silver Spring, in 2001. And back then it never occurred to me to think of it as having anything to do with me beyond the fact that it was a new place I was living. Now I think differently.

At the front of the museum, to the left, one of my books was there, for sale. I offered to sign it, but the man in charge of the front desk seemed unsure about whether that was an appropriate thing for me to do. Which made me doubt the inclination as well. I was feeling proprietary towards something I made but which didn't belong to me. Presumptuous, too. Maybe I was just creating unnecessary complication. So I left it alone, thanked him, and walked on.

There was a particular place I had learned about as I was digging around in stories of Maryland, and I wanted to get to it in order to figure out what I was looking for here. I'd read that there was a pub where founding fathers used to drink, carouse, and sell Black people. And it is still open. My phone GPS went topsy-turvy for a little bit, but eventually I found the tavern.

I stepped inside, hoping to feel something mystical. Nothing. It was dimly lit and fairly inglorious. I sat awkwardly in a black-painted wood chair, alone and facing a young family with a little girl in a high chair, with the bar behind me. I ate fish fried in a thick batter. The pocket of heat under the skin was tongue-burning but increased the sweetness of the flesh. I drank cranberry juice with ice cubes too large to chew. I looked at the fixtures; I looked at the floor. It was disorientingly dark. As historians of slavery have noted, our images of auction blocks are more theatrical than the reality often was. Regular places were sites of the trade in people. The everydayness of disaster was a feature of slave society. We might be inclined to look for somewhere to place a memorial or an altar to the past, that we can treat as particularly hallowed ground. But the truth is that this mundane place where I was served cranberry juice and fish by a young White man with flopping brown hair and an eager smile is exactly where my foreparents might have been wrenched away from everything they loved. Matter-of-fact, like that. When I went outside again, the sunlight felt like it was about to blind me.

Next, I decided, I'd visit two historic museum homes of which Annapolis boasts. The first was under construction. I made it to the second just in time for a docent-led tour. It began inauspiciously. The guide was lovely, but the moment the phrase "Those nasty Indians tried to fight us, and we had to fight back" came out of her mouth, chill bumps raised on my forearms. Well, I thought, this might be some good material. Not a moment later a manager ran up to me: "I heard you're working on a book!" I hadn't intended to be treated as though I was there on an official visit. But I accepted her graciousness. She told me that I could take a hard hat tour of the building that was under construction and gave me her card, which I promptly lost. And then she followed up, explaining, "We are trying to tell the history more thoroughly. That house is where we found artifacts that relate to the history of enslaved people in Maryland." Her words were offered gingerly and with sensitivity. I didn't inquire further. I wasn't interested in making an indictment or issuing praise. I was just trying to see how the back-then is inside the now. I offhandedly mentioned to her that I was just now starting to think of Maryland as the South. "Of course it's the South!" she said, smiling. "And an important part of it! But this is the *urban* South." That struck me. I'd been talking for years about how people forget there is an urban South outside of Atlanta or New Orleans. How often when I went home for holidays people up North would ask me things like "Is it boring in the country with cows and chickens?" And I would have to remind them, I am from the urban South, although, yes, I know what it is like to wake up to the sound of a cock crowing next door and to see a headless chicken running around. But here I was being reminded myself that there always was an urban South, one that went back much further than Birmingham. Strange again, because I've taught Frederick Douglass's *Narrative* more times than I can remember, much of which takes place in Baltimore. But your knowing self and emotional self don't always match up.

We walked through rooms restored with great detail. Historic preservation is a painstaking business, especially when it comes to paint colors and fabrics. It is a matter of samples and formulas, mailing them back and forth and cross-referencing up the wazoo and things being not quite right until they are iterated to perfection. Unexpectedly, the docent turned and looked at me wide-eyed. "I hate to tell you. But I have to talk about"—and she whispered the word—"slavery." I shrugged. "Well, yes," she said, "it did happen." "Yes. It did," I replied.

My companions on the tour were a lovely couple, older and White. They were deeply interested in history and preservation and traveled frequently to experience both. The woman, a Kentuckian with a thin gray bowl haircut and a smile so earnest it looked like it belonged on a twelve-year-old, struggled a bit. These old homes are hard to move about in if you have a physical disability. There weren't many chairs along the way, and her effort to stay standing struck me as heroic. She shared information about the house and its history as we went room to room, from how the table was set to why the beds were so small, but she also had the wonder of discovery. I was amused by the detail that something I had assumed was a chamber pot was actually a child's play seat.

Before we made it to the basement, my bowl-cut companion needed to sit. The docent led her and her husband to the garden. But before that she held my forearm and said, "You really must go to Mount Vernon. It is fascinating." I told her I would, although I was certain I wouldn't.

I walked down a set of stairs and joined in on another tour. A young White couple recently graduated from Georgetown University was listening. They were smartly but casually dressed, with studiously respectful countenances. Standing in the kitchen, this docent told us that the enslaved woman in charge of the cooking slept there, on the floor in front of the hearth. It was freezing cold in the winter and sweltering in the summer. On a kitchen table, which, compared to the elaborately set dining table upstairs, was rough-hewn, a feast awaited delivery. I wondered who brought up the sumptuous meals replicated in plastic.

Then she said something that stuck in my craw. Slave cooks had to possess a great deal of knowledge. They had to understand science and math, even though they were illiterate. They had to keep track of proportion, the distribution of heat, and the ingredients to every meal they made. The docent pointed to a device, gleaming metal with a pulley, that was used to turn meat in order for it to be fully cooked, and though it aided the task, cooking still required rapt attention. Maybe because I have spent my entire adult life studying and researching with the control and aid of books, archives, and computers, the colonization of this Black woman's mind hit me hard. I have long known that each purchase of a slave was an investment. The feeding and clothing of one was as well. The task was to keep them alive enough to work and procreate, and cheap enough to yield the highest profit margin. Also, they were supposed to be abused enough to terrorize them out of retaliation. It has often been noted that slaves were denied knowledge as a way to keep them docile. But some, like the builders, the blacksmiths, the plantation botanists, and the cooks, were required to hold vast knowledge and steady it in their minds and memory because pen and paper were denied.

My college friend Adam Rothman, a professor of history at Georgetown University, is one of the people who has catalogued how Georgetown reaped their investment in the slave trade. Georgetown has decided upon a form of reparations for students who are descendants of their human property, a too-late but nevertheless welcome and important correction. The desire to make sense of this is so great that I watched in one evening how, upon offering a bibliography of books on the history of slavery, he gained tens of thousands of social media followers in the course of a few hours. People hunger for details about what it meant to be born, raised, and die a slave.

The life task of the enslaved person was to stay alive and where possible love and find some joy. I imagined this cook lying on this intact ground, shivering, sweltering, alone, and knowing. An archive in her head, her name left on no ledger, no wall in this house. There is no recording of the precise color of her flesh or apron. I imagined her smacked for an error or patronizingly praised, and aching. Eventually arthritic, smiled at for making the loveliest cakes, until, like her birth, her death came and went without public notice. Tears welled up in my eyes, and I am somewhat embarrassed to say that I felt a momentary relief that if my ancestor, Easter or Esther, worked here, I didn't know it.

I wonder if Easter or Esther looked at the ships, like Frederick Douglass did, longingly. I wonder if she dreamed of boarding one and finding another place to be or returning to her mother's home. Easter Lowe, or Esther Watkins, is my ancestor and my muse. I set her alongside the documented stories of Harriet Tubman and Frederick Douglass. Home is such a jealously guarded concept in my life, so specific. I don't know how it was in hers. Did slavery make home always somewhere else? In *Barracoon*, Zora Neale Hurston made clear that "home" for the last Africans brought here on slave ships was different than it was for African Americans, for whom this was the only place they knew. Home was vexed but here. For the Africans, it remained out there. Without knowing how close or far Africa was in Easter's life, my thoughts could not even be convincingly speculative.

Of course home isn't just a concept of feeling. It is a physical space. For Americans, property ownership has become the symbol of that. Black people have never stopped having a vulnerable relationship to home in that sense either. Property ownership is cherished and vulnerable, often fleeting, for us. I started reading about the Saving Slave Houses project led by architect Jobie Hill, in order to think about the idea of home for my enslaved ancestors. In her project, as it is described:

"Slave house" includes all buildings in which housing for enslaved people was one of the functions. It was very common for enslaved people to work and live in the same space. This is especially true for kitchens and wash houses, because these services were always in high demand. Today, slave houses and the stories that they encapsulate, are safe places that allow all of us to heal as we reflect on the sacrifices of the past and the racism and inequality that continue today.

At the time of this writing, the project has accounted for over seven hundred dwellings. That so many are intact is an indication of the skills that enslaved people had. They built many homes that survived despite the willful neglect of their history by the powers that be over multiple generations. Jobie Hill's project is a relatively new kind of preservation, one that changes the archive of slavery by unearthing its neglected architecture. One of the most intriguing aspects of the project is that the researchers cross-reference the buildings with interviews of formerly enslaved people that were collected by the WPA, matching homes to people who occupied them. When it comes to memory and slavery, there are people who center their concern on the gaps and absences. They dwell on the grief of silences. And there are people who every day are fitting puzzle pieces together to find as much truth and detail as possible. Both are essential.

We, descendants of the incomplete puzzle, know a good deal about dwelling in rough, negotiated spaces. Trapping places where intimacy existed despite the fact that law did not recognize its sanctity. Places where life and death and woundedness and love all persisted. But did our ancestors truly feel at home? (Do we?) Was home some affect in the ether, hard to hold, or a future perfect tension, imagined as part of some freedom to come? This word that I hold in my mouth, ever and always meaning the state where I was born, "home" is not something I am sure can be assumed to have had meaning before freedom. Familiarity, reliability, even *love*—these are not the same as *home*. Nor is home the building where one sleeps, necessarily. Prisoners, interned people, the involuntarily committed and institutionalized are not at home, are they? I think of the gospel song "Ain't That Good News," which goes, "I got a robe in that kingdom, ain't that good news. I'm gonna lay down this world, gonna shoulder up my cross, gonna take it home to my Jesus, ain't that good news." Maybe faith was the antidote to homelessness.

Easter/Esther probably didn't live in a big urban house like the historic home I visited but the "but" or "maybe" still thumped in my chest. Not knowing specific ancestral details makes me claim an inheritance in every piece of the history of enslaved people I encounter, which is probably more of a virtue than genealogy is anyway. It is more likely my Maryland ancestor was in the tobacco fields, fields that cramped your fingers and made your head swim with nausea as the potent crop passed across the barrier of skin and into nasal passages. This work was probably worse, barring circumstances in the house being intimately brutal. On tobacco plantations, seedbeds were prepared when the year was new, in January or February. The seeds were then sown, and the beds covered with pine boughs for protection. In spring the plants were transferred to fields. As it was getting hot and the work became more arduous, the enslaved made hills of soil to host the plants. Then they tended them, keeping away pests and weeds. They cut the plants at the place flowers were poised to grow because allowing such beauty to bloom would have been a waste. Come harvest time, there was a lot of back-and-forth, to make sure the yield was right, as a matter of growth and time. Finally the leaves were sweated and pressed and sorted.

When Maryland was still a young colony, King Charles I of England was loath to invest in this vice, as he found smoking vulgar and filthy. But the nicotine business became too valuable a prospect to do anything but invest in. A begrudging greed took hold. And since it appears my ancestor was born in Maryland back when it was close to 40 percent African, the odds are good she worked in

the tobacco fields. Still, for whatever reason, imagining that sicken-
ing air doesn't bother me like this kitchen did. It's just I knew that if
I knew my mother's mother's mother's mother's father's mother had
been cast on that floor in that grand house, sweltering and lonely
as she made lavish meals for her owners, I probably would want to
smash something to pieces in this beautiful restoration.

I went to the garden. From the back, I saw men in muslin shirts
and work pants, wearing straw hats. Were they reenactors? What
an odd means of bringing this place to life. Then one of the men
turned around. His face shone, golden red, square. He spoke to his
colleague in Spanish. I sighed deeply, sad and also relieved. Workers, not reenactors. Walking around the manicured plots, each with
tiny written tales of what each plant and flower was, I contemplated
what gets named and noted and what doesn't. Swamp rose, Burgun-
dian rose, Tuscany superb gallica rose.

There are still people, including children, working in Southern
tobacco fields. The past isn't even past, as Faulkner put it. Recently,
public health researchers have called attention to the poison seeping
into the bodies of the children in tobacco fields, who are now mostly
Mexican and Central American. Children have never stopped being
in American fields, nor have they ever stopped being held captive
on American soil. How often are we attentive to the fact that there
are still child captives? In a conversation with a friend, I remember
talking about the child-removal policy of the Trump administration.
And he responded that it was harrowing indeed, but how new was it
really? Yes, he was right. Democratic presidents have had the same
practices, only less cruelly enacted. But also, we remove children
from their homes and incarcerate them all over the nation and have
for years, whether immigrant or juvenile detention. That, too, is
an inheritance of slavery and colonialism. The difference is one of
degree but not kind. That blind eye, we turn it until we don't. But
we turn it every day.

I promised the head docent I would return to Annapolis when

the new information about Black people was integrated into the old, and lingered over the photos I'd just taken before I started walking out to the waterfront. Annapolis is most famously home to the Naval Academy, so I also snapped some pictures of a bunch of Navy-related signs. It's not a branch of the service that I know well; only one relative that I'm aware of has served in the Navy. When I have contemplated what it is like to be a sailor, my thoughts have mostly dwelled on the confinement that seems to be the lot of the soldiers who serve. And the way they guard entry and exit of ports, human borders. Sort of like what that Mason-Dixon Line once was.

I looked up and saw a used bookstore, which seemed like a place I ought to enter, given my subject. There were regional titles, books about the military, maps and such. Near the front, there was a copy of *The Life of Johnny Reb* in red with a cartoonish script. Near the center of the shop, on display, was *The Practice of Klannishness*, which announced itself as the first lesson in the science and art of Klancraft. I didn't want to buy it then. For some reason, at that moment, the fact that it was on display seemed to me a tacit affirmation of its content. I wrote down the title. I'd get it somewhere else. I entered and exited without a peep from the proprietor.

On the water, I thought, where Frederick Douglass imagined freedom, the quaintness of Annapolis is given a broader scope. A vision of water as far as the eye can turn sweetness into the sublime. Here is a pretty life, on the cusp of an ocean. Historically, in the coming and going, I imagine, everyone was reminded that things could change. One of the commercial centers on the water is Market House. It was established as a place for people to sell their wares, and was also once a meeting place for slaves, who could trade news and be social as they ran errands, mostly for masters. Some were even allowed to sell chickens they had raised at the market. Additionally, Maryland had the largest free Black population in the late eighteenth and early nineteenth centuries, so they gathered there, too. The reins of participation in society were not held as tightly as in the Deeper South, where my ancestors were moved at the beginning of the nineteenth century.

Market House was renovated in 2018 and now has all the luster of a revitalized modern food court with a communal eating space and classic Maryland food. I looked about a bit and then left. Dusk was falling, and I can't see very well at night, so I made my way back to my car. But I couldn't find it. I'd tried to protect against my propensity to lose my bearings by taking a picture of its location. But that didn't help me because the picture I took, while pretty, didn't include a street sign. It was just a picture of my car. You could see that the blocks were cobblestoned in it, like the ones all over town. I wandered up and down those pretty uneven bricks in block-heeled sandals that were giving me big blisters. It was growing darker and I was tired. Annoyed by my ridiculousness, I started to cry, and then suddenly there was my car. I sat inside and caught my breath before driving home. Relieved, the questions came: Where was I? What was this place that I was trying to recall and name and put into a new fabric not just of self but of home? What was I trying to accomplish by being here? I still wasn't sure. I ate a few pieces of my Harpers Ferry candy.

Back in my house, in front of my computer, I tried to find out more information about Easter or Esther. In a database of runaway slaves, I found the record of a woman:

ESTHER: Charles Cty runaway notice, July 27, 1790-a runaway Negro woman who calls herself Stace, she is known to be the property of Mr. Abraham Lowe of Calvert county. Her owner is requested to pay charges and take her away.

I felt a rush. There she was! Then I chastened myself. The record was circumstantial evidence, not definitive. But I speculated anyway: Where was she running? Was she trying to make it to the Great Dismal Swamp, where Africans had built their own fugitive society? Or did she imagine there would be someplace much farther north, in Canada or Europe, where the European society would have her? Maybe she wanted to go to an Indigenous group into which she could fold her future? Or to the Bahamas, with the Black people who had fought for Great Britain in the Revolutionary War and now lived free on one of the many islands of that nation? What kind of woman, caught, tells you her slave name and then her true name, reminding you that no matter how the law might grant you a sovereign claim to her flesh, she remains her own? One whose mind was set on freedom.

Until recently, it was thought that the Dismal Swamp, which stretches from south Virginia through North Carolina, was a modest settlement at best, and that Maroon communities founded by runaways were rare in United States slavery. But recent archaeology has revealed it was a settlement that was sustained over generations. Literally thousands of people escaped to and lived within the swamp from the seventeenth century through the conclusion of the Civil War. It is a challenge, with the many generations of land clearing, to precisely detail the original size of the swamp, but by some estimates it was once over a million acres in size.

There is a lot of swampland in the South, all along the Atlantic Coast through Georgia, the Carolinas, and reaching down into Florida, and across through Alabama, Mississippi, and Louisiana. Like others, the Dismal Swamp is storied for its peril and its refuge. George Washington once tried to raid the swamp and cast out the Africans. Sometimes raiders made a discovery and arrest, but they never fully usurped the hidden colonies. Harriet Beecher Stowe's character Dred, the opposite of the kindly Uncle Tom, dwelled in these swamps while plotting revenge against the cruelty of slavery. A composite of Nat Turner and Denmark Vesey, Dred was the heir to revolutionary sentiment, a fugitive in the wetlands because the slaveholding civil society was barbarous in contrast.

Guests can tour the Dismal Swamp now, for wildlife or hiking, or as one of the stops on a driving route that reaches into where the Maroons once were. You can read about their lives on a historical marker. The water is a deep golden color, pure and healthy and once prized as such by ship crews. Notwithstanding the definitiveness of a sign, this is a changing story; the swamp coughs up knowledge unevenly. Sometimes a utensil or a tool appears like a puzzle piece and is placed in the disjointed fabric of history. Today it is a place of both excavation by archaeologists, and wild growth. Birds nest in the witches'-broom, speckled with round white berries that are poisonous for humans. Hummingbirds with iridescent green breasts and reddish-pink throats suck nectar from the flowers. Humans must stay on the paths to avoid getting trapped or lost. The good news is that since 1973, this land has been assiduously preserved. If Esther were ever here, odds are that whatever was left of her has been overgrown or has been eroded to such an extent that it cannot be retrieved. As the South always reminds us, the land provides another place for recounting. Even without formal archives, one can mine it.

* * *

I TOOK A RURAL TRIP to Boonsboro, Maryland, in order to visit the Crystal Grottoes. They are what geologists refer to as in-line sinkholes. They formed centuries ago when the earth collapsed above an underground river. This labyrinth is owned by Jerry Downs, the third-generation proprietor, who I met as I walked up to the entrance, but I didn't know he was the owner then. He was sitting on a scooter, hearty with a red face, a trucker cap, and a broad grin.

"Is this where I take a tour of the caves?"

"Sure is."

"Can I go on the tour in an hour?"

"Why don't you just go on the next one?"

"Oh, I guess I can do that!" We laughed.

He said, "Girl, I can look at you and tell you're high mainte-nance!"

That's when I really cracked up. And I can't tell you why. Be-cause I don't ordinarily feel okay with strange White men calling me "girl," or anyone for that matter who isn't a Black woman of a certain age. And I wasn't sure what he meant by "high maintenance," but I had a feeling he was slyly calling me some kind of fancy-pants lady. There was a familiarity to him that wasn't about putting me in my place. He knew I wasn't to be trifled with. So we had established a mutual understanding.

I had a problem, though. I didn't have any cash. "Cash Only" was written plain as day in front of the register. "Aw, man, I don't have any cash!" But then the woman, rangy and blond, so skinny as to be concave, said with her gravelly voice, "Hear, that's all right, I'll take your card!" "Here" or "hear"? I didn't know which it was in that moment. She probably didn't think about it either 'cause it could have been either. When Southerners say "Y'all come back now, hear?" it means "Do you hear me?" But "here," often uttered like "huh," means 'give it here' or "take it." Either way, I listened and gave her my card and I got in line, and we, the tour takers, made our way down. Maryland in that instant definitely felt like the South, hear?

Our guide was a younger woman. Half her hair was platinum; the other half was bright red. Her pale eyes were rimmed in heavy black liner, and she rolled them up in her head repeatedly. I think it was a tic, to remember what she had to say and to avoid having to look at us in the eyes. She talked us through geology, sharing quips and making metaphors to help us make sense of what we saw. One that stuck to me was the "bacon strips" of frozen rock. And then, as if we were in the clouds instead of down in the earth, she asked us to see figures in the grottoes. There were dolphins and ducks swimming all butter and tan. Notwithstanding the effort to make it plain, the geological history she described was complicated. It was a delight for the eyes, though—like something you might imagine of outer space, light reflecting and strange, formations reaching and receding, and sometimes spiraling up beyond our gaze. One formation looked like a man on a throne. "He's all white and sparkling, just like a king should be!" No one else seemed to flinch. Shouldn't have been surprised, I guess.

There were two couples along on the tour with me. One of the men was Black, too, about my age and height, portly, with a long curly ponytail, a green football jersey, and a cocaine pinky nail on his left hand. He and I joked about how often tall men didn't like to play football. I told him none of the big dudes in my family played football, and he, no more than five foot six, said, "All of us did."

The tallest of the group, a dirty-blond young man, was chivalrous, always wordlessly stepping back so I wasn't in the rear. He was with a small mousy brown-haired woman who reminded me of Velma from *Scooby-Doo*. She had a lovely smile and was soft-spoken.

The energy started to inch tenser and tenser, the farther into the grottoes we went. Finally we reached a place around a sharp turn that we were allowed to touch. "That's dolomite," she said. It was black, cool, slick, soothing. I wanted to linger, but soon we were off to the next room. This one was vast, almost like a clearing. The air was sweet. We stood in a circle, and she switched off the light. "Try to put your hand in front of your face. You can't see it, can you? That's because no natural light gets down here. If you stayed down here without lights, you'd turn blind pretty soon. 'Cause that's what our eyes do, they look for light. If they don't find it, they stop working." We were silent. I imagine we were all wondering if we could crawl on all fours and find our way out of a hole without being impaled by a jutting slab or terrorized by impending blindness. She switched the light back on. The caught breath wasn't audible, but you could see it in the jerking of the shoulders. We made our way out.

Driving home in early evening, I took the Chesapeake Bay Bridge. I don't like bridges, but I wanted to cross the bay for one last vantage point. Over the side, I imagined I could see the land if not the precise place where Easter/Esther/Stace probably once labored and maybe where she once ran.

The landscape was otherwise uninspiring. But along the side of the road, I was surprised to see cornfields for miles. And roadside trailers, mostly a dingy white color. Maryland is now more of a corn- than tobacco-producing state. Given the perils of high-fructose corn syrup for American health, it seems vice still is a money-maker here. And corn is where the money is.

Corn is the primary US feed grain, accounting for more than 95 percent of total feed grain production and use. More than ninety million acres of land are dedicated to corn, with the majority of the crop grown in the heartland region. Most of the crop is used as the main energy ingredient in livestock feed. Maryland isn't a leader in corn production by any means. But agriculture writ large has played an important role in Maryland since its founding in 1634. While tobacco then was the main crop, wheat, corn, fruits, and vegetables were also farmed. By steadily supplying flour to the Continental Army, Maryland's Eastern Shore earned the title "Breadbasket of the Revolution" during the war for independence.

It's also a reminder that Maryland isn't just suburban DC, Baltimore, and Annapolis; it is also cornfields and trailers and country folks. This rural part of Maryland is still open and wide and made for the kind of work that people close to the land do. The bridge is long and narrow, and the water spills out beneath your gaze to the left and right as far as you can see. I've read that it is polluted by agricultural runoff. Toni Morrison wrote that water has perfect memory. I wonder if this water in this bay remembers the people who once came to its edge to wash their clothes or rinse their tears and stinging, cut flesh, or have the toxins eaten away at what was once grace and is now yet another repository for a history of using the earth until it is dried up hard, a hull of thirsty dirt? I hope it remembers. Not nostalgically but in the manner of scar tissue.

She came before the constitution. What would it mean to cultivate a sense of nationhood that would honor Easter/Esther/Stace—the ones who labored in these fields? It would require us to put aside our focus on powerful individuals in favor of a collage of historical meaning, allowing for what will remain unrecorded, and what will come to the surface unexpected. Until I was nearly done with this book, Easter was the furthest back I'd been able to trace in any branch of my family tree. I'd grown comfortable with that. Until one day another ancestor showed up in the digging. Her name was Mary Richards. She was born in Virginia, and her daughter in South Carolina. New questions came. More than answers.

I also eventually ordered the book I avoided in Annapolis. *The Practice of Klannishness* offers a tidy lesson. We think of the Klan as the violent thugs of history, because they were. But the familiarity of their ethos should shake us to awareness. Their practice was described as generous, family-oriented, and respectable. The Klan is so very American. We are used to making virtue out of shameful ways. And justifying brutality for the sake of virtue. It is easy to see the deception with the Klan, but imagine all the other ways those habits are made manifest in our culture.

When I had asked about what the future of the Crystal Grottoes would be, after our tour ended, the guide looked circumspect. The owner was aging, and managing the business was hard with a disability. She didn't know who was going to be equipped to take over. "Maybe us, but I don't know." It would be easy to classify this as a problem of succession or business design. We could call it a lack of sophistication. But isn't this uncertainty universal? We choose, daily, to sustain or neglect some detail of our lives and experiences. In this period of history, in which some people are clinging to the past and others are expunging it, perhaps we need to learn to acknowledge that most of us feel uncertain and even uneasy about what we will sustain and what we will leave behind. I'm talking about places like caves and historic homes, but also practices like electoral processes, courts, and constitutional interpretations. I'm talking about heroes of history and our consensus narratives about how we declare ourselves as a nation. I'm talking about local cultures and collective values. What will we make of those things that we decide to keep intact? The moment we refuse the idols of history, we are faced with the question of whether we ignore that it ever was, or turn to crafting a memory of it. I mean, I needed to caress the cool dark dolomite in order to feel the cave. And if we aren't careful about what we are doing and where we are going—ecologically, politically, socially—we might find ourselves in a clearing that could be a trap. Without a lit way out.

IRONIC CAPITAL

Washington, DC

THOMAS JEFFERSON HOSTED JAMES MADISON and Alexander Hamilton one evening in 1790. The dinner was an occasion for dealmaking. In exchange for siting the nation's capital along the Potomac River, the Southern states would pay the Revolutionary War debts of the Northeast colonies. The Residence Act was approved by the Senate and House in July.

Jefferson asked Andrew Ellicott to survey the land chosen by George Washington. And Ellicott hired Benjamin Banneker. Some of the land for the capital came from Maryland and some from Virginia. Maryland laws applied on the east of the Potomac, and Virginia laws applied on the west until the government was permanently situated there. After that, Congress would legislate for the federal district.

The cornerstone was laid for the White House in October of 1792, and building continued over three decades, a labor extended in part due to the British army setting it ablaze in 1814. It was designed by architect James Hoban, and much of the physical labor for building the edifice was done by the enslaved, along with some free labor. Its halls were filled by workers and aristocratic self-proclaimed everymen, citizens with enough money to suck up the power of the democracy, and their families, servants, and slaves. Maintenance of the building, two hundred years later, continues to be a challenge. Every so often one reads a news report about the cyclical disrepair of the White House, and it is always tempting to read it as a metaphor, but it's not clear for what exactly. Commitment? Instability? Patriotism? Rot from within?

Washington, DC, the White House, the Mall, the monuments and the museums—these are the places Americans and international visitors come for patriotic tourism. I must admit, as many times as I have been on the Mall, sometimes for protests but more often for tourism, I always remember it differently than it is. My mind's eye never records it as a green place, but of course it is extremely green. White stone and marble in the blazing summer sun is what I register.

Everywhere one turns in DC, one witnesses the history of the South: the Lincoln Memorial, the Washington Monument, the Supreme Court, the American Indian Museum. There are histories of all the regions here, and the nation's consensus narrative is made plain. Sectional conflicts and regional distinctions are therefore reconciled in stone and artifact. The official story is embedded in the buildings, in the bodies that have passed through, and in the self-conscious appraisals and encomiums. Here is where the people gathered to protest Jim Crow. There is the court where Jim Crow was once approved and where it was dismantled, at least by law. There is where the Southern strategy won and Nixon lived until he left disgraced. There is where two "New Democrat" Southerners, Clinton and Gore, hailed the Southernization of American politics, and where, eight years later, an Andover-Yale man called Dubya convincingly portrayed himself as a better sell to the South than the Tennessean. There is where Woodrow Wilson watched

The Birth of a Nation railing against the rudeness of Black freedom, and there is where, in order to prove the arc of the moral universe is bending, a statue of Martin Luther King Jr. was placed. I am perhaps too cynical, but I do like that his face is soft and his eyes are reflective in the middle of all this stone. It is an aspirational monument, yet also potentially deceptive. As a country, we have not yet embraced Dr. King.

However, the Confederacy is not celebrated on the National Mall. One of the sharpest signs of the tensions in federalism is how often Confederate monuments were placed at Southern courts and statehouses in contrast to Washington, DC. Being the nation's capital muted its Southernness at least in that regard. Confederate monuments were toppled all over the South in the spring of 2020. It was a redux of a few years prior, when the flags began coming down. Finally, it seemed, the lost cause was being released. In the midst of all this, one evening I sat down with my son Freeman, a deep-brown-skinned child who is descended from slaves, abolitionists, sharecroppers, communists, civil rights workers, and signers of the Declaration of Independence. He spontaneously announced, "I kind of understand why White Southerners are so invested in the Confederate flag as a sign of Southern heritage and claim it isn't about racism." I have learned, over time, to sit quietly and let my children finish their thoughts even when I am immediately alarmed and want to set them straight.

"I mean, I think the Confederate flags and monuments are terrible and I hate them," he went on, "but what's the difference between that and any American monument?" He went on to talk about how slavery was a national institution. That many of the founding fathers were slaveholders, that it was central to the wealth and power of the country. "The only difference between the two flags is time period," he concluded. Freeman was correct, of course. The Confederates may have been traitorous, but they believed themselves to be following constitutional precepts. And even though the fifty-state flag is post-slavery, it certainly isn't post–Jim Crow or post-racially-discriminatory-federal-policy, and it always implies the earlier flags, the one flown over the slave nation from the beginning. My child argued that Southerners who lay claim to Confederate heritage and honor—their commitments to distancing themselves from the nation's name and focusing instead on bravery, leadership, and even heroism, their appeal to the ideal of state self-determination—have a lot in common with *all* American patriots. After all, when American exceptionalism is extolled, it requires us to set aside genocide, slavery, colonialism, and all manner of shameful deeds to trumpet national honor. And when the ugliness is brought up, you can always expect the "men of their time" line will be dropped, as though accountability for destruction has an expiration date.

But a distinction is made when speaking about the South in this regard. The South is not afforded that troubling grace *except* when we are talking about that legion of Southern founding fathers (they are counted differently). And here's why, I think, as I stated before, there is a consensus that the South is supposed to bear the brunt of the shame, and that the nation's sins are disposed upon it. So the South in the founding is muted. But if we are to tell the truth about how central the region is to all of us, we have to be honest about the shared habits of the past and their justification.

I myself have made the distinction between the sins of the founding fathers and the Confederacy by saying the "lost cause" is worse because they celebrate traitors to the nation. But that is, in a sense, a victor's skewed logic and not compelling even to me. The Revolutionary War soldiers were traitors to the Crown. We celebrate it otherwise only because they won and we became what followed.

In a sense, Martin Luther King Jr. on the Mall is a subtle corrective to the sins and faith of the fathers when it came to the social order. The Black Southerner is, in him, included in the national architecture. One might read this as a path towards the ever more perfect union. One might read this as a means of legitimating the earlier half-truths. I don't think an either/or conclusion is necessary. What does occur to me, however, is that any monument is in a sense both an icon and a grave—a burial vault, in which the messiness of history is often dispensed with for the sake of the imagined community. And that should always concern us.

You could draw an isosceles triangle between the King Memorial, the African American Civil War Memorial, and Howard University. Every time I visit the Civil War memorial, I am afraid that I will not find my ancestors' names, that somehow they will be erased. And yet there they always are: James Garner and Washington Walls. Surnames didn't belong to the enslaved. As men who freed themselves, they chose their own. I suspect they used the names of masters, but still they have two names each, etched in stone.

On Howard University's campus there is another kind of monument. It looks stately and unflinching. The African American sculptor Richard Hunt's piece is metal, copper burnishing into green. Industry and nature against the blue sky. It is called *Freedmen's Column*. It honors the emancipated. The names are important on the memorial to Black soldiers, but part of me thinks that a memorial to the unnamed might be more so. Unnamed human value is the truth of how the enslaved who became freedpeople were treated by this nation. And we shouldn't forget it.

For generations we have grasped at words to explain the evil of slavery. Our hands and minds falter. Look, we say, they are nameless on slave registers. A rough age, a sex. I cannot even trace my ancestors, we say. They were not seen as human, we say. They were socially dead, we say. Efforts at explanation of horror indeed. But these words are far from fact. Look at the kind of details one could find on a wanted poster for a runaway instead of a register.

'RUN AWAY . . .

Copper	Corpulent
Very Black	Lean
Chestnut	Stout
Dark	Five Five
Light Brown	Five Seven
Mulatto	Five Two
Bushy Headed	Speaks Easily
Indian Hair	Intelligent
Long	Eyes Half Closed . . .
Curls naturally	Green
Can be Brushed Straight	Velvet
Hair divided on one side	Waistcoat
Limp	Checked Shirt
Scar	Branded on Both Cheeks
• Over the right eye	Likely
• On the left cheek	
• Across the lips	

Words of precision. These were known people. Called by names: Solomon, Thomas, George, Minty . . .

With attitudes and tastes remembered, those nameless registers were acts of historic aggression. They were not, however, true. And you know why that matters so much? Because every brutality was human to human. And they knew it. When Marse Thomas sold Susie's baby, he already knew the sounds of both of their cries.

And known Black people once marched past the White House in coffles. Richard Hunt sculpted wings, appendages for escaping, to honor them. Wide like the span of our national bird: white-headed and black-bodied, bald eagles.

Sterling Allen Brown, a man who became a storied professor at Howard University, was born in 1901, five years after the Supreme Court decided *Plessy v. Ferguson*. Back then, the Supreme Court met in the old Senate chamber in the Longworth House Office Building. That building was also infamously known for being the location where, in 1856, Preston Smith Brooks, a South Carolina planter, nearly beat abolitionist Charles Sumner to death for delivering an anti-slavery speech. Brooks became a hero in South Carolina. And the story has become apocryphal, one of the indicators of the coming Civil War.

Forty years later, the court, having gone through the upheavals of war, Reconstruction, and what Southerners called "Redemption," put the final nail in the coffin of the promises of Reconstruction with *Plessy*. Louisiana's separate-cars statute was upheld, as was the ejection of Homer Plessy, a white-skinned homme de couleur from New Orleans, from a train car reserved for Whites.

Sterling Brown's complexion was not far from Plessy's. Nor was his pedigree, though he was a child of the Upper South and not a Louisiana Creole. Brown was bourgeois. He came from once en-slaved people who became elites. However, he spent his life deeply immersed in the fact of his Blackness. And if one looks to the lu-minaries of twentieth-century African American literature, Brown's imprint is on many of them.

When James Baldwin was going to the Deep South to become a witness and seer for the fight for freedom, and to write, he visited Sterling Brown. Brown, by then corpulent and irreverent, was an institution at Howard. Baldwin once reflected on Brown, saying, "If I were a Professor, he's the sort I'd like to be." Though famous, Baldwin was small, dark, raised (and often remained) poor. Brown was big, light-skinned, influential but not famous, and a graduate of the most distinguished Black high school in the country, Paul Laurence Dunbar in DC, as well as Williams College. He also earned a master's degree at Harvard University. Baldwin's life had him in all sorts of bourgeois European circles. As an adult, Brown spent most of his life in Black schools and circles. In the conversation between Baldwin and Brown, Brown said to Baldwin, matter-of-factly, "Of course DC is the South." He let it roll off the tongue without hesitation, but in doing so it is clear he was making an argument to Baldwin as if to say, "Don't be confused by the whole capital thing. You're already here."

Howard, founded on March 2, 1867, just after emancipation, is a gathering place, one of those precious ones, for Black people, American and beyond. This is where William Leo Hansberry, the Mississippi-born father of African studies, taught leaders of African independence movements. This is where Charles Hamilton Houston crafted the *Brown v. Board of Education* litigation strategy. This is where the nation's first Black sorority was founded. And though it may seem counterintuitive to many, Howard is one of the places that makes DC lean Southern. Sites of Black higher education are overwhelmingly Southern. When Toni Morrison left home, she went south, not as far south as the place her foreparents began, in Alabama, but to a place that had some old ways made of Maryland and Virginia. Countless others did the same. The South, even if it did not necessarily house the bulk of the Black middle class through the twentieth century, certainly educated them.

And you simply cannot tell the full history of HBCUs without noting that they were and are international institutions. Black young adults from all over the colonized world traveled to the United States to study at Black colleges. They were often funded by the Phelps Stokes Fund, a philanthropic organization that supported the education of African and African American students. Like much in the South, HBCUs are often deeply embedded in the local context as well as standing at the intersection of global forces. That challenges what people think about the South inherently. Whether by way of the Gulf Coast, the Atlantic Ocean, or the Mississippi River, it's a place created out of people being carried from there to here and back. As an example, in 1939, in Birmingham, Alabama, during the Southern Negro Youth Congress convention, W. E. B. Du Bois told the young people, many of whom were students at HBCUs, that they must stay in the South instead of lighting off to what were ostensibly brighter destinations up North. That they must stay and fight, that the South was the gateway to the Caribbean and the rest of the Black world; it was therefore the site of possibility.

Even now, in very different times, there is a lingering feeling on the campuses of thriving HBCUs that echoes Du Bois's words. There are, of course, also divisions among students based in class background, ethnicity, and politics. But it matters that they are incredibly diverse places for Blackness in a nation that often flattens Blackness of every sort into something simplistic and two-dimensional.

When I spoke at Howard in the spring of 2019, I asked students the question I'd started asking anybody I saw in DC. Is DC the South? One of them, from DC, said, "I never thought of this as the South until I went up to college in New York, and everybody said, 'You got a Southern accent.'" A graduate student from South Carolina said, "Absolutely not." Of course it's a matter of perspective. As I walked through campus and literally saw people I'd known from nearly every stage of my life—my mother's friends, a professor who was a student at Marquette University in Milwaukee when my mother worked there, the daughter of my childhood babysitter in Boston, a niece of my friend from Alabama, one of my teaching assistants from college who I called by his South Carolina nickname "Squirrel"—it occurred to me that the tight network of Black life that Black colleges and universities make is a Southern thing, even if it's not always precisely happening in the South. These institutions built up from the striving and hoping of freedpeople, under the constant threat of White supremacist violence, training against the odds of doors ever opening, are home places.

At Howard there is perhaps a parallel to Ellis Island of sorts, a place through which a person might travel to become something—not an American, per se, but rather to become a person who understood her relationship to empire, including the American one, that power that reached all over the world from the dawn of the twentieth century forward, and which had been born out of European empires. Even in the periods in which they have had conservative administrations, HBCUs, simply by their composition, facilitated a critical look at the global order: whether it was the students from Howard who went to the Deep South in Freedom Summer, or the independence movement leaders who fought against colonialism in Ghana and Nigeria, or the protestors who struggled for Black studies, Howard University in particular makes a potent case for a more complex reading of Washington, DC, than that to which the official story attests.

I was in DC on the day that the National Museum of African American History and Culture opened, but I didn't have a ticket to attend. I still felt the buzz. The building itself holds a symbolic weight. It had two architects: Philip Freelon, now deceased, one of the most prominent African American architects of the twentieth century, and David Adjaye, a Ghanaian global citizen who has lived in England, Tanzania, and Egypt. They imagined the building as a synthesis of design elements of West Africa and the Americas. It marked a change. Not protest or monument, but Black people filling a whole building with our history in the nation's archives. For months and months it was hard to get tickets. The museum broke attendance records. People wept upon entering. Suffice it to say this is evidence of the significance of being acknowledged as part of the national story.

The physical experience of the museum itself is a matter of ascent or descent, and that I think is perhaps the most intriguing part of its design. One can start from the bottom and make one's way to the heights Black people have attained. That is the triumphant story. Or one can start at the top, reading it as perhaps a view of where we are, and then walk down, reaching deeper into the depths of history.

The thing I am most moved by in the NMAAHC is how it is filled with personal heirlooms. They hold the dress Carlotta Walls wore on her first day at Central High School in Little Rock, Arkansas. It was store-bought for the special occasion. The waist is tiny, the skirt bells to midi length, and the sleeves are puffed. The sweetest details are blue and teal letters and a floral scrawl on the midnight background. The smallest one of the students, she entered into the maelstrom of a mob outside and tormentors inside, café au lait, steely-faced, and delicate. She made the honor roll at Central High and graduated from the school in 1960.

Preservation reflects values. For Black Southerners, preservation has been challenging, even at an institutional level. Take, for example, the bounty that historically Black colleges and universities possess: papers, photos, all manner of artifacts. The wealth gap is evident. Lacking the capital of their White counterparts, Black institutions, even with the most careful of handlers, are fighting against the hands of time—and I mean that literally. Erosion threatens. The processing, maintenance, and preservation of these materials requires money. Think back to the mini scandal over Toni Morrison's papers going to Princeton instead of her alma mater, Howard. The practical argument was about resources. But there was a sense of frustration in many quarters, that an institution that had always been the keeper of our stories had been set aside for one that had only recently admitted they were of value. I think the resource matter is a serious one. But what interests me about that moment, and this museum, is that when describing its artifacts, it also describes how Black people held fast to what mattered. A people who, at the dawn of emancipation, were assumed to be without relevant history or culture to speak of. People who were relegated to the back of the closet of national formation understood the value of their own artifacts.

In 1965, a Democratic senator from New York, Daniel Patrick Moynihan, authored a report on the Negro Family. He was a liberal reformer, and the report was a response to the unrest in parts of the freedom movement. One aspect of the report is famous or infamous, based upon your perspective. He argued that the rates of out-of-wedlock birth among African Americans was a consequence of the damage slavery had done to Black families and in particular to gender roles. Black women, he argued, were matriarchs, and Black Americans would never fully assimilate in society so long as Black women had so much domestic authority.

The response to the report among leading Black intellectuals was fast and furious. There's a whole counter-Moynihan genre of Black writing. But it comes to mind for me in light of this museum. I think about all those mothers and grandmothers who held on to artifacts that likely seemed as though they were worth very little and which are now held in the nation's capital. The women and men who kept the artifacts and the traditions and the old ways and the stories and who held blankets of tears and stanched blood and survived the killings and lived to tell us made this possible. Because underneath the grandest of proclamations is always the living. And the holding on despite the process of being erased.

If Moynihan had listened to the historians who recounted the desperate attempts to find family after emancipation, to quilt it back together, I wonder if he might have come to another conclusion. I wonder if he saw the grief in the eyes of Black men. Like in Roy DeCarava's photo *Five Men*, taken at the funeral for three of the girls who perished in the 16th Street Baptist Church bombing. A sadness so authentic that it doesn't look like a single image of ideal manhood in American culture. It is human . . . and their skins are charcoal to glistening black. A museum like this gives you the evidence necessary for a better story.

DC has changed in many ways over the decades. So I asked two friends, both Black men in their fifties and native to the city, if DC was the South and they both said, after pausing, "Yes. Upper South." Their DC was Chocolate City, less gentrified, less international than it is now, with a much sharper distinction between the city and its people. I asked Ibram X. Kendi, a DC transplant at the time, and he said, "Yes and no." Tanya McKinnon, a DC native, says no with her classic smile, raised brows, and gleaming eyes, which I took as a gesture towards the very particular citified toughness of DC folks. As we reflected on the not-fully-Southern Southernness of DC, she told me about the "garden sheds" advertised in DC house listings. They are rustic and rectangular. Tall and narrow, with askew planks, and often painted in surprisingly sweet colors. Those, Tanya taught me, were backyard privies not long ago.

I posed the question to my former student Malachi Byrd. "No!" Then he told me that's part of why he didn't like the pop concept of the "DMV" meaning: DC, Maryland, and Virginia. Dee Cee (as locals say it, as though its name is made of two crisp separate words even more than initials) is a different kind of place altogether.

Then I asked a Lyft driver. He was exactly my age, and driving in a cloud of weed smoke. He said, "What the fuck they talking about?? Who said that?! South?? Compared to what, MAINE?" He waved his skinny arms off the wheel and shook his head. And yes, I thought, compared to Maine, it definitely is the South. After some time fussing and ranting, he said, "Well, now, DC *is* country. I got that all the time when I was out in Vegas. They be like, 'You from the South!' Naw, motherfucker, I'm just country!" I *had* thought of a slice of DC folk as country, even though it is very urban. In fact, I couldn't ever quite get over the fact that when I was living there, the drawling people on the corners, though they walked with a slow-motion bop, called folks "Bama" (as in my birthplace) as a synonym for "backwards."

The distinction between country and Southern is a fine one. Southern is regional and cultural; country is a disposition. There's an earnestness to country, more often found in rural places, though not exclusively by any means, an ease combined with backbreaking work. A knowing that doesn't announce itself unless and until you take somebody for a fool or they're trying to hustle you. Highly ritualistic, what you see is what you get, and sometimes what you don't see is why you get the ass whupping you gon' get. Southerners are more open about the fact of being country than DC folks, but many are not country at all.

It is not incidental that when I asked people if DC was the South, there seemed to be a generational distinction and a differential assessment based upon what "Southern" means—and to whom one is being compared: Northerners coming down, or people from the Deeper South coming up. But what struck me as most immediately important to locals was not the matter of North and South but the loss of communities they call home.

DC is being gentrified like major cities everywhere. It raises the question: To whom does this place belong? That is a local question, but it is also an existential one. We are literally still fighting over whether Black people belong to their home places and whether their home places belong to them. Once, the formerly enslaved migrated to DC with the hopes that, as the seat of the federal government, it might be a place that brought them a little closer to freedom. They built communities, universities, institutions, and networks. Gentrification threatens it all. When DC natives look back wistfully, remembering what is no longer there, I am reminded of what Raymond Williams calls a "structure of feeling," a sense of a time and place that is only fully available after things have already begun to change.

There are now monuments and museums, as well as laws and

ordinances, that tell a truer story than the myths circulated about the Union in the past. But when the fateful 2020 season of discontent and racial upheaval arrived as a result of more Black death at the hands of "law and order," my mind soured on all remedies. In every corner, books were bought, forums were held, opinions shared, new jobs and new opportunities came. And people took to the streets. And yet virtually nothing happened to arrest the forces displacing Black people in any of the cities we saw rise up in rage.

In 1975, the funk band Parliament released the song "Chocolate City" about Washington, DC. It sounds innocent in its optimism decades later, with lines like "They still call it the White House / But that's a temporary condition" and the refrain "Gainin' on ya." But it has a subtle prophetic message: "To each his reach / And if I don't cop, it ain't mine to have . . ." The truth is, all the learning in the world won't create a new set of race relations if so much remains out of the grasp of those on the disfavored side of the color line. In 1970, DC was 71.1 percent Black. In 2017, it was 47.1 percent Black. Chocolate City is slipping away. Just take a look at the astronomical real estate listings or the "revitalized" neighborhoods. There are no historic firsts, no grand gestures, no monuments or museums that undo generations of exclusions under law, policy, and practice, or that stop the expulsion. It makes me wanna holler. Tell the truth. What is this symbolic republic?

II

THE SOLIDIFIED SOUTH

THE CLEARING

Upper Alabama

WE WERE MOSTLY GIRLS. So we took turns dancing the hustle with my boy cousin Durrell, who knew how to do the dance. It was one night, after hustling and watching cartoons, when we were outside, and I found myself ashamed. I hadn't meant to kill, only to catch, that lightning bug. I meant to cup it delicately and open my hands slowly, revealing the softly bright creature. Instead I smashed it, and my left hand glowed.

Writers have praised the Alabama sky at daybreak. Pure blue. I always preferred the night sky when the deepest indigo is broken by heat lightning. The lit sky flashed sharp and angular, a blaze without a sound, and the lightning bugs danced. We ran across grass so green it gleamed in the dark, wet and redolent. Every sound, no matter how close, had an echo. This is the place where my grandparents came from, and so my relationship to it feels ancestral. Perhaps that is why my memories of times there are impressionistic. They merge with how I have imagined my grandparents' lives in rural Alabama.

Huntsville sits along the Tennessee River. The river courses through both states, Tennessee and Alabama. Its most prominent landmark, the Redstone Arsenal, takes up 1250 acres along the river. It was built in 1941 as the second US chemical weapons plant, completed prior to the nation's entrance into World War II but certainly in preparation. When the Army occupied the land, over five hundred families were displaced, most of them tenants and sharecroppers living in small rural communities. They had lived among their dead. It is estimated that forty-six distinct cemeteries were on the land. At first the Army planned to move the bodies. But that didn't happen. Remains remained. In 1988, road building outside the arsenal uncovered one of these cemeteries. Fifty-nine bodies were found, most of them Black people. We know this, even though their flesh was long gone. Forensic anthropologists make racial assessments using calipers to measure the nasal bones, chin, skull, and brow. Upon encountering these skeletons, the road was taken in another direction. The arsenal had already been a site of disruption for generations.

Immediately after World War II, and after my grandparents had already left, German scientists arrived in Huntsville as part of Operation Paperclip. First the scientists built ballistic missiles and other weapons. Later they worked on establishing NASA.

The leader among them was a rocket scientist named Wernher von Braun. A Nazi, he was a master of rocket technology in Germany and was brought to Alabama to do the same. Although von Braun claimed that his Nazi party membership was solely utilitarian, concentration camp victims remembered that he selected prison laborers for his laboratories. And he worked mere steps away from torture facilities and walked among the corpses. It is bad enough that Nazi Germany adopted racist ideologies from the United States, but it seems worse still that after they committed genocide, their scientists were invited to Jim Crow Alabama, to plot their way to the sky.

Von Braun was a cautious researcher, and some of his colleagues believed that caution was what allowed the Soviet Union

to beat the United States in the first major step of the space race
by launching Sputnik on October 4, 1957. Americans feared the
implications of the Soviet achievement: the first man-made satellite to orbit above the earth. Astronaut Frank Borman recalled, "I
was teaching at West Point when Sputnik was announced . . . The
Cold War was a very real thing and there was a very great concern
of a nuclear exchange and all of a sudden this country that was our
real enemy had jumped the gun and launched a satellite, and it
was an enormous impact." However, when the United States one-
upped the Soviet Union in the moon landing, from farther south,
on Florida's Space Coast, it wasn't a victory in everyone's eyes. The
event was protested by an Alabaman civil rights leader. Ralph Ab-
ernathy arrived outside the gates of the Kennedy Space Center with
five hundred people a few days before the launch. They brought
two mules and a wooden wagon to illustrate the contrast between
the gleaming white Saturn V rocket and families who couldn't afford food or a decent place to live. It was a theatrical repetition of
Gil Scott-Heron's pointed phrase "A rat done bit my sister Nell with
whitey on the moon." Though the protestors were invited to watch
the launch, and they were disarmed by that invitation, the point
they tried to make remains poignant. The future had arrived, and
the rural Black South was stuck in the past.

How do we consider Nazis in Alabama? Where does their presence lie in the story of the state? Is it simply an alarming fact that
they moved from one hateful, murderous order to another? Or is the
better lens one of relationship? The cold political calculus of how
to achieve global power included a sign that the proclaimed democratic values of the nation weren't as deep as declared (something
that Black people in Alabama already knew quite well). Or—and
this might be the most frightful and the most honest option—
maybe it simply indicated that anything, absolutely anything, could
be justified for empire.

I imagine the ancestors haunting space flight. Maybe they have also gone up into the night. Huntsville's ghosts have a story that one finds all over, of being suffocated under the weight of ambition. It was true during slavery. It was true afterwards. Von Braun, making himself into an American, told the people in Alabama to pronounce his name "Brown." And he was fully immersed. Signs of his influence are everywhere. He created a research center at the University of Alabama, and various institutions bear his name, such as the Von Braun Center and the Von Braun Astronomical Society. In 2014, von Braun's custom-built house in Huntsville was up for sale. I looked at it on Zillow. The nearly three-thousand-square-foot ranch on Big Cove Road is a large mid-century modernist home with a two-car port and built-in bookcases in the den, set back behind cedar trees. A moss carpet lies before it. It is an understated but historically recognized dwelling. Yet there is no marker out front bearing his name. It doesn't matter; local people know.

The relation between the powerful and the less so is, in part, about sowing, reaping, and building. It is also about death, burial, and rebirth. My grandmother used to tell me about the house her family owned in Huntsville and the acres on which it sat. I'm not sure how they acquired so much land, although I've verified that they were landowners through census records. When I was younger, the stories were a luxury for me. You'd hear so much about the way life piled up on Black people that the sounds of a life of abundance gave ease. "It was a raggedy house," she said, "but a big one." There was a fireplace in each room, a farm outside. And the trees were heavy with fruit.

We do not own that land anymore, but there are artifacts of our history in Huntsville. The church my great-great-grandmother would take my grandmother to is still in operation on the very same property where it was located in 1869, then called African Baptist Church, now called Indian Creek Primitive Baptist Church. Black folk in Huntsville were Primitive Baptists and building churches even before emancipation. (Incidentally, the difference between "folks" and "folk" is the difference between a collection and a collective. Folks can be relatives or a community. Folk is never just family; it is always the larger group.) Primitive Baptists are old-school foot-washing people who take "primitive" to mean not undeveloped but original. They believe that only those elected by God will experience salvation, they await the Second Coming, and they profess the virtue of acts of humility. Primitive Baptists initially rejected dancing and music, making rhythm only with voices and hands. That has changed, however, in many congregations, including Indian Creek.

Indian Creek Primitive Baptist Church has had fewer than ten pastors since 1869, and that is but one example of its traditionalism. Another is its conviction to divine purpose. In 1952, the church was destroyed by lightning with nothing saved except the piano. Taking that as a sign, they rebuilt quickly on the same spot, creating a more elegant edifice with multiple rooms and bathrooms as well as a balcony. The same building remains.

I do not know why my grandmother converted to Catholicism. I have speculated that the relative quiet of Primitive Baptists among Black Protestants when it came to music might have made the transition easy. But she told me a few stories about the old church in the place that she called home. And she maintained some of the Primitive Baptist sensibilities. For example, she always warned us against telling our personal business in confession and drinking from the Communion cup. Primitive Baptists disagreed with the idea that church should interfere with the dominion adults had over children. For Black Primitive Baptists, I imagine this doctrine resonated deeply. They had been disallowed possession of their own children for generations prior.

Churches in Huntsville and throughout the South are places in which people make sense of history. Theology is professed more often than the past is invoked. But the past is ever present. A mile and a half to the south, a mile to the east, there is another site for old-time religion in Huntsville: Oakwood University. It was founded by the Seventh-day Adventist denomination in 1896. The specific mission of this denomination in Huntsville was to educate freedpeople. The sect purchased 380 acres of land that was once a plantation and named the school for the huge oak trees that cover the campus. In slavery times, the most famous Black plaintiff, Dred Scott, lived on Oakwood's land. Born in Virginia around 1799, he was brought by his owner Peter Blow to Alabama in 1818, along with five fellow bondspeople. If you know the Dred Scott story, you may have heard the name of his second wife, Harriet. She was much younger than he. Together with their daughter, they litigated for freedom. The Scotts had been taken to free territory, and precedent suggested that this should have made them free. But they lost their case before the Supreme Court. Justice Taney, writing for the majority, declared that not only were they not free, they didn't even have standing to bring a case before the court because Black people were not and could not become citizens of the United States.

Before Harriet, Dred Scott, then called "Boy Sam," reportedly had another wife in Alabama. And two children. By some accounts, they were sold away from him in 1840. By others, they died and are buried here on the campus of Oakwood. Their names and fate remain unknown, subject to conjecture and dispute. But whether their bodies are among those interred here or not, there are gallons of sorrow in the soil. Including Dred Scott's. Perhaps, as religiosity promised, his wife and children rose into freedom in the heavens, a freedom in death unattainable in life.

Oakwood grew over generations. Its history tracks along with the larger history of the nation. It became a junior college in 1917 at a period in which there was a substantial uptick in college attendance in general and for Black people in particular. The footprint expanded to accommodate more students in 1918. Still a firmly Christian institution, Oakwood experienced the rumble of protest from students in 1931. Nine Black youth had been falsely accused of raping two White women on a train nearby in Scottsboro, Alabama. The Scottsboro case became a national and international story, an example of the racism of the American justice system and social order. Arna Bontemps, a Harlem Renaissance poet and a native of Alexandria, Louisiana, was on the faculty of Oakwood at the time, and hosted protestors from across the country, agitating the school administrators further. Their request that he burn his radical books eventually prompted Bontemps's resignation. He went to the Midwest.

The students went on strike during the annual Board of Trustees meeting, refusing to attend classes, chapel, or work assignments. They organized speeches and prayers among themselves, putting faith to the purpose of freedom.

Their statement of protest read as follows:

> We are tired of lying. In view of the fact that conditions at Oakwood Junior College are not favorable to mental, physical, and spiritual advancement, we the student body, are appealing to our interested brethren in the field for help. Too long, Oakwood has had to feel the brunt of despotic rules. Too long, we have been living under conditions entirely contrary to God's plan of operation for Christian institutions.

These events led to the ouster of the president and the installation of the first Black president of the institution. Though consistently a conservative institution, Oakwood was also the site of student political organizing in the 1960s, as was common at HBCUs during that time. But even after the social transformations of the '60s, it remained deeply conservative, at least on social issues. Today it is a university. Oakwood serves an 86 percent Black student body, and remains a Seventh-day Adventist institution. Although it is the only Seventh-day Adventist HBCU, Black people have been an important part of the denomination for generations. Currently, the Seventh-day Adventist Church is diverse: 37 percent White, 32 percent Black, 15 percent Latino, and 8 percent Asian. Its congregations are primarily in the South and West. Though segregation remains (as the saying goes, Sunday morning is the most segregated time in the United States), much continues to bind its parishioners. For Adventists, like evangelicals, churchiness, including sect and gospel, is common ground between Black and White people in the South. In fact, in virtually every cultural arena, there is both common ground and disaffection between Black and White Southerners. As Albert Murray said, "American culture, even in its most rigidly segregated precincts, is patently and irrevocably composite . . . the so-called black and so-called white people of the United States resemble nobody else in the world so much as they resemble each other."

However, when it comes to race relations, Black Southerners often struggle against what White Southerners try to maintain. Nevertheless, many more old ways, in one way or another, are treated as virtuous. And the old ways can be a recalcitrance when it comes to progress. They are also found in wearing slips and girdles and pantyhose, in still having rollers to place in one's hair. They are in eating the evening meal early, and disconnecting all electrical devices when it's storming out. It is putting "Miss" in front of an elder's first name. And, when your mother or auntie or any elder woman to whom you owe respect calls you, answering, "Ma'am?" Black Southerners lament the land that was swindled or in a moment of desperation sold away for a pittance, but even without a foot of property to your name, the old ways become properties, constitutional and therefore more intransigent than the intimacy with land. Massive resistance to desegregation and devotion to lost-cause history is the ugliest part of this disposition. However, I refuse to call its expression, in the large sense, "backwards," when "traditional" is far more apt.

* * *

IN MUSCLE SHOALS, ALABAMA, beginning in the 1960s, two of the most famous music studios were situated: FAME, founded by Rick Hall, came first in 1961, and then the Muscle Shoals Sound Studio in 1969. At FAME the group known as the Muscle Shoals Rhythm Section was founded. They were a shockingly good collection of White studio musicians who played background to soul, R&B, and country artists. The first group of musicians was lured away to Nashville. Another group replaced them. Then four of those members went on to create the Muscle Shoals Sound Studio. These musicians, collectively, played on over five hundred records including songs by Aretha Franklin, Wilson Pickett, Joe Cocker, Willie Nelson, and many more. Audiences were frequently surprised, at least until their reputation was solidified nationally, that they were mostly White. But perhaps they shouldn't have been. In the rural South, musical inheritances are not neatly segregated. Rising in popularity over the 1960s, they went most often by their nickname, "the Swampers," because that's how the music sounded. Blended and muddy like a swamp, a jambalaya, a gumbo of the sounds of the South. The Swampers played on at least seventy-five gold and platinum hits.

When I first heard the Alabama Shakes in 2012, they reminded me of the Swampers. They were a White band with a biracial Black front woman, Brittany Howard, who belted like a blues queen, and moved her voice across gender and genre lines with elision, rising and falling, wails and howls. Her falsetto is gender- and genre-bending, sounding like a gutbucket Smokey Robinson as she sings, "I just wanna stay high with you."

One of my favorite musician interviews was with Brittany Howard. The interviewer asked her about growing up biracial in the South, and she answered thoughtfully that she didn't much think about it. That she was more aware of being poor and raggedy: the kind of dirty-kneed kid who other folks didn't want their kids playing with. In another interview, Howard said she thought she was getting away from racism when she traveled to the Northwest but then realized that "[t]he South has tons of black people, so even if you're racist, you're still down with the black people. But up there, they ain't got that many black people so they don't even know how to act." There is simultaneously a jealously guarded color line and an ease between Black and White in the South. It has to do with both numbers and history, including the ever-present knowledge that that which is prohibited has always happened, especially when it comes to sex. This is not progressiveness, though. It is the matter of fact of living. So while that's true on the one hand, we are still careful driving through Cullman County right by Madison County, where Huntsville is, because it was and is known as Klan country. You make do with each other, and you've been in each other's families for a long time on opposite sides of the color line. Howard's voice is a testament to that. She can belt, round and strong. And she can holler, too.

Howard's point is about history and genealogy, but not in the way people tend to find most fascinating. The one-drop rule is a source of endless speculation and spectacle for Americans because miscegenation titillates. You'd be hard-pressed to find an article about Brittany Howard that doesn't mention that she is biracial. It is as though the South is misunderstood as an absolute racial border and therefore the consensual interracial relationship is posited as a heroic narrative. That is simply historically inaccurate. Interracial sex is a complicated but persistent reality through Southern history, ranging from frequent rape to true love. But once the fact of sex and procreation across the color line is set aside, there is a larger genealogical and historical point. We lived together, Black and White. We traveled from the Upper South to the Deep South together. We died together. This intimate garment is a lesson. If you think, mistakenly, that American racism can be surmounted by integration, by people knowing each other, even by loving each other, the history of the American South must teach otherwise. There is no resolution to unjust relations without a structural and ethical change.

Now, even though I assert the intimacy across the color line, I do not mean to suggest that cultural differences don't exist. They did and do. This is what one hears in the voices, eliding with distinction. A White Southerner is more likely to have a twang, and a Black Southerner is more likely to have a drawl. A White Southerner's sentences end up high, on average, whereas ours have a lower-register refrain, "mmm-hmm, uh-huh," sometimes said round-robin, sometimes staggered, sometimes in unison. And we know sayings like "If somebody shows you who they are, believe them" are not famous people's quotations but Black aphorisms. Black Southerners laugh from the belly; White Southerners' shoulders shake. But if you say, "Put it up," a Southerner on either side of the color line will hear what Northeasterners think should be "Put it away." If you say, "I got strangled on some water," nobody will look at you funny in the South. Because "choked" isn't the only way to express water making you cough and sputter. "Cut it off" is the way you turn off a light, and "cutting up" is a vivacity that might be amazing or a mess. "Alley" is an adjective for street life, as well as kind of place. If you "wasted" something, you spilled rather than misused it. "Quit" is the imperative that is always "stop" in other regions. If a Southerner says "skeet," you should know it means ricochet and not just a sexual reference from a rap song that got to the mainstream in the early 2000s. No matter who, you can respond to someone "Did?" and it will qualify as a whole sentence, just like "So." Which is also a dare. We both talk alike and talk different; tongues mix and tongues lash against each other.

Down here, Black and White folks both use the word "nigger." Not in polite company, of course. And I want to explain it. Do we begin at the beginning? Or do we begin where we are today? It is a slur that demanded the tongues of Black people at the outset, forced to wear the mask of subservience. Some of those tongues turned in on themselves, forked, sucking in poison; some others—more I believe—began to speak on two registers, or three, or four. In case you haven't noticed, Black American language does that frequently. Our words mean multiple things, sometimes opposing. Of course they would. How else in this nation could there be a way for Black people to both love themselves and stay alive?

Language has direction. It demands a listener, or a reader, and it lands accordingly. That isn't just a matter of intent. It is a matter of the wind. There is a reason we say, "Who are you talking to?" as a way to say "I am turning your ugly words back into the air, they won't touch me. Ever."

"Nigger." It repeats, again and again. And people opine or snigger. The opinions are political and social. Some of them ask, "Well, if the Blacks say it all the time, how come we can't?" It strikes me as envy about the way Black people have figured out how to bend language so hard. I wonder what would happen if we disinterred an old field hand, at the arsenal or at Oakwood, and placed her in the middle of deliberating about that word as a sort of inheritance. Because she is there already; we just don't acknowledge the way she haunts. We acknowledge the master's ghost more frequently. We remind the young, or the uninitiated, that the word was an appendage to his property right. For shame, we say. But remember, in the language of the old South, "Black," "African," and "Nigger" were roughly equivalent words of degradation, precisely because the charge was that Blackness itself was inferior, that Africa was the dark continent from which niggers could and should be stolen because it was without human value, like them. I think—and of course this is speculation, but it is a speculation that comes from both my study of history and my study of the elders—that if we put the old field hand at the center, this is what she would tell us: "Baby, they think of everything to tear you down. You got to stay alive, but you also got to offer your testimony. Hold your head high. You may not have much, but you are a child of God, nothing more, nothing less." She would be the one to know how to shelter the fugitive and the insurgent, and to offer poultices to the whipped. To see what has to be done, now, and do it. She would say to choose your words with care, even when you curse fate.

The descendants of that old field hand, and thousands upon thousands of others, fought hard to not be called "nigger." They fought for "Negro" to be a word of respect, and "African," and "Black." They fought to be American, and they fought to be free of America. I can say it that way because they weren't all fighting for the same thing, even when fighting against the same thing. I won't tell you what to think about the word itself, but I will tell you to think about what it does, inside history, with all the ghosts intact.

Hip hop is filled with the word. And hip hop is global. So the word is as well. Some elders ask if the young who use it with such aplomb have any sense of its history, especially down here. One might even think there is a world of difference between the vulgarity of hip hop and the foot-washing evangelists, but there is a common ground between what James Brown's sideman Fred Wesley referred to as "Alabama conservative" and the most stratospheric riffs on the planet. We are the slim, clean-cut, elegantly suited pastors and mayors as well as the sparkle-toothed wildly suited pastors and tattooed rappers like another Alabaman, Gucci Mane, who is fresh like new money, with icy diamonds clutching his neck and wrists, draped in gold like an Akan king. From 2014 to 2016, he did a two-year bid in prison for illegal possession of a firearm and weed. Gucci came out fit and got married to the woman who stood by his side while he was away. They had a televised wedding ceremony of unrivaled ostentation. It was a reminder of what he had already told everybody: "We got so much money 'bout our money, so money, more money, dummy!" Like so many rappers, Gucci revels in excess and accumulation. This is one of many sides. Alabamans in the everyday know to stay gracious and humble. And yet we also say with praise that someone "looks like new money" when they are sharply dressed and floss at the club. Crisp. For the children of slaves, this, too, can be a virtue and a supreme fuck-you.

When you dream yourself into a kingdom that doesn't include you—whether it is an empire or the "Kingdom of God," as the evangelists say—there are myriad permutations and paths. You might imagine yourself the king. Or you might imagine the peasants having a revolution, making the kingdom for everyone. If I tell the truth about Black church, not just my experience but all of it, I promise that both imaginings are found aplenty. The figure in the pulpit might imagine lighting the castle on fire, or walking across the moat for another land. That Lyft driver in Virginia and I, I realize, might have more in common than I first thought.

* * *

IN APRIL 2019, I LEARNED that a child at Huntsville High School had died by suicide. Nigel Shelby was openly gay. He was bullied at school and, according to his mother, told by school officials that his sexuality was a choice. The school district claimed to know nothing of the harassment he experienced at school. It is hard to imagine that's possible. Homophobia tends to be performed in humiliating episodes. The shunning is public and brutal.

After his death made national news, his image came across screens. His eyes in every photo shared were bright. His luminosity in photographs reminded me of Emmett Till's, as did his death. I prefer not to think of one death as more tragic than the other, but instead to realize that they are layered. The rules of manhood and the rules of race grow into a monstrous beast, begging for our destruction in dozens of different ways. And the resulting grief notwithstanding, it seems to be so hard to pry the cold wet hands of death-dealing from our throats.

I do not know the scope of Nigel's faith, but he was immersed in the religious culture of the South, having been baptized at age twelve. When he died, he was a member of Greater Fellowship Church. A young church in an old faith community. Religion, in Black Southern life, has always been a lifeline. It kept hope alive in the slave and Jim Crow past. But it can and could also destroy it. As I said before, some Black Southerners have embraced their own version of the God of masters. After all, grown in the thick of a slave society, they came by it honestly.

When I heard about the suicide of Nigel, I thought about the ways people join forces of shared bigotries across the color line. Not all interracial cooperation is decent or good. So much was piled on this beautiful child. Hip hop is populated with men being declared inadequate because they are bitches or bitch-made—so many homophobic slurs that in truth, after I hear stories like Nigel's, I can't even type them. I can't stand to read them even in citation. I wonder about what happens when the direction of profanity slips from the "we" to the other. "We" are N-words versus "you're a . . ." I don't think we can describe it in the same way. I think it becomes akin to the White folks saying "nigger." It becomes a mimicry and a mockery. You don't get to claim innocence when adopting the ways of masters. At best you get to be a trickster, and not a subversive one. Sacred and profane ugliness are conjoined.

What price faith?

Several years earlier, in 2015, the United States Supreme Court declared in *Obergefell v. Hodges* that a fundamental right to marry is guaranteed for same-sex couples, much to the chagrin of many in the Bible belt (and elsewhere). In his dissent, Chief Justice John Roberts likened the decision to the Dred Scott opinion, by now considered one of the worst-decided opinions in the history of the United States Supreme Court. Roberts likened the substantive due process of allowing a same-gender couple to be a "we" to human bondage. The analogy is so strange that it defies coherent interpretation. It must have been based in the anchor of faith, or in his self-constitution, rather than the Constitution of the United States.

There's an artist who I now associate with Huntsville, Toyin Ojih Odutola. She is Nigerian—Yoruba and Igbo—yet also Alabaman. She has a painting called *Anchor*. It is a stunning portrait of a dark-skinned Black women in a white dress before a fragmented geometric background. We do not know precisely where she is, but the light comes from behind her and echoes in the whites of her eyes and attire. Ojih Odutola was raised in Huntsville, and was in a grade between my two cousins at the Catholic school they attended. Her father brought their family to Huntsville because he took a job as a professor at Alabama A&M, the school where my grandfather once studied. Ojih Odutola often wears a gele and insists that you use her Yoruba middle name as well as her Ibo surname so that you call her genealogy correctly. She values her tradition.

Anchor is a piece that followed from her *To Wander Determined* series, which tells the story of two families. One is an Ibo family, landed gentry. The other is Yoruba, a minor aristocratic family. They are joined by marriage. One son with another. In the series of images, the artist contests the law in Nigeria, which does not recognize same-sex marriage. And although the prohibition has been struck down by the United States Supreme Court, plenty of Alabama judges have diligently evaded granting marriage licenses to same-gender couples. They are both "traditional" places in the ways that the British colonizers first imposed on both. In Western art history and conservative theology both, stories are filled with Black bodies appearing as capital in captivity—the story of the transatlantic slave trade and the age of empire. Looking at these paintings that bear the name *To Wander Determined*, I could not help but think about the biblical wandering in which the children of Israel spent forty years seeking the land of milk and honey. There is a destination in these paintings, an alternative vision of human relations. The colors—a spectrum of red, electric blue, and the blackest black—are brilliant.

This is what I think about the legacy of Nazis in Alabama: we should curve our imaginations against lynching, cruelty, and the desecration of the dead, and towards electric beauty. That is tradition, too. It is what can be heard from the body that shakes in religious or erotic ecstasy; in those moments of transcendence is possibility. It is possible that the ways of holding on—music, dance, God—can unearth the fullness of desire. It is where we look for the resurrection of the dead and the life of the world to come.

TOBACCO ROAD IN THE BIBLE BELT

North Carolina

H. L. MENCKEN, one of the sharpest critics, satirists, and scholars of the first half of the twentieth century, frequently derided the South. It was provincial and feudal, in his estimation. But in 1935, Mencken wrote an article titled "The South Astir," and in it he offered a glimmer of hope. The center of his hopefulness was in North Carolina, where the academic seriousness of the university and the growth of industry (specifically the military) were a harbinger of cosmopolitanism. He wrote:

> Carolina had a State university that had inherited a tradition of free speech from a forlorn and almost forgotten little Methodist college, and the State itself had long been notorious for its bellicose and often somewhat uncouth independence of judgment. It was less affected by the ancient Southern langours than any of its immediate neighbors, and it had more money than any of them, and hence more assurance. Moreover, it lay at a sort of cultural crossroads, halfway between Virginia and the Deep South, and it is

always at such crossroads that new ideas are most plentifully hatched.

Mencken was partially correct but barely prophetic. North Carolina has gone through waves of transformation, including a substantial in-migration from other regions in the last thirty years. But those transformations did not, as he expected, change the operative logic of the state. They became part of it. That's not unusual in the United States. Local cultures and power structures are remarkably resilient. The God of masters, as it were, has kept a hold on power. Hence, North Carolina has experienced what Amiri Baraka referred to as the "changing same." He wrote, "Just as the God spoken about in the Black songs is not the same as the one in the white songs though the words might look the same. They are not even pronounced alike." We Americans continue to be at odds despite claims to common purpose.

North Carolina is in the Bible belt, that region that reaches from the Southeast into the Midwest with a shared Protestant conviction, still, Mencken's warnings encouraged Carolinians to grow beyond evangelical moral certainty and into the curiosity and deliberation of rationalism. He wrote:

Helping to get rid of this incubus is the first task of every enlightened Southerner today. It stands in the way of every free functioning of the mind, and is an impediment to all genuine progress, on whatever plane. I'll begin to believe in the prophets of Regionalism when I hear that they have ceased to fever themselves over the sins of New York, and applied themselves courageously to clearing the ground in their own Region. Let them begin at home.

Mencken died in 1956. It was at a time when the massive resistance to desegregation was felt all over the South. The promise of

Brown was not speedily pursued. The evasion was deliberate. Segregation academies, private schools established as a form of resistance to integration, were built. White flight from the cities would come. And evangelicalism would soon have a revival.

The growth of the religious right in the 1970s was in large part a backlash against the civil rights movement and women's movement. To this day, in North Carolina, 65 percent describe themselves as very religions. Three-fourths say they believe in God with absolute certainty. And 77 percent of the adult population identify as Christian, the majority evangelical. The religious right makes a virtue of White supremacy. And perhaps the best evidence of that is the combination of scapegoating and sexual scandal in their ranks. The religious right leads coordinated attacks on those they deem sinful: queer people, trans people, nonevangelical Black folks, and those who have had abortions. Evangelical preachers' revelations of queerness, adultery, and breaching of various religious rules are accompanied by tears and shunning. A more complicated dynamic is that the distinction Mencken saw, between business and higher education on one side and religion on the other, is not so tidy. All ways of "knowing" in this country, not just articles of faith, are shaped by the histories of race and racism.

I've described the God of masters and the God of slaves. They each are the product of impassioned beliefs, but theology is also a product of the distribution of power and politics. The story of David Walker, the landmark Black abolitionist, is a potent example. He was born in Wilmington, North Carolina, to a free woman. Walker argued in his classic 1829 manifesto that if the promise of the nation could ever be actualized, it would require a redemption in the eyes and experience of Black people. The same was true of Christianity, in his estimation. As a young adult, he witnessed an enslaved man forced to beat his wife to death. The redemption of a society that could support such cruelty would require mighty effort and a rebalance of power. Walker's theology had older roots in North

Carolina. There are two Black men who lived in Fayetteville, North Carolina, in the eighteenth century who both articulated an early Black liberation theology.

The first, pastor Harry Hosier, born in 1750, was never literate, but he preached the gospel with a preternatural ability to memorize long passages of Bible verse. He became a noted Methodist circuit rider during the Second Great Awakening who ministered to both Black and White audiences. One of Hosier's most famous sermons came from the book of Luke and the parable of the barren fig tree. He preached that you can plant a faith, but if it does not bear fruit, you cannot consider yourself saved. Hosier testified that repentance requires work. Notwithstanding his popularity, long after his death, the enslaved were still told by White Protestant preachers that they must honor their earthly masters in order to be good Christians, no matter how much those masters refused to repent the violence of claiming ownership of souls that were supposed to belong to God.

The other, Omar Ibn Said, was a scholar. Captured from where Senegal is now and sold into slavery, Ibn Said escaped his first owner in Charleston, South Carolina, and found himself incarcerated in Fayetteville, North Carolina. He wrote in Arabic on the jail wall, presumably by candlelight. Remarkably, we have his written story. Though Muslim, Ibn Said describes Jesus as the Messiah in its pages. And yet we cannot read this as a conversion narrative, from Islam to Christianity. The duress of enslavement may have determined or even distorted his testimony. Ibn Said wanted to be free in a slaveholding Christian society. His declaration might have been an effort of appealing to the theology of the master class rather than an assertion of his own. The word of God remained ambiguous.

Broadly speaking, the interpretation of political and theological principle has been an essential division in the history of North Carolina. And it pivots around White supremacy. The theology of resistance, however, did not depend solely on a counternarrative in Christianity. It included other traditions. Charles Chesnutt, a writer and activist, captured this in his 1899 short story collection, *The Conjure Woman*. Chesnutt was born in Ohio, yet he moved to North Carolina, where his roots were, during Reconstruction. He taught at the school that would become Fayetteville State University. He became well-known, however, for his conjure tales. Chesnutt was African American, but white-skinned, educated, and Midwestern. In contrast, his protagonist, Uncle Julius, was an elderly man, emancipated from slavery as an adult, unlettered and living where he was born, raised, and held in bondage.

Uncle Julius, a strange exile, free but squatting at the site of his plantation home, entertained the married Northerners who now owned the place. In his storytelling, Uncle Julius managed to convince the couple to give up some of the bounty of that land. Negotiating around property rights by telling stories about conjure gave him access to scuppernong grapes, his old cabin, and a church, if not legal rights to them.

The scuppernong detail came from Chesnutt's experience. It is native to North Carolina. When English colonists first arrived in Roanoke, they reported delighting in the abundant grapevines. That original settlement in Roanoke was "lost." But there is a vine that witnessed the English arrival and kept growing long after those settlers disappeared. It is now known as the "mother vine." A canopy holds the strands up along the pathway it follows across an island road. It has been weakened by pesticides and a past effort to destroy it, but now it is cared for. The sweet-sour fruit is bronze-green. The first layers under the skin are slightly translucent but then deepen into opacity. In Chesnutt's tale, a grapevine is "goophered," meaning that it was covered by the power of conjure. Only the knowledgeable could safely partake. By implication, Chesnutt drew a distinction between those who knew the land through their hands and their labor, and the new owners, Northerners who came down, ignorant of Southern ways, and couldn't safely recognize the dangerous spells of the state.

Though the stories are quaint, they also teach us about the dance of navigating Black dispossession. Julius relies on his savvy and his ability to appeal. Repeatedly.

But Chesnutt's greatest work of fiction is the 1901 novel *Marrow of Tradition*. And it rests upon another kind of appeal. *Marrow* follows a bourgeois Black couple and draws from the story of the 1898 Wilmington, North Carolina, race riot. Chesnutt's characters are representatives of the thriving and prosperous community of African Americans in Wilmington, who had political power as well as economic stability that far exceeded most members of their community in the nation. Black Wilmington raised the ire of local Whites. But it was an article written in a local Black newspaper, the *Wilmington Daily Record*, that precipitated the violence. The writer, Alexander Manly, was responding to a speech delivered by the writer Rebecca Latimore Felton, a White supremacist. Standing before the Georgia State Agricultural Society on Tybee Island, Felton advocated the lynching of Black men, who, she said, had a habit of raping White women. Her speech was reprinted in regional newspapers. In response, Manly defended Black men against this charge, saying that the relationships between White women and Black men were overwhelmingly consensual. The *Daily Record* had been circulated among Black and White residents. It was well regarded across the color line. And Manly was reputed to be a direct descendant of former governor Charles Manly. But the White community immediately cut ties and denounced the paper after he published his editorial.

The violence was savage. Alfred Waddell, a local champion of racial resentment who drummed up outrage, declared their achievement in grotesque terms. He bragged that the White rioters "choked the Cape Fear [river] with [Black] corpses." Estimates of Black death range up to 250 people. Three White people were wounded. In the end it was not only a massacre; it was a coup. The multiracial Republican government was overturned, and the all-

White Democrats succeeded in what was often called "Redemption."

Before the riot, Wilmington was an integrated city in which Black people thrived, a metaphoric oasis in the dry desert, a coastal town with a river that spilled into the Atlantic Ocean. A multiracial fusion ticket had led the city, a rarity in the post-Reconstruction South. After the riot, commerce survived, but the oasis was shattered.

The broken oasis is a motif in the post-emancipation South. Wilmington is but one example. Others include Tulsa, Oklahoma, and Rosewood, Florida. And Little Hayti, not the one in Miami but the long-lost Black town near Durham, named after the first Black republic and birthplace to *Vogue*'s André Leon Talley. And Zora Neale Hurston's Eatonville, Florida, and the coastal Alabama Africatown. These communities were efforts of Black Americans to become incorporated into American politics and commerce as well as independent. They embraced the social and moral norms proclaimed by the nation. They were destroyed by the habits of White supremacy. Some of the towns were destroyed by massacre; some were less dramatically but just as insistently dug up or torn down to support new industry, or faded by loss of industry, or dismantled by highway building, or grown sparse by traumatic echoes of the past or the pull of someplace with more going on. The documentary filmmaker Michelle Lanier's *Mossville*, for example, tells the story of a once-thriving community in Louisiana. It was necklaced by petrochemical plants, which killed the land and the trees: a post-apocalyptic true story.

The deeds of the rioters of Wilmington were illegal. But they went unpunished because the de facto law of the land had always been the respect of White grievance and the destruction of Black flourishing.

Just as White Wilmington residents reared up in outrage as a response to a changing lot for Black people in 1898, they also did so in 1971. Then the trigger was the gains of the civil rights movement. Ben Chavis, a former director of the NAACP, comes from an old North Carolina family. His ancestor John Chavis fought for the Continental Army in the American Revolution and, between 1792 and 1794, was the first Black man to attend Princeton University. John Chavis subsequently made his way in the world as an educator and preacher until he was killed in the aftermath of Nat Turner's slave rebellion, ostensibly for preaching the gospel of the God of slaves.

Ben Chavis was a civil rights organizer in 1960s Wilmington. Despite the legal guarantees of integration, the coastal town balked. Black people stayed poor, and the schools stayed segregated. The city ultimately decided to implement desegregation in a cruel yet common way in the South: by closing the cherished Black Williston Industrial High School, firing Black teachers, coaches, and administrators, and distributing Black students in small numbers among the White schools. Black people in Wilmington were outraged by this move, which amounted to more deprivation rather than actual inclusion. The Klan rode again. Black students boycotted the White schools.

A White-owned grocery store was firebombed on February 6 of 1971. An uprising ensued, with Black and White people in conflict, again, and the National Guard was called in. Ben Chavis, eight Black male high school students, and a White woman civil rights organizer were charged with arson. At trial, most were sentenced to twenty-eight or twenty-nine years. The White woman received fifteen years, and twenty-four-year-old Chavis was handed the longest sentence: thirty-four years. Unsurprisingly, the trial was flawed. One of the "witnesses" who testified against the ten said he was promised a minibike in exchange for saying they were guilty. The other recanted his testimony on the stand.

This was the decade we now know advanced mass incarceration. And events like this were powerful harbingers of how states would respond to the freedom movement. The case drew international attention for its obvious illegitimacy. After an appeal to the Fourth Circuit, their convictions were finally overturned nine years later, and the defendants were released. The surviving defendants were ultimately pardoned in 2012, forty-one years later.

By the time I was a young adult, however, in the early 1990s, what I most heard about North Carolina was that it was part of a "new South," with a growing business sector and an increasing number of transplants from other regions. When I visited in 1994, I was twenty-one years old. I had been admitted to Duke University's graduate program in literature. Though the program was known as a home of cutting-edge postmodern theory and cultural studies, I thought I would be immediately comfortable there, being Southern. In fact, I found it terribly intimidating. Dressed in black, Europhile, and using words I just didn't know, the students I met were unlike anyone I had ever encountered in the South. I most remember them talking about Neufchâtel cheese. They said it, and I couldn't even imagine how the word was spelled. I hadn't heard of it, even from upper-class peers at prep school or my parents' European leftist friends, i.e., the most cosmopolitan people I thought I knew.

I went to an appointment with one of the faculty members in the program. I was starstruck. I'd read her writing, and though I was sure I didn't understand everything, I'd found her ideas illuminating and exciting. She said to me, "You have a very impressive dossier." This was before smartphones, and there wasn't a dictionary nearby to look up the word. Then I glanced at the pages she was turning. It looked like my application. Maybe that's what "dossier" meant.

That evening, I found myself confused and upset. This was a department that was devoted to critical theory. These were scholars who had been shaped by the intellectual movements of the late twentieth century. Their ideas and theories were made in light of decolonization movements. I'd applied there because I wanted to

study theory in ways that would help me understand racial and gen-
dered domination and the history of struggles against them. But
here I was, feeling as though I was an outsider to the intellectual
space of the department, despite being inside my region of origin.

I took a long walk through campus. It was spring. I remember
the magnolia blossoms on trees, a firmer and whiter variety than
the loose pink to brown blooms I was accustomed to. The students
I passed were what I had expected: preppy, clean-cut, affluent. A
legacy of tobacco-money opulence hung over the gorgeous buildings
and greens. Many of them were designed by Julian Abele, a man
from Philadelphia who was not invited on campus to celebrate his
architecture because he was Black. He was good enough to make
the place but too Black to be acknowledged. Trained in the beaux
arts, Abele brought grandness and flourish—porticoes, balustrades,
columns, and quoins—to a campus that didn't want him. Though
Black labor had built the buildings in both design and construction, and unfree Black labor was responsible for the wealth of the
state that had been poured into Duke, and though social theory
had emerged from the intellectual imaginations that grew in the
thick of independence movements of Black and Asian people, I felt
a profound invisibility.

And so, in 2006, when I learned about what has become known
as the Duke lacrosse case, I immediately believed the testimony of
Crystal Gail Mangum. A Black woman and a college student at a
nearly historically Black college, North Carolina Central, Crystal
said she had been hired as a stripper by the Duke lacrosse team,
then brutally raped. Given the routine sexual assault of Black
women in Southern history, and of women by college athletes more
generally, the story seemed more than plausible. People I knew who
were affiliated with Duke jumped into action. President Brodhead,
who had taught me Charles Chesnutt's writing when I was an un-
dergrad and he was a professor at Yale, was outspoken in his support
of victims of sexual assault and racism. It was a moment in which it

seemed that the university would, in its punishment of the lacrosse players, signal itself as no longer being the bastion of White patriarchy and the descendants of the planter aristocracy. It would not allow, as had happened all over North Carolina for generations, for a Black woman to be subject to sexual violence in service of elite White men.

Then the prosecutor's case began to fall apart. His argument rested upon evidence that the DNA of one of the defendants was found on an artificial acrylic nail Mangum had worn that evening. But the prosecutor had suppressed evidence that on her underwear, DNA of four unidentified men was found. Mangum also offered conflicting accounts of the evening. She could not properly identify her attackers. Her behavior was consistent with the victims of trauma, but inconsistent with what is necessary for conviction in a rape case. When it was all said and done, the lacrosse players were found innocent and in turn sued the university, reportedly receiving millions of dollars in recompense. The impulse to support Mangum was decried as political correctness run amok, the prosecutor resigned, and faculty who had spoken in support of her were singled out for harassment. This moment was understood by many right-wing pundits as a redemption moment, restoring sanity over liberal hysteria. Some demanded the resignation of all Duke community members who had supported Crystal. Some in fact did leave.

But so much was left untouched. A few details worth pondering remain: The lacrosse players reported that they immediately had buyer's remorse. They asked for White strippers and were unhappy that the women who came were brown, leading one of them to say, according to court testimony, "We asked for white, not niggers." That loud diminishment of Black women as compared to White, even in exploitation, reaches far back into American history. And it echoed in this particular young woman's life. Crystal had been sexually assaulted on multiple prior occasions. The trauma of those events might well have shaped her perception of that night, or perhaps there were perpetrators who were left undetected. Or maybe she just spiraled into fiction. Or maybe the evidence didn't tell the whole story of what happened that evening. Truth doesn't always comport with the rules of evidence. At any rate, something was still awry after the case and the public spectacle were over. No one wanted to return to the house where the party had taken place. It was demolished in 2010. The detective who worked the case committed suicide. A widespread unease remained. In 2010, Crystal was arrested on charges of attempted murder. She was cleared of that charge but was convicted of lesser charges: contributing to the delinquency of a minor, injury to personal property, and resisting arrest.

In 2013, Crystal was charged and found guilty of second-degree murder for stabbing her boyfriend to death. She said it was an act of self-defense. Her sentence was fourteen to eighteen years. At the time of this writing, she is in prison.

I still have questions about wealth and the use of poor people for pleasure, about desperation and excess. About whose vices are protected because they can afford them. I've also wondered about Crystal: Did a wild panic rule her life? How is it that she is responsible for her crimes when so many crimes against her left her without sanctuary, literal or emotional? She didn't have to be a sympathetic or infallible defendant for me to see generations of Southern Black women's woundedness in her. There is no moral in her conviction because what went wrong cannot be repaired, as far as I see it. My takeaway is that there is no recompense for Crystal. There is no accountability built to protect her according to the dominant logic of the South. We have not had rituals of remedy; the brushfire of sexual humiliation belongs to the race and has been described for hundreds of years at this point in slave narratives, memoirs, and histories. But healing? We have no ready ways for offering it up.

In 2012, the Wilmington Ten were finally pardoned. Progress of a sort. However, by 2016, political scientists were saying that North Carolina was not a functionally democratic state. This was the product of politicians elected in 2012. It was also the first time since 1870 (back when Republicans were the progressives) that Republicans controlled all branches of North Carolina government. They moved quickly to assert their power. They removed environmental regulations, cut unemployment benefits, refused to expand Medicaid, decried immigration, and targeted trans people with a notorious bathroom bill, insisting that people use the bathroom facilities of their gender assignment at birth. Their brand of reform focused on targeting extremely vulnerable populations, exploiting widespread and unfounded fear and hatred. Many leaders proclaimed that they followed Christian religion in this effort. Their policies became an altar to the God of masters and the people of plenty. People wondered how this could happen in North Carolina. But it ought not to have been surprising. It was part of a long choreography in which wealthy North Carolina elites respond harshly when threatened.

In 2020, I spoke to Wright Thompson for a piece he wrote titled "A History of Flight," about Michael Jordan, who is a son of Wilmington. We talked about how his disposition as a player, avoiding every action that was overtly political, might have been a strategic effort shaped by the repressiveness of Wilmington. Jordan came of age in the place where his ancestors were enslaved and Jim Crowed. Wright and I talked about the racial politics of excellence that are so central to one of the forms of defiance commonplace in the Black South. Certainly Jordan's work ethic is an example of that. It was not the politics most Black Americans wanted of Jordan, especially not when, right outside of where he balled in Chicago, housing projects ate away at the lives of the descendants of migrants; especially not when in his home state Harvey Gantt, a Black man, lost in senate races to Jesse Helms, a former Klansman, twice. When appealed to for a Gantt endorsement, Jordan famously said, "Republicans buy sneakers, too." It was profoundly disappointing that he withheld his influence. After all, the whole world wanted to be "like

Mike." Many of us thought that Jordan could have applied his race-lessness to the persistence of racism to make a difference. But who knows? Perhaps an outspoken Jordan would have broken the spell of his widespread mainstream popularity and everyone would have remembered he was just a country Black boy who first balled on the land where his forefathers felt the lash.

One of the phrases I live with is this: "Trauma repeats." PTSD returns us to the time and place of a life-shattering moment or moments. We are snatched back psychologically. Sometimes we replay the moment by making ourselves the perpetrator, the destroyer, the powerful. More often we quake. This isn't just a mind game. It is often a doing. I am old enough and young enough to remember the police killing of Bonita Carter in Birmingham on June 22, 1979, when I was six, and the Greensboro massacre of November of 1979 in which the KKK killed five people, when I was newly turned seven, and the way Liberty City, Miami, exploded in the spring of 1980, when I was still seven, because of the snuffing of Arthur McDuffie—every instance a straight line from lynching and burning that we want to cast way back. But I remember. Murder is a tool of White supremacy. Some of us don't recall living without it. Some of us saw camera phones as recordings of the tapes that were already in our nightmares, in our bodies, in our adrenaline systems. We already knew. Some of us who watched *Roots* as little children had nightmares because it wasn't just a story of the way back then; it was "let me explain to you so you can understand what is happening right now." You see, there is no point in the entire scope of magnificent events when we—and I mean Black people homegrown over multiple generations rooted in the Deep South—were ever under the delusion that racism was gone rather than sometimes, temporarily, quieted.

At the crossroads of culture, history, industry, nature, and humanity, we (and this "we" is the national we) repeat injuries as the way it always was and ever shall be, world-ending again and again.

My grandmother and mother came of age in Jim Crow; I came of age in the violent backlash against its undoing. There is a gospel song that asks, "Will the circle be unbroken?" or, in some versions, prays, "Let the circle be unbroken." It is a song about the repetition of death. Salvation, life after death, is a promise, a balm in the middle of grief that is unrelenting.

James Taylor, who, like me, is a Southerner mixed with New England, famously sang of going to Carolina in his mind. The words "Can't you see the sunshine? Can't you just feel the moonshine? And ain't it just like a friend of mine to hit me from behind?" are at once nostalgic and bittersweet. It isn't a "redneck" anthem like "Sweet Home Alabama," or a cheesy ditty like "Chattanooga Choo Choo." It's a romantic song in the deeper meaning of "romantic," in which emotion in all of its complexity, including horror and grief, provides the grounds for poetry and aesthetics. "Can't you just feel the moonshine?"—does that mean the heat of the liquor coursing through your body or the delight on an indigo night of the moon illuminating the water? I don't know that my New Englander friends, the ones who love James Taylor more than anyone else I know, hear it that way. But it is an exile's ballad. I'd like to lay claim to that tradition. Critical theorist Walter Benjamin once distinguished between two types of storytellers: one is a keeper of the traditions; another is the one who has journeyed afar and tells stories of other places. But there is a third, and that is the exile. The exile, with a gaze that is obscured by distance and time, may not always be precise in terms of information. Details get outdated. But if the exile can tell a story that gets to a fundamental truth and also tell you something about two core human feelings, loneliness and homesickness, along with a yearning for a place where they once belonged and/or a reality that has evaporated, then they have acquired an essential wisdom, earning them the title of storyteller.

Michael Jordan matriculated at the University of North Carolina, where a prominent Confederate statue called "Silent Sam" was a fixture. Silent Sam was dedicated by Julian Shakespeare Carr in 1913. He was the son of slaveholders, and a wealthy businessman. As the owner of the *News & Observer* newspaper, he was largely responsible for the fury whipped up against the Wilmington fusion government in 1898. Having had a hand in a coup, he did not pause his vociferous advocacy of White supremacy in the intervening years. Carr was not only an advocate of the lost cause; he supported lynching and other forms of racial violence. On Duke's campus, a library, designed by Julian Abele, is named after him. On UNC's campus, there is an administrative building that bears his name. There is even a town in North Carolina, Carrboro, named after Carr.

In his dedication speech, Carr waxed poetic about the Daughters of the Confederacy and their service to the cause. He also praised college students who joined the Confederate Army, and President Woodrow Wilson. Prior to his presidency of the United States, Wilson had been president of Princeton University, and when Carr graduated, he reflected, he wore his Confederate grays. Carr reported that his Confederate loyalty moved the president to say, "[I]n many years nothing had so much touched and warmed his heart as the sight of that Confederate uniform."

There was one mention of a Black woman in the speech.

One hundred yards from where we stand, less than ninety days perhaps after my return from Appomattox, I horse-whipped a Negro wench until her skirts hung in shreds, because upon the streets of this quiet village she had publicly insulted and maligned a Southern lady, and then rushed for protection to these University buildings where was stationed a garrison of 100 Federal soldiers. I performed this pleasing duty in the immediate presence of the entire garrison, and for thirty nights afterwards slept with a double barrel shot gun under my head.

It isn't so surprising that he took pleasure in whipping a Black woman out of her clothes in front of a hundred men. But that he would fear retaliation afterwards sounds absurd. As if anyone was punished for wounding and humiliating Black women.

On April 4, 1968, when Martin Luther King Jr. was killed, Silent Sam was defaced. Jordan was five years old. In 1971, the year of the Wilmington Ten, Silent Sam was again defaced, and Jordan was eight. The monument was defaced once more on March 30, 1981, the day Ronald Reagan was shot, and the day UNC won the NCAA basketball tournament with the freshman Jordan making the game-winning shot.

In 2018, when the statute was toppled, a nationally known North Carolina activist, the Reverend William Barber, quoted the words of a young White pastor who graduated from UNC, Chris Furr: "As I looked at Silent Sam, face down in the dirt, all I could think was that it was the end of another battle in a war we just can't quit fighting, because we can't tell the truth about why it started." It is true, even in the progressive Southern state, the act of dying in the service of White supremacy is lauded and its resurrection keeps coming. The virtue of racism is proclaimed through thinly veiled proclamations. In that case, it was the decision of UNC to give the statue to the Sons of Confederate Veterans and to offer the organization a $2.5 million trust for its care and preservation—in other words, a windfall. Members of the UNC community who were outraged by this gift spoke up, and the settlement was soon overturned. But the Sons of Confederate Veterans already had the money and the statute. Refuge from White supremacy remains elusive in North Carolina. Refuge for White supremacists seems to be always available.

But those who were assigned to inferiority have not been silent. Reverend Barber, a descendant in form, if not genealogy, of Hosier and Ibn Said, has revitalized the message of the God of slaves. A leader in the local NAACP, he stood at the helm of Moral Mondays, a coalition of a variety of progressive constituencies—queer folks, trans folks, Black folks, Latinos, environmentalists, and pro-choice people—in the tradition of the civil rights movement. Barber lives with ankylosing spondylitis, an inflammation of spinal joints that tilts the body forward, shifting the center of gravity and gait. Perhaps it is my way of making meaning of my own disabilities, but I think pain that shoves itself into your consciousness around the clock, especially when it's at your center, can make things clearer when you are seeking a moral witness. That's not an idyllic observation. Pain forces you to pare down to the essence of every question, to feel the stakes, literally. And every time I hear Reverend Barber speak, no matter to whom, the God he invokes does not equivocate on law and expediency and social order. His God is a God who brings people together, each in their fundamental human vulnerability.

The pushback against the undemocratic order in North Carolina was at least in part successful. In 2016, a Democratic governor was elected, but before he took his seat, the incumbent who lost, along with the Republican legislature, stripped the office of much of its power. They passed the notorious bathroom bill, too, targeting trans people. I wonder what North Carolinian Pauli Murray, the first Black woman Episcopal priest, a pioneer in civil rights law, a professor, and, as their personal papers reveal, genderqueer, would have said about it all. How would they martial faith in response to persecution? Murray was rejected from the University of North Carolina law school in 1938 because of their race, and from Harvard because of their assigned gender; they'd faced bathroom crises in their life, dressed in conventionally masculine attire and often read as male. Would they feel fit to battle now? Or would they be struck dumb by how much hadn't changed? The battle wages on. And it is and was one that is a matter of law and policy as well as symbol, still.

In 2016, Duke recognized its Black architect by renaming the section of campus for which he was primarily responsible Abele Quad. He'd designed those buildings between 1920 and the mid-1950s. Early in that period, the lacrosse players' house had been erected. Abele's work stands; that house has been dissembled. Abele's historic marker includes the phrase: "If you seek his monument, look around." That sentence on Duke's campus reverberates. Some monuments have been hiding in plain sight. Some monuments are not human likenesses but the persistence of creation. Some monuments are destructive or ambiguous. Some are an aspiration as well as recognition.

The God of masters, I imagine, approved of the reward to the Sons of Confederate Veterans. It was a nod to the original logic, one of which the elite White planter class would always have a place to grow rich and build mansions, to work the slaves and the land in service of the intoxication of nicotine, a treasured monument tucked away but still dearly held. The God of slaves continues to fight back, persistently creative, refusing idolatry in the service of those who have been worked, those who have been used, those who find themselves still hungry and dizzy even if not picking nicotine, creating something worth holding on to instead. Followers of the God of slaves can feel the words of the classic gospel hymn (written by Tommy A. Dorsey, a groundbreaking composer of both secular and gospel music, alternately known as Georgia Tom and Reverend Dorsey) "Precious Lord," which recites, "Precious Lord, take my hand, lead me on, let me stand, I am tired, I am weak, I am worn." In order for them to win, in the words of gospel, they have to be "more than a conqueror" and also "more than a conjurer," standing in the house of the Lord as human equals, monumental spirits.

I like that the Duke quad is named for Abele. But it can't erase the prohibition of the architect any more than affirmative action can be an adequate compensation for all of the tobacco plantation workers dizzied in those fields, sweating in those rows, who labored for the prosperity in these grand buildings. Necessary but insufficient. And not a justification for the American habit of putting blinders on one's cruelty. Self-soothing to prevent self-loathing. North Carolina speaks to Faulkner's assertion that the past isn't even past. We live in it as a changing same. The only possibility is reinterpretation of the scriptural underpinning. Making sense of it in the words as understood by the God of the slaves in the present as much as our repudiation of the past.

How naive we were to think that all of those transplants from other regions without twanging or drawls in their speech, without elision in their gait, were the sign of a "new new South" in North Carolina. Maybe they came because they were drawn to the old South. There are people who resettle in the South precisely because its reputation jibes with their values. Some come because it's a place that they imagine makes it easier to express the bigotries that are generally held close to the vest elsewhere.

In one of Chesnutt's conjure tales, titled "Po' Sandy," a conjuring woman named Tenie turns a fellow slave, Sandy, into a pine tree to protect him from the hardships of slavery. Each night she turns him back to human so they can keep company. Until one day Sandy, living as a tree, is chopped down for lumber. His body can never be reassembled. Bereft, Tenie sees Sandy mangled, neatly planked, and turned into a small building: a monument to suffering. Uncle Julius tells this story to his Northern neighbors in order to prevent them from tearing down that very structure, which is now on their property. His effort to sway the Northerners is successful. They grant him, the native, authority over the building. And Julius, pleased, goes on to use it as a church.

I first read about "the trees older than Jesus" that were along the Black River with amusement. The wonder at the formulation "older than Jesus" is possible because Christian theology usually avoids both history and nature. That something, many things, were "before" is an uncomfortable detail. Still, out in the Black River swamplands, at Three Sisters swamp, where vireo and warblers sing, and otters splash, there are trees older than Jesus. The gray-bodied, wide-bottomed bald cypresses have grown for two millennia. At base they are mossy and separate; up towards the sky, their finger-like branches twine together. You can take a ride through them. The trees older than Jesus are treated as a tourism opportunity for the state, but the locals worry that the price of their seduction will be the lives of the trees themselves. And who knows what life comes after that death? Perhaps there is a lesson in holding a certain reverence for something that came before the faith we hold on to. Such non-theological mysteries should make us all quake before the smallness of our humanity, the necessity of our codependence. They were here before the dominant faith of North Carolinian settlers and their descendants was established. They remind you that the state was made, in a particular way on particular terms, out of nature but not according to nature. Therefore, it might be remade. And North Carolina might be remade through the wonder of the unknown. Perhaps even though Mencken was wrong, he was right.

Scientists have discovered that trees themselves breathe. They know by means of the subtle respiration-like movement the trees make at night. What, we might wonder, other than the sun and the soil, keeps them going? Feeling that wonder, we ought to contemplate the fact that it is possible that we are guilty of suffocation. Probably we should still ourselves. The human desire to build a world around greed makes our behavior sloppy and cruel. It could even be, and was, deadly.

I do not claim a firm theological doctrine. This is a choice. I believe—despite my Southern-rooted habits of proclaiming "Lord, have mercy" and "Thank you, Jesus!"—that it is good to be skeptical of religious rules and exclusions and the way they might keep us from discovery. And yet, in the tradition of conjure and hoodoo, I firmly believe in the signs of death approaching. When a bird flew through a window of my house, death arrived soon. And once, when a bird collided with an especially clean window, failing to understand the barrier set up to avoid a message, my aunt died anyway.

There was the squirrel, too. It had a field day, running everywhere, and one time, one was in the walls. I don't know what happened. At first I assumed it didn't expire in there because no stench followed. Until death did. When I got to college and read about Uncle Julius, he was a familiar figure, not in an academic way but in a soulful way. In the way of being Christians but holding on to this kind of knowing that is, like the bald cypress, older than Christ. As much as we want articles of faith to tell our stories, the most important thing is to be honest that they don't tell them all. The origin story is incomplete. We make do with the threads of wisdom. Southern mysticism, our esoteric ways in hoodoo, conjure, astrology, and religion, our ideologies, might keep us aloft, but they also are our tools for negotiating a private need. That is where our skepticism is requisite, and being ecumenical has to extend even further than the boundaries of Christianity to all belief systems. And why nature is always an essential reminder. When forests die and when trees live, we learn something about the gaps between who we are and who we take ourselves to be. When the vulnerable are marked as guilty and the wealthy as innocent, we do as well. When the crop that brought wealth under the banner of Christianity is found to destroy human lungs but trees older than Jesus breathe, it makes me think the meek might inherit the earth. I just hope it's still living then. The trees don't know your race or your gender identity or your sexuality. The trees don't expel you for rumors or bigotries. Book pages like these, stripped, pressed, and printed upon bits and pieces of trees, are filled with ideologies and hierarchies, debates and attitudes. But maybe we learn as much, if not more, by the ones left whole and rooted.

KING OF THE SOUTH

Atlanta

IN THE SUMMER OF 2020, Atlanta's mayor, Keisha Lance Bottoms, said in an interview for *Harper's Bazaar*, "Atlanta will be known for lemon pepper wings and great strip clubs if we're not careful." Some critics of respectability politics balked at her cautioning. To me, it exposed what I once thought was a fault line in the city between its establishment and its excess. Now I see it as simply a part of its choreography of self-creation.

In 1903, W. E. B. Du Bois cautioned his readers about the shiny spectacle of the city in an essay called "On the Wings of Atalanta." It is as though he prophesied the sumptuous greedy drag of reality television: *The Real Housewives of Atlanta* and *Love & Hip Hop*. They showcase a prosperity that some foolishly believed can transcend race and history. Case in point, Soulja Boy, an Atlanta rapper, once said, mortifyingly, "Hold up! Shout out to the slave masters! Without them we'd still be in Africa. We wouldn't be here to get this ice and tattoos." He drips in mess, gold and diamonds. Other rappers, gifted with second sight, like Outkast, always understood "the South got something to say" that ain't all about "pimpin' hoes and slammin' Cadillac doors," and like Ludacris, they will explain "country shit" as a gleaming surface with a lot of roiling underneath: "In Atlanta we get that paper, can you haters say 'cheese'? 10,000 watt amps, 6 15-inch kickers, my truck bumpin' like injecting ass-shots like a stripper. No insurance on these whips, tags all outdated. I might not be shit to you, but my mama thinks I made it." It is a quick quip, but it matters. Underneath all of the glamour is his mama's baby who wasn't likely to make it at all. That's as much of the story as anything else.

Atlanta bustles. Before, in the 1930s, it and my hometown, Birmingham, were the same size. Now the Birmingham metro area is about a million people, and Atlanta is six times its size. Birmingham lost a bid, which it only offered in lackluster fashion, to become a Delta Air Lines hub in the 1940s. Birmingham gave financial preferences to the coal industry, which included a fuel tax, and with that, Atlanta emerged as the regional hub. Atlanta runs on commercial prosperity. It is the home of Coca-Cola, the most popular soft drink company in the world, and CNN, the business that revolutionized the news, paving the way for our reality-show-like attachment to information.

Walking through the airport, which bears the names of a White former mayor and a Black former mayor, it buzzes with its importance and exhausts with its color-coordinated symmetries. One has to "get through" the Atlanta airport, narrowly avoiding collision with others doing the same. Seems like nearly everybody moves through there for coming to and leaving the South.

Culturally speaking, Atlanta is the bright star of the South that we steadily watch, even if with disdain. Atlanta is the cutting edge on unsteady ground. The Black queer mecca, the heart of the Black music industry, the place where McMansions are maintained, pristinely, by the descendants of domestics who now pay somebody else to clean their houses. Atlanta is an in-the-flesh Disney World, a spectacle of American consumption and ambition. It is not, as some are wont to say, the "Black New York." Shops close early, public transportation is minimal, there's something quaint about its boast-fulness. People from larger metropolises often like it and yet are amused by its self-conception. But they might not want to be so smug. It's not incidental that it is the birthplace of a King, the iconic hero of civil rights, who, though he always labored in community, burnishes brightly as singular in our national story.

Atlanta was named by an executive in the Georgia railroad, J. Edgar Thomson, after a mythical figure known to run too fast to be made into a matron. That is until she, seduced by the allure of golden apples, allowed herself to be overtaken. There is a lesson in that. Atlanta still runs, though, and one is reminded of Ted Turner's absurdly colorized classic films. Absurd but so pretty to watch, the precursor to his cable news network. Business has been its engine, and it has shaped the city in every fashion. But even in industry, the quixotic quality of Southern life is evident.

In the case of Coca-Cola, a doctor named Pemberton was stabbed in the chest during the Civil War. He survived but covered the pain with morphine. Soon addiction posed another problem. So he experimented with alternative pain-management systems, including the coca and kola plants. It was a syrup and then a beverage, advertised as a form of medication to deal with all the emotional as well as physical ails that lingered in Reconstruction-era Georgia. In 1886, due to regulation, the alcohol had to be re-moved from Pemberton's drink, and the preparation was revised to include carbonation and remarketed as a sweet indulgence rather than a medicine. The name changed from French Wine Coca to Coca-Cola. In 1888, Pemberton was still suffering, jonesing for morphine, and hadn't made much money, so he sold the rights to what would become the most popular soft drink in the world, even though he suspected it would become a big hit. Atlanta is now a Coca-Cola city, literally and symbolically.

But Coke isn't the only game in the region. Soft drink (some-times just called "drink") companies of all sorts come from the

South. The number two, PepsiCo, hails from New Bern, North Carolina. Caleb Bradham invented Pepsi in 1893 in his drugstore and marketed it as a digestion aid. RC Cola, the first canned soft drink, first made in Columbus, Georgia, became a favorite among Mountain South miners through clever marketing that claimed a MoonPie and an RC would keep you going all day deep in the pitch-dark earth. The Chattanooga Bakery has been making MoonPie since 1917. Marshmallow and cookie covered by a stiff frosting of chocolate or banana, washed down by the sharp, not-quite-as-sweet-as-Pepsi cola, provided a burst of energy. There were even songs written about it, and the MoonPie is now an iconic Mardi Gras treat on the Gulf Coast, and has its own eating contests in Alabama and Tennessee. Mountain Dew took its name from a nickname for moonshine, and it has so much sugar, it nearly can make you feel high. Southerners drink more soda than anybody else, and I do think it's because it has a way of "keeping you going," especially in the heat. Personally, I'm partial to Faygo and Grapico—the former came to Alabama via a reverse migration of all of the Alabamans in Detroit, and Grapico is the only grape soda that rivals Nehi Grape (of the RC company) in my estimation. It's of Alabama vintage, as is Buffalo Rock, a ginger soda so potent that it makes Jamaican ginger beer taste like Canada Dry.

If you take an "Are You Southern?" data-mining-type test on social media, one of the questions will inevitably be: "Do you call soft drinks soda, pop, or coke?" The last one is supposed to be the correct answer, but that's not true everywhere in the South. Rather, it evidences the power of Atlanta as siphon and signifier. And it underscores one of the complications of a word like "Southern" any-way. The South is extremely diverse and complex. It is multilin-gual, speaks different dialects, and has different histories. But we do call certain things Southern in a broad way, some because they are quintessential and some because they're a marker of "not that," as in not Northern, which really means not Midwestern, Northeastern, mid-Atlantic, Northwestern, Californian, or far Southwest in general.

Atlanta has a way of sucking in features from here, there, and everywhere of the South, repackaging it, and selling it to the world. Coca-Cola is one of those global tastes of the United States. Its ads have always been cheerful and refreshing. Its tendency to erode away tooth enamel and weaken systems has not dissuaded the public from its taste. I, like my grandmother before me, prefer the sweeter Pepsi. My mother, however, has always liked Coke. We mostly quit the habit years ago, but if I get the chance to have one in another country, where they're still flavored with sugar rather than corn syrup, I can't resist the taste of nostalgia. So American.

Right now, Atlanta is also a center of Black music production. It is the place where Southern hip hop was shined up. T.I., the self proclaimed "King of the South," branded trap, that music about hustling and dealing in the urban South inside trap houses, once crack houses, once the spot, once shooting galleries, once-once-once something else, but always re-created places for business and destruction, which would eventually take the world by storm. Under the gaze of the Northeast, Southern hip hop was mocked almost from the outset. The repetitive vulgarity of Miami bass was deemed corny by Northeastern hip hop heads. The slower pace of Memphis crunk and the lean, dragging sound of Houston was called less than lyrical. But the truth is, no matter what New York says, hip hop has always owed a debt to the South as per Kiese Laymon's classic essay "Hip Hop Stole My Black Boy." You cannot get to hip hop without James Brown and his funky drummer, the sonic foundation of the art. Brown, country as he wanted to be, with his greasy perm, spangly suits, and gravelly drawl, was Augusta-bred. And the children of the Great Migration and the civil rights movement loved him to death for two generations straight. Then there was also Gil Scott-Heron, the Tennessean poet, who, reared by his grandmother, talked about revolution. His father, a Jamaican soccer player, heralded from the other root region of hip hop. I've always said that it was the common aesthetics, the beats and sounds that resonated for the diaspora here and there, where rhyming and boasting were held aloft, that made hip hop a national art for Black people in the US, and eventually a taste for the whole world. But there's something else that would come later. We say the only difference between Black folks in various parts of the diaspora is where the boat stopped, but we don't say that the boats, and the marches through land, didn't ever stop. Slavery controlled movement and moved people across water and across language. Fugitivity did, too. And so of course there are rhythms that would be found here and there, though a different blend. This is, I think, the thing that Albert Murray got wrong about the South, even as he described those rhythms with a seriousness and precision unlike anyone before and likely since.

And yet I find myself looking for the genealogies, searching for how to make a point that is an argument. When I first heard that Prodigy, the brilliant emcee from the duo Mobb Deep who suffered from sickle cell disease, a New Yorker in every curve of his tongue, was the descendant of William Jefferson White, the founder of Morehouse College, I was intrigued. I considered it a novelty, I suppose, one of those moments—like when I learned that the Queensbridge rapper Nas was the son of a Natchez, Mississippi–born jazzman—in which I could say "Aha!" But my intrigue turned into digging, because by now you have probably ascertained that nosiness is at the heart of my gift for research and association. Prodigy's grandfather was the bebop saxophonist and clarinetist Budd Johnson, who worked with everyone from Count Basie and Earl Hines to Billie Holiday. His great-uncle Keg Johnson played trombone for Booker T. Washington's vocalist daughter Portia Pittman before working with his own roster of famous musicians, like Dizzy Gillespie and Ray Charles. Later he produced beloved bands in the

'70s and '80s R&B world, like the Sylvers, the Brothers Johnson, and Shalamar.

One way of noting this history, of course, is to use it to challenge the mythology that hip hop is not a part of the long genealogy of Black American music. I think it should be obvious that it is. Another way, however, is to think about the web of connection between William Jefferson White and Booker T. Washington, founders of what would become rival institutions for their different models of education, both intertwined in the life of the Queens rapper Prodigy, who narrated his intimate knowledge of incarceration and street life. Such connections are evident everywhere in Atlanta, a city in which hip hop and highbrow are both rooted in and routed through Black life.

W. E. B. Du Bois was introduced to Atlanta through Atlanta University, the preeminent Black institution of higher learning. Though somewhat overshadowed by a shifting racial landscape, it remains *that* institution. Look anywhere where there is a preponderance of Black achievement, and graduates of Morehouse and Spelman are disproportionately represented in that number. Unsurprisingly, those campuses that produce the Black leadership class in this country are also sites of the growing pains of Black America, places where sexuality, gender, and class are played out in challenging interactions between students, between students and faculty, and between the university and the city. It is as though, even with all the ways the world has changed, Atlanta University's talented tenth, that elite vanguard of Black aspiration, still holds down the fort for Black America. In virtually every competitive professional school in this country, one will find a critical mass of Morehouse and Spelman graduates; the same is true of investment banks, corporate law firms, and doctoral programs.

Even if students are only in Atlanta for four years, the sheen of that place, the discipline, doesn't rub off. And it does strike a contrast, a dramatic one, with the strip club, spangle-bra, ass-shot, iced-grill Atlanta of popular culture. But they can't be tidily disentangled. When Migos chanted "Bad and Boujee," a knowing listener could tell you boujee is an attitude that is a citation of "bourgeois." She is a bourgie woman who shares some uncommon tastes with elites. When Trinidad James chanted about being covered in gold, he shouted the "bad women at Onyx" as well as the "freshman at Spelman" on Instagram flexing.

Regina Bradley, author of *Chronicling Stankonia*, identifies the foundational moment at the 1995 Source Awards when André 3000 of Atlanta's Outkast responded to boos with a proclamation: "The South got something to say." It was a turning point away from the subgenres that characterized Southern hip hop, a coalescing of the articulation of the urban South that could only come from Atlanta.

Like virtually all Black people of Generation X, I suspect, I remember the Atlanta child murders vividly. Over two dozen children and a group of adults, too, were killed. It was a terrifying time, and it was difficult to stomach the idea that a Black man did it after so many generations of such terror being inflicted upon us from outside. And in Atlanta, no less. We didn't know if it would stay there, but in those years between 1979 and 1981, Black families stayed on edge. Once, at a gas station in Chicago, a man came up to me and asked if I was okay. I was with my father, a white Jewish man who there was not, as sometimes happened in Alabama because of the coarseness of his hair, thought to maybe possibly be a very light-skinned Black man. This other man, with terror in his eyes, told me he was just checking because of these child killings in Atlanta. My heart swelled rather than contracted. It was a moment of tenderness.

I assured him I was safe with my dad. But I was scared in the world. We believed Atlanta was the place of Blackness rising. An oasis. And if we weren't safe there, it didn't seem we could be anywhere. The resolution of that case was supposed to restore that comforting myth. Wayne Williams was convicted, but many of the cases remain unsolved. He claims his innocence. The killings stopped after he went to prison. The jury consisted of eight Black people and four who were White. That alone was a change. For generations, sham trials without a Black peer on them had convicted Black innocents. This looked like a tragic reversal.

Writers took up the case. Southern writers always have—they narrate terror and injustice, restoring a moral center when it seems as though it has toppled. Tayari Jones, an Atlanta native who has returned home, made it the subject of her first novel. Toni Cade Bambara wrote about it as well. And James Baldwin, who kept returning to the South to find himself and his country, described the period in *The Evidence of Things Not Seen*. The book is an exemplum of being shattered, by death, by Reaganism, by the dashed hope of freedom in the moment. Like Bambara, he is skeptical of that which is taken as prima facie truth about what was going on, in Atlanta and elsewhere. One of his lines, among many, still resonates loudly:

> It is a very grave matter to be forced to imitate a people for whom you know—which is the price of your performance and survival—you do not exist. It is hard to imitate a people whose existence appears, mainly, to be made tolerable by their bottomless gratitude that they are not, thank heaven, you.

I wonder then about the allure of Black prosperity in Atlanta. Especially for its most successful agents. A quiet reconciliation, I suppose, that their possession of so much rests upon the bulk of their folks having so very little, even within the city walls. And a louder proclamation of the glory of not being boxed into the constraints of racism. But perhaps that is worse than a delusion. In

Atlanta, 40 percent of Black households have incomes of less than $50,000, whereas only 20 percent of White households do. Look at corporate boards and corporate leadership and you will see that they remain overwhelmingly White in the city: 80 percent of White Atlantans have a college degree; 27 percent of those who are Black do. And it is a city with one of the lowest percentages of Black homeownership at roughly 25 percent, even as rates of homeownership are higher in the South for Black Americans than other regions. One day, listening to the Atlanta gospel singer LaShun Pace's "I Know I've Been Changed," I noticed the line "God's chemical laboratory of redemption took my black soul and dipped it in red blood / And I came out white as snow." I knew that in the song, whiteness was intended as a metaphor of spiritual purity, and blackness as sin. But I heard it differently. Atlanta is over 50 percent Black, it is luminous with Black celebrity and iconography, but the unbearable Whiteness of its being—and by that I mean a very old social order grown up from plantation economies into global corporations—still leaves most Black Atlantans vulnerable. No matter how it might look, Atlanta still comes out white as snow.

Hip hop in Atlanta threads aspiration together with stratification. Atlanta, and Black entertainment in general, is serious business. And there are moguls. When decrying Black protests against police brutality, T.I. referred to Atlanta as a real-life Wakanda, a place "we" shouldn't tear up because it is ours. He was wrong on multiple counts. His "we" is a small group. They, however, seem outsized because their impact is literally global. Tyler Perry established his empire there. So did Jermaine Dupri. And there's Magic City, which is probably the most famous strip club in the world. It is the apotheosis of sexiness on display. I mean that, because its lore reaches into every corner of the globe where hip hop has reached. Cultural and social capital takes on different forms. Just as a particular university on a sweatshirt or pearls have exchange value, so, too, does a snatched waist, iridescent coffin-shaped fingernails, and a perfect lace front wig cascading all down a woman's back. Du Bois's warning still matters. Dollar bills paper the air, the waistlines, and the wallets. They gush, more aerodynamic than doubloons, more sensually appealing than a regular piece of paper or a business card. The dancers have their own fame. Under the haze and colored lights, they are monuments of self-creation, wigs with seamlessly lacquered edges, geometric curves, skyscraping shoes, and very small clothing. They set the pace, and the audiences, men and women, are rapt by their acrobatic gifts. Michael Barney, a Duke University class of 1978 graduate, founded the club in 1985. I have been told it has come a long way. Though his aspiration to provide a high-end lust-filled experience was there from the beginning, it had a humble start before becoming the most distinguished geography in contemporary hip hop.

In the light, the corners crinkle. Feet hurt; life is a hustle. And that is Atlanta, too. There are lots of poor folks, particularly among the residents whose families have been there the longest. And whether it's in comparison to the nouveau riche or the old money, there is a resentment there as well as an attraction to the unfulfilled promise. The kids who wander around Lenox mall, often with very little in their pockets, have eyes filled with possibility. Hotlanta, ATL, ATLiens, ALANNA . . . the major metropolis of the South doesn't have a sufficient mass transit system or a polyglot culture yet. What it does have is a lot of really nice shit. And listen, dirt roads will not let you forget to appreciate that.

Rappers tell hood stories of Atlanta. That is what rappers do. We hear tell of local places and events. But if you've only gone to Atlanta to be seen, you might not know how it is in person. If you've gone just to be, you've seen the children in a casual moment. You've seen hair that hadn't been combed in the summertime, the stick of a sucker (lollipop) hanging out of mouths. Ashy knees. Riding on the back of your cousin's bike. There's a boy named Anthony who is called Amp, not Ant or Tony. There is a girl whose knees are set wide, leaning over on the stoop like her mama, skirt tucked down in modesty but sitting like much more than a lady.

Behind Atlanta's shine, whether we are talking about social media, the spectacles of pop culture, elegant fine dining, global corporations, or icy diamonds dripping from necks, there are myriad stories and relationships. We know that intuitively, often shaming the artifice in our midst. But I'd like to think, more specifically, that Atlanta makes it obvious that being American is being a trickster. Fashion a self, hopefully a compelling one, out of the messiness of your life. Hold the things that make you most vulnerable close to the vest unless and until you can control how they are received. It's what we do because the rat race is everywhere. I guess the saving grace is that there are places where we can let the funk settle and shed some tears.

MORE THAN A MEMORIAL

Birmingham

I WAS BORN IN BIRMINGHAM because my grandmother believed in the promise of a bus ticket. Of love. Her life was probably harder than she could have anticipated when she was riding there on a Greyhound in the colored section. Twice I also rode a Greyhound bus to Birmingham, though departing from much farther north. I tried to sit as close to the front as possible, so as not to smell the bathroom and to get into the store at the rest stops quickest. It is a long ride. And you've never heard resigned melancholy like the kind on a bus riding down I-95 in the middle of the night. A faint ammonia in the recycled air, a whining toddler, and shadows everywhere.

The Great Migration was not just to the Midwest, Far West, and Northeast. It was to Southern *cities*. My family migrated to the urban South. And mostly stayed there, with exceptions I can count on fingers.

My grandparents settled in Birmingham and went on to have thirteen children. She gave birth to twelve. He made shoes to support his kids. She cleaned houses before becoming a respiratory-therapy staff member at the hospital. She used to tell me that when she worked as a domestic for a Syrian family it was the hardest.

Because they got on the floor with her to work. They beat the rugs every week. She told me that even though they had straight hair, nearly white skin, and big houses, they faced discrimination. When she worked at Syrian church events, my grandmother's employer offered leftover food, which she would accept, then throw away. My grandmother was gracious but not interested in charity. But their coffee, she said, prepared in the way of the old country, was delicious. I liked tea. One day she looked at me matter-of-factly and said, "White folks like a lot of tea." We both laughed. I'd picked up some different ways up North, which stayed charming, I suspect, because she knew I'd never forget where I came from.

Her table never changed. Were it wood, dust would have streamed, littered the shop floor, and muscle would have been spent to make those rounded corners. As it was, the plastic top had been factory-produced dark, with black lines to look like planks, in the prefabricated shape. That, and the spindle legs were sturdy. Not a nick, not a buckle. She would sit there in the kitchen. Small and solid. She hated gluttony and ate on a saucer, or sometimes out of a small bowl. Her newspaper would be in front of her, and she proceeded deliberately through life until it was over.

I always studied her hands and her voice. Her ring fingernails were ridged like mine. Her beds were wider. I can still call them up in my mind's eye. I liked to stand behind her chair, in the mint-green kitchen, as she ate or drank coffee. As a little girl, I would say it this way, in competition with my cousins, elbowing them to the side: "I want her back." Which is now, years after her death, true in another way. As she lived, I sucked down every story she ever told me about her life, wrote them down, over and over, so much so that now they are imprinted not just in my mind but in my fingers, a muscle memory.

Birmingham is called the Magic City. It is a place known for coal and steel mining. It is known for four little girls. It is not as well-known for the two boys who died the same day. Or for Fred

Shuttlesworth, Birmingham's civil rights leader who made clear to Martin Luther King that he wasn't in charge when he arrived, even though our airport bears Shuttlesworth's name. It is not well-known for Mayor Richard Arrington, who kept the city afloat after White flight and the crash of mills and mines, and never once got ensnared in a scandal despite being under surveillance every day of his tenure.

This is the place I call home. I bristle whenever people use the word for me elsewhere: Cambridge, Boston, Chicago, Philadelphia, all places I've spent a whole lot of time. "Home" is one word for me. It is not a physical architecture, though 2345, our house number, and yellow, our house color, matter. Home for the Southerner eases into the cracked places like Alaga, thick and dark sugarcane syrup. Woundedness is pro forma; disaster touches everyone, even if only because you caused it. The unregulated emissions gather in your chest. The blood is so deep into the red earth that grief spirals into madness. We Alabamans have the highest rates of mental illness and the lowest rates of medical care. Inside home, terrors happen and repeat. That is what is neatly called trauma. But its facts are never neat. They gurgle and spill. Whispers are loud, often things you don't want to know because after you hear, in that tinny scream, it's always there right under the surface. ("She woke up in the middle of the night to find . . ." "It turns out her daddy was really . . ." "Let me tell you how Mr. Greg died . . ." "By the time he got to the hospital . . ." "Wasted all over the floor . . ." "The smell . . .") We will tell you about the warmth and charm more easily, but you cannot understand what a remarkable grace they are without the other part. Murderous home, sweet home, old home week, home.

On board the ship, in Melville's *Moby-Dick*, was a cabin boy named Pip. Of him, Ishmael said, "Nor smile so, while I write that this little black was brilliant, for even blackness has its brilliancy; behold yon lustrous ebony, paneled in king's cabinets." Pip is baptized into madness after being cast into the water. Or maybe into a different clarity: "Man's insanity is heaven's sense." He has been reminded that a whale, their prey, would sell for thirty times what Pip would in Alabama. But in his new reckoning, having survived the water, Pip earns second sight.

That's who my people are. You hold your people close, but that, too, is a matter of understanding that they have been ripped out of your arms again and again over generations: sold away, killed by a grinding gear, a careening car, off in the labor camp, off on the chain gang, down from the lynching tree, away to the prison, dead from the sugar, from sepsis, from cancer, from a broken heart. The way life kills, with unapologetic abandon, is precisely why we hold each other so close. And get so angry when our love is riven. In Ralph Ellison's "Harlem is Nowhere," he thinks about how the Black Southerner is ill equipped for the North. According to Ellison, his subtle devices become laughable or even simpleminded there. I doubt that was true, even at the time. But in any case, a Black mind built to handle absurdity is a wonderful thing to maintain. And you need your people to show you how.

These are the things I always knew. A relationship failed. My mother, a paragon of self-regard in a generation that denied that for women, went home to have me. There she and the father who would raise me fell in love and built a partnership that was ahead of its time, almost European in the way each could pursue their life courses until the end. He remained my dad; I retained her and my grandparents' name.

But there is so much more. My father, the man who raised me, had witnessed the Black Panther trials in New Haven. Had railed against the war. And when the choice came to either go into private industry or go down South, he went south. At his job interview at Miles College, when they told him what his salary would be, he laughed. His interviewer looked at him in complete seriousness. He took the job anyway.

At the new faculty orientation, he told me, he saw my mother and thought, My God, she's so beautiful. She was. And he also thought, She's probably not smart. He was sexist. She was, he would soon learn, brilliant. He shared it as a lesson for me, to not see myself from the outside in. Who I am belongs to me.

She'd also made her way from New Haven to Birmingham, under different circumstances. For her it was a journey home. For him it was a journey to becoming who he would be. The rest of the story of my own beginnings has come in bits and pieces over the years. The thing about having organizers as parents is they are not inclined to dwell on the highlights of their lives. You have to discover them on your own.

In 2020, Tom Gardner came to my house on his way to Charlottesville. He was depositing documents for a University of Virginia collection on the civil rights movement and wanted to bring me some materials related to my parents' organizing work along the way. Tom is a professor and has lived in Massachusetts for many years. And I assumed he was a New Englander until, fairly soon in our conversation, he said the telltale word "lawyer." As it turns out, he was born in New Orleans but was a child of a military man and so moved around the South a bit.

There is a natural affection among movement people, a sense of family even at first meeting. I don't know how to name it exactly: common cause, fellow feeling, a shared grief.

Tom had been a member of SNCC and then later president of SSOC, the Southern Student Organizing Committee, a group of White Southerners who were civil rights organizers. Despite the common perception that only Northern White students were involved, there were young White Southerners who aligned themselves with SNCC and understood the importance of organizing among White people.

There are more gaps. Such as people believing that the alarm around mass incarceration did not begin until the '90s and that it slowly morphed from the cause of political prisoners. But there, in the papers of the Southern Conference Education Fund, is my mother talking in 1974 about the indigenous prison struggle, meaning Black Southerners recognizing that locking people up was a tool of social control. As it had been, right after slavery with the convict labor system, and then yet again with chain gangs. And then as a tool for punishing civil rights organizers. And in the '70s as a backlash, coming from left and right, at the prospect of society opening up, ever so slightly. The portrait of my parents in the records is illuminating. They were not pious. They speak assertively, sometimes critically, to people who are now lionized in the stories of the movement. There is a refreshing honesty that precedes the days of sainthood. People could disagree and be on the same side. Everyone was part of trying to figure things out.

I called my mother after Tom's visit. I laughed as I recounted reading her remarks about the difference between White revolutionaries and "White boys playing at revolution." There was something in those pages that put me back to seeing her then, my earliest memories in Birmingham, head covered in a West African gele and ears dripping with long gold earrings or liquid silver from her time living on an Indian reservation out West. So slender that she looks like someone who ought to be in *Vogue* rather than riding the bus in Birmingham. Yet there she was.

She asked me if he knew anything about what happened to Claude Williams. Williams was a White Presbyterian pastor who lived in a trailer out in Alabaster, remote since people had tried to bomb his home so many times. The child of sharecroppers in Tennessee, Williams was a social gospel evangelical who struggled for over fifty years to save the soul of the nation, which meant he was beaten and brutalized a lot over the years. By the time my parents knew him, he was in his seventies and his organizing was focused on police brutality and Black landownership. He'd been defrocked and refrocked, decried and rejected, and was still living with the Holy Ghost.

Williams's conversion to a belief in the living God had come, in part, through the mentorship and influence of Alva Taylor, a professor at Vanderbilt and a proponent of the living gospel movement. Williams is one among many examples of why it is so insidious to tell the story of the Southern movement as though it wasn't intellectually informed. Study, from the educators who organized the Montgomery bus boycott to the students of SNCC to the freedom schools and citizenship schools, was everywhere. It makes sense, of course; the pursuit of learning was an obsession of the Black South after emancipation. It was understood as a key ingredient of making freedom mean all it could. And the fact that formal education was impeded at every turn never changed that fact. I had to tell her Williams had died in 1979, not long after we moved to Massachusetts. She must have known and forgotten to remember.

I thought, sitting next to Tom, about the cost of writing the White Southerner out of the freedom movement story. Yes, there were many more who taunted and terrorized, more still who silently accepted racial terrorism. But what possibility was foreclosed by not seeing the fullness of what could have been, and what could still be. For all the smug assessments of how poor White Southerners vote against their own interests and hate indiscriminately, how rare it is that we attend to their other stories. In my early childhood I had been given affection by those who chose differently than what the order prescribed. I knew the prospect of love along with the intimacy of the Black and White South.

But I always have to be brought back from my tendency to be romantic in my defensiveness about the region. I'm reminded why when I talk to one of my parents' friends from back then—I will call him Beau. He is a gay White man, Southern as they come, an organizer, still of the counterculture. I would call him a person who is at once beautiful, fragile, and steel strong. He's survived. He tells me stories. He reminds me, a woman who has loved Black men, of how hard it is to disentangle desire from the cruelty of the social order, of relations of power and domination. How hard it is to get truly close. Can anyone be vulnerable in all of this, safely? I shied away from his letters at first because they are hard to read. But they are truthful.

Do you know what surveys of porn searches show? They show interracial desire is deepest where Jim Crow was strongest. The social order we occupy shapes the erotics of our lives. Shame keeps us from telling the truth about it. We want to say that the institutionalized rape of the plantation was back then, but it reaches so close to the here and now, through the Jim Crow era, the rape of girls who cleaned homes, the gang rapes on country roads, that violent desire is still thick in the air.

We tend to think moments of pain provide reckoning. But pleasure might tell us even more. What shows up in the abandon of delight tells us a great deal about who we are, naked. This desire happens over an intimate ground. It isn't a gulf. In fact, it is a very old hierarchy of who is on top and who serves the other. Pleasure in the degradations of that order is an old American way. Sex workers will tell you of a queer mix of bloodthirstiness and vulnerability that exists in their most powerful clients. The sexual economy of the plantation persists.

And it isn't just a dispassionate means of achieving satisfaction. In the process, it kills the beloved. The lover, the mammy, the protector, the one who feeds, the one who works the land, labors for the wealth. The one whose physical warmth was yearned for, the one who rides you, the one who lies underneath. Is it any wonder that gender is as passionately claimed as race down South? This is the place where you will hear of a woman strong as any man, or a Black boy with skin white as snow. And yet "a man is a man," and some will caution that everyone "ought to stay with their kind." Rules keep even the folks on the borders of identity very sharply differentiated. If you've read *Black Boy*, you'll remember Richard Wright's blond peach-skinned cousins. If you've read or seen *12 Years a Slave*, you'll remember Patsey, the master's sexual victim, the mistress's beaten one, as the best picker on the plantation. Amythyst Kiah, a Black woman roots musician, has a song called "Polly Ann's Hammer." It is about the folk hero John Henry's wife. When her man fell sick, Polly Ann worked as a steel driver with a baby in her arms. She declared no one strong as she, and yet she tells the baby:

> *This little hammer killed John Henry*
> *Won't kill me, won't kill me*
> *This little hammer killed your daddy*
> *Throw it down and we'll be free*

In the traditional John Henry song, we "hear tell" of his life. The singer is a narrator who tells the story of a man who dies proving his strength. In this one, Polly Ann speaks up for herself and her family. Kiah, voicing Polly Ann, changes the end from death to survival. Polly Ann chooses life over lore. Her secret is knowing that sometimes survival must be chosen over victory even when you know you deserve to win. We endure.

What make a secret a secret? It really isn't who knows—somebody always knows, usually a bunch of people outside of the secret holder. What makes it a secret is that it cannot be spoken about above a whisper without something breaking. Much of the South's conservatism is little more than an effort to zone where we place the yearnings that we don't know what to do with. Every time a pastor faces a scandal, remember that. No one thinks these things don't happen, but many, if not most, think they are supposed to be hidden. And as long as they're hidden, we are prohibited from creating more loving ways of being with one another; we aren't allowed that joy on the other side of secrecy. We cannot correct the imbalance and violence that happens in the shadows with shame lashing out all over the one who is supposed to be beloved unless and until we decide the truth can be spoken.

In 1964, eight years before I was born, my family moved from Titusville to Ensley. Ours was the third Black family on the block. And the last White man on our block, which changed from White to Black across a few years, diligently kept up a sign that read "Zoned for whites." Each morning on the way to school, the neighborhood boys kicked it down. Each night he put it back. It was a choreography on repeat until the old man died.

In 1970, Johnny Harris's family also moved into a White neighborhood in Birmingham. But Johnny Harris's block had White cops living on it. They didn't like integration, and they weren't satisfied with symbolic hatred. They dealt in vengeance. One day he was arrested while going to work. Harris was shoved into a lineup and told by the cops that if he didn't confess to three nighttime robberies and a rape charge against a White woman, more cases would be put on him. Despite his having a long list of alibis, Harris's court-appointed attorney convinced him to plead guilty in their first meeting. Harris was convicted and sentenced to five consecutive life sentences. He was sent to Atmore-Holman prison, down near Mobile.

In the first few years of the 1970s, Johnny Harris became politically conscious. He studied the struggle for independent Black nations, workers' movements, Black nationalism, and socialism. As these ideas swirled in his head, he organized a prison union, Inmates for Action.

The newspapers of that period would call the protest led by Johnny Harris and Richard Mafundi Lake at the Atmore-Holman prison "Alabama's Attica." The prisoners, tired of ignored petitions to the public and the courts explaining the physical abuse they suffered inside, staged a 100 percent effective work stoppage. While sugarcane rotted in the fields, the prison administration tried to defeat the strike with every tool at their disposal. They threatened mass punishment, pointing their guns at the prisoners sitting down in the yard. The prisoners held firm. They tried to divide the White prisoners from the Black. But they remained unified. Finally they beat, transferred, and isolated over three hundred inmates, hoping to disperse the "ringleaders." The protest turned into a rebellion. A guard was killed. Every single one of the rebels was expected to pay.

Johnny Harris was placed in solitary confinement, a vicious barracoon. There he took the name Imani, which means "faith" in Swahili. There is a picture of me and my mother in an old photo album. She wears a purple gele. My hair is uncombed and my fist is raised. It is 1975. I am three years old, wearing a shirt that says, "Free the Atmore-Holman brothers."

As a child, I used to speak to Imani on the phone. He called collect, his voice scratchy through the heavy black receiver. He reminded me to mind my parents and be good in school over the choppy line. He told me once that my name inspired him to change his and not to forget it. He was from Birmingham; so was I. He was locked up; I was up North. When he was finally released in 1991, he said it was talking to children that allowed him to keep it together after so many years.

I stayed with my grandmother when I was home in Birmingham. I ate grits and buttery white toast. I drank orangeade and picked pecans off the ground. I loved it when my auntie Thelma brought me Andy Capp's Hot Fries from the store on her way home from school. I wore lace-trimmed socks and ribbons. My knees were greased with Vaseline. I said "hey" instead of "hi," and when I was at school up North, White kids made fun of me for pronouncing "ask" as "aks" and thought it was funny I said "pin" and "pen" the same way.

And I also remember when Tapson Mawere, a revolutionary intellectual in the fight for Zimbabwean independence, came to Birmingham to speak of the global African liberation struggle. I remember how my whole life growing up, I saw letters that came from prisons in Alabama. Most came from Richard Mafundi Lake. He was also born in Birmingham, in 1940. As a teenager, he was charged with a $34 robbery and sentenced to fourteen years hard labor. This wasn't unusual in the days of the freedom movement (as the organizers I grew up with called the civil rights movement) and the violence of Bull Connor. When Mafundi organized the IFA, he was punished with twelve years in solitary. His chosen name means "artisan." He believed in crafting a freedom vision. And once constrained, he chose survival:

> For 12 years in isolation I had no books to read. I learned to play chess without a board . . . It would get extremely cold with no heat or blankets in the cells. I slept on a concrete slab. And to make matters worse, the guards would throw water on the floor to make it colder . . . I would shadow box until I would get exhausted near the point of passing out in order to sleep. I would take the little piece of toilet tissue they gave us, which was 3 tiny squares, put it on my chest and psych myself out that it was a blanket.

My point is that some, in the plantation South, saw the struggle not as one about inclusion in the American project. They saw it as the unfinished revolution against the age of empire. Over the years, Mafundi was released, and he went back to organizing. I remember when the Iranian Revolution happened. I was sitting with my dad, watching the news on our black-and-white television. I asked him, "Is the shah bad or good?" "Bad," he said. "So is the Ayatollah Khomeini good?" "Well . . ." he said. And looked troubled. Mafundi was in Florida at the same time at a protest supporting the Iranian Revolution against the shah. The protestors were attacked by flag-waving Floridians shouting, "Sand niggers go home."

Mafundi called himself, like many of the organizers I knew growing up, an Afrikan. And in my family, though only a small fraction were deeply involved in the movement, names changed. Those of us born from 1972 to 1985 mostly have East African names. We are of a time, and of a people, who thought of Blackness as beautiful in the hyperlocal and the international sense. We are people who see no necessary conflict between loving individual White people or the agape love of all human beings, including White people, on the one hand and hating Whiteness and what it has meant for us on the other.

In 1986, my dad and I went to hear Daniel Ortega, president of Nicaragua, speak at Jesse Jackson's Operation PUSH in Chicago, the place Jackson moved after Selma in 1967, and where my dad moved after Birmingham. Reverend Jackson held on to the internationalist reach of the Southern freedom movement for some time (as had King until his death). And he wanted people to hear the perspective of the Sandinista leader. As we walked inside, protestors hissed at us. They were all White, and one elderly woman taunted at us, "Communistas, communistas."

The nation was in the throes of the Iran-Contra affair. Oliver North, a Texan wearing his uniform and a *Leave It to Beaver* haircut, testified to the Reagan administration's illegal deal, selling arms to Khomeini and using that money to fund the death squads undermining Ortega in Nicaragua. I think about the 1980s often. How so much went upside down then, the air sucked from the sails of organizing, the prisons filling up rapidly, the hope that was sustained as Black mayors entered office and universities opened up and the tax base of cities plummeted. We have to learn to tell the story of this decade in a manner this isn't simply deindustrialization, Reagan, new wave, sentimental R&B music, and Wall Street. And I have to tell it because it's part of my life that doesn't fit anywhere out there. But it surely happened.

Decades later, as I was piecing together this book, I got a Facebook message that made my heart drop. On January 21, 2018, guards found Richard Mafundi Lake unresponsive in his Alabama prison cell of thirty-one years. In the following days, his daughter Assata and I wrote to each other, like our fathers before us.

The world freezes Birmingham in 1963. But 1963 alone is insufficient, and even if you tell the story of 1963, you need the stories of 1937 and '79 and '83 and all the other years to understand what it was and what it was not. The fire hoses were only one kind of pressure knocking the people down. The marches were only one of the ways that people stood up. I went home. I saw the street names change, the schools desegregate and resegregate, the hospital system go, the steel mills close.

I went back to Birmingham four times in 2019. In February of 2019, I was called back to Alabama to interview Angela Davis, another daughter of Birmingham. She had recently been awarded a human rights award by the Birmingham Civil Rights Institute, and then had it rescinded for her leftist politics. I was selected to speak for the people of Birmingham in our declaration of love for Angela Davis, a defiant reaction to this humiliation, a beautiful and thick love from a socially conservative but deeply self-protective Black community. This is a Southerner's paradox. We conserve. Holding on is a commonplace of people without a great deal of luxury, for whom disaster is a commonplace. Some of you will make fun of your grandmother's sofas covered in plastic, but how else would we find those living room suites, pronounced "suits," in pristine order long after the furniture man, diligently paid once a month, and his son, too, was dead and gone? The caramel set, scroll-edged and brocade satin, has not a tattered thread on it, since 1964. The South is conservative in the sense of conservation. But what that means is not in fact easily described in political terms. It is more solidly grounded in the withholding and forbearance and tendency to hold on, and depending on the moment, that can usher in radical transformation or leave us stuck.

I took a taxi from the airport to my aunt's house. This is something I never do. Usually someone comes to get me, or I rent a car at the airport. My driver was a White man. I got in and was stricken because I could not remember the last time I'd spoken to a White person in Alabama who was working neither in a store nor a university. He was chatty. I could hardly understand him except for when he said "yonder." "Yonder. Yonder. Yonder." I held my head cocked to hear. I often laugh when Northerners can't understand Southerners, but here I was, confused. Once upon a time, not being able to understand the particular twang and yammer of a White man could have been deadly for a Black woman. Now it just elicits an anthropological curiosity for this one. What was he saying and, better yet, what was he trying to say?

Finally my ear grew accustomed to the pacing of his words, the flat pressure at the back of his throat that made words reedy. "Worked in the coal mine nar thirty yar." Thirty years in the depths of the earth, pulling out coal, is claustrophobic work. I wondered: Have his eyes adjusted to living aboveground? To driving? To Super Walmart?

He is the man I have known to distrust. He is the one whose race and manhood once (and maybe still) made him my ruler and me his mule. He could kill me then, and if he had a badge, he could kill me now. I tasted venom in my mouth when he spoke. I won't even say he hadn't earned it because the odds were good he had. I can guess the words he wouldn't say to my face but most certainly would say. The fact that some tenderness crept into my chest despite myself made me uncomfortable. I know he has struggled. Just like I know that he thinks I am supposed to struggle more than he does because I'm a Black gal. And that, of course, is the conundrum—I am American. That means something to me, some common ground with others of this soil, even as the country feels irredeemably racist and maybe not worth saving. It is what Du Bois called a twoness—two warring souls—Black yet American. You face it in its most raw truth below the Mason-Dixon Line. To be an American is to be infused with the plantation South, with its Black vernacular, its insurgency, and also its brutal masculinity, its worship of Whiteness, its expulsion and its massacres, its self-defeating stinginess and unapologetic pride. What the White South confronted in the movement era was a paradigm shift. There was a model for sustaining White supremacy: terrorizing Black folks, the dispassionate acquiescence of the White North and the federal government, economic control, and an ideological hold on its ranks managed by humiliation and cruelty. But a model only holds as long as its assumptions can be sustained. The terror was confronted by valiant organizers. The federal government began to see its racism as bad for the Cold War, Black people cut into their profits with boycotts, and though the screaming mobs were louder, the stranglehold of the White South cracked.

If we ask the question "Why didn't enough change?" one answer is this: domination is creative as well as consistent. The way the region does working—working people like dogs, working to the bone, working somebody to death, working hard "ALL my life," as the old folks would describe it, for little to nothing—was kept up. Servants became service workers. So did farmers and factory people. The lash and the prison farm became the chain gang and the prison farm and then the penitentiary and the prison farm. Birmingham, once a place of dynamite and industry and social transformation and protest, coalesced in the other thing it has always been: resilient.

Riding aboveground, circuitously and with a bit of frustration because the new highway project had redirected everything, with more sunlight and less stability, the coal-miner driver got me to my aunt's apartment complex. And he waited to make sure I got in the door.

The driver's gentility, despite the fact that he could have, could still, string me up without the world flinching? That toothless smile that could easily accompany either mirth or murderousness, depending on the eyes? This is what Black folks mean when we say we prefer the Southern White person's honest racism to the Northern liberal's subterfuge. It is not physically more benign, or more dependable. But it is transparent in the way it terrorizes. You never forget to have your shoulders hitched up a little and taut, even (and especially) when they call you "sweetheart." Cold comfort.

That night, I went to the Boutwell Auditorium to interview Angela Davis. You might expect it would be an audience of young people who see her as an iconic figure. But the elders were the ones who had made the space for her to come home. Richard Arrington, the first Black mayor of Birmingham, was there, on Richard Arrington Jr. Boulevard. He had once been my parents' employer as the dean at Miles College. My father had been his first campaign manager when he ran for city council. Arrington is a historic figure, and also a living, breathing man with the vibrancy of someone half his age. Judge U. W. Clemon was also there, Alabama's first Black federal judge and the father of my college friend Michelle. He'd enlisted me to interview Davis, and regardless of whether I'd wanted to or not (I did), I would have because of who he was to me and us. Not only was this a man who'd been a leader of the student movement at Miles College, he also was the one who had sued Bear Bryant for the segregation of Alabama football. He'd cracked open the state iconography really, and made way for us to become a part. Davis, who was seventy-five years old, was greeted by her Sunday school teacher Odessa Woolfolk onstage. Davis, whose iconic visual image has always belied a lifelong commitment to freedom fighting, was feted in today's Birmingham by folks who had tended her when she was young, and by young organizers who sought her counsel and thanked her profusely for her legacy.

You cannot resign this place to the past if you are being honest. That was the evening's testimony. Victories were had, some died, some live, and the struggle continues. It was the first time in my life, and probably the only time, that large numbers of the people in my professional world, professors from various places who had come to celebrate Davis, were in the same space as my people. Twice that night, someone I knew through my work life said to me, "I think I just saw your family, everyone in the group looked just like you." Recognition is a powerful thing.

I have told my children, time and again, that I think I have a bunch of diseases because the air quality in Birmingham was and is poor. It was called the Pittsburgh of the South and named after the other Birmingham. Even to this day, one of the world's worst polluters remains atop the totem pole of the city. In Colombia, miners have accused The Drummond Company of murdering protestors. In Alabama, they were charged with corruption, including prostitution and bribery. Those charges were ultimately dismissed. Undoubtedly, Drummond is a behemoth of quiet wealth. The company owns two bituminous open-pit coal mines in Colombia, as well as the Alabama By-Products Corporation, also known as ABC Coke, the largest coke foundry in the nation, which has polluted North Birmingham. Residents have been complaining about the impact of ABC Coke for years. The Environmental Protection Agency began efforts to declare the neighborhood a Superfund site, which would have made the city eligible for federal funds for long-term cleanup of hazardous waste. Drummond leaders, fearful that this would negatively affect their business, allegedly bribed and cajoled the EPA out of protecting the community.

A Drummond executive was criminally convicted. But the company remains one of the most environmentally dangerous organizations in the world. Their avatar is Vulcan, the Roman god of iron, a statue of whom sits above the city on Red Mountain, former site of the Sloss Mines. It is the largest cast-iron statue in the world.

The statue was originally made to represent the city at the 1904 St. Louis World's Fair. And then, when it was returned to Alabama, it was left in pieces at the side of the railroad after a dispute over payment for the freight costs.

Vulcan rose again. This time the statue was placed at the fairgrounds, minus its spear, which had been lost on the way back from St. Louis. And in 1936, it was placed where it is now. Thanks to the tension between its concrete interior and its iron skin, which contracted and swelled at differing rates, the statue started to crack from the inside out and was in danger of toppling by 1990.

Finally, at the dawn of the twenty-first century, Vulcan was renovated to its original glory, spear and all. I've wondered what it would be like to not be inflamed. To not have my insides battling against my outsides, a fundamental tension of living with autoimmune diseases, a condition that I speculate has to something do with being born in a city in which Iron and Coal were twin gods. Always wondering if Vulcan cursed me with his poison—he seems to be Southern industry's graven image. For a highly Protestant region, idols abound. But on a drive between Birmingham and its affluent suburbs, where White flight went, you can see something else. Part of Red Mountain was blasted through in the 1960s to build the expressway, and so on the side of the freeway you have a perfect view of its insides. Pinkish and ice-blue diagonal streaks, the red iron-ore seam, and spidery plant life stripe the rock wall. Here are millions of years alongside you. There is the thing that drove the making of the place, the thing that was taken, used, and then used to death for us to make this place, yet again something older than Jesus.

We, the darker children of Alabama, have inherited the scraps of industry and made something of them the same as we did with the land and African languages and cultures. Our artists have told the story.

My friend Farah Jasmine Griffin and I went to an exhibition at the Philadelphia Museum of Art in the summer of 2019. I'd seen her in Alabama for Angela's homecoming that spring, and she already knew my people. Farah is a native Philadelphian, descended from Low Country Georgians. I met her through the terrain of universities, but the ground upon which I've known her has deeper roots. The exhibition was advertised on the billboards as Black Southern art. But as it turned out, and I didn't know this until we arrived, it was mostly Birmingham and Bessemer art. The industrial cities of Alabama have birthed a legion of assemblage-yard artists. They create grand sculptures made of scattered parts and metal too precious to discard, making something out of some things that together go from a little bit to a whole lot.

You are more likely to be familiar with the quilt makers of Gee's Bend. Some of the quilts were at the exhibit, too. Quilting is a rural art form in Alabama. I once asked Mudeah about it, and she told me about the loom, but that she had never learned. What the industrial art and the fabric art and even the fine art of Alabama have in common is their layering, of texture, color, and pattern. Repetition like the certainty of tides coming in in rapid enough succession that the last wave is still in your mind. It is impossible to call what emerges as wholly African or wholly European, though the art tends to be mostly a Black tradition in the state. That said, how does one decide if the Scots Irish or the West African strip quilting led to the fanciful patterns of the Gee's Bend quilters? One doesn't, in fact. Nor does one choose between Vulcan or Ogun, the Yoruba orisha of iron, who traveled a linked chain from heaven to earth. Both are manifest. Even the gospel sound, one of mellifluous harmonizing as much as wails, groans, or shrieks, follows the ways of Alabama art. But the most dramatic example I've experienced is the African Village in Birmingham.

When I went to Joe Minter's village in 2019, it was the second time. Minter is a master of outsider art, an assemblagist who has built the village on his land at the end of a cul-de-sac. This time Minter was there; the first he was running errands. This day, he told me he was going to drop his wife off at the doctor's, but he would be back. After he drove away in his pickup, my cousins and I fanned out in the village. It is a holy sculpture garden. Their four eyes, of two of the most intellectually imaginative people I know, disciplined my attention. Look, Jill said, at the cyclone. It was made of wire and doll babies, an architecture that made the still air appear wild. Dwayne pointed out an altar of crosses and baby shoes. A remembrance of our lost children.

Minter's village lies adjacent to two historic Black cemeteries. As I walked towards one, a group of dogs appeared. Guardians of the dead, they barked me away. I stepped back; they retreated in kind.

Mr. Minter's house is a saturated blue. He wears a helmet all the time, as far as I can tell. When he came back, I asked him what had made him start to make art. He told me, "In 1989, I asked for guidance from God." As he talked, I followed him up to the second-floor deck. There he gave me a lesson. He drummed, and paused to say the sacred beat had gotten him in trouble with the police. I laughed hard, then he laughed, too, and the lesson continued. We were supposed to listen to the ancestors. I looked out. There were figures, icons of metal. There were scenes, theaters of history. There were Bible verses. There were ancestors' names listed, beckoning for you to repeat them. The words sat inside the landscape. Minter pointed to the cemetery on the right-hand side. "Michelle Obama's great-granddaddy is buried there." I nodded. Although the graves haven't been maintained as carefully as they should, and that's a matter of funding, we must be steadfast in our guardianship. Minter instructed me, as so many have, that we have to listen to them, to the testimony of their lives. Minter talked about the teachings of Jesus, but I couldn't help but see Ogun amid the crosses everywhere, a figure walking through a river of metallic beauty. This was not the work of Vulcan. It was the act of doing more than making do.

Back in the Northeast, I attended a party in New York, celebrating Brent Staples's receipt of the Pulitzer Prize. I'm shy and fairly awkward at cocktail parties, so I mostly stood in a corner by myself except for encounters with a few old friends. I chatted with Monica Drake, who was in my class in college, and my emeritus colleague Nell Painter. But of course no matter how shy you feel, you cannot hold people hostage in panicked conversation, so I reluctantly had to let them move around as I fidgeted with my glass. I did successfully enlist a woman in conversation about chiffon and crinolines.

At dinner afterwards, I was much more comfortable. Seated, one-on-one extended conversations are my preferred form of communication. And I spied someone who I was eager to meet. Howell Raines, longtime *New York Times* writer, and (for me) more importantly the author of *My Soul Is Rested*, a unique record of the civil rights movement, was seated at the same table. *My Soul Is Rested* is a work of oral history—essentially a chorus of voices and a form that is, by its very structure, an honest rendering of a much-misinterpreted time and place. I love that book, and I have my father's copy in my office. I told Raines so.

He was gracious in response. And I went on, "I'm writing a book about the South." He asked me where I was from. "Birmingham, originally. But I moved away when I was a little girl." What neighborhood? "Ensley." His eyes widened, then glistened. "I'm from Ensley, too." His home was two blocks over from mine. The neighborhood had once been zoned for Whites. Now Ensley is pretty much all Black. My mother isn't from Ensley. She is from Titusville, like Angela Davis and Condoleezza Rice. This might not seem like such a big deal because the South often gets talked about in a Great Migration blur. But migration happened within and across the South all through history. And the cycle of desegregation to White flight to resegregation was one pattern.

Ensley is a tough place. Nearby Pratt City, once a mining town, is, too. I had a student at Princeton once who had lived in Alabama and, hearing I was from Ensley, looked at me, mouth agape, and said, "How did you get here?!" and by "here" he meant the distance between the "Southern Ivy" (as Princeton is often called) and the Southern trap, I guess. It's almost like all that mining metal and mineral ore gets baked into jaw clamps. Ensley is a place that is protective of who it belongs to, and cautious about interlopers. And it is pretty. You walk along its streets and you are likely to witness, if the weather is mild, people working on cars or sitting on porches or on fold-out chairs right in the yard, listening to music. There are warnings not to walk around on the street. I still do.

From crack house to trap house, in the 1980s and '90s, the zones of addiction disturbed what little peace there ever was. It would ebb. It flowed. Back in 2004, in Ensley, three White cops were shot dead, and one injured, at a drug den. Word circulated that these were dirty cops who were asking for too much of a cut of the dope business. I don't know if that is true or not, but I know that's what folks said. On March 6, 2020, one of the men convicted of the crime, Nate Woods, was executed. He did not pull the trigger. He was convicted under an Alabama law that says that if you are an accessory to murder, you can be convicted as harshly as the killer himself. Governor Kay Ivey went forward with the execution despite a public uproar. The Supreme Court granted a stay for a few hours, then gave the go-ahead. Ivey said, "This is how we do things in Alabama."

The day after Thanksgiving in 2019, I asked my big cousin to take me to see the Ensley ironworks. Photographs I'd seen showed a shell with light shining through. The vestiges of a postindustrial city that survived because of the hospital system that I was born into. But by then, the city had closed the ironworks off. We couldn't get to it. Dwayne showed me instead where they used to bring Black men to beat them, and then have them walk home. Next we rode to the sewage facility; behind it is a Black community. The stench was so great we couldn't stand it beyond a few minutes.

I think people don't really understand Birmingham's toughness, even when they speak of its heroism. How my mother and Angela Davis both recall the men who patrolled their communities at night, armed protectors against White supremacists. How they, as children, pretended to be speaking another language and sat at the front of Jim Crow buses. Those Birmingham buses, the historian

Robin Kelley wrote, were a public theater, a ritual site of Black resistance. And that was a deadly matter. My mother has described
one of the most harrowing events of her youth happening on a bus.
She was with a group of teens who had decided to exit through the
front door. The bus driver stood up, wielding a knife. He lunged,
and only the protectiveness of one of the boys, who pulled the girl
at the front back by her shoulders, saved her life. All of them witnessed the violent commitment to Whiteness. Those things aren't
forgotten.

When Birmingham came out to see Angela, it was a way to
remind each other that we are still here. Prisoners and freedom
dreamers alike. Migrants and homegirls. Strivers and dope boys.
The spirit of freedom dreams remains, however, if waned and complicated. And it rests on imagination as much as resistance. You
have to have an active imagination for all of that building. Sun Ra,
a man who changed from polished suits to capes and sparkles and
spangles, echoed the famous observation of Zora Neale Hurston:
"The will to adorn is the second most notable characteristic in
Negro expression." Perhaps his idea of ornament does not attempt
to meet conventional standards, but it satisfies the soul of its cre-
ator. In this respect, the American Negro has done wonders to the
English language. No one listening to a Southern White man talk
could deny this. Not only has he softened and toned down conso-
nant heavy words like "aren't" to "ain't" and the like, he has made
new, forceful words out of old feeble elements. Examples of this
are "ham-shanked" (with big thick legs), "bodaciously" (boldly and
physically), and "muffle-jawed" (with a fat-droopy face). That night
Angela Davis said, "I love Birmingham," and it was like the sound
of Sun Ra's "Abstract 'I,'" a blade sharpening for the battle to come.

Like the word, the musical note stretched to capacity allows
the living room to breathe through the incessant unmitigated disaster. Staying alive on the grounds of your ancestors' murder and
abuse is no small matter. It requires a living witness to their al-

chemy. Go into a church, find the old woman singing, listen to how her voice, even if cracking, takes up much more space than that to which she has been resigned. Like the laws of slavery, Jim Crow laws were defied every time people on the darker side of the color line opened their mouths and released sound and air from the diaphragm into the ether. Fighting there is heroic. And I mean fighting for freedom, of course, but also simply fighting to live. That struggle has never ceased.

It teaches. By now we know that the flower children, the yippies, the gay rights organizers, and the second-wave feminists were all inspired by the voices of the freedom movement. But the ripple is much bigger. In each successive generation, expression has pushed past existing boundaries, arguing that their insistence is more than a matter of style or taste, but rather that it is a matter of freedom. It's completely reasonable to argue the point about whether an insistence is frivolous, substantive, or righteous. But it seems to me undeniable that we've collectively taken that reaching voice as a case for living.

PEARLS BEFORE SWINE

Princeton to Nashville

An irritant enters an oyster. As a defense mechanism, it
forms a lustrous nacre, layer by layer. A pearl is born.

DURING THE ACADEMIC YEAR, I drive from Philadelphia to
Princeton at least three days a week. I take 95 North. But it doesn't
feel like I'm going north. From the fictional rumors of slave quarters
in the dorm rooms, to the ghost of an auction block that sits right
outside my office, the one from which Black slave children were
once sold, Princeton retains an echo of the plantation South. Princeton
University's first graduate student, future president James
Madison, brought one slave with him to campus and another to
the Constitutional Convention in Philadelphia. The latter he had to
free: all that talk of liberty had ruined him, a poison to the rest of
the plantation. He took the former home with him.

In the town cemetery, Jonathan Edwards is buried. A president
of Princeton, father of the Great Awakening, he met his maker after
a bad smallpox inoculation. The sarcophagus, heavy gray and
stone, bears a few stilted words. It belies the man. Edwards always
had a great deal to say. He wrote on everything. And among his

possessions, on the other side of a paper that he had cut into quad-
rants to write four good sermons, was a bill of sale for an African
woman named Venus. What a fascinating example of reuse and re-
sourcefulness: a sermon on top of human trafficking. Historians
know nothing of the transit of Venus. Just that she was here and
some other there, as Edwards preached the imminent destruction
of a reprobate American people who yelled "What shall I do to be
saved?!" He thought he knew.

The Princeton and Slavery Project, replete with documents,
plays, and paintings, was an answer of sorts. It told the university's
sordid history, in part. There are now historical markers on campus and special tours. But the full consequences of the slave past
haven't yet been unearthed. They reached far beyond 1865. In the
'50s, James Baldwin felt he had entered the South when, as a teenager, he worked here and was routinely denied service in places that
were "Whites only." One afternoon, at a diner near campus, his rage
erupted, and in response to being denied service, Baldwin threw a
glass at a mirror behind the counter, shattering both. He fled immediately.

Today, if you walk down Witherspoon Street, away from campus, you see where Paul Robeson grew up and the small historically
ghettoized neighborhood that still houses some of the descendants
of slaves and servants. Whether formally acknowledged or not,
there are legacies of both slavery and its aftermath everywhere in
this small town, which is the home of the university, a bedroom
community for New York City, and a dwelling place for professionals who work in the pharmaceutical industry.

Mario Moore first arrived on Princeton's campus in 2018 from
Detroit via Brooklyn. He's a fine artist, a painter of portraits with
historic and political significance. He painted and etched the faces
of Princeton employees who work in the dining halls and campus
security. They are Black people, so much Blacker than the student
body and faculty and often with generations-long connections to

the institution and town. They are legacies without a claim. Now, because the university has acquired Moore's work, some of their faces hang on the walls of the Princeton University Art Museum. In the layered browns of their bodies, and the emotions in their eyes, they are realistic and real, in-the-flesh Black people. Because many are still staff as well, the echo between truth and life when you see a person laboring and then see a faithfully rendered grand portrait of her, it feels like a shifting ground.

Princeton is very polite. And it elicits rage. Until 2020 the policy school was named after avowed racist, and former president of both the university and the United States, Woodrow Wilson. The students who protested the name of the school in the late 2010s called themselves the Black Justice League. The "BJL" posted Wilson's racist words around campus. They sat in at the president's office. They were shunned by classmates. One professor called them "terrorists."

Several years prior, as a gag, the swim team dressed up as tribal Africans for a talent show, apparently thinking something just shy of blackface was good fun. On a social media platform, Yik Yak, anonymous students chatted about which Black girls on campus were worthy of "doing," and then, when an African student spoke out about the ugliness of campus racism, they talked about how she was worthy of "doing in." Bomb threats, but not yet actual bombs, have come when discussions of race intensify on campus. Some faculty have proclaimed themselves concerned that people like me will feel inferior because standards have had to be lowered so far for our participation in the community. Literally. They've said that.

In one sense, Princeton is rarefied air. In another, it is the thick of things—public policy makers, presidents, and good old boys have emerged from its Nassau Street gates to shape the world. And so have descendants of colonialism and slavery, alongside sons and daughters of the American Revolution and the Confederacy. Some of us are both.

All of this is to say that in order for me to talk about Nashville—the next stop on our journey—I have to tell you something about the Department of African American Studies at Princeton. From 2009 to 2021, African American studies was housed in Stanhope Hall. This building is named for Samuel Stanhope Smith, the seventh president of Princeton. It received that designation in 1915, over a hundred years after Smith oversaw its construction. Smith was not a polygenist. He'd argued against the idea that humans of different races belong to different species. Rather, he posited that environment was responsible for variations in skin color. And speculated that slaves who worked in the field were darker than those in the house because of the cultural benefits of proximity to masters, rather than evidence of the institutional rape that was central to American slavery. Smith also brought his slaves with him to Princeton. But he defended Phillis Wheatley against withering attacks from Thomas Jefferson. I guess he has a mixed legacy.

The mixed complexions in our building directly contradict his assumption that close proximity to White people of fine education and high status would morph our bodies, making the "huge freckle," as he described brown skin, shrink down to nothing. The people who worked in Stanhope Hall—Black, White, Latinx, and Asian—were and are various shades of brown, and Princeton has not changed our external bodies.

Both the demographics of the bodies and the artifacts of Stanhope Hall changed. As African American studies was institutionalized there, a bust of Frederick Douglass was brought in. Abstract art from Richard Hunt and photographs of Angela Davis, Lorraine Hansberry, Stokely Carmichael, Mamie Till Mobley, and more marked a different sense of history than the vast majority of buildings on campus.

The fourteen professors in the department made their way to Princeton's African American studies department from various places. From the West Coast, from West Africa, from the Far East,

East Africa and the East Coast, from the Midwest, and from the Deep South. Unlikely as it is, a small place in Nashville threads a group of us.

Let me go back and go south.

When my grandmother was a teenager, she was sent to live with her aunt in Nashville. I wish I had asked her more details regarding her time there. But after she passed away, I latched on to one detail. She was always prideful about her high school. She would say, with a smile, that she had attended Pearl High.

Pearl, I learned through research, was one of those special Jim Crow–era institutions, a superior segregated school built against the odds, a feeder for higher education and respectable working-class employment. Most of all, it was a place where the intellect and the spirit were nurtured. So when I was invited to Nashville to speak to Jon Meacham's class at Vanderbilt, I decided I had to visit Pearl, too.

It was only by chance that I took a look at my grandmother's marriage license the night before my flight and realized that it had her Nashville address on it. Kismet. I would go there, too! My grandparents had met in Huntsville. In eighth grade, she sat next to Sadie—that was my grandfather's sister. He passed my grandmother notes when he came to see about Sadie. Dan Perry, as she would say his name, used to come see about his sister and pass notes to her. Courting was frustrating for Neida Mae: her folks would not let her turn off the porch light when he came by the house. She worried that his attention would be drawn elsewhere, to the girls who had privacy and dark porches. And then she moved to Nashville.

He wrote letters. He sent for her. She told me, "He wrote me a letter asking me to marry him with a bus ticket inside. And I was so stupid I went. He could have done anything to me."

He married her.

The geography on a census document is highly organized, general, and speculative. Personal stories have to be threaded into them along with the idiosyncrasies of physical architecture, bodies, and plant life. I cross-referenced the address on my grandparents' marriage certificate with census documents in order to try to get some information about the aunt she stayed with in Nashville and what their lives were like. I looked at the occupations of her family members: a cook and a janitor at Vanderbilt University, and indeed their home was just a few blocks from Vanderbilt. I was literally bound to visit a house that was down the street from where I would be speaking.

The plan for Vanderbilt predated the Civil War. But when it came time to build a school meant to train Methodist ministers, the economic consequences of the Civil War posed a huge impediment—that is until a New Yorker, Cornelius Vanderbilt, stepped in. Vanderbilt was married to a lady from Mobile, Alabama. And he was a philanthropist. In 1873, he endowed the university that would eventually bear his name.

It took me no more than ten minutes on foot to get from my hotel, adjacent to the Vanderbilt campus, to where the house once was. Where the block once was. A Vanderbilt building is there now, but you can see the old street marker. I shouldn't have been surprised that the building where my grandmother lived is no more. Nashville is being built up constantly. I looked up, and cranes filled the sky. At street level, hot chicken spots were everywhere with blazoned signs of such good eating. Down-home and cosmopolitan at once.

I hadn't asked my grandmother about Nashville, but I experienced a bit of it with her when I was a little girl and we watched *Hee Haw* together. It was a television show that came out of the Grand Ole Opry. That most significant country music institution in history is located in Nashville. The Opry was a polished and storied, although self-consciously humble institution, too respectable for Elvis or Jerry Lee Lewis, and so White that only a handful of Opry singers have been Black. Yet she slapped her knee at the country "opera."

When Linda Martell, the first Black woman to perform at the Opry, was on *Hee Haw*, she sang "Bad Case of the Blues," but it wasn't a blues song. It was a yodeling bluegrass up-tempo song about a girl who followed a two-timing city boy to urban despair. Martell herself had left rural Leesville, South Carolina, for Nashville. I wonder if the song was partly autobiographical. Whether it was or not, it was a common story sung by a woman in an uncommon situation, smooth medium brown in a shiny bouffant wig, ladylike and "po'," meaning skinny, as my grandmother would say it, singing at the Opry.

In our family, we watched Southern TV of various sorts. Like *The Waltons*—a show about John-Boy, the writer to be, and his big Virginia family—and when it was just us kids, we watched *The Dukes of Hazzard*, though I don't remember anyone saying a thing about the General Lee, the orange getaway car we all rooted for emblazoned with a Confederate flag. It just was what it was. Then there was *The Beverly Hillbillies*, about Ozarks folks who went out to California after making a heap of money from oil on their property. At the time, some White Southerners were offended by their representation on television. As with Black people, some worried about being made into caricatures and how some authentic cultural features were rendered as signs of stupidity. Others embraced the stereotypes, even turned them into a sign of honor. The comedian Jeff Foxworthy, for example, built a whole career off of proclaiming the identity of redneck and poking fun at "his own kind."

My favorite cast member on *Hee Haw* was Minnie Pearl. I loved the way she screeched out "HOOOOWWWDDYYY." Her frilly dresses and her flowered straw hat with the tags still on it were warmly familiar. The earnestness of country folk, something unfettered about her, pulled at my heartstrings. It was the bit of truth in the stereotype.

Back then, the South on TV was virtually all White. The Black South in public was more sound than image. But when it came to

Black sitcoms? Nothing was ever Southern. Black people on TV were exclusively migrants now residing in Northern cities. The majority were just a generation or two removed from the Deep South. For example, James and Florida Evans on *Good Times* often talked about having come up from Mississippi, but their show was framed around living in Chicago. There was, in contrast, something immediately familiar about all those White Southerners' lives on TV that had its own comfort. I suppose that was ironic given that we lived in the midst of a very clear and angry backlash against the civil rights movement. It isn't unusual to note that racists often love Black art. But it is a bit more surprising how White folks who performed with so many of the signs of racism, as in the near absolute Whiteness of the Opry, could still entertain Black people.

I do not believe in American exceptionalism. But Black Americans belong to so many places in which we have been subjugated. And there's something rare about that. We are not seen as interlopers, as not belonging, but rather as belonging stuck to the bottom. My grandmother's refusal of the bottom is storied in my family. And Pearl High, I had gleaned, was part of how she became that way.

I told my colleagues about this planned pilgrimage. It was research with a personal meaning. One evening, I had dinner in Princeton with Reena Goldthree, a historian who specializes in the Caribbean. I told Reena that I was fascinated by this high school my grandmother had attended in Nashville, Pearl. She smiled broadly and said, "My parents went to Pearl too," along with at least 5 other relatives. Reena hails from St. Louis, but this Nashville school was also in her family tree. When I told Keeanga-Yamahtta Taylor, a colleague from Dallas, a sociological historian who specializes in housing and the history of social movement, about this remarkable coincidence, she held her head to the side and slightly back, as she tends to, and said, "My parents and grandparents went to Pearl." It was uncanny.

Right before I left for Vanderbilt, I was talking about the research I was planning on this trip with our department chair, Eddie Glaude. We sat in his office on the first floor of Stanhope Hall. He is a Gulf Coast Mississippian by birth and rearing. He speculated out loud, "You know, my mother's family is from Nashville. I wonder if any of them went there."

I asked him to find out.

I reached Pearl High and stood at the street corner, seeing the lines of the building reach far back. It is an impressive edifice, dark and stately, haunting in the middle of a bright day. The historical marker read:

> Named for Joshua F. Pearl, the city's first superintendent of schools, Pearl was established in 1883 as a grammar school for Negroes and was located on old South Summer Street. It became a high school in 1897 when grades 9 thru 11 were transferred from Meigs School. In 1917, the 12th grade was added and Pearl moved to 16th Ave. North and Grant Street. In 1936, the school moved to this location.

My heart fluttered. Maybe this was the place where Mudeah fell in love with reading. Maybe this was the place where she learned to draw lifelike faces. Maybe this was the place that convinced her of the power of education and gave her the conviction and dedication to ensure that all twelve of her children would attend college. The building invited the most wonderful speculation.

Not long after my visit, Eddie visited his grandmother. He said he asked her, "'Dear, did you go to Pearl High?'"—addressing her with his family's version of the contraction "Mother dear." He said she said, "Sho' did, Bay-bay." But her memory was failing by then. He told me he wanted to follow up again—she might have been mixing up details. I was already planning the paragraphs, eager to flesh out the marvelous coincidence.

But also, I learned his grandmother lived a mile from where my grandmother lived, before his went back to Mississippi and mine went back to Alabama. Reena's family had come from Alabama and some returned, becoming a Tuskegee family, like my own, as well as a Tennessee State University family. My cousin Jill, who is from Huntsville, like Mudeah, whose parents attended Tuskegee, attended Tennessee State. Keeanga's relationship to Pearl was one that also took her family members on to Tennessee State University, the state's only land grant HBCU, where her ancestors served as educators and administrators. It was a remarkable architecture of relation in a place that none of us called home. Not unlike Princeton.

Eddie's grandmother died before he could ask her the question again. Precious probability and possibility, but not the precision, struck again. Likely true, but with a question mark. Just like finding my grandmother's street with the building long gone, such that I could never see its color or shape. I have no idea how many rooms were in that house. The way some histories are left untraced while monuments to other histories pile up tells you a great deal about what we call "the uses of history."

A Southern childhood changes across the generations. The things that some of us had and most of us knew, like getting trench mouth from eating dirt, or sneaking Argo laundry starch that our mamas and big mamas ate with big spoons, are old Black rural habits. And before us, old women knew how to eat dirt without danger. And did so because dirt was full of nutrients that satisfied the cravings of the poor. On the other hand, the starch, like ice, soothed the cravings felt by anemics. Another hazard was getting a case of the worms because maybe we went barefoot in the mud. This is why they told us to stay out of it and to keep on some shoes. Like the others, that risk has receded.

The plantar aspect, the base of one's foot, is a mark of generations and paths. The flat, calloused soles are now less common than they once were. My grandmother's foot, by the time she passed, was knotted, grown thick with labor and babies, out from the size-4 shoe she wore on the day of her wedding to a 7. Sometimes she said she regretted not getting her bunion fixed while she still worked. We soft-shoe in comparison, even though we've traveled far.

On the day of my visit to Vanderbilt, Andy Lack, then the chairman of NBC News and MSNBC, was also visiting Meacham's class, and over lunch he told me that a great-grandfather on his mother's side had been mayor of Greenville, Mississippi, one of the first Jewish mayors in the South. Like the history of Asian Americans, Jewish Southern history is barely known to the public, including among Southerners. But it is there. The history of Jewish people in the South reaches as far back as the eighteenth century. In 1735, for example, Congregation Mickve Israel was founded in Savannah. In Charleston, Kahal Kadosh Beth Elohim was founded in 1749. The congregation at first was comprised of Sephardim from Portugal and Spain. Other colonial and antebellum Jewish communities were scattered throughout rural towns. They remained small, and antisemitism was always a threatening undertow. But it was a distinct status. In the context of slavery, Jewish people were understood to be White, with higher rates of slaveholding than their Christian peers. They had some access to political power, notwithstanding the existence of antisemitism. In fact, the second in command of the Confederacy, Judah Philip Benjamin, was Jewish, born in St. Croix and reared in Charleston. His ascent speaks to the particular status of Jewish Southerners. He married into an elite Louisiana family, and yet their marriage contract depended on prospective children being raised Catholic. Benjamin studied law and became a distinguished contracts scholar, and both a sugar plantation owner and a legislator. He eventually became a US senator for Louisiana until he resigned along with other representatives from the Southern states at the dawn of the Civil War. He was referred to by abolitionists as an Egyptian in Israelite clothing—implying that his service to the Confederacy was inconsistent with the biblical history of the story of Exodus. Jefferson Davis said he was the brains of the Confederacy. Interestingly, he appears to have not been invested in slavery—he sold all his slaves a decade before the war—but rather Southern autonomy. In fact, he advocated for the Confederacy to offer Black people the opportunity to enlist as soliders in exchange for their freedom. His proposal was ultimately victorious, but it came too late. Defeat was already near. Benjamin drafted the Confederate surrender and then left for Europe, spending the remainder of his life abroad.

The contradiction of being included in Whiteness in relation to Black people, but also subject to virulent antisemitism at times, continually placed Jewish Southerners in a liminal status. In 1868, Samuel Bierfield was lynched in Franklin, Tennessee, largely on suspicion that he had aligned himself politically with Black people. The most impactful example of a Jewish Southerner being treated in ways usually reserved for Black people was the 1915 lynching of Leo Frank in Atlanta. Frank was born in Texas, raised in New York, and settled in Atlanta. He, a prominent member of the local Jewish community, was accused of killing a thirteen-year-old girl, Mary Phagan, who worked at a pencil factory. The fervor of anti-Jewishness in response to the case makes clear that hostile attitudes were just under the surface of White Christian Southern tolerance of Jewish communities. In a certain sense, Southern Jewish life, historically, provides an example of the outer limits of Whiteness. That is to say, Jewish people became "White" in a way that was at that time largely impossible in Europe, but a latent otherness, particularly in the Bible belt, also characterized their social position. To the extent that Jewish people were overrepresented in leftist politics in the early twentieth century, anti-Jewish skepticism was heightened. And in the context of the civil rights movement, when significant numbers of the White students who joined Freedom Summer were Jewish, the alliance with Black people placed their Whiteness in further jeopardy. My father, who arrived in Birmingham to teach at a historically Black college, with a strong Brooklyn accent and wiry, curly hair, was acutely aware of the venom directed at him. When he was living, he would tell me the story of traveling to Atmore, Alabama, late one night for activist work around prisons. He'd always cry, recalling how when he left that evening, he worried that it might be the last time he'd see me and my mother. Being killed was a real possibility. This was a decade after the murders in Philadelphia, Mississippi, of Goodman, Schwerner, and Chaney, three civil rights workers, two of them Jewish. Even after all of the legislative and social change, he was aware of being an outside agitator.

My parents' friends Marshall and Gail Goldberg, now living on the Upper West Side of Manhattan, were back then supporters of civil rights causes in Birmingham. They owned a children's clothing company and outfitted me in beautiful dresses as a result. My favorite was a two-piece. It had a white puffed-sleeve blouse and a contrasting apron on top of it in peach and green, with a crinoline holding the skirt away from my knobby knees. It was a dream dress for a little Southern girl, and precisely the sort of adornment that declared the dignity of the Black Southerner who was so often defiled.

I attired myself more formally to visit Vandy than I generally do for my own classes. This ratcheting up felt necessary for me, being in the South. It was the day after one of the 2020 Democratic primary debates, which had been hosted by MSNBC. Andy Lack shared his thoughts about how to fashion such events for television in ways that are politically useful. He talked about the mechanics of production, a word for putting together a film or television show. I thought about it as a gift or a showing. I was here in Nashville, I understood, to produce something.

In John Steinbeck's book *Travels with Charley*, he moves across the country with a black dog. And the repeated joke he depicts, and it is nauseating, is that when he stopped for gas in the South, people kept saying, "I thought that was a nigger in your car." The joke was a warning. Charley could not, after all, be in the front sitting alongside a White man with any decency were he a Black man. A dog was okay. There is a Southern saying for being dismissed: "You didn't care enough about me to say 'Hi, dog.'" But what happens inside when the dog has more precious status than you? The chorus of Jim Crow living: if you didn't know your place, you were put in your place. Four generations of my family were part of this place. My great-aunt and -uncle—I guess they witnessed a lot of conversations, sweeping and mopping, cooking and wiping from their place. Things to know, but at best only to stow away or navigate around. My grandmother remained outside of Vanderbilt gates, but was held by Pearl, a place of their own. Then my aunt Jacki, who came to Nashville from Alabama, crossed a color line to attend Vandy because they were not ready for her, a Black woman, to be there. She returned home, to Tuskegee, then moved to Boston, went to Boston University for medical school, and became a powerful diagnostician, an ER doctor, and a constant font of essential knowledge for our family. And then my cousin Rasheeda, whose name means "righteous," enrolled in Vanderbilt, coming from Atlanta, the big city that my aunt Regina had moved to with her family, as part of her long career working for Southern Bell. She earned a BA, an MD, and an MBA from Vandy.

One could tell this story as progress. But instead my mind lingers on all the dashed possibilities, the extra work, the workarounds. Whatever I produce, I've always known, has something to do with that. But it also has to do with this.

When my ancestors worked at Vanderbilt, on the margins, there was a group of White male intellectuals who hated being mocked as backwards Southerners and called themselves the Fugitives, people who were running away from what beleaguered them and towards a vision of beauty and freedom. The Fugitives met every other week to write and discuss poetry. "Fugitive" was an odd designation, given the history of the South, where fugitive slaves were escaping elite White men like them. But really, they saw themselves either romantically on the outskirts of the literati, or as outsider intellectuals of the South, or of a flipped fortune as lost cause, the thinking often went.

The Fugitives eventually made a literary magazine bearing their name that became the home to a host of important American writers. Some of the Fugitives also became members of another Nashville group of students and faculty who called themselves the Agrarians, a more appropriate name, perhaps, even though Nashville was urban. Their manifesto was a collection of essays titled *I'll Take My Stand* that featured Robert Penn Warren's essay "The Briar Patch," which was a defense of the segregation laws that defined the US South. The Agrarians took exception to those who cast aspersions on Southern culture. And they took it upon themselves to defend their traditions in literary form.

Theirs was both a new and old way. In the late nineteenth century, the Confederacy was an object of near sacral devotion, a patriotism to a resurrected system with a host of saints standing in stone throughout the South: Stonewall Jackson, Nathan Bedford Forrest, and so on. The Agrarians reveled in the honor and militarism, but studiously avoided the temple of slavery.

It should be no surprise then that when the Agrarians turned to literary criticism, they avoided the matter of context. In the "New Criticism," the term applied to their school of thought, analysis was text, text, text, never intent, never context. It wasn't a bad school of thought. There is a great deal to understand about literature when narrowing in upon the words and their architecture, without always seeking authorization from the author or the politics of the time and place. But how convenient for writers of the Southern gentry to not have to acknowledge the scorched earth and beaten bodies, and the Blackness all around. Famously, Robert Penn Warren, whose work sat somewhat awkwardly among the Fugitives, stepped away from them. His article "Divided South Searches Its Soul" appeared in the July 9, 1956, issue of *Life* magazine. In it, he rejected his earlier "Briar Patch" stance, and became, at least formally speaking, a supporter of civil rights. Albert Murray, "[a] Negro," as Warren described him in a letter to Cleanth Brooks, reviewed Warren's 1965 book, *Who Speaks for the Negro?*, which extended his pro-civil-rights position. It was a series of interviews with civil rights organizers and other prominent African Americans.

Murray was a bit more generous with Warren as a person than some others. He wrote:

> Robert Penn Warren, a white Anglo-Saxon Protestant Southerner, a one-time apologist for segregation, a long-time colleague of the old agrarian romantics and a sometime friend of countless white supremacists and even Dixiecrats, has written a new book which is perhaps the very best inside report on the Negro civil rights movement by anyone so far. In spite of several ridiculous flaws, which are much more characteristic of certain New York indoor intellectuals than of the worldly, realistic and thoughtful son of a hard-headed old Kentucky dirt farmer, *Who speaks for the Negro?* deserves the widest possible circulation.

Sterling Brown would remember Warren bitterly as someone too quick to distort the legacy of those who fought more valiantly and consistently for freedom, as per his depiction of John Brown as a lunatic. But there was a tempered grace in how the Black writers saw Warren's much vaunted conversion.

The Fugitives and Agrarians sought reclamation and recognition. Black people like my ancestors labored with neither option in their midst. In Black studies, we have countered the lie of inadequacy. We repair the breach. Hortense Spillers, one of the leading thinkers in the field, holds a distinguished professorship at Vanderbilt. Her work in Black studies has taught us to understand what it means to stand in the vestibule of the Southern order, to be inside of it but outside at once, and to see this as a position of critical insight and deep understanding.

A few miles away from Vanderbilt, Fisk University stands. It was once the nation's premier historically Black college. Founded in 1866, from the beginning it promised a liberal arts education unlike the vocational emphasis of many other early Black institutions and sustained a reputation for excellence. The buildings, still Georgian and refined, are in need of renovation. They have been well tended to. But despite having one of the most important archives of Black history in the world, and having graduated generations of extraordinary scholars, the wealth gap between Black schools and White ones is apparent at Fisk. Cross the vestibule into this historic institution, and you will find the words for what has transpired. Fisk's library holds Benjamin Banneker's 1792 *Pennsylvania, Delaware, Maryland and Virginia Almanack and Ephemeris*, the print slightly off with yellowed pages, chains used in slave coffles, the records of teachers in Jim Crow schools, the correspondence of Charles W. Chesnutt, and one of the only extant "slave Bibles" provided by masters to those they held in bondage, a version with no references to freedom.

For generations, Pearl graduates made their way to Fisk University or Tennessee State University. Other students came from much farther away. W. E. B. Du Bois, one of the greatest intellectuals of the twentieth century, arrived in Nashville to attend Fisk, from Great Barrington, Massachusetts, and found himself forever transformed by encountering Blackness not as "otherness" but as culture and community. There he found intellectual peers as well as political opponents. Among his political rivals who were also associated with the university was Fisk's first African American president, the sociologist Charles Johnson, who was named to the post in 1946. Though Johnson was not as strident and outspoken as Du Bois, he is remembered for drawing some of the greatest Black intellectuals to the Nashville campus: lawyer, novelist, and NAACP secretary James Weldon Johnson; painter Aaron Douglas; poet laureate Robert Hayden; and Sterling Brown (though Brown didn't stay—the rules of the South deeper than DC were a bit too much for him).

In African American studies at Princeton, there are no Fisk graduates. But we as a department have all followed in the tradition of that institution in growing the field of African American studies. There are no Vanderbilt grads either, but we have hungrily read and reread Hortense Spillers. It is also true that many of us, whether we are literary critics or not, have adopted methods of "close reading" proposed by the Agrarians, even as we believe context is key. And four of us are attached to Pearl High in Nashville. The ways we came to sit in the same buildings, writing our books and teaching our students, are varied. But this coincidence is not in fact coincidence. The reach of institutions that nurtured Black children in the wake of a White supremacist order is much broader than most of us, even in African American studies, realize. The people who came through that school were socialized into grace, dignity, and intellectual aspirations that shaped their families' trajectories even if they did not change their families' class positions in that generation or even the next. Abstract values and virtues were made real in the fabric of Black living.

At the airport, leaving Nashville, I had a taste for something sweet. I stood in front of the vending machine, trying to find a treat that was both satisfying and not too bad for me. Ridiculous, I know. To my left, a White man hovered. He was pale and small with a drawn face. He had a cap on, and a dark blue uniform that hung on him, leaving his britches puddling over work boots and a set of keys jangling at his hip. "Oh, I'm sorry," I said as I stepped back, realizing he was waiting to fill up the machine. "No, you can g'on and get you something." He smiled a sweet smile with a few missing teeth. His eyes crinkled—I assumed he knew what it was to have a hankering for sweets. "Thank you, Imma be quick." I selected a honey bun, huge and covered in frosting. We nodded at each other once again quickly and I walked on.

Whatever it is that I'm saying about the South *as* America includes that, too. Were I to do an assessment based on that man's demographics, the odds are he wouldn't feel so warmly about me. He might look at my life and think, Where's my affirmative action? He might bitterly think that the wages of Whiteness didn't do him much good, while the remediation of them did me a lot of good. We were in roles that to a certain extent were a reversal of the promises of the place from its beginning. And the odds are pretty good that I would be irked by the things he thinks about the world. But the softness with which we could speak to one another is something, not that we would in all circumstances. We could spit words. He could threaten and terrorize me. I could lord the fact that Whiteness failed to give him something over me, sneer about it with my designer shoes and Ivy League pedigree.

Ask any Black student at Princeton or Black students at any peer institution the same, and the odds are quite good that the celebration of their admission was diminished by a claim of unearned benefit. "Affirmative action" is said with a sneer. It is a straw man of the right wing. Because of course college admissions are not an exercise in fairness, no matter what the brochures claim. They are a product of all sorts of inequality. It is not as though labor and talent are inconsequential; it is just that they don't count for nearly as much as opportunity. But let's stay for a moment with the potential complaint of the man who was working the vending machine while I was flying back from teaching a class at Vanderbilt to my regular life as a faculty member at Princeton. Because the fact is that he does have a meaningful claim against the nation; the problem is that the claim is misdirected when it comes to me.

W. E. B. Du Bois taught us this, and we teach it to our students. Whiteness was offered as a promise. Precarity makes it less sturdy. There are White people who work hard all of their lives and

Whiteness gives them little materially. On the other hand, there are White people who come from powerful edifices, who can point to paintings on Vanderbilt's or Princeton's walls and see their genealogies. Individuals like me, the descendants of those who cleaned the toilets who happened to make their way into the classrooms, are distorted images of some remarkable transformation, but in truth we are the exception that solidifies the rule. We have departed, taking pearls with us, but Nashville's Black people remain largely poor. Many are imprisoned. The North Nashville zip code has the highest incarceration rate in the nation. It is where Black Nashville was shuttered and ghettoized when I-40 was built through their older neighborhoods. If I can show you how I owe my purpose not to an elite university (or two or three) but to the fabric from whence I come, I think you might see why I see fit to tell stories that haven't been told, of the people who clean the toilets and those who fill the vending machines and what keeps them from standing alongside one another. Then I will have produced something useful.

WHEN BEALE STREET TALKS

Memphis

There's a great text in Galatians,
Once you trip on it, entails
Twenty-nine district damnations,
One sure, if another fails . . .

—ROBERT BROWNING

THE BLACK COMMUNITY ON BEALE STREET in Memphis dates
back to the Civil War. By the first decade post-emancipation, twenty
Black-owned businesses and a freedman's bank graced the district.
Black people were excluded from Main Street by law and custom.
Beale Street was it. There they could buy food and clothes, as well
see medical professionals. By the turn of the century, the days were
for commerce and the evening for entertainment. Down on Beale
Street, history happened.

Though flourishing, it wasn't safe from the terror of Jim Crow.
The journalist Ida B. Wells was run out of Memphis, damned for
telling the story of its racial violence. In 1892, there was a successful grocery store owned by three Black men, one of whom was a
friend of Wells. A rival White grocer, resenting their success, gathered a mob to enter their shop. After the tussle that ensued, several

members of the White mob were injured. As a result, the Black grocers were arrested. The mob came back to the jail, and while the men fought valiantly, they all were killed.

Ida B. Wells wrote of her friend Thomas Moss:

A finer, cleaner man than he never walked the streets of Memphis. He was well liked, a favorite with everybody; yet he was murdered with no more consideration than if he had been a dog . . . The colored people feel that every white man in Memphis who consented in his death is as guilty as those who fired the guns which took his life.

And then she offered an indictment of the entire system governing the city:

. . . with the aid of the city and county authorities and the daily papers, that white grocer had indeed put an end to his rival Negro grocer as well as to his business.

Wells was best known as a journalist for exposing the lies behind the justification for lynching. Negroes charged with recklessly eyeballing a White woman, or worse, were often people who had found prosperity and respect despite the constraints of Jim Crow. The lynchings put them back in their place. Wells nearly met a similar fate, but escaped as a fugitive to Chicago.

Those who stayed continued to build. They made their own way, excluded from the main drag. It was a Black area, but as was the case with Jim Crow, White people always had access to it. As a teenager, Elvis Presley used to walk up and down Beale Street, looking in the windows, wishing he could buy the fine clothes. He'd been an outsider his whole life, poor as a church mouse and living up close to Black folks more often than not. He was mocked in school. And when was on the precipice of fame, the country establishment were not interested in him at all. He was far too close to Black folks' ways of moving, moaning, and shaking.

The stretch of I-40 between the Nashville and Memphis is called the Music Highway, and that road tells a story. Nashville is country, whereas Memphis is where the Rock & Roll Hall of Fame should have been, as it is the home of the music that was birthed by the blues. But Memphis was and is poorer than the city that won that distinction, and now Blacker than the classic American form that came from Black people. Doesn't change what it was and is.

When I was coming up, in part because of Public Enemy, specifically Chuck D's words, "Elvis was a hero to most, but he never meant shit to me. Straight up racist, the sucker was simple and plain, motherfuck him and John Wayne," Elvis was a subject of scorn for Black people. And even though *Jet* magazine announced that he'd never said, "The only thing a black person can do for me is clean my blue suede shoes," the rumor persisted. Rumors, even when not based in fact, are often based in truth. This one reflected the economy of race and entertainment, and the history of the way they were intertwined. Elvis, the man they called the King, somewhat erroneously, knew what was happening with him. When asked about his popularity, he would say he was an apprentice to Black musicians. He knew why he could get what they didn't.

Dominion over the land and labor were ongoing expressions of White supremacy in Memphis. Nowhere was this more apparent than in the working conditions of Black sanitation workers. Their jobs were deplorable compared to their White peers'. They rode the back of the truck, with the trash, vermin, and maggots, in the rain and terrible summer heat, while their White peers sat in the cab. They were paid less and treated worse. In 1963, thirty-three sanitation workers were fired for attending an organizing meeting. The city leaders refused to recognize their union.

By February 1968, some of the Black sanitation workers began holding nonviolent marches; the use of mace and tear gas against demonstrators galvanized support for the strike. One hundred fifty local ministers, led by the Reverend James Lawson, a friend of King's, organized to support the workers. King came to town and delivered a speech on March 18 to a crowd of around fifteen thousand people. He returned ten days later to lead a march. Though King's hallmark was nonviolent protest, the demonstration turned violent, with stores looted and the police shooting and killing a sixteen-year-old. Police followed retreating demonstrators to a landmark church, the Clayborn Temple, entered the sanctuary, released tear gas, and, per one authoritative account, "clubbed people as they lay on the floor to get fresh air."

The marchers paraded down Beale Street. King was at the head of the column. Then a number of young African Americans began breaking storefront windows. James Lawson was leading the march with King. When they turned onto Main, Lawson says, they saw "lengths of police in riot gear across the street."

Remembering a violent crackdown by Memphis police during a protest march one month earlier, Lawson feared the police would attack again. He recalls telling King, "You must leave. They are going to break up the march and go after you more than anyone." A reluctant King was led away. The marchers turned around. Then police abused marchers with tear gas and clubs. One teenager, a suspected looter, was shot to death. Dozens of protestors were injured, and nearly three hundred Black people arrested. Stores in the Black section of town got looted and burned. Tear gas drifted across the neighborhood. Journalists captured the debacle on film and broadcast it live on local radio.

When King returned, on April 3, he delivered his famous mountaintop speech. The one in which he said, "I may not get there with you, but . . . we, as a people, will get to the Promised Land." We think so much about how it seemed he prophesied his death, perhaps because it allows us to avoid thinking about how the promised land is ever elusive. King was murdered April 4, on the balcony of his room at the Lorraine Motel.

I do wonder what Elvis thought when violence broke out on Beale Street, or when Martin Luther King was killed as he was supporting the cause of Black sanitation workers, who, though working the same job as many White men, had far deadlier and more humiliating circumstances. Or when the city's arteries were cut in half to maintain segregation after the de jure rules were scrapped. I wonder if he simply turned his head, or if he shook his head.

Elvis's life before fame featured repeated experiences with humiliation, but he also experienced something else characteristic of the South and the United States in general: the wages of Whiteness. An effort to place Elvis more accurately in history doesn't just require a recognition that he saw his indebtedness to Black musicians. It also means thinking about how he stands in the American imagination above Black musicians who were his forebearers and peers. Now and again, popular media will point out Big Mama Thornton, Sister Rosetta Tharpe, Chuck Berry, and the most famous among them, Little Richard, as masters of the form of which Elvis was deemed King. And music critics will continue to restore them to their rightful place in history. But there's something to be understood just in noting the difference. Even with his poverty, even considering how he was an outsider, Jim Crow logic created a different trajectory for Elvis. And that phenomenon is now built in our popular culture, even with the progressive erosion of a color line in music. For example, Justin Timberlake, a Memphis native whose style is deeply rooted in the traditions of the Black South, does nothing quite as well as Usher (from Chattanooga) in terms of song and dance, and yet Timberlake is tens of millions of dollars wealthier.

Little Richard reminded everyone, during his life, of the indignity he was forced to endure in comparison to Elvis. Never granted his rightful place in the history of rock and roll, he resented Elvis and he told the world about it, too. Little Richard's prettiness was a transgression, and his profane and electric performances were provocative. He held a note, high and right, as long as a wail with vibrato on the top, perfectly coiffed and adorned. I recall him saying in an interview I heard as a kid that when he was growing up, he always took on the role of Mama when playing house. And that is a particular role in the South. The mama sets the pace for family living, dictates the order and the cycles. She is a choreographer even more definitively than a nurturer. And Little Richard taught Elvis how to dance by example.

The man who really deserves the criticism Elvis got was Pat Boone. But we've mostly forgotten him, so he doesn't come up that often except among those who think like he does. Pat Boone, a descendant of Daniel Boone, was born in Jacksonville and raised in Nashville. He had a very lucrative career doing covers of songs first recorded by Black artists. A conservative Christian, he has spent his later life making birtherism claims against President Obama, and charges about homosexual agendas and the existential threat anyone who speaks Arabic poses to Americans. This is simply a continuation of his past. Listen to his renditions of Little Richard's "Tutti Frutti" or "Long Tall Sally." They are, frankly, sad, stripped of every tinge of eroticism till they sound like spoiled milk.

The Lorraine Motel, where Martin Luther King Jr. was killed, is now a museum. The facade of the motel has been left intact. Visitors are allowed to enter room 306, where Martin Luther King stayed right before his assassination. The image you have seen of him standing there, on the balcony in front of his room, is a still in the middle of motion. Jesse Jackson is burly standing adjacent to King, ever small-statured, ever polished even in the humblest of photos. It is as though there couldn't have been blood, but of course there was. Of course it seeped from his body, hot tragic rivulets, as with the striking sanitation workers.

In 1969, a statue of Jefferson Davis was installed in "Confederate Park," a section of the 342-acre public Overton Park in Memphis. Davis lived in Memphis for three years. Like Confederate statues across the South, the Daughters of the Confederacy were primarily responsible for it being erected. City leaders had approved the statue two years prior.

Inscribed on it were the words "HE WAS A TRUE AMERICAN PATRIOT." In 1967, that inscription could not have been clearer. The branded proclamation to Southern heritage is a joining of Whiteness and Americanness. There are artifacts and there are people making do in Memphis. I asked the poet and professor DaMaris Hill, who used to live in Tennessee, if she could tell me something about Memphis and its distinction from Nashville. She said "Memphis ain't Nashville," and knowingly looked at me. "Memphis is Black." It is, literally—65.5 percent Black in a state that is a bit more than 16 percent Black.

The largest employer in Memphis today is FedEx. It was founded by Frederick Smith in 1973. Smith, who was from nearby Marks, Tennessee, decided Memphis was an ideal location. It is near the center of the country but, unlike the Midwest, doesn't frequently suffer inclement weather. He came from a business family—his father had been one of the founders of the Southern regional branch of the Greyhound bus line, Dixie Greyhound, as well as a chain restaurant called the Toddle House. And perhaps that, plus the access and knowledge that came from an elite education, assisted the success of his venture. Within ten years, it was a billion-dollar company. In contrast to Dixie Greyhound, FedEx described itself as "federal," a business that would have national impact. By 1985, its reach began to extend beyond the borders of the United States.

The growth of FedEx was a consequence of deregulation. The Carter administration began a process that would be ramped up further in the Reagan administration, unleashing businesses from federal government control. One consequence was that new airline carriers entered the market and could fly where they chose and charge what they wanted. Federal Express bought a fleet of Boeing 727 planes and went public.

Now it is the largest airline by freight. And in the top ten by fleet. "Free markets" and free movement allow businesses to soar. It is funny then to think how unfree movement about the city of Memphis can be. Over the first decade of the growth of FedEx, the powers that be in the city managed movement on the ground.

I-40 was supposed to pass through Overton Park, but local residents protested. Among the institutions the highway threatened were the zoo, an art museum, and the site of Elvis's first paid concert. The park was beloved, and locals litigated to protect it all the way up to the Supreme Court, which decided in 1971 that the highway commission had not explored alternative routes to justify taking twenty-six acres of a public park. While the highway commission explored various options, including the prospect of still building the highway through the park, the Citizens to Protect Overton Park won their effort to have the park named to the National Register of Historic Places in 1978, guaranteeing that I-40 would not go through the park.

"People's Days" had been going on for several years in Overton Park at that point. Weekends and holidays, the park was closed to automobile traffic. Eventually the closures became permanent. Hein Park, a small residential community off the west side of Overton, closed the main thoroughfare that ran through it and led to the park's entrance, completely walling off Overton Park, a place preserved for public enjoyment, from the Black community. A group of Black residents sued the city, and again litigation went all the way up to the Supreme Court. They lost. Thurgood Marshall's dissent described the city's behavior as White citizens preventing "Negro citizens from traveling through their 'urban utopia.'" It's more than a metaphor to think on the one hand of those who clean up the city being crushed and on the other hand the fleet of planes venturing everywhere from the city, to witness a deliberate split in the geography and a split in the heights to which its locals scale. There is a cycle that seems unrelenting. Race cuts up.

Memphis is not just aesthetically a far cry from Nashville; it is Mississippi much more than Tennessee. People there reference Mississippi frequently. They have family there, they travel there, and Memphis, like Chicago, was a Great Migration destination for African Americans from Mississippi. One train line took folks from Mississippi to Memphis or Chicago. Another took folks from Alabama to Detroit. But there were exceptional paths. Aretha Franklin, Detroit's greatest voice, was born in a Prussian blue shotgun house at 406 Lucy Avenue in Memphis. The birth home of Elvis in Tupelo, Mississippi, is smaller than Aretha Franklin's in Memphis. His is a shotgun with a porch in white. Hers is blue and wide enough that there are three windows facing you when you look at it straight on. When she died on August 16, 2018, mourning fans made a pilgrimage to her first home and found its blue ashen from dust and debris, its windows all boarded up. All the grass in the front yard was eaten out. Just dirt remained. Elvis's birth home is always covered in a fresh bright white paint, and alongside it there is a historic marker. The last sentence is "He died Aug. 16, 1977, at Memphis, Tennessee." Where he died, at his home in Memphis, there's a formal tourist site: the mansion he called Graceland.

Aretha and Elvis are both one-name icons. They call him the King of Rock and Roll because Beale Street infused his White body. They called Aretha the Queen of Soul because her voice refused a choice between the secular and the sacred. She was exacting, precise, disciplined in her song, and also knew how to shout heartache, grief, and exultation, sometimes all at once.

They both sang a song of Memphis, but the condition of their homes? That is also Memphis.

Plans to convert Aretha's home to a museum are challenged by a confusing chain of title and the size of the home. It is small. It is humble in a community that remains humble. We could build a massive edifice to honor Aretha's gift. But this little house is an instruction. One could tell a Horatio Alger story about talent rising from humble beginnings to become globally famous. But that would be inadequate, I think. Inside the little house is where the magic happened, as it were. This was the term of creation. There are thousands of little houses like this, all across the South, most without historical markers or fundraising for preservation or a famous name attached to them, and they are the places of creation still.

Lil Buck, an astonishing contemporary dancer, a beautiful young man, is of Memphis. His style is called jookin, and he cuts up. That's not a new word: "jookin," sometimes pronounced "joogin," can mean a whole bunch of things. It can mean knocking somebody hard, and in the early twentieth century it meant a form of leaping-buck dancing, but in this case, it's the movement that goes along with "buck," which is a synth-laden version of crunk, mixed with snatches of New Orleans bounce. It is bass-heavy, repetitive, and guttural. The body goes up and down, moving balletically and athletically, with an arrogance of masterful relation to rhythm. Lil Buck looks like he flies on a hinge. He is the master of the form. And, as happens from time to time with Black popular culture, he has caught the attention of the high art world. Lil Buck dances at museums and with ballet companies. The marketing of these moments is akin to folk art's place in fine art museums. A shock at what comes from a Black vernacular space is implied. But that should not be the shock. African American social dance is a stern discipline. It demands precise isolations of extremities and joints, grace and excellence of form. Black dance around the world is rule-bound, and so it should be unsurprising that there would be points of commonality to be seamed together between the rigors of one dance tradition and another. Black children grow up learning dance combinations for talent shows or their own entertainment. And there is no ridicule like failing to master the basic elements of rhythm and style. What made Elvis remarkable is that he moved past the amateur stage of these movements. He made his body respond appropriately and on time to the rhythm.

The prevalence of "Lil" and "Baby" as prefixes throughout hip hop tells you something about Black language, especially as rendered in the South. You are defined by your relationships, by your people. To be a "lil" version means there was an elder to whom you belonged, from whom you learned. There's a history in your name, and an honesty about your apprenticeship. That said, in the world of popular culture, it appears to also suggest an eternal adolescence, a role-playing immaturity sustained for the amusement of audiences. But one thing is clear: Lil Buck, Lil Wayne, Lil Baby, DaBaby, and so on and so on, will offer apprenticeship, literal or by virtue of recorded sound and sight, and the traditions they carry will likely endure, even as the form is altered by the moment in time and the latest innovations. These are the symbolic children of the men who carried signs at the sanitation workers' strike that read, "I am a man." It is an elegant cycle, to the earth, to the concrete, from acoustic to electric. It is a disobedient art of movement, searching for something and still sitting up close to the land. It is the sound of porches and dusk.

Funk or fly.

In 2018, the Jefferson Davis and Nathan Bedford Forrest statues were removed from Memphis city parks. It was in the evening, in front of crowds who had been organizing against monuments to the Confederacy there. Yet do I marvel at the claims of patriotism under the banner of a traitorous flag. Of course Confederates saw themselves as holding on to principles set forward at the founding. The Constitution was written to make space for a slave society. Today both those who lament the failure of the Confederacy and those who decry its intended ends might both call themselves patriots.

"Patriotism" is a confused word. Is it virtuous? Is it found in the effort to make the nation live out the true meaning of its creed? Is it found in holding the nation true to how it was made, suffering and all? Would that make it a scandal? Is it looking at its documents, with a passionate fervor, or refusing to let its people going hungry?

There are many Southern words that mean a lot more than they seem. Take, for example, "Mississippi" and "Louisiana." They are, of course, both states. But Louisiana was also a land deal. In exchange for $15 million, France granted the United States 828,000 square miles, including a lot of territory that didn't belong to them. Most, in fact. With Louisiana, the US doubled in size and spread west of the Mississippi.

And that is another word that means more. The river's name comes from the Ojibwe word meaning "Great River." And it is. It reaches through ten states now, much of the terrain of the purchase. And you cannot understand the history of the nation without it. Mark Twain's greatest contribution to Americana is perhaps alerting the culture to its centrality, not just as a matter of commerce but as a way of being. Human cargo, Africans, were carried down it, if not marched, when the promise of cotton grew deeper South. Cotton was carried back up.

And there are things that are important for us to know about the Mississippi River now. It has been invaded by carp, bighead carp, black carp, grass carp that leap into the air, as well as zebra mussels, gobies, walking snakehead fish, all imported for various reasons—aquariums, food markets—and then loosed or escaped into the river. Wild hogs, which were imported there by Spanish explorers in the 1500s, and the big mammalian nutria, which were brought to the US for fur in the late nineteenth century, spread disease, destroy levees, and chomp up crops. The Mississippi River has been called the most tainted coastal ecosystem in the world. In 2013, an oil spill from a barge that hit a railroad bridge near Vicksburg, Mississippi, poured tens of thousands of gallons of crude oil into the water. In 2015, near Columbus, Kentucky, 120,000 gallons of oil poured into the river after two boats collided. More disaster is coming.

The use of the great river to fill coffers and steal lives has been

the American way for a long time. You could anticipate it, the way
Mark Twain reflected on the vice and greed, as well as the science and beauty. He wrote about the riverboats that brought one to
Memphis as exempla of the spirit of the city, a drink-induced social
order:

> How solemn and beautiful is the thought, that the earli-
> est pioneer of civilization, the van-leader of civilization, is
> never the steamboat, never the railroad, never the news-
> paper, never the Sabbath-school, never the missionary—
> but always whiskey! Such is the case. Look history over;
> you will see. The missionary comes after the whiskey—I
> mean he arrives after the whiskey has arrived; next comes
> the poor immigrant, with ax and hoe and rifle; next, the
> trader; next, the miscellaneous rush; next, the gambler, the
> desperado, the highwayman, and all their kindred in sin of
> both sexes; and next, the smart chap who has bought up
> an old grant that covers all the land; this brings the lawyer
> tribe; the vigilance committee brings the undertaker. All
> these interests bring the newspaper; the newspaper starts
> politics and a railroad; all hands turn to and build a church
> and a jail . . .

Another ambiguous Southern word is "favor." It can refer to being in God's good graces, looking alike, or treating a wounded part
of oneself more gently, as in favoring a broken foot. "Blessed and
highly favored" is a common phrase, as is "She favors you" or, if that
is your child, "You spit her out."

The new Beale Street favors the old one with conscious kitsch
of the South. You can eat at the waterfront at Beale Street Landing in Memphis. Development projects promise more tourist at-
tractions and gentrification. And in recent years, with old projects
demolished, the push-out goes further. Development is promised

again, new businesses, restaurants, and entertainment venues. The city promises it will all be diverse.

Beautiful at sunset, fresh air, easy walking. Memphis may be Black, but the waterfront is Whiter than the city. Though that's not surprising given the history of the place. Its name means more than blues and fun. Like Memphis in Egypt, it's on the river and therefore made for trade. And then the railroad came through, the first in the South. And the up and down and east and west were all serviced by the ones who would make the poetry of the river city but reap very little.

The difference between Nashville and Memphis, between Elvis and Pat Boone, between the Alabama-to-Detroit ride and the Mississippi-to-Memphis-to-Chicago ride, between the riverfront and the rest of the city, and between both cities and another—Knoxville, home to the South's favorite baking flour, White Lily, a product that looks as pure as the driven snow though first made in Knoxville's vice district—could be told in thousands of different ways. These places remind you of both their particularity and their interconnectedness. There would be no rock music without Memphis and Mississippi and no Motown golden oldies without Alabama. There would have been no national uprising of "burn, baby, burn" all across urban centers in 1968 without what was done to Martin Luther King Jr. in Memphis, and no ripple across the world either.

A tourist visit to Memphis will tell you some exciting stories about the history of American music, and the same is true of Nashville. You will bop around with familiarity, whether you are American or a tourist from another corner of the world. Everybody moves to our music. Just remember, the sounds of this nation that captured the whole world were born out of repression. Up from the gutbucket, as it were. You know the song, maybe even the story, but I want you to study its provenance. Because it belongs to you, too. And so you are implicated; we all are. But will you serve as a witness?

SOUL OF THE SOUTH

The Black Belt

Others fell among the thorns, and the thorns came up and
choked them out.

—MATTHEW 13:22

[T]he world grows darker; for now we approach the Black
Belt,—that strange land of shadows, at which even slaves
paled in the past, and whence come now only faint and
half-intelligible murmurs to the world beyond . . .

—W. E. B. DU BOIS, *THE SOULS OF BLACK FOLK*

I WANTED TO READ *BLACK BOY* when I was in the fourth grade,
because of the title. My father said no; my mother said yes. So I
read it. I started working on this book and read it again, for the
fourth time. The first time it was a story. The second it was a lesson.
The third, an argument. This time it was a testimonial. A part of
our history that ossified aching, the times when we are less sure in
healing and loving than we are in lashing out, is explained through
the bones that lie in the dark soil.

The Black Belt is a crescent-shaped stretch of land from Virginia through to Louisiana and Arkansas, where the head turns

into a sickle. Or like the hammerhead of a shark. Because slavery was concentrated in the Black Belt—it was good land for growing cotton—the name acquired a double meaning. It grew to refer to the counties of the South with majority-Black populations. The blackest soil and the Whitest people. The Blackest people and the whitest cotton.

In the 1930s the Communist Party of the United States—and, more importantly, Black communists of the South—began to develop the "Black Belt theory," which argued that the Black people of the Deep South constituted an internal colony of the United States. Some argued that they should embrace an independence struggle like the rest of the colonized world. These ideas continued to be circulated well into the 1970s. Mississippian writer Richard Wright was first drawn to the CPUSA in Chicago, and then later disaffected by them; regardless, the particularity of the Black Belt as a place of beauty and terror remained inside him.

The collision of the body, heart, and mind is the place where Wright always becomes spectacular. When he wrote, "Hunger has always been more or less at my elbow when I played, but now I began to wake up at night to find hunger standing at my bedside, staring at me gauntly," it is not merely physical hunger he speaks of. It is existential, too.

Wright describes how his mother's pain became his own: "My mother's suffering grew into a symbol in my mind, gathering to itself all the poverty, the ignorance, the helplessness; the painful, baffling, hunger-ridden days and hours; the restless moving, the futile seeking, the uncertainty, the fear, the dread; the meaningless pain and the endless suffering. Her life set the emotional tone of my life, colored the men and women I was to meet in the future, conditioned my relation to events that had not yet happened, determined my attitude to situations and circumstances I had yet to face. A somberness of spirit that I was never to lose settled over me during the slow years of my mother's unrelieved suffering." The words echo in your chest. Some sadness and deprivation digs so deep in your spirit, Wright tells us, that it won't let you go no matter how many books you sell.

When I entered higher education, I was taught to treat Richard Wright with skepticism. He was not a vital force in the African American literary tradition according to the canon I was taught, but rather a flat-footed Marxist (in contrast, elegant Marxists were allowed). I'm glad I studied him earlier. In high school, Mr. McFarland gave me a part of *Black Boy* to read. He wanted me to study it for the writing itself. "The sentences," he said, "pay attention to the sentences!" Their length varied. Wright animated the landscape. My sensorium was riveted.

But the higher education consensus narrative was that, in *Native Son*, Wright had made a character for whom he tried to deny the prospect of sympathy, much less empathy. Bigger was not supposed to pull a single heartstring or resonate like a guitar one. Wright failed at that enterprise. *Native Son* was extremely successful as a bestselling selection for the Book of the Month Club. And readers cared about Bigger. I did.

Black Boy was published five years after *Native Son*. It begins in the Black Belt, and it provides a sober picture. But that isn't unique. When W. E. B. Du Bois traveled from Atlanta to the Black Belt in the 1903 book *The Souls of Black Folk*, red clay gives way to the darkest soil. The badges of servitude that the Thirteenth Amendment were supposed to erase were found at every turn. Jean Toomer, in his 1923 novel, *Cane*, modernist to Wright's naturalist style, to Du Bois's realist style, shares the feeling that the landscape weighs, dizzies, sucks one into a terrible unrequited yearning. It is as though it is near impossible to distinguish the self from the earth. The founder of the Nation of Islam, Elijah Muhammad, emerged from Sandersville, Georgia, a place that was demographically, if not geologically, the Black Belt, and is said to have witnessed three lynchings before adulthood. It was a town through which General

Sherman had slashed in his March to the Sea, and the White folks never stopped making Black people pay for that humiliation. No wonder so many left.

The poet Margaret Walker, who loved Richard Wright, spent years trying to figure out his refusal to see any beauty in what it meant to be Black. Others simply rejected him. But I have come to the conclusion that Wright was telling us something about the Black Belt in particular. That what he showed about it didn't have to refer to all of Black life to be centrally true. And while plenty of folks in the Black Belt found a way to love and transform—the most transformative work of the freedom movement took place there—it is plain to see how it could break a spirit.

Wright wrote of his homeland:

The land we till is beautiful, with red and black and brown clay, with fresh and hungry smells, with pine trees and palm trees, with rolling hills and swampy delta—an unbelievably fertile land, bounded on the north by the states of Pennsylvania, Ohio, Illinois and Indiana, on the south by the Gulf of Mexico, on the west by the Mississippi River, and on the east by the Atlantic Ocean.

Our southern springs are filled with quiet noises and scenes of growth. Apple buds laugh into blossom. Honeysuckles creep up the sides of houses. Sunflowers nod in the hot fields. From mossy tree to mossy tree—oak, elm, willow, aspen, sycamore, dogwood, cedar, walnut, ash and hickory—bright green leaves jut from a million branches to form an awning that tries to shield and shade the earth. Blue and pink kites of small boys sail in the windy air.

Set against all of this majestic beauty was an irredeemable hunger. And I choose that word deliberately. There is nothing to justify, in all that abundance, that people would be made half crazy with hunger. It is that condition, so fundamental for so long in Black life in the Black Belt, that Wright had to testify to even if it was horrifying to witness as well as acknowledge. Beauty is a tortured thing in the Black Belt. This is the place, the core, that we mean when we say "the South" as a historic location. So it must be told.

The cotton gin ramped up what had been a dying institution. Eli Whitney, a New Englander staying at the Mulberry Grove Plantation in Savannah, had tried and tried, and quit, disillusioned. Then Black people, slaves, helped him identify the problems with the gin and refined the process of technologizing agricultural society, to their great misfortune. Planters fanned out into the Black Belt, where the soil was best for cotton growing. The Cherokee, Choctaw, Muscogee, and Seminole were forced out of their national territories in the Southeast because of cotton greed. Through the 1830s, Indigenous people were removed, White people settled, and Black people were brought in to build the wealth. So many Black people arrived that this region became the beating heart of Black culture: blues, spirituals, gospel—the forms that grew all the subsequent forms, from rock to jazz to R&B and hip hop—depended upon their seeds.

In the nineteenth century, cotton "came to dominate world trade . . . the factory itself was an invention of the cotton industry," according to Sven Beckert, author of *Empire of Cotton*. And the rise of the United States as a global power rested upon cotton. "What distinguished the United States from virtually every other cotton-growing area in the world was planters' command of nearly unlimited supplies of land, labor and capital, and their unparalleled political power," said Beckert. "The insatiable demand of cotton planters dominated the politics of the new nation not just because of their reliance on the state to secure and empty new land, but also because of their need for coerced labor."

As a result, the Black Belt became the destination of the internal slave trade. In the second great forced migration story, a million people were "sold down the river" via steamboats or marched, often chained together, to serve King Cotton. Africans were marched in, Indigenous people were marched out, and fugitives scattered to swamps and remote settlements. Even now, after the early to mid-twentieth-century Great Migration of Black people north, and the late nineteenth and early twentieth-century migration of Europeans into the South, the region remains very Black and very rural.

Cotton blooms twice. The first bloom begins white. The next day it is pink, and becomes steadily lusher and wider until it strikes magenta. Then it withers and dies. The boll grows tight. It pulls in and thickens. Its color is dark: purplish brown. Eventually it cracks and pushes open. This is a different kind of flower, rough like lambswool and fat, though white. The fiber cuts fingers. Wearies souls. It clothes us all.

I looked over the more than 250 years of my genealogy, and not one person was born and raised in the Black Belt. And it made me wonder if I and perhaps we, some of us Black people and students and educators of Black culture, just do not, did not, understand the circumstance that Richard Wright was explicating. Had we, from our oppressed yet demonstrably less so, family histories, misunderstood the fundamental terror and violence of that place? After all, those were the folks who left the South in the largest numbers. But long after slavery ended, Black folks stayed close to the land. They wanted land. They wanted to be able to move freely and also to lay claim. They wanted to build family. The lore of the Great Migration is that Black people just left for a better life. But the numbers suggest that a lot of the movement was simple necessity prompted by the boll weevil. White folks moved, too, in even larger numbers. As James N. Gregory wrote of the Southern diaspora, "In the Great Migration era of the early twentieth century, when African Americans moved north for the first time in large numbers . . . less-noticed white southerners actually outnumbered them roughly two to one. The margins became larger after 1950 and still larger as the century drew to a close." White people, however, often came back. Richard Wright wrote in *12 Million Black Voices*—and this makes my heart ache every time I read it—that the Black migrants' mistake was thinking the North would be better. And they would be stuck there too.

This was the heartbeat of the Great Migration, the heart of American darkness. I have grown more inclined to trust Wright as time has gone by. And as I've read him alongside Du Bois and Toomer's narration of the Black Belt, I trust them, outsiders looking in, more, too.

In 1941, four years before the publication of *Black Boy*, *Let Us Now Praise Famous Men* was published. James Agee and Walker Evans had been sent on assignment for *Fortune* magazine to depict the conditions of tenant farmers in the American South. They spent eight weeks in the Black Belt, in Hale County, Alabama. Their coverage was of White families exclusively. It was odd, given the demographics, to depict the life of the poor in the Black Belt without Black people at all, where Black people were a supermajority. The passage from the Wisdom of Sirach, a collection of Jewish ethical teachings from which they named their book, seems almost like an admission: "Let us now praise famous men and our fathers that begat us. The Lord hath wrought great glory by them through his great power from the beginning . . ." *Our* fathers are worthy of praise, too, not just famous men. Yet "our" did not include ours.

Even in the devastation of the Depression, there were some whose misfortune mattered more than others'. The New Deal had been designed, in deference to Southern political authorities, to exclude Black people from the welfare state. And, in Agee and Evans's book, from public concern. But if you read further into the Wisdom of Sirach, there are other words that offer a deeper truth: "And some there be, which have no memorial; who are perished, as though they had never been; and are become as though they had never been born; and their children after them." This was

Wright's testimony. Agee wrote: "For one who sets himself to look at all earnestly, at all in purpose toward truth, into the living eyes of a human life: what is it he there beholds that so freezes and abashes his ambitious heart? What is it, profound behind the outward windows of each one of you, beneath touch even of your own suspecting, drawn tightly back at bay against the backward wall and blackness of its prison cave, so that the eyes alone shine of their own angry glory, but the eyes of a trapped wild animal, or of a furious angel nailed to the ground by his wings . . ." Despite himself, the aperture opened: shining black eyes of grounded Black people are all around this story, invisible but essential witnesses. I am telling you now that Wright's scaffolding of *Let Us Now Praise Famous Men* is more than a corrective. It is a potent unmasking of the wages of Whiteness. Du Bois explained that in the Redemption South, the White worker was offered Whiteness to set himself apart from the Black worker. And no matter how hungry, how imprisoned by labor, how deprived he was, that was his gift, or grift as the case might be. One way to read this is in simple Marxian terms: the working class was divided against itself by means of the false consciousness of race. But that is too easy an interpretation in a society that had been forged by race. Whiteness was an article of faith. It redeemed suffering. And afforded compensation in the ability to feed bloodthirstiness—lynching, burning, beating, raping, humiliating—which also became matters of faith. That might not provide a tidy economic explanation, but it became an undeniable and central aspect of the social order. It was material.

Two weeks before he was murdered, Martin Luther King Jr. was in the Black Belt. He was in Hale County specifically. King had traveled to Greensboro for a Poor People's Campaign rally. And the Klan came after him with the intent to kill. Locals hid him in a little clapboard shotgun made of naked pine. Without those two weeks more of living, in which he went to Memphis, we wouldn't have the mountaintop speech to remember. Usually "The Mountaintop" is called prophetic because it is the speech in which he anticipates his death. But maybe the speech was prompted by the danger he felt in the Black Belt, in Hale County. He'd argued in the past that in the protracted struggle for civil rights, its most pointed battles were waged on the grounds where Black people had been enslaved and bound to cotton. They taught the rest of the South what it meant to refuse the government in service to the plantation.

For Agee and Evans to tell stories of the White Black Belt as though they were not in symbiotic relationship with the Black Black Belt was a convenience perhaps, or maybe a revelation of common-place values. On the one hand, the White Northerner often seeks to find sympathy and common ground with the White Southerner by disappearing the Black Southerner. On the other, the White Northerner seeks to express solidarity with the Black Southerner by turning the White Southerner into a caricatured demon in comparison to his own virtue. Both are insidious. In the Black Belt, you cannot separate out what happened to the Indigenous and what happened to Black people. To kill and push out, and then to bring down, to wear the earth down. You cannot separate out the hand-to-mouth of the tenant farmer, with nothing but his Whiteness, told to thrive on that when there is no thriving to be had, thus turning what is supposed to be a blessing of birth into a bitter gall. It is all the same theater of creation.

Now, the Black Belt will remind you of the cruelty that is the changing same. Like the swallow-tailed kites, birds with white bellies and black-tipped wings who follow the tractors. They swoop from the sky, tailing the sound, so they can eat up the insects kicked up into the air like they've been doing for decades. And yes, slavery was abolished, Jim Crow is over, but the prisons, the persistence of poverty, are constant reminders of how the past made the present.

The Alabama Black Belt is roughly 50 percent African American, and nine of the ten poorest counties of the state are there. Through Mississippi's Black Belt, all the way up in the Northwest alluvial plain with the most fertile soil that is called the Delta, you can trace the blues. There are 187 sites along the Mississippi Blues Trail, and Parchman Farm located dead set in the Delta, the most notorious penitentiary in the history of the South, has one at the entrance. The labor at Parchman was, and is, akin to slavery. Back-breaking, hot, cruel. But the cruelty is not slavery. Don't call it that. The cruelty is in being caught up in a system *like* slavery when you are called, by right and law, free. Parchman blues were different from old plantation work songs, which were sung to make the work go by, different songs from the ones that could keep you swinging or shucking or pulling. The blues were songs of the interior. Shared, they were sung on a common ground, but with private memories and longings; the things they knew about each other included the fact that there were things they would never know about each other—joys and hurts and wants. The prisoners drank chicory coffee, ate beans and gristle and some cornbread, and were worked half to death from "kin see to cain't." They drank moonshine in the evening, hollered, moaned, and strummed.

I cannot get to Parchman's fields—they are five miles from the road—but the blues makes me know that that is where *it* is. Where we have to go if we want to ever approach freedom. I am, like so many now, thank God, someone who believes that people should not be held in cages or barracks or on plantations. In 1974, when my mother referred to "the indigenous prison struggle" in political meetings, she meant those who had been returned to captive conditions and were fighting the ice-cold civil war on plantations yet again.

Take one word: "commissary." The same word was used for share-croppers, soldiers, and prisoners to get provisions. Modest means of sucking the poor into indebtedness. Coercing them to buy here, because where else are you going to go? Some people are required to do for their country without their country doing much for them.

It is a cruel truism to say that the beauty of the region is what makes it bearable, or a sign of the glory of the South despite its hauntings. At best, the beauty is the promise made to us, if we can get humanism right. If we don't snuff out all the people and kill all the land, we will finally get to revel in it. Have you ever wondered about the high register of men's voices in Black music? They call it a falsetto, but I resent that name because it isn't falsification. I think it is just how the mouth opens to let out the tenderest part when they all told you that stoic and hard was the only way to live. People weep in prison. They fall to their knees, too. And sing. Listen.

Professors teach "the blues" in a range of different ways in African American studies. In *Blues People*, Amiri Baraka teaches the history of Black people through sound, a narrative of alienation and self-creation, migration and class. Albert Murray was skeptical of Baraka's style criticisms of the Black middle class. Baraka saw the Black middle class as assimilationist, and too eager to give over their culture for the allure of White ways. Murray, perhaps because he had grown up in a Jim Crow society where all Black folks lived behind the veil, as it were, didn't emphasize class distinctions among Black Americans.

Both Baraka and Murray seemed to settle in the idea that Black American music is deeply American, though Baraka was more troubled by the ruptured connection to Africa, a near complete loss resisted against by the power of rhythm. To Baraka, blues was the product of Black resilience against all odds. Murray, more fundamentally literary in his account, sat with the hero's journey and the meaning of democracy to Black people. The bluesman (and he is a *man* for Murray) is a sort of everyman who contends with the American dream and the creation of the self that is at the heart of the American project, from George Washington to Emerson to Davy Crockett. At least according to the self he creates in song.

They each get themselves into trouble, and I know that trouble myself, because it is hard to make a political argument through a body of art. Yes, closely reading a specific recording often gives you the political ideas quite readily. But the blues, a composite form into which its men and women poured their individual selves, had a lot of different ways of seeing, doing, thinking, and feeling. It is challenging to hold them to one particular truth.

It is unquestionably true that the blues was music of the incarcerated and also of the roaming. And the Great Migration wasn't the only way folks took to the road. The history is full of traveling seasonal labor across different types of farms and fields, and also the bigger migrations to cities within the South. Escaping the plantation didn't necessarily mean escaping the South for many. Richard Wright wrote of the 1890s:

> . . . wandering from Natchez to New Orleans, from Mobile to Montgomery, from Macon to Jacksonville, from Birmingham to Chattanooga, from Nashville to Louisville, from Memphis to Little Rock—laboring in the sawmills, in the turpentine camps, on the road jobs; working for men who did not care if we lived or died, but who did not want their business enterprises to suffer for lack of labor . . . more than a million of us roamed the states of the South and the remainder of us drifted north.

Between drifting and captivity, there is an undeniable melancholy. The blues is testimony to the possibility of a laugh, a sweetness in each place. A libation poured for the dead. And joy. Of course the lost-cause narratives of "happy slaves" on plantations were false. But it is true that the culture made by enslaved people insisted upon joy. It was not a naive childish satisfaction. No, it was, it is, the joy of a voice that could soar one moment and growl the next, giggle and holler. It's the joy of dancing in a whip-scarred, food-deprived, achy body. The joy of love, of the binding between souls across the borders of flesh and the rules of society. It was a refusal to be rendered entirely in the image of White Americans, even when completely beaten down.

I love Bobby Blue Bland and B.B. King's version of "I'll Take Care of You." Bland dropped out of school in the third grade to work in the fields in Tennessee before moving to Memphis with his mama. There he found Beale Street. Bland was his stepdaddy Leroy Bridgeforth's last name. After slavery the land kept snatching Black folks back, and the way names came and went, based on to whom you belonged or where you went, was also sustained. Bland was the name that came from Bridgeforth. These are the terms of belonging rent apart by law, but made by promises, of people who still knew the cost of being counted as chattel. They made do. Bland had a half-brother, James Cotton, from Tunica, Mississippi, who played a beautiful blues harmonica. I can't recall the connection. Families fragmented, and claimed each other still. Informal kinship was created, too, when people lost track of legal connection.

When you hear Bobby Blue Bland sing, you understand why they called him Blue. His voice is like daybreak. It cracks, but with sweetness. In footage of them performing the duet, Bland has a drink in hand, and wears a leisure suit, the glassiness in his eyes dancing in light-reflecting unison with the golden hues of the liquor. They tell bittersweet jokes between songs. A good time doesn't require abandonment of the hard time that settles inside your chest. Forever. This is what I think the blues are. I think it is the magic of believing that B.B. King was not, in fact, ventriloquizing his guitar, Lucille, but that he conjured her to talk nice to him. He knew how to press and pluck her strings to make her wail. Electricity, a music technology, yes, but also a harnessed power under his hands. That is the blues, I think. I know what Murray meant by saying it, but I don't think it is at heart a hero's journey. I am less concerned with the twelve-bar structure and the standard form than with what the eyes and the fingers do all along.

Inside of the Delta Blues Museum, they have the remnants of

Muddy Waters's old cabin, including a guitar once made for ZZ Top out of some of its planks. And it hails to a time even before the shot-guns, when a home was a rough-hewn rectangle. I wonder about that balance, between the precision of a shape that holds together and the organic uneven shapes in real, worn wood. It forces you to remember that there is math in even the most organic of forms, ge-ometry so minute that you forget, from the angle of a jagged toenail to the curve of a bump on your chin. What many of us urbanites take as a feature of the past is living here, and it is, in fact, like the minute geometry, more sophisticated than we have been trained to see. You can turn on the radio and listen.

The story of the last man executed by Mississippi is a blues song. Or, better yet, a murder ballad. Or both. He was White. Gary Carl Simmons Jr.'s final meal was this:

One Pizza Hut medium Super Supreme Deep Dish pizza, double portion, with mushrooms, onions, jalapeno peppers, and pepperoni; pizza, regular portion, with three cheeses, olives, bell pepper, tomato, garlic and Italian sausage; 10 8-oz. packs of Parmesan cheese; 10 8-oz. packs of ranch dressing; one family size bag of Doritos nacho cheese flavor; 8 oz. jalapeno nacho cheese; 4 oz. sliced jalapenos; 2 large strawberry shakes; two 20-oz. cherry Cokes; one super-size order of McDonald's fries with extra ketchup and mayon-naise; and two pints of strawberry ice cream.

Simmons was a butcher who owed a debt to his drug dealer, Jeffrey Wolfe. When Wolfe and his girlfriend came to collect, Sim-mons and his friend killed Wolfe. They cut him up and fed him to alligators. They hog-tied and raped Wolfe's girlfriend, who, against all odds, escaped to tell the story. After Simmons's death at Parch-man, no one else has been legally executed.

Rural people live with the knowledge that they are understood as both of the past and invisible in the present. The same mass culture and popular programs air here and elsewhere. Simmons ended his life with brands: McDonald's, Pizza Hut, Doritos. In the flesh it probably didn't feel so abundant or comforting. He died without fanfare.

In the fall of 2019, people began dying at Parchman—nine, twelve, twenty. There's nothing new about Black men being killed violently in Southern prisons. In the same season at Elmore, in Alabama, drug addiction was taking lives, too. Some who die in Parchman or Elmore lived most of their lives in prison. Others who survive prison are released without a home to return to. Have you noticed how often people who were once incarcerated describe their time locked up as being "away"? Like another dimension. When prisons are now where slavery was, what is that place? Has time warped? Or just betrayed us?

Towards the end of his life, Richard Wright turned away from his sociopolitical narratives and wrote haikus. Many were about his home state. Number 782 reads:

From the dark still pines,
Not a breath of autumn wind
To ripple the lake

And if you know the region, you feel much more than what the few words say. The stifling heat even in the fall, the thick scent of trees, and still waters that run deep.

Number 725 reads:

From a cotton field
To Magnolia trees,
A bridge of swallows

This last one requires you to understand that in the South "swallow" does not only refer to birds but also to gulps of something to

drink. Often pronounced "squalla," as in, "Give me a squalla of water." Our people were swallowed up by the drive for cotton. Taken
into its fields, barely making a living or none at all from its bounty.
Abundance wasn't found in prosperity but instead in the lushness
of the magnolia tree and the glory of birds flying overhead. Most of
all it was found in the stuff of their imaginations.

The South has remained the region where the majority of Afri-
can Americans live. And even with the declining population in the
Blackest South, the Blackest Southerners remain. So the question
I always ask is not why did Black folks leave, but why did they stay?

The answer is home. If everyone had departed, no one would
have been left to tend the ancestors' graves. When you walk past
a plantation, even if not outfitted soberly or joyously in the history
of slavery, you are forced to remember something. And it is a vile,
bloody remembrance, but it is also one that should strike awe at
the human mastery of existence that is evidenced in the blues, in
the experience of the divine in the spirit-body, that keloid-covered,
scarred Black body, that violated, hungry, sparely clothed body, the
labor-flattened, thick-soled feet. Had these graves not been seen,
daily, over generations, had we not been witnesses to them, I do not
know how it would have been possible to sustain hope, or at least
to pretend to.

American exceptionalism, that sense that we are somehow special and ordained as such, is a myth sedimented on Southern prosperity: oil, coal, and cotton. Every piece of evidence of our national
distinction has relied upon this wealth of the nation. As you certainly have already gleaned, I do not think genocide, slavery, and
exploitation were worth it. Nor do I believe they should be tidily
set aside in moments of patriotic fervor or national piety like the
Fourth of July or the following days: President's, King's, Labor, or
Memorial. But even if you are a lover of the national romance, integrity requires that the stories be at least halfway honest. It is not
enough to set aside a little time or attention here or there to grieve

our national sins, then, soft as butter, turn back to proclamations of greatness. Because history is an instruction. And what you neglect to attend to from the past, you will surely ignore in the present. If you doubt what I'm saying, look into the production of your computer and desk, your kid's toys. Look into the kitchen staff at your favorite restaurant, the revenue streams your state gets from prison, and the workers at the side of the highway as you speed by.

* * *

WHILE I KNEW TUSKEGEE WAS PASTORAL, I was surprised when I first visited Montgomery right nearby. It is the capital, and so I expected it to be like Birmingham. Bustling, though green. Built up, yet still gracious. But Montgomery is very much town-like. It has everything but not too much or too big.

This time when I arrived in Montgomery, it looked distinctly more developed. Newer, shinier, not simply a maintained plantation elegance. Something had changed. Also, I realized that I had brought the wrong suitcase. A nearly empty one left over from my last trip instead of the one I had packed. So I went to a drugstore to get myself together. I bought banana crème cookies, Goody's headache powder, Tussy deodorant, underthings (a three-pack of drawers to be exact), a toothbrush, and a Faygo red pop. There was a White lady at the register. Older yet girlish. Southern ladyhood entails a high-pitched singsongy way of talking and walking and flirting. The face wrinkles, and the voice still lilts. She was worried for me, after she put the items in my bag. "Let me get you a double bag," she said, "so folks can't see all your business." And I thanked her. She meant it. I meant it, too.

I was hoping on my most recent trip to Montgomery, colloquially known as "the Gump" (can't tell you why), to get a chance to visit Tuskegee because I heard that they were filming Bob Zellner's biopic there, based upon his memoir, *The Wrong Side of Murder*

Creek, about being a White Southerner who was deeply involved in the civil rights movement. My curiosity was sparked because my parents had known Bob and his wife when I was a small child, but I didn't know much about his personal story.

As it turned out, my visit was too short to travel to Tuskegee. The first night I arrived in Montgomery, I delivered a short talk in honor of the state's bicentennial and then had a public conversation with the actor André Holland, of *Moonlight*, *Selma*, and *The Knick*, also an Alabama native. It was something, Black Alabamans talking about the state of the state, in the first capital of the Confederacy. This is the place where a provisional secessionist legislature was established just forty-two years after Alabama joined the union.

Holland and I talked about "Zoom." It is my favorite song, and the Commodores, the group who sang it, were founded when they were undergraduates at Tuskegee University. The lines "I wish the world were truly happy, living as one. I wish the word they call freedom someday would come" end with a drift. It is the sound of hope, which has always been at least as important as struggle.

The streets of downtown Montgomery were empty on my way back to the hotel. The hallways were silent. Things weren't animated until morning time, when I ate a breakfast of grits and hash browns before going to the Alabama Book Festival.

I showed up to the appointed place early. And as it turns out, under the awning where I was supposed to be speaking, there was Bob Zellner. Kismet. Zellner sat at the front with his interlocutor. He waved at me in recognition. And I waved back. And then he began to tell his story.

Bob was named for the famous Methodist evangelist Bob Jones, a native of Dothan, Alabama, who at age twelve gave a defense of the populist party in front of a dry goods store and remained a segregationist until his end. Zellner's father was a follower of Jones. He was also a Klansman. Bob's mother was "part Indian." Everything changed when Bob's father went on an evangelical trip to Europe, hoping to convert Jewish people to Christianity in order to protect them from Nazis, which of course drips with irony and yet is wholly Southern. This Klansman was terribly homesick and grateful to run across a group of Black Southern evangelicals while there. They got to talking about food and home ways, and suddenly the color line started to melt. At first, Bob's daddy planned to just set it aside for as long as he was in Europe. But eventually he knew he couldn't go back to a Jim Crow ethos.

Zellner's daddy came home, and his wife turned his Klan robes into shirts for the boys. The family was done with that hatefulness. This alienated them from their relatives, including a cousin who told Bob that it was only because of Southern family ways that he hadn't killed him. Zellner stayed in Alabama and attended Huntingdon College in Montgomery. But the college also denounced him once he became part of SNCC.

At a certain point, Bob's interlocutor, the film director Barry Alexander Brown, an English-born Alabaman, was asked to speak about his own life. He talked about having worked with Spike Lee for three decades. Bob interjected in his charismatic raconteur style, turning to the audience with "And y'all know Spike Lee is from Alabama!" Barry answered, "No, he's not, he's from Brooklyn!" But the audience, nearly in unison, filled mostly with White senior citizens, chimed back, "His people are from Alabama." And that is the truth of the matter. (Later I learned from someone who remembered Lee from his visits to his grandmother's block in Atlanta that he tended to turn his nose up at his country kin. She said, "Didn't you watch *Crooklyn*? That's what he thought of us.") Still, I figured—no, I knew—that Lee's sensitivity to Southern Black sensibilities, whether in *4 Little Girls* or *When the Levees Broke*, has something to do with how he's felt the region.

One of the things my folks had told me about Bob Zellner is that while his ex-wife, Dottie, had been deeply hurt when SNCC members decided it was time for Black people to organize separately from White folks, as she had been especially close to Stokely, Bob understood it and even was supportive. I think, being a Southerner, he understood the importance of self-determination for Black people. He'd been a witness, up close, to living under the thumb of Whiteness, to the daily indignities, the ritual violence, that existed long before the freedom movement. Although all the White members of SNCC I've ever known have easily referred to it as a "Black movement," meaning Black-led and -imagined, some struggled with the fact that there were conversations that had to happen without them, that their Whiteness could not be erased even when they shared mutual love with other organizers.

I walked up to speak to Zellner after the panel. "Where do I know you from?" he asked, grinning, and I reminded him that he used to give me saltines at his kitchen counter. He said, "And look at you now! Writing books and everything."

And everything. By implication that big word reminded me that what to write is a serious question, made fraught by Alabama for me. Alabama is iconic, both Birmingham and the Black Belt. It is where Martin Luther King Jr. cut his teeth, home of Rosa Parks, John Lewis, and a host of no less significant figures of the civil rights movement. It is dignified in its legacy and also shorthanded to the (16th Street Baptist Church) bombing and the (march across the Edmund Pettus) bridge. We participate in it, too, holding the state's legacy aloft like a banner of pride, while on-the-ground living has made it a more difficult story.

Though my time was short, while in Montgomery I also had to visit the institution that is responsible for Montgomery looking so different from the last time I'd been there, the Equal Justice Initiative. Bryan Stevenson's fingerprints are on the city, molding it into a site not simply of historical remembrance but of reckoning. An attorney who has devoted his life to addressing the scourge of racism via mass incarceration, he leads an organization that has revitalized

Montgomery. I went to the museum first. It was around the corner from my hotel. I didn't have a ticket, and there weren't any available, but I was waved in on a pass for local residents. The beginning was backlogged, so I went around the back way, stopping first at the object by the exit, a sculpture by Sanford Biggers, the Morehouse-educated artist, called *BAM*. It is an homage to Michael Brown, who was executed and left for dead on a Missouri street, igniting the Black Lives Matter movement. As with Missouri, Stevenson's home state of Delaware is a former slave state that isn't fully Southern in culture but certainly was in deed. Stevenson attended segregated schools as a child, became a lawyer, and now has built institutions in the Deepest South to address the lingering badges and incidents of slavery that the Thirteenth Amendment promised and failed to eradicate, particularly with its exception to the law against slavery. Prisoners, it says, can be held in involuntary servitude. And the United States has a lot of prisoners. Bronze layers move across Bigger's figure like ropes; a stepping left leg stops at the ankle. It is one of the most harrowing truths of American life. All of those years of struggle, and yet here we are again.

There is a part of the permanent exhibition, near the center of the museum, where you can sit on the phone as though you are visiting an incarcerated person and hear their voice. Prison takes the ease out of your voice. "I didn't want nothing, I just called to see how you was doing" is the Southerner's sign-off at the end of a call. It is a mannerable way to get off the line. And it is a reminder of the everyday living of checking up on your people. Prison dislodges the everydayness of family. Love has to be scheduled when it comes to people who are locked up. First you hear "Do you accept the charges?" and then the awkward yet rushed exchange. I remember when my father's answering machine message began with "I accept the charges" so he didn't miss a call from inside.

Across the street from the museum is the corner where the artist Bill Traylor used to sit and sell his paintings. He'd been a slave in

Lowndes County, and then a sharecropper. Traylor came to Montgomery after everyone he was close to had died or scattered, when he was seventy-five years old. First he worked at a shoe factory, but within ten years, disabling arthritic pain made it impossible. Traylor slept in the back room of a funeral home and sat in the Black business district during the day. From age eighty-five to eighty-eight, he could be found at the corner of Lawrence and Monroe Streets, drawing and painting. He achieved some notoriety in his day, if not much money. Long after his death, his extraordinary talent was realized, and his paintings became valuable. Among his pictures is one in which every figure is blue. Two round-headed people and one with a farmer's hat are up in a tree. Legs and arms are splayed in panic and attempted escape. They share the branches with birds, relatively calm in comparison. Below, two men in top hats: one has a rifle; the other is pointing up at the fugitives. Three dogs bark at them, and one has made its way halfway up the tree. I suppose, just as I conjure Traylor up in my mind on that corner in 1940, he conjured or, more likely, was haunted by this image, either from hearing of it or witnessing it. The economy of his form and the power of his symbolism means that even all in blue, you can see the structure of racial terror, from top to bottom. Southern trees bear Southern fruit.

I walked to the lynching memorial. I could have taken a bus, but you don't get the same feel when you ride through a city as when you walk through hot streets. As with many Southern cities, the blocks were sparsely populated. Most folks were driving, and I felt both deep comfort and unfamiliarity as I made my way. If someone had talked to me, I could speak the language, but I didn't know the geography. I relied on my GPS to get me to where the proverbial bodies are buried.

The memorial is deeply affecting. Marble slabs the color of Alabama red clay are suspended from above. Each has names of the lynched carved into it. They are gathered by place. You follow them along a descending ramp to a lower level, and with the sun ob-scured, you get cooler the farther down you go. If you look up as you walk down, you feel your neck stretching. At several points, I froze and stiffened, craning my head to look past the ceiling to the sky.

Alongside the installation, the same names are laid out on slabs lying flat instead of hung from above. The practical effect is that you can see all of them clearly. The emotional effect is that it is a graveyard, where you might place flowers for the departed. I was struck by where "unknown" is written. Somebody was lynched without a name recorded. Like the slave ledgers, disregard dumped on violence.

There are words at the exit. Baby Suggs's sermon in the clear-ing, from Morrison's novel *Beloved*, comes first. This is her gospel of self-love of the flesh that has been desecrated, a gospel preached to the formerly enslaved who have made it to Ohio. Then we read an invocation from Elizabeth Alexander, summoning the ancestors. Among the lines: "Ancestors, you will find us still in cages / despised and disciplined / you will find us still mis-named." Though the me-morial is grand, we are reminded that the past is not past. The final lines are: "The wind brings everything. Nothing is not lost."

Cat-a-corner to the museum is the parole office where Mont-gomery ex-felons must check in, bearing the badges of their incar-ceration. For many this is the case long after they have served their sentences. You must show up at the parole office even with the em-ployment discrimination that often leaves ex-felons penniless and sometimes with no option but to return to the "streets," as it were. Standing between the parole office and the lynching memorial, I ask myself: What does one call this mix of past and present sitting against each other? I believe it stretches the meanings we make of museums in a profound manner. This is not preservation; it is inter-vention. On the grounds of the denial.

Though I didn't make it to Tuskegee, I visited another HBCU on the same trip. Alabama State University is in Montgomery. My

friends Tarana Burke and Yaba Blay were on campus that day doing a daylong workshop that was part of the #metoo HBCU Tour. I
wore overalls, and Tarana teased me, "Okay, you're doing the SNCC
look." I was, perhaps subconsciously. It was one of those quiet ac-
knowledgments that we share, of what it means to be grown and
shaped by Southern movement people. And while we live in the
history here, time moves on and the young people make sure we remember. For instance, in the audience, there were two young men
attired with brilliant pink handbags and tight pants. Their gestures
were like those of ballet dancers, their skin brilliantly sheened.
They were undoubtedly pegged as gay as they navigated the world,
and whatever their sexuality, the way they moved struck me as a
step closer to freedom compared to generations past.

I sat down in the back of the auditorium. Alongside me was
a group of young men who I figured by their clothes and postures
were athletes. They chatted anxiously and then walked out together as a group before the conversation began.

The program was extraordinary. Loving, nuanced, and deliberate. This was not Twitter. Not combative or confessional, but a process. And that's important because there is a challenging question
underneath all of it that Tarana has spent years working through.
What do we do with #metoo on the grounds of the lynching tree?
We have, by means of abundant horrifying experience, learned
that the accusation of rape has been thrown at the innocent and
led to death sentences, summary executions without a drop of
process. It is easy to say that we aren't back there now, that we have
to go through rather than put our heads in the sand about how to
manage that past and the reality of a culture that breeds violence
indiscriminately. But to do so is much harder. As recent histories at-
test: Rosa Parks was first an organizer for the NAACP who investi-
gated the sexual assaults of Black women by White men. Rape was
a ritual of racial terror wielded against the spirits of Black women.
Accusations of rape were a tool of racial terror threatening Black

men. What remains harder to address is the way sexual violence exists inside Black communities in the United States, although it does in every community in the United States. The challenge is that we are still afraid. False accusations of rape directed at Black men were a commonplace of the lynching era. We want to heal communities without falling into the old patterns of demonizing Black men that destroyed communities. This is what makes an internal conversation like the one I witnessed so important.

The ethics of building a just society begin at the place where you can touch another person, and the moral imagination reaches out further. This is what is meant, as far as I can tell, by the importance of "grassroots." It is not simply that struggle should not be dictated by elites. Of course that is true. But it also means that we must become different kinds of people in relation to one another, that we become the people suited to the society we want to create. That is the best of the tradition of the Southern movement. It lives even though it has been forgotten by many, including many who lived it. It is necessary to build ethical relations despite or even because of the fear they might elicit. In some ways, Tarana is the daughter of Rosa Parks, a woman who began by working on issues of sexual violence as an arm of White supremacy, and worked her way into what would be the mainstream of the civil rights movement. Except her course was reversed. Tarana began with the movement folks of the Black Belt in Alabama, in that iconic place, Selma, and progressively deepened her work by organizing around the sexual violence experienced by Black girls and women. Tarana's work focused on the wounds that persist and fester within the people of the Black Belt. And moved from there.

There are so many things that were made here that are so tragic because of what they symbolized or what they did to people. The big houses. The plantation roads. The slave. The master. The colored section. Even with housing projects that are prettier than in the rest of the country, and even with the fact that you can always

238 SOUTH TO AMERICA

find a pale pink house or a baby blue one, or one the color of a lime, a lemon, or the flesh of a blueberry, so much of what has been built is a shrine to violence. Race still matters, enormously. The historical marker of the exact location where Emmett Till's body was found kept getting shot up and down, replaced, and shot up and down again. It puts one in the mind of Jeremiah 12:9: "Is my heritage to me like a hyena's lair? Are the birds of prey against her all around?" When it comes to landmarks, the one for Glendora Gin is still intact, even after the cotton gin once was partly dissembled to punish Till. Till's murderers took a seventy-pound metal fan from Glendora and tied it to his body so he would be anchored to the bottom of the Tallahatchie River. The Southern repetition for emphasis is tragically appropriate here: "They killed him dead."

* * *

I HEARD HIS VOICE OVER the PA in the airport and I wet my eyes. "I am Chokwe Antar Lumumba," the mayor of Jackson welcomes you when you arrive. He is one of a growing number of young Black Southern mayors. Mayor Lumumba, like my uncle Cornelius, went to Tuskegee for college and Texas Southern for law school. He was nurtured in the tradition of HBCUs. And he is a scion. Sons have a certain importance, culturally. Patriarchy, that fundamental structure of the West, was denied to Black people during slavery and has remained fragile ever since. Money, protection, domestic authority—these are elusive, though cherished things in the face of poverty and prison. As much as I have written about escaping from patriarchy's hold, I can't pretend to not understand the deep yearning for a son to take on the leadership role of the father when it comes to Black people. To "carry on" in a picture of respected manhood. I do not mean this as a criticism of scions themselves, who may very well be feminists or iconoclasts, but rather as an observation as to why they're so important even to an avowed feminist.

In Jackson the mayor's father, the elder Chokwe Lumumba, had spent decades in the service of the freedom movement. The attorney for revolutionary Black activists of the Black Power movement like Assata Shakur and Nehanda Abiodun, he was also a leader of NAPO, the New Afrikan People's Organization and notably carried a chosen surname that was the same as that of Patrice Lumumba, the Congolese anticolonialist movement leader who had been murdered in 1961 by Belgian and US forces.

NAPO was a coming together of different communities in the New Afrikan Independence Movement. The Republic of New Afrika was imagined in 1968 as an independent Black-majority nation in the Southeastern United States. The first vision was articulated at a meeting of the Malcolm X Society in Detroit. The states they imagined as being part of this new nation: Louisiana, Mississippi, Alabama, Georgia, and South Carolina. They shared goals of self-determination, landownership, and an independent nation-state for New Afrikans, who were colonized by US imperialism, in line with the older Black Belt theory. They believed in Democratic centralism, socialism, and reparations, as well as humility and self-defense. One of its founders, Queen Mother Moore, was a native of New Iberia, Louisiana, and is considered the mother of the reparations movement. She moved to New York, became a Garveyite and an internationalist, and involved herself in a host of educational and political organizations. Political power, even among those who questioned the political economy of the United States, was a meaningful tool for shaping how people could live. The elder Lumumba was elected to the Jackson city council in 2009, and then to the office of mayor in 2013. He died under mysterious circumstances soon thereafter. The latter two events were national news, but I'd heard about the elder Lumumba repeatedly from my parents and their friends. Of his brilliance, courage, and commitment to "the struggle" to "free the land." And now here was the voice of his son, bearing a shared name, welcoming us to Jackson.

If there is one egregious miscasting of the Black Power movement, it is the neglect of the South in that history. The action was not all on the coasts or major cities. Once upon a time, emancipation and its consequent constitutional amendments promised life, liberty, and the pursuit of happiness, only to be dashed when Reconstruction ended. Black people turned to building internally—schools, churches, civic organizations—so that they were ready when it was time to take up direct action again. Once upon a time, Black Southern organizers, leaders, and laypeople faced death and confronted evil. They changed American law. In fact, I would argue that 1954 to 1965 was the most significant decade in the history of US constitutional law and legislation. Black people's protests offered the prospect of an equitably heterogeneous society. Nominally embraced, it was socially and economically refused. Enter Black power. Or perhaps reenter. Black nationalism and Black secession and Black armed self-defense had always been a part of the political imagination of the Black South, from Martin Delany through Nat Turner and Denmark Vesey and the Stono Rebellion and Garveyism and the Deacons for Defense. For some reason, folks want to act as though Black power started in New York and Oakland, even though the Black Panther logo came from the Lowndes County Freedom Organization in Alabama, and even though Huey Newton was born in Louisiana, and Sundiata Acoli in Texas, and Eldridge Cleaver in Arkansas, and Kathleen Cleaver in Tuskegee, Alabama, and Gil Scott-Heron was raised in Tennessee, and Assata Shakur in Wilmington, North Carolina, and Geronimo Ji Jaga Pratt in Louisiana. Sterling Brown commented in the earlier civil rights era: "It is a mistake to believe that this protest in the South is instigated by Negroes from the North . . . I found a large degree of militancy in Negroes who were Southern born and bred, some of whom have never been out of the South . . . I found this protest natural since the Southern Negro is where the grip is tightest and the bite goes deepest and most often." Stated another way, Southern Black people learned steeliness the hard way, under the thumb of Jim Crow. And perhaps from seeing how the North wasn't much better, if at all. They learned there was nowhere to turn and no option but to fight back.

The vision of the Republic of New Afrika was to build a place where Black people could implement a cooperative vision of social organization not unlike what folks on the Sea Islands did during the Reconstruction era. There they built workers' collectives out of the land they'd once worked as slaves, until the property they'd earned was returned to the master class. Such visions always lived in the shadow of the Confederate fantasies that continue to animate White Southern politics. The movement of Black radical politics into electoral politics and policy made sense in the Black Belt.

Before the 2020 election I came across a news report that warned about Russian trolls planting the idea of an African republic in the Southern states. They claimed we would be flooded with messages about being taken for military training on the continent. I wondered if whoever was reporting had looked back in history to our wildest dreams and decided to see if they might be seductive yet again, and therefore disturb the vote. Or had the idea of Black self-determination and self-governance become so preposterous that it was the wildest trick imagined? Better yet, perhaps they took freedom dreams as foolhardy fantasy and thought they could sprinkle them anywhere, tapping into anxieties about Black discontent. Whatever this moment of moral panic meant, in the present and in retrospect, the Republic of New Afrika has never been established. But Jackson has stayed on the move. It is part Chicago and mostly Mississippi, a place where, like the first Chokwe Lumumba, people reverse-migrate, either to start a revolution or because life in the North was too cold.

Jackson is urban, but it is also country. Naipaul referred to it as "the frontier." It was where he was introduced to the classic architecture of the Deep South. "There were streets of 'shotgun' houses.

It was the first time I had ever heard the expressive word: narrow wooden houses (like mobile homes or old-fashioned railway carriages) with the front room opening into the back room and with the front door and back door aligned. On Sunday afternoon the people were out on the streets, so that the effect of crowd and slum and blackness was immediate: as though outdoor life, life outside the houses, was an aspect of poverty." I wouldn't call Jackson the frontier, but it might be something else: a sort of reverse metropole, a substation of the people.

I have had bantering exchanges with Mississippians for years. Eddie Glaude reminds me, "Your blues ain't like ours." (True enough, but Motown is the baby of Jefferson County, Alabama, gospel.) Kiese Laymon told me, "Mississippi is Alabama's mama." Which is in a sense also true. Alabama was carved out of Mississippi. I feel competitive sometimes, but the fact is that Mississippi is the only place that has ever felt so akin to Alabama to me that, if dropped in the middle, I might confuse it.

The first time I ever met Jackson native Kiese was on Vassar's campus. He had invited me to talk to his students. We talked about virtuosity, the striving for excellence that sits at the core of Black Southern aesthetics. It was a conversation about art, but also about identity. The fact is that we come from a tradition that treated beauty as a form of refusal. And in refusing White supremacy with our beauty, we are a people who are exacting critics. We are withering and hyperbolic. A perfect example is how often we'll describe a vocalist who is competent, if not outstanding, as someone who "can't sing worth a damn." On the other side of that judgment is the requirement of humility. And the requirement of humility poses some challenges to self-esteem. If you get a big head, you'll be admonished about getting too big for your britches, either directly or slyly: "You might can sing alright, but you ain't got nothing on X" or "Who told you to wear that?" Implicitly "that" undermined whatever success you may have had. And the consequence is that striving for excellence and even achieving it leaves one still on un-steady ground.

The second long conversation I had with Kiese, about eighteen years ago, was about my flailing efforts to write a novel. I'm embar-rassed about the failures of that artifact. I knew less than zero about composition and form back then. But the most interesting part of the conversation we had was about what was the most interesting part of the novel, the way it pivoted around a character who was a New Afrikan. Kiese told me his daddy had been in NAPO. Al-most immediately there was another layer of familiarity between us. It should have been anticipated, though. Southerners choosing African names for their children—like "Imani," meaning "faith," or "Kiese," meaning "joy"—were signals, for a time, of twin commit-ments to roots and rootedness, as it were, the people and the land, here and there.

Then one day back in 2018, Kiese posted a photo on Facebook of a drawing someone from Mississippi had sent him as part of a re-quest for money. The sender was a visual artist who wrote on lined notebook paper. Within an hour or two, I sent Kiese a drawing that the same artist had sent me. It was nearly identical but not. Each had been hand-inked in pen rather than photocopied. On the draw-ing he sent me, the artist had run the pen back and forth to correct a mistaken line: the artist's hustle had to be respected. I'm guessing he thought that these two Black writers, obviously stuck on home (the idea, the topic), might be willing to redistribute a little bit. And it was a good gamble because I sent him money, more than made sense. Kiese did, too.

The formula of the drawing was rudimentary, a pen drawing of a cabin in the rural South. It's an architectural form that re-mains, though just barely, and doesn't withstand history that well. In contrast, plantations are preserved with urgency. But now they're farms. The only real difference between a farm and a plantation is how it's used and who it uses, nothing else. Still, real estate brokers sell working farms as "plantations." I suppose it gives some buyers a rush, a delightful turn in the past. It turns my stomach. The brokers will describe the vastness of both the home and the empty space around it. They promise things like: "This one has it all, luxury, beauty, recreation, fishing, hunting, guest quarters, timber. You name it and it's here. The only way you are going to understand this property is to take a look for yourself. Paradise . . ." All that is missing is us.

I had heard about children being charged with building plantation dioramas as part of science projects in Southern schools. So I googled, following the mothers' anxious questions asking how to do this. You cannot buy a plantation kit from anywhere, I've found. You perhaps could turn a farm kit into a plantation, by placing Black figurines about. But you would also need cabins and ragged clothing to be authentic. For the resourceful parent, however, there are plenty of guides online about how to make one from scratch. It seems less offensive than buying a slaveholding landscape already prefabricated. Dollhouse fantasies are generally expected to be idyllic, except when used by child therapists as a vehicle to open up about trauma. I'd pass on that exercise.

One of the big three craft stores, Hobby Lobby, has all the supplies you need. Crafting is big in the South. Its kitsch is not, however, self-mocking. There is honest joy in the ritual of making things. Hobby Lobby sees itself as wholesome. Its Oklahoman founder, David Green, and his executive offspring and siblings live the gospel as they see it. The stores are piously closed on Sundays, and donations go to megachurches and institutions like Oral Roberts University and Liberty University. Green even funded the building of the Museum of the Bible in Washington, DC, where you can take a virtual tour of the Holy Land. The museum opened in 2017. But thousands of Hobby Lobby–owned artifacts, presumably intended to be housed at the museum, were confiscated by the FBI because they had been stolen from Iraq. Hobby Lobby paid a fine and returned the relics. The museum claimed no intent to ever hold them. It did, however, feature fifteen Dead Sea Scrolls. As it turns out, those were all fakes.

But it's still filled with other stuff. A story is crafted in this museum, as with a plantation replica or a site of historic preservation, of a particular tradition. We all have to accept narrative histories can never be comprehensive. But choices are made that reveal values and priorities. And I suppose what I find so compelling about Jackson is that there is no avoiding the truth that there is a battle still being waged over the story. Jackson is named for Andrew Jackson, though, like many parts of the South, it might just as easily have been named for Stonewall Jackson. Though one was formally a president and the other a secessionist general, they shared plantation values of domination. For me, that heroism is shameful. For others, it is to be lauded. Thus, the battle is over truth. But it is also over decency. If you make sin look pretty, that must mean you love the devil.

The generations of freedom fighters in the Black Belt continue their work. And in Mississippi, they have made it the state with the most extensive Black political representation in America. It is the closest we have to a realization of full Black political citizenship. And it is the only state with a scion of Black nationalism as the executive of its capital. Jackson is publicly, unapologetically Black, even for Mississippi. It evidences itself in culture as much as politics. For example, the marching band at Jackson State University is called the Sonic Boom of the South. When the male dancers jump, in navy and white so crisp it could not have possibly touched dirt or concrete for how pristine it is, they are suspended in air, time stands still, and yet the music goes hard and unceasingly. When the women dancers dash a hip, to left, to right, it is sharp, taking back the lasciviousness teased in an instant, a taste before magisterial precision; as the horns gleam, the musicians are consistent as seasons of crops. They march, left right left right. The band does not make the flesh crawl; it revels in it. Love this flesh, it says. It makes sense that this is where the great chronicler of Black history in poem and fiction and prose Margaret Walker made her home as a professor at Jackson State University. She was one who saw the glory of the eternal coming of Black people. The exultation.

They march through the streets, not just in stadiums, and you can always see the dirt high-stepping underfoot. There is no easy resolution between beauty and terror, between poverty and abundance. And just outside of the city, you find yourself looking around and saying the South would be worth holding close even if only for the trees. You can see it. How before all the building, the Piney Woods once stretched across five states. And as chopped down as they are now, their sharp warm scent and sight wraps around you even when you're standing from a distance. They emanate fragrance that you feel in your eye sockets and above your socks. They are a fortification against climate change. The scientists say these trees are in a desperate battle against human green, slowing the pace of destruction by literally killing greenhouse gases with their scent. If only we were willing to reblanket the Southeast in conifers, we might save ourselves.

Knowing this, however, doesn't really make it better. Because while we have won, we lose. We still are being killed by what the land won't bear for us. We bear the wounds offered up as data or statistics. The life expectancy for Black men in Mississippi is 66.71. In Alabama it is 66.66. I stare at the statehouse, with its golden orb at the top. It is imposing, and yet it also looks like it could be peeled like a fast-food wrapper, to find some chicken inside. The interior rotunda in the seat of Mississippi government has a statue of the blind goddess Justice lit by over seven hundred lights. Around her are two Indigenous people, a European explorer, and a Confederate soldier. There is no African. Look up at the top of the gold leaf copper dome and see our national symbol: a white-headed bald eagle.

We haven't outrun or outlived the plantation, although it looks a little bit different. Now the fugitives are from Central America, and the unfree laborers are in prison. Some kids are still hungry, even so many years after the breakfast programs and Head Start and all of the gains fought for by Black elected officials, because the gag is in the money and the land, and it still isn't free. There's an honesty to Mississippi about all of this. The triumph is not in ends; it is in the fact that we are still here.

To the east of Jackson, in the center of the state, in 2019, ICE raided chicken factories. They were populated by Mexican and Central American immigrants, doing jobs once done by Black folks. If you've ever read Anne Moody's memoir about growing up in the Black Belt and joining the freedom movement, *Coming of Age in Mississippi*, you will remember her summer of working at a chicken factory in Louisiana. The workers, who were White, went on strike. And Black people were brought in as scabs and, more importantly, as people hungry for work. It is awful work. Going to work in the chicken industry made up for the loss of fieldwork. The mechanical cotton picker made much of the human work unnecessary.

Though less backbreaking than picking cotton, the work was dizzyingly rapid and unrelenting, and the stench of diseased flesh seeps into the workers' pores. Moody said she couldn't eat chicken anymore after that. Chicken production remains a dirty business. Five companies—Tyson Foods, based in Arkansas; Pilgrim's Pride, a multinational company that began as a feed store in Pittsburg, Texas; Perdue of Salisbury, Maryland; Sanderson Farms, the only Fortune 1000 company in Mississippi; and Koch Foods of Illinois— all with processing factories in Mississippi, together control about 60 percent of the entire US chicken market. It is a Southern industry in location and orientation.

Now, often the people brought in to undercut the cost of a living wage, people who are exploited, are immigrants. Different people, same choreography of suffering. The children of those raided workers were abandoned by the law and swept into its disorder. There was tearful footage, as though it is enough to tell the story of what happened. As though it is enough to care. The workers were deported, lives upended. The chicken factories continued their business, though the profit margin was temporarily unsettled. You must never let the orchestrated story of the journey from slavery to freedom or from Jim Crow to civil rights keep you from seeing what remains the same even when things change. The storied places do not serve you best as sites of commemoration. They are much better as sites of instruction.

I was in Jackson for the Mississippi Book Festival in 2018, And I was a little bit huffy at the festival because they had Margaret Walker's face on a banner as a Mississippi author. Of course she spent more years there, in Jackson, than she did in Birmingham. And my claim to her was tenuous even on that count because she was born in Alabama to a Floridian mother and a Jamaican father. But Alabama has relatively few writers to our name. As the saying goes, "Mississippians love their writers the way Alabama loves football." In Alabama, Joan Didion noted "[t]he sense of sports being the opiate of the people. In all the small towns the high school gymnasium was not only the most resplendent part of the high school but often the most solid structure in the town, redbrick, immense, a monument to the hopes of the citizenry." And the people yield accordingly. It has occurred to me that Mississippi's comparably vast literary tradition has something to do with it being the Blackest state. Storytelling is a critical feature of African diasporic culture, and what greater melodrama exists in modernity than the elliptical tale of the slave yearning to be free, killed dead for it, then rising again. Maybe it's because it is the least industrialized part of the South. Plants, in the sense of production, came late to the state. Agriculture remained its mainstay. Folk living is good for writing. Or maybe I'm counting wrong. Maybe I ought to count Alabama's songwriters as our writers: Lula Mae Hardaway, Stevie Wonder's mother; Mattie Moss Clark, the Clark Sisters' mother and the mother of modern gospel music; Big Mama Thornton, the Mother of Rock and Roll; W. C. Handy, the Father of the Blues; Nat King Cole, father of Natalie Cole; and Lionel Richie, son of Tuskegee and therefore son of the Black Belt.

For lunch I fixed my mood with a big cup of lemonade and a delicious catfish sandwich from a food truck. It worked. Part of the brilliance of Kiese Laymon's book *Heavy* is that he tells you about what eating means in the South. It is refuge, distraction, but it is also what is forced down your throat. You can work to get it out and sweat it out. It is what you yearn for and what you hate about yourself. And one of these days, it won't be long, someone will write the text about our eating disorders, and not just obesity but binging and purging with laxatives such as Feenamint gum chewed piece after piece, after the slice after slice of cake, after the battering of catfish.

Mississippi has the most catfish farming in the country, with Alabama coming up close behind. In both places, catfish took up some of the slack left by the decline in cotton prices. From above, catfish farms look like marbled cerulean and pale sapphire rectangles, like a mild Mondrian painting. Cormorants shoot down from the sky and feast on catfish, costing harvesters thousands. And yet a catfish sandwich is easy to find. The fish themselves, at least the varieties that are whiskered and sharp-toothed, look like disgruntled old men. I used to watch them swim figure eights in tanks in the basement of my friend's parents' house. I loved to look in catfish eyes, but they never caught my gaze. I liked to watch them. I never had an aversion to eating them.

Sitting cat-a-corner from her table, I watched the genius chronicler of Southern lives Jesmyn Ward and her daughter, a near exact replica of her but tiny, with her hair in two ponytails instead of Jesmyn's cascade of curls. Together they signed books. Most people in line were waiting for her to sign *Sing, Unburied, Sing*, a novel in which a child ghost of Parchman lives alongside a boy today who bears the weight of loving and caretaking alongside the trauma of addiction and the fact of poverty. As I watched her and her baby girl signing books, I felt history's layers seeped into the moment—the prohibition of literacy, the denial of a history, captivity cum freedom cum captivity again, a yearning to end the sorrow, and ultimately, in the act of extreme grace, the art. She smiled and gave me a little wave. Her beauty and gentle, humble poise alongside such incredible power is a quintessential form of Southern womanhood; it is a thing I cannot quite explain but that I know when I see it.

Years ago, I noticed that when Black men from the South are about to fight, physically, they hold their mouths in, whereas Black men from the Northeast tend to poke their mouths out. There is that knowing restraint, telling you: "You don't want to make me do this, but I will." I am sorry people mistake withholding for timidity. I hope you know better now.

III

WATER PEOPLE

HOME OF THE FLYING AFRICANS

The Low Country

WHEN I WAS SEVEN YEARS OLD, I danced with Bessie Jones. By then she was well into her seventies, older than my grandmother. She traveled, city to city, teaching children folk songs and clap games that were traditional to the Georgia Sea Islands. Her visits to Boston were some of the few occasions when I vied to be in the front. I was usually shy and quiet. But I needed to catch her eyes. I wanted her to notice me and think, Here goes a real little Southern girl, what's she doing up here? She didn't say that. But Ms. Jones always smiled right at me.

In her younger days, outside of singing, Jones did odd jobs and worked as a moonshiner. She was a real short woman. I could nearly look her in the eye when I was in elementary school. Her voice had gravel in it, a throaty alto. She wore a wig that sometimes was a tad askew but looked just like the hair underneath: straightened, strong, chin-length. She shuffled when she walked. She clapped her hands in layered syncopation, changing rhythm mid-phrase like the soul clap in Chicago house music, like the echoing clap in the break in Nina Simone's "Sinnerman." We children danced the choreography accordingly. That clap has been traced all the way back to the

Mende people of Sierra Leone. But here is the thing with that kind of tracing: the markets for human flesh and labor, the way they ruptured and burst and bled out people, refused a single straight line from then to now. There was a lot of re-creation.

One of my favorite songs, "Old Lady from Brewster," tells the story of an old lady who had two hens and a rooster. The rooster died and the old hen cried because she couldn't lay eggs like she used to. The culprits were two boys with "a red cap on." As punishment, they were hit with a hickory stick. And we repeated, as they repeated, "Pain in my head, ranky tanky. Pain in my shoulders, ranky tanky. Pain in my waist, ranky tanky. Pain in my feet, ranky tanky." I didn't know "ranky tanky" even meant anything. But it means to get down. The beatdown leads to dancing.

I met Gullah Geechee culture through Bessie Jones and the Sea Island Singers before I knew much about the people and their history. I'd read their stories, too. My mother bought me a book when I was twelve years old by Virginia Hamilton, called *The People Could Fly*, and it told the story of Ibo Landing on St. Simons Island, a place I'd first see as a teenager. In the fictionalized version I read, the Ibo people, brought there on a slave ship, witnessed the brutality of a slave plantation and turned around to fly back to Africa. In the historically recorded version, a group of Africans arrived in Savannah on a slave ship called the *Wanderer* in 1803. They were bought by merchants and resold to plantations on St. Simons. On the ship transferring them to the island, the Ibo rebelled, drowned their captors, and grounded the ship. They disembarked, singing and marching.

Roswell King, a White plantation overseer, then witnessed the Ibo refuse this land. They walked into Dunbar Creek. And didn't walk back out. King said he dragged dead bodies back to land. Black folks said that some of them walked all the way across the ocean floor back to Africa. The people of St. Simons have kept the memory of the flying Ibo alive and created something new, at once distinctly

African and Black American, on their island. They have collapsed the space between life and death when it comes to freedom. Their spirituality touches the realm beyond this physical world. That is what I take of the story of Ibo Landing and the acknowledged presence of the dead in the culture of the people on the Sea Islands. With majority-Black populations, and after generations of absentee landlords during slavery, their language and folkways are more distinct here than anywhere else in Black American life. They are called Gullah Geechee people, a portmanteau of two traditional names for the language and the culture. Even their tongue is most distinct, a language that the Deepest South Southerner from the mainland doesn't understand without some intimacy. Their home is an enchanting place. Walking along their water's edge among the knobbed whelks, fluted shells that end in a point like a bloom or a seed, I felt like I was sitting in the decorations of history. Swirling, haunting, repeating, eerie and magnificent. How, I have wondered, having walked on these islands, could we maintain the myth that the "heartland" is the place *farthest* away from the water? Is it because of the American habit of running away from the truth? There on the water is where alienation was first felt. There is where encounter, discovery, disaster, and wonder hit those who came to shore. Often all at once. There are tears in that salt water. Fear, of course, and lust for what might be gained were also feverish at the coast. The Ibo walked away from greed. And the Gullah Geechee held on to hope, but even in the best of circumstances, terror threatened. That terror pivoted to ugliness so often. Against the backdrop of the water, beneath which lie the remains of African bones, they survived.

The Gullah Geechee worked in tandem and in mutual aid. The owners who had had them chained and stacked left them on the island on their own. Owners distanced themselves from the evidence of the fetid hold, the salt-soaked death on their skin, satisfied with the proceeds of their labor: indigo, rice, cotton. This absenteeism was common on the Sea Islands during slavery. The Africans who were left there became water people, people who lived by fishing and tides, but also people who understood water to be the most feasible path to escape. Seeking freedom, some made their way to Mexico, the Bahamas, Trinidad, even as far as New York, swimming and sailing out of constraint, like gigging flounder or frogs at night. Wandering in the water, you might catch a print in the sandy bottom. Flounder lie sideways, one eye peering up. A print tells you they are there, in your midst. Under the sand they think they are camouflaged. They are for some viewers. But the very same habit lets the fisherman know exactly where to stab. Stab, pull it up by its punctured side, hold it still, a victory. Like flounders, some made a way while staying here, on the islands.

Long before I learned I descended from water people—St. Helena Parish, Louisiana; Maryland; coastal Virginia—I secretly wanted to belong to them. It was back when I believed that the mystery of how one comes to be is genealogical. It isn't. But water people do often hold their ways and truth close to the vest, to protect them from the chaotic frenzy of modernity. I thought maybe through family trees I could get into it. After all, it isn't always easy to access. But I knew more than I thought, earlier than I thought.

There is something else, about the thread of connection. I don't have known roots on the Sea Islands or in the Black Belt. But I am a descendant of the culture. That is what it means to be Black American: the hidden virtue of an unsure genealogy is a vast archive of ways of being learned from birth. We dance in all of our ways when we are together. That a people choose to dance is not a mark of simple happiness. That a people still sing is not a picturesque story of their satisfaction. It is art. To this day, the children of the children of the children of the slave South, in ghettoes and hoods across the country, will clap and stomp in unison. They will "cheer," as the expression goes, and rhyme. They will study for hours how to make their voices careen and their bodies work in tandem precision. They will evade boredom and desperation with the stern discipline of kinetic beauty. We do not know empty hands. Our bodies do not gleam and muscle because of genetics; it is because our ways of being, our singing, maudlin or joyous; is a disposition towards the fact of living that persists no matter how much changes.

The Bilali document, written in the nineteenth century by Bilali Muhammed, who had been enslaved on Sapelo Island, is a partial recounting of Islamic law. It is part of the fabric of a pious improvisation, a holiness unbound by law but made anew in the stutter steps caused by enslavement. Look up on porches on St. Simons, Sapelo, Edisto, St. Helena, and you see another thread. The ceilings are often painted in blues, blues called "haint blue," but in fact not all exactly the same color. A sensibility as much as a color, haint blue was traditionally made of indigo, lime, and milk. Of course paint companies have taken up the color, as have the affluent. Their versions tend to be paler. The reason for the blue is that ghosts, or haints, as well as insects, are warded off by the tint of water and sky. It's a warning: Don't cross over into this world with your wailing, your unsettlement. There's enough suffering on this side. On the trees you can sometimes still find cobalt-blue milk of magnesia or Blue Nun wine bottles resting on branch tips. Inside them the ghosts reflect and gleam. Old ways collide with the fact of resort culture. Some people want their vacations with more ornamentation than chain restaurants and Bibles in tan-colored rooms. And so this, the African part of the South, is encroached upon.

The resorts and golf courses and budget luxury—a hotel style first innovated on Tybee Island, Georgia—have creeped up on Sea Island after Sea Island. This was where the forty acres and a mule were promised. And where, after emancipation, the formerly enslaved tried out a collective model of ownership, something that we clunkily call "socialism," before the land was snatched back. Now, as the younger ones do not want to stay, and the older ones die, and the developers push, the hard-fought-for pieces of land and ways of being are vulnerable. Gentrification is often the enemy of history and honor. And yet visit the islands and you will see herculean efforts to keep tradition alive.

One afternoon in the fall of 2020, I was talking to Tina McElroy Ansa, a Macon, Georgia, native who lives on St. Simons. For years I devoured her novels; now I count her a friend and play auntie. She told me to come as soon as possible, that back in the woods the ancestors were waiting for people who could tell their stories. I thought of the trees. The oaks whose branches reach way out before touching down, and the way the sun shines through their moss. I swear it looks like you're in heaven. I can't wait to go back.

* * *

IN THE SUMMER OF 2018, I was traveling to Savannah to participate in a writing retreat. And so I decided to reach out to David Blight, the historian who wrote the groundbreaking biography of Frederick Douglass, *Prophet of Freedom*. I'd noticed that he dedicated the book to Dr. Walter and Mrs. Linda Evans, who live in Savannah. Walter is a collector of African American art and artifacts. Until recently, when they were acquired by the Beinecke Library of Yale University, Walter owned the family photo albums that Douglass had maintained, along with other personal effects. For Blight, learning about this trove made writing the biography an imperative. I was curious about what else Dr. Evans had and how he'd gotten it. David made the introduction.

Walter told me, soon after we met, that he doesn't meet with everyone who wants to meet with him. He spoke to me in a way that is common among Black Southern people of a certain generation. Their skepticism comes with a smile. It is a warning that decency and sincerity are expected of you and you just might be dismissed if you don't know how to conduct yourself. He also didn't exactly trust that I'd be able to find his home myself, so he came to pick me up at my hotel. As I expected, when he arrived, he stepped out of the car, walked around to the passenger side, and opened the door for me.

But one thing was unusual. Though a general surgeon, and over twenty years my senior, Walter did not want me to call him Dr. Evans. After I did it about five times, he said, insistently and with his brow furrowed, "Just Walter." He puts on no airs. Once we became friends, and that was quick, he said to me about my professional life, "Those folks are working you hard 'cause they know you're an Alabama Negro," and we both shrieked with laughter. It is the kind of humor you acquire when you come from a place that is frequently mocked. Think about how Muhammad Ali, from the Upper South city of Louisville, Kentucky, mocked the Beaufort, South Carolina, Low Country–born Joe Frazier, calling him dumb, slow, and ugly. Ali described himself as slicker, prettier, lighter, and better as a boxer and person. It is mortifying to recall that time when a hero diminished himself with an outsized ego. Joe Frazier was still talking about how deeply it hurt him three decades later. But this is what we of the Deep South have lived with, in dozens of different forms, hierarches among the diminished, along with the burden of sobering up those who mock us to avoid the truth of who they really are. Sometimes they're drunk on the wine of self-delusion. I mean, you already know how Southern Louisville is.

Walter's home sits up from the ground, as grand homes in Savannah often do. High ceilings, large windows, and a raised first floor characterize fine Low Country houses. Everything sits close together in Savannah, at least compared to other parts of the South. It is an old and urbane place, established in 1733. In 1864, Union General Sherman marched to Savannah after the burning of Atlanta. Upon reaching Savannah, I have read, Sherman was taken by its beauty and could not bring himself to destroy it. I have also read that Savannah's mayor offered immediate surrender in exchange for the Union Army keeping property and person undisturbed. Perhaps both details are true. In any case, it is one of the best-preserved cities in the South.

Walter directed me to look at the front of his house. "Do you remember the scene in *Glory*, when Frederick Douglass is speaking to the Black troops of the 54th regiment?" I did. *Glory*, released in the Christmas season of 1989, is a Civil War film starring Denzel Washington, Morgan Freeman, and Matthew Broderick. It was, at the time, one of the few depictions of Black soldiers during the war. "That scene was shot right here." I'm sure my eyes widened. The Evans home *did* look just like it could be in colonial Boston. I loved *Glory*, and I held special regard for the 54th regiment. In my teenage years, after tooling around Downtown Crossing, I would stop and visit the memorial for them that sits on Boston Common. My mother and I had gone to see the movie at a theater nearby a few days after Christmas in 1989. As Walter talked, I imagined the scene with Douglass. I wanted to step down, to be at the vantage point from where the soldiers watched him. But we were already at the threshold, and I didn't want to behave too idiosyncratically on our first meeting. Walter pointed at the live oak. "They had to remove the Spanish moss from the tree in order for the scene to look like they were in Boston. It never grew back."

The first time I ever came to Savannah, I was starry-eyed about the Spanish moss, like fine lace decorating the city. I would walk looking up everywhere I went. When two West Indian SNCC members, Stokely Carmichael and Michael Thelwell, recalled moving to the Deep South, they both commented on the moss. Thelwell said it frightened him, duppy-like in its sheer cascade. Carmichael said, ". . . you know what really represented Deep South to me: my first sight of tall trees festooned with beards of Spanish moss. The mere sight of those moss bearded trees etched against the rising sun said *Louisiana, plantation, slavery, bayou, swamp, lynching,* the mythical South." I'd been born in a lynching place, and spent plenty of time in Louisiana, and ridden past more than a few plantations, but when I went to Savannah as a teenager, it was the first time I'd seen Spanish moss. I hadn't even imagined it. It was indeed something mythical. Though its moss is now gone, the live oak outside the Evans home, thick with branches like massive tentacles, is still magnificent.

How to describe the Evans home inside? I will fail. It is stately. But also fantastical. The furnishings are heavy, ornate, works of master cabinetmakers and designers. The wood is rich, vivid, as though it is still reaching into the soil though it has been cut, shined, glossed, and fashioned. And then there is the art. I would find out that it reaches to the tippy-top of the house, and also gathers in rooms with closed doors. A house filled with the work of African American artists from the eighteenth century to the present—and, to be precise, the greatest of that tradition.

I could hardly catch my breath. On the wall there was a William H. Johnson piece that caught my eye. In middle school, I'd bought a pack of postcard images of Johnson paintings and took them out of my desk drawer, frequently, to admire them. "I've never seen a work of his that had that color flesh in a subject," I commented. Walter's eyes smiled a little, and he told me about the piece. Part of how I'd introduced myself to him was through my love of African American art. And I wanted to be an interesting guest. I told him I'd even begun collecting. I shared details of my modest yet serious purchases. "Oh!" he said with a grin, "You know what you're doing!" I smiled back. "Yes, I do."

I explained to him that I was trying to write something in the vein of Albert Murray's *South to a Very Old Place*. "Let me show you something." We walked up to the second landing, and there was a vast streetscape. He stopped. "Do you know whose this is?" I think he knew I knew.

"Bearden, of course."

"And where?"

"From Albert Murray's window, in Harlem."

If you've seen Romare Bearden's *The Block* at the Metropolitan Museum of Art in Manhattan, you've seen a version of this painting. Except this one, in Walter's home, is even more complex. Its rendering of a mid-twentieth-century street in Harlem, the rhythm, the motley of people, the trials and dreams, seems to reach beyond the frame. I'm not sure how Bearden did it, but the painting feels bigger than itself.

In Atlanta, a few months after my visit with Walter, I would go to a Bearden exhibition at the High Museum. The pieces depicted his youth in Charlotte, North Carolina, before his family moved north. There was also a video installation showing in the center of the exhibition room. Albert Murray sits alongside Bearden in much of it. They talk about how Murray named almost all of Bearden's paintings and that they were the closest of friends, something that Walter would affirm to me in one of our many conversations over the following year.

They were different. Murray elegant, Bearden sensual. Though the same could be said about either, one sensibility dominated in each. Murray was from coastal Alabama, Bearden from farther inland, Charlotte, North Carolina. He was pale, where Murray was the most oakly solid brown one could imagine, with sharp birdlike features. Bearden's face was full of rounded shapes: a nose and chin that recalled the hips of the women in his paintings. These friends were not identically Southern by any means, but together they told you something that was true across all the differences. And it was more than anything about the poetry of Black life. Both the thing and the way you said, showed, or sang it. The valence and its expression, whether you were talking about the trade of the woman of ill repute or the oration of a pastor. It's about the common affirmation and aphorism that "Mama didn't make no junk," including the junk you acknowledged you made in your life. Yes, there was a particular friendship, and there was also a legacy crafted in between their arts.

Walter, his wife, Linda, and I went to dinner. Linda is a tall, ele-gant Detroiter, soft-spoken and sweet yet steely with jet-black "blow hair" (as we Black folks traditionally describe natural straightness) brushed into a chignon at the nape of her neck, polished in that way that Detroit, or what I like to call Alabama North, specializes in: bourgeois and butter-hued, but not dicty at all. Kind, humble, and gracious, she had been a science educator before they retired back in Walter's hometown in Savannah. It was the second marriage for both of them, and they've spent their time together creating a life and a legacy. Talking with Walter is like going to a library. He is an endless font of event and detail. Linda's reflections are lingering in contrast; she fills in narrative and comes to conclusions with careful pacing. It is clear she was a masterful educator.

We ate in a trivia-themed restaurant in a property that the Evanses used to own. They'd renovated numerous buildings in Sa-vannah that were previously in a state of disrepair, and sold a num-ber of them afterwards. I had fish and chips and lemonade. And I asked about the beers they had selected. They taught me what it meant for a beer to be hoppy, how one could taste earth or fruit along with wheat. We went from topic to topic like that, back and forth with curiosity.

After our meal, Walter and I walked outside for a moment so he could show me the restaurant's garden. He'd planted it as part of the building's renovation. These were not a few pretty flower beds. They were stunning large-leafed tropical plants. "Now, this," he said, reaching for the ground, "is Savannah gravel. We were known for this." Once it was cheap; now it is cherished.

Walter was born in Savannah, but raised partly in Beaufort, South Carolina, which, he asserts, is the most beautiful city in the United States. I wouldn't argue with him on that. Everywhere you look, Beaufort has the perfection of a painting, with some of the trees arcing up and then all the way back down to the ground, beards dripping, a lush frame to greenish sky. When Walter was a child, his father died in a storm, and he, his mother, and his siblings moved around as a result. His mother, a nurse, sought opportunity to support her family. In addition to Beaufort, part of his youth was spent in Philadelphia, and part in Hartford, where he finished high school, faced what he describes as the most overt racism he ever encountered, and spent summers working on tobacco farms with migrants from Puerto Rico. But Savannah remained home in his own estimation, and he returned there after building his career in Detroit because there was no place he'd rather be.

I asked him how he began collecting art. He said, "I had just finished Howard, and I was working in Philadelphia for the summer. I wanted to take a girl out on a date. And she wanted to go to a museum. We didn't have museums down here for Black folks, not down South. So, I went to the Philadelphia public library, the big one on the parkway, and read everything I could about the Philadelphia Museum of Art. When I took her on the date, I could talk about everything in that museum." He paused. "The girl is long gone, but the art stayed." It was a charming, somewhat apocryphal story. And didn't answer my question really, but who could push past such a delightful memory?

He told me he was also drawn to books by his Philadelphia sweetheart. His habit began with the *New York Times* bestseller lists. After time in the Navy, he went to Howard University. He was well-read, and well versed in fine art. But Howard led him in another direction. The thrall of the freedom movement was everywhere on campus. He listened to Sterling Brown hold forth and witnessed the fiery Black liberation preaching of Stokely Carmichael. His nascent love of art and literature dovetailed with his growing race man sensibilities—that particular traditional African American orientation to life in which, whatever endeavor one pursues, the uplift of one's people remains at the forefront. He turned to reading Black books. He began to collect Black art specifically, inspired by the movement. Walter became a person at the crossroads of two histories. He situated himself in the tradition of forerunners like W. E. B. Du Bois, who saw his charge in life as documenting and preserving the artifacts of Black people precisely because their significance had been obscenely discounted and diminished, and of the Black power activists of his own day, for whom that tradition shaped how they lived and worked in an unapologetic commitment to self-determination. He told me he even chose his medical school, the University of Michigan, in large part because of the ministry of Albert Cleage, a Black nationalist Christian minister and writer who renamed himself Jaramogi Abebe Agyeman. And although Walter was a general surgeon, he served as Agyeman's personal physician at his insistence.

Over the years, long after the end of the Black power heyday, Walter sustained relationships with a wide range of extraordinary people. In Detroit, his home became a salon in which artists and writers would come and stay in residence for a week or two. He'd become friends with Bearden that way, and the writer Margaret Walker, among others. I was dazzled by the stories, and a bit envious. "Why," I asked, "do you think we don't have that anymore? I mean that kind of space, for Black artists and writers and thinkers to gather together and share with each other and the larger community." "Well, Black artists don't need Black patrons in the way they once did" was the first part of the detailed answer he gave me. And it explains how he, a doctor and not a corporate CEO, was able to acquire such an extraordinary collection in the days before Black art was astronomically expensive. The prices were relatively low, and the community could grow intimate. The same was true of housing in Detroit. He said, "White flight meant we could live in mansions." And since he had no aversion to living in a Black community that was healthy, solidly working class, and filled with homeowners, it was in some ways an ideal circumstance.

One of the difficult side effects of desegregation—and you'll hear it again and again from Black people who lived in the before time—is that something precious escaped through society's opened doors. Even acknowledging how important desegregation was, the persistence of American racism alongside the loss of the tight-knit Black world does make one wonder. What if we had held on to those tight networks ever more closely, rather than seeking our fortune in the larger White world that wouldn't ever fully welcome us beyond one or two at a time? Such reflection often leads to a sorrowful place, though not what I would call regret. Black folk knew they had to push the society to open its doors. They just didn't know how much it was going to cost.

In Savannah, I also spent time with my cousin Nichelle Stephens. She'd returned to the South from New York, first to Atlanta and then to Savannah. It suits her. She is counterculture, an accountant by profession with a penchant for comedy and music, an early adopter of social media and immensely knowledgeable about food and drink. Savannah provides outlets for all of her interests. When we were small, on holidays we'd sleep foot to head on my grandmother's sofa in the den. And at her house, in a hilly section of Birmingham, we would clean—wiping counters, vacuuming, taking laundry from the line and folding it—and then, late in the evening, after everyone else was asleep, we would bake cakes and make sweet flavorful iced teas. Chelle always thought up ways to make recipes better. She was the one who taught me creativity when it came to making a home for oneself. In Savannah, she recommended that members of the writing workshop eat at the Grey Market, where she worked part-time. It is a New York bodega-inspired offshoot of the Grey, Mashama Bailey's fine-dining Savannah restaurant. Bailey, a Black woman who moved between Georgia and New York throughout her childhood, learned to cook first from the women in her family and then through formal training at Peter Kump's New York Cooking School and Château du Feÿ in France. She won a James Beard Award as the best chef in the Southeast in 2019 and also serves as the chair of the Edna Lewis Foundation, named for perhaps the most influential Southern Black woman chef in history. Both women trip up hokey or sentimental images of a Southern Black woman sweating away in the kitchen that anyone might want to hold on to. They evidence that appreciation for the earth's bounty and humble ingredients can and often do coexist with a sophisticated palate, intellectual curiosity, and a sense of glamour. Lewis, once a member of the Communist Party and a fashion designer of West African ankara dresses, wore her abundant gray hair in a swirling cinnamon roll that dipped to the bottom of her shoulder blades, and rubbed elbows with the likes of Truman Capote and Gloria Vanderbilt. Bailey is often photographed in her aprons, chic with a crisp, short-sleeved, white dress shirt underneath, gleaming mahogany skin, and coiffed and coiled hair. There is an ease to her presence, and to her food. Bailey's flavors struck me as sensuous, not so much subtle as unfolding and layered, distinct from both the rich creaminess that defines so much of New Orleans cooking and the spicy-sweet umami blend that I knew best as mainstream food of the Deep South. Her work is to home cooking as jazz is to blues. In the more experimental and widely ranging version of the tradition.

One afternoon, I walked past Flannery O'Connor's childhood home. The thing about O'Connor, as devoutly Catholic as she was, is that she exposed some of the vulgar innards of the South that most try to ignore. The practices of Southern humility, of grace, of conformity, can be so great that madness is often a necessary refuge. O'Connor talked about that. The Southern gothic is grounded in eccentricity, that extravagance of strangeness that lives among us, often a source of irritation but always tolerated, until it isn't. You can *be* crazy (and I use that ableist word deliberately because that is how the struggle with reality is described, but other words like "teched" or "not right" or "off" are options), but self-consciously acting too free might land you in a world of hurt.

The South is a monster of a place that one cannot help but at least partially revile. And everybody knows it, no matter how much they might glory in neo-Confederacy. The Janus face of Southern Whiteness—they *know* what they've done wrong, and they know you know; they hate you for it, and hate themselves for it, too—is strange. The way Flannery O'Connor overtly despised Black folks, the way she was as racist as could be, had a teasing and tenacious venom to it. Critics fairly studiously avoided it until the *New Yorker* published a piece dedicated to O'Connor the bigot in 2020. I spoke to Walter on the phone about it, and he said he was glad. That perhaps people in Savannah would cease treating her like some sort of local saint. I was glad, too, but also I felt that familiar disappointment that a writer who I not only liked, but who I believe understood and explained Southern idiosyncrasy and violence so well, had been such an utter failure when it came to what might be the most basic moral question in the history of this country: Can it ever be remade in the image of the Declaration of Independence? Or will the founders' racist sins taunt us always?

In O'Connor's short story "A Temple of the Holy Ghost," two Catholic girls are accompanied by two neighborhood boys to the county fair. While there, a member of the "freak show" raises her skirt to reveal both male and female sex organs. News of the salacious event spreads far and wide, and the fair gets shut down. But the smaller girl, who has been taught to read her body as a temple of the Holy Ghost, surmises that the intersex body is also a temple of the Holy Ghost worthy of protection. It is such a delicate inversion, beautiful even, and plainly, though strangely, wrought. I read this story again and again.

I imagine O'Connor crossing paths with the Grand Empress, another one of the most famous residents of Savannah. She was a slender, Black trans woman originally from Florida. She became a celebrity under the name the Lady Chablis, which was taken from a sibling her mother had miscarried. The Lady Chablis performed across the South, winning drag beauty pageant titles. Settling in

Savannah, she became well-known as a fixture there, in large part because of being an actor in the film adaptation of *Midnight in the Garden of Good and Evil*. O'Connor would sneer at her, I imagine, this person with the courage for an even greater creation: not just a literary imagination but a free life.

Here is another contradiction. The South is home to some of the richest queer culture in the world, and some of the deepest intolerance to any order other than patriarchy. I suppose that is why the Lady Chablis was wont to say, "Two tears in a bucket, motherfuck it." Every cruelty is also an acknowledgment that the thing or people reviled are there, and ain't going nowhere. I think this was Flannery O'Connor's point when she said, "Whenever I'm asked why Southern writers particularly have a penchant for writing about freaks, I say it is because we are still able to recognize one." Lest that sound too glib or cruel, she also said, "I think it is safe to say that while the South is hardly Christ-centered, it is most certainly Christ-haunted." The God-as-big-man voice taunts and picks at us through all matter of human variation. Some people just have enough soul to them to resist. And they get punished for it, even if everybody knows they have to be as they are. Or sometimes strangeness grows precisely where people can't simply and comfortably exist. For example, I know of a woman who had a security gate installed in her bedroom doorway to keep her husband out, but neither left nor divorced him. What cruelty had he committed? Had she lost touch with reality? Had he? What happened when the company came to put in the gate? Did they mind their business, or did they mock her? Was she able to sleep for the first time in years once she locked herself in? Did it feel like a chosen prison? Did he taunt her from outside the gate? Did he cry? Did they cry together or apart at the same time? Did she ever lose the key? O'Connor would have had a field day with this. But what she wouldn't have given much thought to, or lent credence to, were the layered wounds of a husband taught a cruel lesson about what it is to be a man and then denied it. Or a woman so afraid of leaving she would lock herself inside, risking fire and disappearance, eating what had to be her own rage, or terror, at every meal. I had to try, I thought, to add to my picture what O'Connor refused to reckon with.

In one of my many conversations with Walter, he told me of his first time treating a trans man patient many decades ago. His ethical grace was evident in how he cautioned me, as he spoke, to regard his former patient with care. He didn't want me to see the man in any way other than who he was. Walter told me about telling his patient that, as challenging as it was, he must seek reproductive health care. Walter advised the man to bring his wife along to the gynecologist's office in order to avoid the probing gaze of others in the waiting room, a plan that turned out to be successful. He reminded me then, and again, that there are ways to tell difficult stories about who we are that are tender rather than gothic.

Savannah was first laid out in squares. Twenty-four at the beginning; twenty-two exist now. They are neat compact squares, but things are more raucous inside each one. On virtually every square that I visited, there were at least four different types of people honored from at least three different historic periods. A monument here, a placard there, oak trees everywhere. At first slavery wasn't allowed in the city, and then of course it was. The "peculiar institution," as it was called, was too lucrative to turn down. At first lawyers were kept out, but that became impractical. Ordered places require advocacy. And Savannah retains a tension: this is a city from the age of revolution, and a city that got its luster in the age of cotton. Of course there are many American places like that, but it's rather rare to see both so clearly in one place.

Square by square, I walked to a church. I'd been there twice before. But the details keep it from ever getting old. Outside there is a monument that was erected to the "Chasseurs-Volontaires de Saint-Domingue" of the Battle of Savannah during the American Revolutionary War. Eight hundred men from what is now Haiti alongside three thousand Frenchmen joined the five hundred American troops at the Battle of Savannah in 1779, allowing the Americans to take back their city. A number of the Haitian fighters went on to fight and achieve victory again in the Haitian Revolution. It is a monument that reminds you that Haiti ought to always be included in our accounts of the age of revolution. You walk around the octagonal monument as though traveling a vortexed Easter ritual of the Stations of the Cross. National memory is jogged up that you didn't even know was forgotten.

Behind the monument was my destination: the First African Baptist Church of Savannah. It is the oldest Black church in North America. It was constituted in 1777, but first organized in 1773 by Pastor George Leile. Leile departed several years later. After fighting on the side of the British in the Revolutionary War, he was granted his freedom and, avoiding potential re-enslavement, abandoned the States to become the first US missionary in Jamaica. Leile is remembered as the man who spread the gospel on the island and who once served three years in prison for agitating Jamaican slaves towards freedom.

I waited in the foyer until it was time for the tour. This habit of not planning my excursions often had me waiting. It wasn't bad, though. Observing both tourists and workers at historic sites is something I enjoy. This time the woman who sold us tickets was White, but all of us visitors were Black. Our guide was a young man, a native of Savannah and a student at Morehouse College in Atlanta. Though he was casually dressed, his posture and crisp enunciation, more Black Panther than John Lewis in cadence, marked him as well suited to the designation "Morehouse Man." Glasses, short dreadlocks, and the way he talked about the importance of community service made me think he could easily have been of my generation, X. The one in which we wore Malcolm X hats and crisp baggy jeans and often preached a mix of hip hop intellectual nationalism.

First African Baptist was built by enslaved people, he told us, gently pantomiming as he spoke. They worked long hours under captive conditions during the day. And overnight they made bricks by hand and carried them to the church site. Sleepless nights and days of labor. We sat in pews and listened to the young man. He continued, telling the history of church leadership. He allowed us to ask questions that were mostly testimonials of appreciation to him for keeping history intact, reminding him of tidbits we knew or recalled about Black Savannah history.

With care, we walked up to the balcony. The steps are steep and the seating narrow and tilted. Those pews are original to the church, almost 250 years old, and smaller, like people were back then. At the ends of many of them, underneath scrolled arms, there is carved lettering, though the meaning remains inscrutable. Mostly Arabic, some Hebrew. Maybe they are the names of families. Maybe there are messages in them. At least they've been kept in good enough shape that eventually someone will be able, with diligent study, to decode them for us.

Down in the basement, there are holes in the floor. I know what these mean because in my first year of college I'd taken a course with Robert Farris Thompson. Thompson is a White Texan who had built his career as an historian of Afro-Atlantic art. Slides shown at the front of the darkened lecture hall in which I sat featured line drawings and circles on a white background—the cosmograms of the Kongo people. Each had a cross at the center. One line is the boundary between the living and dead; the other, its intersection, is the path between us and the departed. The circle around is a sign of continuity, the cycle that continues whether we are in these fragile human bodies or not. Here, on the floor of the basement in the First African Baptist church, we peered at the holes bored in the formation of the cruciform Kongo cosmogram.

I could feel the meaning everyone felt. For us Black Americans, song, ecstasy, and syncopation are so incorporated into our lives that they hardly register as forms of African retention. After all, they've been remade and repurposed as much as they've been sustained. But confronted with ancestral legacies that have receded into mystery, we caught our breath, held it tight in our bodies, before releasing it in a collective wind.

On my walk back to the hotel, I came across two women, Jehovah's Witnesses, sitting in the park with their literature. I don't remember what exactly I said to engage them in conversation, but my intent was to learn more about Savannah. They warned me not to go down to the waterfront at night. "It's too wild down there!" I said I wouldn't. They sat and I stood for hours. The two women were friends and retired. They told me they relaxed in that square frequently. Were it not for the sign and copies of *The Watchtower*, I wouldn't have known they intended to encourage me to join the ranks of the 144,000 who will make it home to Jehovah after death. Both were easy conversationalists. One looked like a Southern urbanite, wearing green separates, tortoiseshell-patterned glasses, and a straightened, coppery tapered haircut. The other was more country. Her arms and long fingers stretched out along the back of the bench. Her afro was salt-and-pepper, her skin a remarkably smooth blue-black. Her voice was deep, but raised in a singsong whenever she cooed over the tiny dogs that led their owners past us.

Savannah's problem, as they described it, is shared by a lot of tourist destinations in the South. Visitors, released from the shame and shreds of dignity they carry at home, came there to get wildly drunk. They didn't know how to act, didn't have any home training, and cut up badly. Southerners are, generally speaking, both exacting in their judgment and good at alcohol. These people from out of town, however, couldn't be trusted. I, however, trusted the women's judgment—"You a little bitty thing, too, and look like you from around here"—and really did avoid the waterfront at night.

I must admit, I was a little bit surprised when the women started talking about a new health food store that they enjoyed. It had good prices, they said, even though it was part of gentrification. I wasn't surprised that they liked the healthy food, mind you. I've always rejected the tendency to talk about Southern food as unhealthy. Greens, beans, corn, and even freshly slaughtered meat, the mainstays of our foodways, are, relative to the standard American diet, quite healthy. Our nutritional deprivation these days is more than anything a consequence of fast food, mass production, and poverty. But I think of the health food *industry* as very White, Northeast, Northwest, and West Coastal, bourgeois, moralizing, and, as I said, gentrifying. This place, however, was nice. The country woman said a young man who worked there gave her an effective cure for her constipation, and the other, while approving of the rates for green beans, cautioned that you have to be careful when it comes to taking vitamins, "'cause you can't be sure what all they're putting in there." Which is true. The farther you are from the place of production, the less you know, no matter what the packaging claims.

Expectations of Armageddon have come and gone for Jehovah's Witnesses in the past. In retrospect, those events are now understood as having separated wheat from chaff, as described in the book of Matthew. According to them, the prophesy hasn't failed. Rather, ongoing preparation is necessary because the people aren't yet ready. Collecting and writing history has a similar pattern. We think we have come across definitive stories, and then there is a disruption. New details, new artifacts, new attentions, new timelines. In Walter's home, there is a box with a letter that Napoleon Bonaparte wrote to Toussaint L'Ouverture. And in another, letters Romare Bearden wrote to a lover. There's a first edition of *Incidents in the Life of a Slave Girl*, by Harriet Jacobs, which is perhaps the most significant slave narrative written by a woman. His version was the pseudonymous one, bearing the name Linda Brent, because when Jacobs wrote it, she still had to worry about recapture. Inside of each, there may be something that has yet gone unnoticed, adding details that could turn a story on its head, or at least begin to unravel it.

As a surgeon, Walter excised expertly. He removed bad organs, cancerous tissue, and rotting innards from the body, leaving it healthy and intact. And as a collector, Walter curates expertly. I think these are companion tasks. Especially when it comes to histories of suffering. In the surgical theater, the conditions are important. You have to prevent disease from spreading; you must not allow carelessness to lead to infection. Some frame is necessary to hold things together as you try to address the violence and, after excision, dress the wound. The contrary move is to curate, bringing the things we need together. Out of a vast, complicated array of objects and events, Walter has curated a precious set of documents and artworks with Blackness at the center of his concern. This is the kind of attention that has prepared a place for me, a writer, a thinker, and a daughter of the South.

One afternoon, many months later, when I continued interviewing Walter for a profile I decided to write, I blurted out to him, "I love Charleston, but it feels different from Savannah." He said, "Charleston has a lot of transplants. People from up North." Characteristically he withheld what might be a withering judgment. No excess needed.

I didn't know about the transplants before. But Charleston had always felt newer to me than Savannah. So geographically close, they were visibly different. In Charleston, stores are higher-end. The housing projects look pretty even though they are built on low-lying land that floods. People don't always speak on the downtown streets. They walk faster. You have to read it with a sharp eye. Everywhere that gorgeous black metalwork, scrolls and decorative twists, you are told, came from the handiwork of skilled Black folks. Philip Simmons alone, a famous metalworker, has his imagination all over Charleston in one thousand gates, balconies, and fences in the most affluent parts of town.

Charleston is like a topsy-turvy doll from the plantation South, one head Black, one head White; below the torso they are conjoined twins, but you rarely see them together because the skirt always covers one head or another. One of my favorite sights here is the line of crape myrtle trees on Rainbow Row, because they are as cultivated as Charleston feels. Imported trees, they were brought from Asia in the eighteenth century and have been grown for their flush of brilliant color in spring: salmon pink, hot pink, red, white, and electric purple. The gray bark feathers off under my fingers, and there is a powdery cinnamon-colored dust. The thirteen Georgian row houses are maintained in comparable glamour, in buttercup yellow and periwinkle. These colorways were a choice to clean up the slum reputation of the block in the 1930s. But there are hints of what was before, as historic districts always provide. On the same street, East Bay, there's also the Old Exchange and Provost Dungeon. At different times both prisoners of war from the American Revolution and slaves were held in its foundation, the latter until the time for a public auction where they were displayed and sold. George Washington dined upstairs where South Carolinians debated the Constitution. Topsy-turvy.

If you take Bay Street north, parallel to the river that is out of sight, you pass through the Historic City Market. For years I thought, apparently like many others, that this was once a slave market. And I felt disgust. I'm not sure the mistake matters much in retrospect. Commerce in Southern cities is always shaped by that legacy, if only because of how common it is for people to work their fingers to the bone for a pittance and die while others feel pleasure. This error didn't change a bit or a whit about the cruelty of Southern history.

Keep going and make a left on Calhoun, named for, you already know, the South Carolinian vice president of the United States who loved slavery and built the architecture of Indian removal to the West. If you took a right, you would eventually come to Liberty Square. But left, you get to Mother Emanuel Church. Long before Dylann Roof came, I had visited Mother Emanuel Church. As with Savannah's First African Baptist, it is hallowed ground, a church made by a fire-and-brimstone resistance. The self-effacement of the Black and holy is only one side of the story, and if you think all they ever did was pray and forgive, you really do not know the story.

Denmark Vesey, one of the South Carolina's most significant enslaved insurrectionists, was once a member of Mother Emanuel. It had been founded in 1816. City leaders forced them to close their doors in 1818. Too much freedom happened there. And after Vesey's revolt, the building was burned to the ground in 1822, only to be rebuilt. The parishioners persisted.

But you also have to understand that, before Dylann Roof, the termites had taken over. They had eaten Mother Emanuel from the inside out. The wood could have been struck, and it would have given way, bending back into the imprint of a hand or a foot. History sometimes tends and sometimes distends. Sometimes repairs are done to physical structures that also ought to be done to human ones. And Dylann Roof is and was the product of an American house eaten out by its choices and built atop the graveyard of what came before. He, too, was called an outsider by locals, rather than an alarming testimony to American violence. This vanity of innocence is like guarding a gate when the warriors are already inside.

Roof says he thought that his prison sentence would not be carried out because of the coming race war. Denmark Vesey could never have approached "the Rising," what he and his compatriots called their planned slave insurrection, with such confidence. It was always a gamble for freedom. Vesey had bought his own freedom with his earnings from a local lottery, but hadn't been able to free his first wife and children, or the members of his church. The revolt he planned had the ultimate goal of, after freeing the enslaved, sailing to Haiti. The plan was squashed before it began. Thirty-five Black people, Vesey among them, were hanged in penalty for plotting their freedom.

Roof is alive. I'm not saying he shouldn't be, just that he is.

Historians think Vesey was born in Bermuda in 1757. He was sold to a planter in Haiti, who ultimately returned Denmark to his original owner because he had epilepsy. Once Vesey's master settled in Charleston, a cosmopolitan hub, Vesey became literate. At a crossroads of history, his story is yet another reminder of the breadth of the antebellum Southern world. After Vesey was executed, one of his sons was deported to Cuba. One of his wives went to Liberia. One of his children helped rebuild the historic African Methodist Episcopal Church, where Roof enacted a time-warp revenge against Black freedom.

Long before Vesey, there was the Stono Rebellion in South Carolina, in 1739. Those insurrectionists, led by an enslaved Angolan named Jemmy, planned to go to Florida, another nation then, where freedom had been promised. But they were intercepted and killed, or deported as slaves to the Caribbean. Prohibitions on gatherings, education, and group movement for Black people were legislated. A ten-year moratorium on importing Africans was implemented. The point is that there were, of course, cycles of repression and cycles of resistance. I suppose the thing I most want to say is that it is rarely acknowledged that every time that group of parishioners gathered in Mother Emanuel, they stood in a tradition of refusing to be rendered soulless and unfree. No gentrifiers, no hierarchies, no displacement, no new arrivals, and no, not even massacres that laid bodies low, one on top of another, can erase that. Their testimony is already embedded in the land.

PISTOLES AND FLAMBOYÁN

Florida

FLORIDA IS A PISTOL. A body of stories, words, and deeds. Along its back handle, the Atlantic runs. Across its panhandle, cultures blur. It reaches as far south as the Southeast can go, and almost as far west as the west coast of Alabama. It is the evidence of an untidy history: the enticement of the Spaniards, the envy of the British, the resistance of the Indigenous. It is the beginning of what would be both the destruction and genesis that made the United States. The gold glinted in Spanish eyes. They looked for the Fountain of Youth. Theirs was a thirst that couldn't be satisfied, but they made do, killing and driven by a vivid imagination. Long after the Spanish and French were gone and the British laid claim, remnants of the older empires remained: ornate architecture; gold pistoles, also known as guineas, coins for which Africans were traded; and a sense of always being pulled by another's tongue. Britain ultimately won, but France and Spain laid claims to the territory repeatedly. Indigenous people were not singular; they were multiple nations, and they negotiated in ways that sometimes had them allied and sometimes in conflict. The Africans varied, too, in language, in culture, in how they came to be new groups, here in the Americas.

In Florida, where there are large numbers of Latinos, the US habit of neglecting history becomes woefully apparent. The same is true in Texas. Just as we speak English in most of the United States because of the British empire, Latinos speak Spanish because of the Spanish empire. Historically, we have twin relationships to colonialism. But the relationship between the United States and much of Latin America is in many ways like one of colonizer to colonized.

As in the United States, in countries that were colonized over the long term by Spain, a racial stratification was built that included Indigenous people and African people in varying arrangements at the bottom, and Europeans at the top. Though the bulk of the populations are classified racially as mestizo or otherwise racially mixed (including significant African ancestry in the Caribbean), history is confounded when Latinos are categorized as being "like Black people" or "like Asian people" in the listing of racial groups. There are Latinos who are positioned as White according to their historic origins and social location, who, as much as any White Americans, have committed themselves to protecting that status. The fact that Spanish language makes many White Americans skeptical of their "Whiteness" doesn't change the fact that Europeanness can be and often is a strongly held and beneficial identity.

Furthermore, distance from Indianness and Blackness can be and is drawn by people who identify as mestizo or trigueño—i.e., a wheat- to brown-colored, curly-haired kind of "mixed"—in Latin America. It is analogous to the color and genealogical stratification that once shaped life in New Orleans or Charleston. Moreover, the growing migrations of Mexican and Central Americans as well as immigrants from the Caribbean to the US South is tied to a long-shared history between these closely connected landmasses, one of which began in the colonial era.

Beyond the sociology, the evidence is clear. Look at that florid landscape; look at all the earth would yield! It makes for greed.

Over and over again, push them out, make them work or kill them, suck everything out of human and land until it is all but spent.

Jacksonville is two hours south of Savannah on I-95. It is the largest city in the United States by area, and at nine hundred thousand residents, it is the most populous city in Florida and in the Southeast. Before it was named after Andrew Jackson, it was known as Wacca Pilatka (Seminole), Fort Caroline (French), and Cow Ford (British). Now it has more Walmarts than any city in the country and is home to twenty-one military bases and a deep-water port. In the early twentieth century, it was hailed as a resort town for visitors from up North, and so Jim Crow was not as violent there as in many parts of the South. Beyond the strip malls and golf courses today, its beauty remains undeniable. Jacksonville sits along the St. Johns River, and even the toxic algae blooms are pretty—a green just a bit richer in color than the surrounding leaves. As fertilizer runoff drains into the river, the green blooms grow. Disturbing it, breathing it in, can poison your liver and damage your nervous system permanently. A delightful killer, like a menthol cigarette.

Home-design magazines often create nostalgia, and Florida is a favorite. Look, the articles often instruct, at this old-fashioned homely style made new! They proselytize about how they have both retained historic visual interest and served up contemporary comfort (those are the necessary components to the romance). In one, I read about the revival of nineteenth-century "Florida cracker" architecture in Jacksonville. The name unsettled me at first, although the provenance is apparently not a derogatory epithet for working-class White people of the South. I was always given the impression that the etymology of "cracker" was the crack of the overseer's whip during slavery. And it developed to mean a low-status White person in general who took on the task of striking fear into the hearts of Black people. That, I had been taught, was a cracker. But I have been told in Florida it refers to the sound of the whip on cattle, not chattel slaves, wielded in the Florida backcountry. Maybe. Some Floridians who've been there for generations wear the name as a badge of pride. By other accounts, "cracker" is a carryover from the Scots Irish meaning of the word: boastful and bloated with oneself, applied to nineteenth-century Florida settlers.

The architectural heritage, the Florida cracker house, is, like the shotgun, a smart form of building that allows for indoor and outdoor living. Cracker houses are cedar and cypress with metal roofs and floors raised up off the ground with oyster-shell bricks. A straight line down the middle of the house from front to back, like the shotgun, is characteristic. Porches wrap around the perimeter. The scene of the Southern porch depends on where you are. Once upon a time, I remember, everybody would be sitting on their porches, looking out. Waiting for breezes, neighbors greeted each other from a short distance and the privacy of their homes. Now you have to get pretty rural for such ritual.

The guidance offered in magazines about how to return to the Florida-cracker-style house in a de la mode contemporary fashion includes instructions like "Honor tradition," "Don't change a good thing," "Hide the modern elements," and "Bring in the haint blue."

The *Wall Street Journal* published a piece several years ago commenting on the revival:

> Virginia has Jefferson's Monticello. Georgia has the graceful antebellum homes of Savannah. But until recently, nobody much celebrated rural Florida's contribution to architectural history. Now, several upscale developers and homeowners are embracing the down-at-heels look—right down to the outhouse, although all these designer projects have plumbing. The trend has even attracted its own, somewhat controversial name: Cracker style . . .

In *Seraph on the Suwanee*, Zora Neale Hurston's only novel that has White protagonists, the characters are "Florida crackers" and identified as such. The protagonist is a woman named Arvay who is longing to be rid of the constraints of being a poor Southern woman, and for whom religious fervor is an escape hatch. Act like you got the Holy Ghost and men will leave you alone is the trick she's learned. The house into which she is born is a metonym of her existence:

> The family lived in a clapboard house more than two miles east of the heart of Sawley and nearly a mile from the Baptist church. The house had been a dark ugly red when Brock Henson, promoted to over-rider, had moved in ten years before. It had not been repainted since and was now a rusty, splotchy gray-brown. Only one room in the house, the parlor, was ceilinged overhead. In the two bedrooms and the kitchen the rafters were bare and skinny. Water for the household came from a well out back, and the privy-house leaned a little to one side less than fifty feet from the kitchen door. A fig tree, two pear trees which bore pears that were only good for preserving, were scattered far apart in the field back of the house. There was a huge mulberry tree that redeemed the very back of the unkempt garden space.

The mulberry tree, which grows to fantastical proportions, is a more reliable refuge for Arvay than her home. She is regularly bothered by men but loved by the tree. When she finally does choose a husband, she remains skeptical of their union, through both children and tragedy, almost until the end.

Nature provides a sanctuary of sorts, as unreliable and wild as it is. This is a common motif in Hurston's work. And that makes sense for a Floridian. Florida is a paradise of a landscape, abundant and beautiful even after generations of development. Though she was born in Alabama, Hurston was raised in Eatonville, Florida, an independently settled Black town, and spent several years of her youth as a boarding student at Florida Baptist Academy in Jacksonville. Hurston loved Eatonville. She disliked Jacksonville so much that she essentially removed it from her personal narrative. She also disliked Jacksonville's most famous Black son, James Weldon Johnson. She called him the Whitest Black man she ever met. Erudite, multilingual, and bourgeois, Johnson irked her with his formality, though, like her, he often testified to the beauty of Black vernacular culture and incorporated it into his poetry and music. Both were intellectuals and scholars. Johnson was a graduate of Atlanta University who later did graduate coursework at Columbia; Hurston attended Howard University before Columbia. Both documented the Black South and were explicit about its connections to the Caribbean, probably as a result of being Florida natives.

The pride Hurston took in being from Eatonville was due to how she saw it. It provided a much different origin story than Jacksonville could give. Eatonville was the first incorporated Black town in the United States. It was established in 1887 by freedpeople who, through collective purchases, established and advertised their town as a place of possibility for African Americans. They built wood-frame houses, schools, and a municipal government. It provided a refuge from the violence just outside their borders. Orange County, in which it sits, was once the center of racial violence in the South. Florida had the highest per capita rate of lynching in the South, and Orange County had the highest number of lynchings in the state between 1877 and 1950. You can understand why Eatonville was precious to its daughter.

Hurston set her most famous novel, *Their Eyes Were Watching God*, in Eatonville. The town still exists. It is small and overwhelmingly Black to this day, but isn't defined by a story of racial violence in the way many of the other incorporated Black towns during Jim

Crow were. There is no Tulsa- or Rosewood-massacre-like story. Rather, with time and lack of industry, folks departed.

When Eatonville was founded, settlers made their way through dense woods active with wildlife. Now, if you want to visit, you drive down 95 South or Highway 1 to get there. If you were traveling there in the 1950s, Zora's last decade, you would have seen Black artists selling paintings made on Upson board along the way. Just twenty-five men and one woman, they sold impressionistic images of the Florida landscape framed by metallic-colored crown molding while in the throes of the shift from Jim Crow to what has come after. Out of their trunks came images of the Everglades. If you look at them now, the landscapes are still accurate. There are the crashing waters, the brilliant sunsets, the moonlit coastal spots. I am fond of the poinciana trees. The highwaymen painted them at water's edge, and each one, through their distinctive styles, depicted the organic geometry of the trees. The red is rich, like what we imagine blood to be but almost never is. Crisp, though made by nature, the flowers bend, a pyramid reaching out over the trunk that, no matter how ample the flowers, never looks overweighted. The poinciana species reaches through the whole region, and though it changes its name (I am reminded of this every time I go to Puerto Rico, where it is more aptly named flamboyán), it grows in Jamaica, Barbados, Cuba, and South Florida, cooling fevers and inflammation for those who know the old ways, brightening the day for everyone else. I think of Zora, traveling down and through color. Remember Alice Walker gave Shug the words "I think it pisses God off if you walk by the color purple in a field somewhere and don't notice it." Because Florida trees remind you that God pleases us, the same must be true of the poinciana, with its delicious red, and the jacaranda, which is blue-purple. The jacaranda gives, at least to me, a more drunken feeling than the red perhaps because its color is at once hot and soothing. In any case, Zora, arguably the best interpreter of Florida, saw how it opened its mouth to the world, and how the world streamed inside it.

Hurston traveled to Suwannee County in 1952, four years after *Seraph on the Suwanee* was published, in order to follow a story. Ruby McCollum, while living in Live Oak, Florida, shot Clifford Leroy Adams Jr. to death. He was White, a physician, and a state legislator. She was Black and the mother of his child. Her husband was an entrepreneur, Sam McCollum, a Black man who ran numbers Florida-style in a game called bolita that originally came from Cuba. McCollum was the richest Black man in Florida. The gossip was that her husband and her boyfriend (the White Dr. Adams) worked together in illegal gambling. Ruby McCollum had a conflict with Adams, obviously, shot him, and was arrested. The next day her husband died unexpectedly of a heart attack.

Zora Neale Hurston had studied interracial intimacies in Florida in the past. She'd spent time in the timber camps of North Florida observing "paramour rights," the structured, though not wholly consensual, relationships between Black women and White men in those settlements. Now she was sent by the *Pittsburgh Courier* to cover the McCollum case. Hurston sat in the colored balcony section for the first trial. McCollum was found guilty of murder and sentenced to die by electric chair. Financially struggling, Hurston couldn't make it back down for the appeal, and so she collaborated with William Bradford Huie, whose book *Ruby McCollum: Woman in the Suwannee Jail* is the principal account of the case. Bill Huie, an Alabaman, was one of the progenitors of checkbook journalism, i.e., paying for a good story. He never interviewed McCollum directly. His book was a bestseller. Huie based his account on Ruby's charge that Dr. Leroy Adams was not her boyfriend; he was her rapist. Ruby had letters and witnesses to the fact that she said he had assaulted her repeatedly from the outset. She testified that she had one child by Dr. Adams and was pregnant with another when she killed him. She wanted him to leave her alone. This was more than American courts could handle. Gag orders were handed down to Huie. He was deemed an outside agitator. On appeal, Mc-

Collum's murder conviction was overturned due to a judgment that she wasn't competent to stand trial. McCollum was sent to live in a mental institution. Huie tried to interview her there, but was denied access.

However, in 1958, Ruby was interviewed for *Jet* magazine, a popular African American weekly. They told the story as if Sam McCollum had simply been cuckolded, focusing on how the doctor told him to leave Ruby alone when she gave birth to his daughter, and quoted him saying that he loved his children, "white and nigger alike." The reporter commented on how healthy Ruby looked, and how much she wanted to go home.

It isn't until the end of the piece that there is a crack in the surface. Ruby says she misses her children and her home in Live Oak. And then how she never wants to hear her surname again. Her infamy has caused her great distress. Ruby's brother Matthew moved to the town where she was institutionalized to take care of her. Matthew brought her meals three times a day, reluctantly. He said, "I love my sister, but I don't want to see her. I'm trying to pick up the pieces of my life and go on living. A man can only stand so much without cracking up." But continued because, "She was my sister, what could I do?"

The various renditions of McCollum's story, like the competing descriptions of cracker architecture and people, are a reminder to those of us who want to tell a story about this state and the varied states of its people. Interpretation is challenging. Maybe McCollum didn't say "no" every time, but what did that mean when "no" wasn't ever a real choice? And though it was far less harrowing, one also wonders what it means to be proud of being a cracker when you can't ever expect to be a member of the gentry. Answers aren't easy to glean from court testimonies or architectural descriptions. I am reminded of what the novelist John Edgar Wideman said when describing Zora Neale Hurston's writings about Florida Gulf folklore. He spoke of the difficulty of rendering folk speech in published form: "Translations ask us to forget as well as imagine an original. The nature of this forgetting varies depending on the theory of translation. The inevitable awkwardness of a literal rendering, emphasizing ideas and meaning, asks the reader to forget the evocative sonorities of rhythm and rhyme or rather recall their presence in the original as a kind of ennobling excuse for what often appears on the page as a fairly bare-bones, skimpy transmission of thought. Freer translations posit themselves as admirable objects of consideration within the literary tradition of the language into which they have been kidnapped, and to that extent ask readers to forget the original, except for acknowledging the original's status as a distant relative or a celebrated ancestor." That is to say: language and the relations between people that exist in living words are dynamic in a way that denotation and the formal interpretation provided to an unfamiliar audience can't replicate. This is why it will never quite be enough to tell you what was said or what happened, why Hurston, and I think Wideman agrees, had to do more than anthropological work; she had to create fictions. Art gets closer to the sensuousness of talk and presence, echoes them in a way that the formal study of language as structure misses, and the constricted utilitarian approach to faithful transcription ignores. They say that Southern speech is songlike, but in fact our songs are language-like. They are better mimics of our living than dictation could ever be.

In *Their Eyes Were Watching God*, Hurston revealed the rhythms of workers through the dispositions of her characters. Those who were Eatonville residents sat on porches and conducted themselves with some reserve. The migrant laborers who lived from day to day, crop to crop, season to season, were prone to, as Southerners describe antics, "cutting up" and "acting out." They drank and rested before moving on to the next task. Today, when people use the term "migrant labor," it comes with images of Indigenous or mestizo people from Mexico or Central America. But for generations migrant laborers were both Black and White, and in their own way often people without papers. No birth certificates, no permanent addresses, more coins than dollars.

In terms of crops, Florida was once best known for its oranges. When Andrew Jackson took control of Florida in 1821, he established two counties: Escambia and St. Johns, with the Suwannee River as the dividing line. In 1845, when Florida became a state, Central Florida was organized under the name Orange County for its abundance. But now Florida's distinction as the "orange basket" is under threat. The work is not simply underpaid; it is diminishing. The trees are suffering from an epidemic of citrus greening. The disease first stifles the ability of the trees to make fruit, then begins to kill the trees altogether. The growers are trying to fill the economic gap with different crops. Some options are beans and hops. The seasons of history change things.

Florida is the second most popular tourist destination in the United States, after California. The appeal is remarkably diverse: beaches, islands, nightlife, and theme parks. The most iconic one is Disney World, in Orlando, Florida. Orlando is seven miles south of Eatonville, and is the county seat of Orange County. Everywhere there are dollar stores. I've always thought that was a good thing, too. They offer much better prices for snacks and kitschy items than the theme parks. Families don't have to completely break the bank. But then I learned that dollar stores are by some accounts the top link in the sweatshop chain. They provide affordable goods to poor people in the United States made by poor people in poor countries.

The dollar store is one of many business models given to us by the South, like Walmart but far more modest and even cheaper. Dollar General began in 1939 in Scottsville, Kentucky, as J. L. Turner and Son. In the mid-'50s its name was changed to Dollar General, and in 1968 the company went public. Family Dollar is younger. It was founded in 1959 in Charlotte, grew through the '60s to have stores throughout the South, and now serves the entire nation. Across the country and world now, there are tens of thousands of dollar stores, many filling a void left by grocery store closings and food deserts.

In my experience, they are usually darkly lit, as though there is some subterfuge to the bargains. It is remarkable how much cheaper so many of the same things you get in brightly lit, mainstream stores are if you buy them in a dollar store. Dollar stores are a bonanza for candy, sponges, party favors, plastic tablecloths, and some cleaning supplies routinely offered in both Spanish and English. There's a willful disorder, again to produce the bargain effect. If there are White people in them, they're often the White people who other White people put down or mock. They have twangs or drawls or heavy local idiosyncrasies in their speech that remind you that White folks do indeed have a lot of culture when they don't run away from it for the faceless bounty of being simply "White." The washrags and towels are rough, precisely how I prefer them to be. Roughness cleans you, your children, and your household items better than thick, lush things. I hate a soft "washcloth."

It's worth it to stop at a dollar store before you get to Disney World, or Miami's South Beach, or any of the luxurious sites in Florida. The state got its name because of the florid landscape. Its abundance is irrefutable. And the Magic Kingdom, Disney's signature attraction, extends its glory even further into a sensory overload. Lights and characters and pristinely maintained buildings and heaps upon heaps of sugar. And everybody is arguing. The expectations of fun are just too extreme. People melt down. It's too hot, the line is too long, the kids whose vacation you broke your neck to pay for are whining, and all of this is for them, and you would much rather be on a beach than in this melee.

I have imagined myself inside the character costumes, a massive black rodent's head covering mine, too wide to press the sweat from my face, or as it dribbles down my ears. My underwear sticking, alternately radiating heat and uncomfortably cooling. An itch under my clavicle will go unscratched, my headache will go untreated, until somewhere in this place I escape to a break room, into which I slip silently so as not to break the fantasy for the children I see, tiny through those holes, who pose with me. Being a guest is a disappointing fantasy, but a worker in the fantasy? As far as I can tell, that's much worse.

On the guest side, the respite, at least in my anecdotal memories, is always in the "It's a Small World" ride. The ride actually began in New York, as a UN exhibition put on by the PepsiCo company, before it became a Disney World mainstay. A boat carries you through lands, many of which are, to say the least, deliberately ambiguous notwithstanding the national attire on the thousands of puppets who sing about the universality of the world. It's small after all! They are different colors. And there is a sweetness to it. Because it lets you imagine that Florida is just that, just all the colors together, cheery and painless.

The plan to establish Disney World in Orlando was announced in 1965, after the Disney corporation had covertly bought up land in Orange and Osceola Counties through dummy corporations. They drained swamps and set upon building. The doors to the Magic Kingdom were opened in 1971, with other theme parks to follow. Disney World was also a means through which Orlando became a city with one of the largest populations of Puerto Ricans in the United States. Puerto Ricans were recruited to work and vacation there. That Florida already had a significant Spanish-speaking population and was a tourist destination for Latin Americans also fed this population growth. Additionally, Landstar, a real estate development company that was primarily based in Mexico, actively recruited Puerto Rican families to its developments in Central Florida. Spanish-speaking US citizens were good prospective buyers in Florida.

To that point: every major political season, the United States population reveals its ignorance when it comes to Latinos. News reporters comment as though they are unmasking a great mystery by announcing that different demographic groups among Latinos vote differently. The lilt of astonishment in their voices is annoying: "Cubans tend to vote Republican, but Puerto Ricans, concentrated in New York and Central Florida, more often vote Democrat! Wow." The surprise is evidence of the American habit of making history so simplistic that it explains very little.

Cuban conservatism has everything to do with the Cuban Revolution and the early departures of certain sectors of Cubans from Castro's Cuba. First it was largely elites, those classified as White or nearly so. They set the terms of the Cuban American community. Later, as Cubans felt the brunt of the US embargo and the fall of the Soviet Union, Cuban exiles became increasingly more African. Cuban Americans are largely either those who fled revolutionary ideas or those who were starved by the US because of them.

In contrast, Puerto Ricans have been written into the nation-state as second-class citizens of the United States since 1917, with formal full citizenship but only partial voting rights as long as they live on the island. They are the victims of racism everywhere. More interestingly, I think, is how, despite the history and present of Florida and Texas (as well as California, Arizona, New York, Connecticut, and New Jersey), Latinos and, more broadly, Latinidad is depicted as "other" rather than indigenous to the United States, even as our three most populous states (California, Texas, and Florida) have undeniable Spanish influence and have been de facto bilingual states from the outset.

Adding to the strangeness of our national mythologies is how Spanish, a colonial language, has been racialized in US popular culture. The most common visual image of Latinos in a mestizo body, or sometimes with African ancestry, renders theirs a "colored" rather than colonial language. And as with all architectures of colonialism and its aftermath, the colonized and post-colonized find themselves tethered to the colonizers. For much of the Spanish-speaking Caribbean, the colonial legacy today is felt in the power of the United States as well as their European national elites. With respect to the US, military bases are an especially powerful form of evidence. Many US bases in the Caribbean were explicitly acquired through the 1898 Spanish-American War, when this country labored to build itself into a modern empire. If you had a map of the Deep South and Caribbean with no state designations but simply dotted with military bases, you'd see the common landscape.

The military is central to Southern culture. Southerners are most likely to enlist. Southern presidents are more likely to wage war. The martial orientation is generally agreed to be an outgrowth of the aristocratic culture of honor among the planter class. It is intensely patriarchal and tends towards authoritarian ways. But the militarism is also an everyman and everyday sort of thing. Each man imagines himself as his own general, but most will defer to the alpha man. Or be forced to. The obligation to "honor" in terms of enlistment is nonpartisan in Southern culture insofar as it consists of the duty to save face for the nation more than an articulated political ideology. And such service often requires self-effacement and suffering as well as great pride. "How long were you in the service?" is a deeply respectful question, laden with admiration in the South. The person who decries militarism, and I am one of them, must understand that Southern notions of valor have a logic that sits outside of what we call "politics." It's all politics, of course. But you will talk past many a Southerner if you claim to be a pacifist as a political value because it will most likely sound like cowardice or selfishness rather than principle.

On June 12, 2016, a young man with militaristic aspirations used his gun to do grave violence. He had previously tried to become a Florida corrections officer, but was terminated from the training program. He twice applied to the police academy. Eventually he became a guard for G4s security Solutions in Jupiter, Florida. The young man had appeared, briefly, in a film about the BP oil spill that was an effort, by the company, to minimize its impact. He was working security in the footage.

It was Latin Night at the Pulse nightclub. And there the would-be soldier sprayed bullets at the largely Puerto Rican Orlando crowd. Fifty died at his hands, and he did, too, from a bomb. It was easy for public opinion to attribute the massacre to his Afghan heritage and Islamism. It was harder to manage what seemed closer to the truth, that Omar Mateen was tortured by his own judgment against his attraction to men. But he didn't just turn that misery onto himself. Maybe all of the not-so-subtle messages about the violent hero, the king of the wild frontier, worked their way up into his insides, and he figured if he couldn't create himself as he'd imagined, he could destroy the sources of his torture: beautiful queer men. There isn't any safe place when the instruments of war are always within reach. They promise a fantasyland of power and action films, and underneath there is always wasted love.

George Zimmerman was originally from Manassas, Virginia, home of two major Civil War battles won by the Confederates. He called the gun he used to kill Trayvon Martin an "American firearm icon." Certainly, many treated Zimmerman himself as such: iconic. A half-Peruvian man who reportedly voted for President Obama and later called the forty-fourth president a baboon, he likely has no warm feelings for Omar Mateen (he doesn't care for Muslims) and hasn't prayed for his soul. But he had a similar military desire. Zimmerman was once a Junior ROTC officer and wanted to be in the Marines, but somehow didn't make it. Then he tried a criminal justice program and was one credit shy of completing an associate's degree when he killed a Black child named Trayvon Martin. In the aftermath of his acquittal, right-wing fans made him flush with money, donating to him from across the country through a crowdfunding site.

What hubris followed being found not guilty? Everything be-

came fantastical then. I assume Zimmerman fancies himself a figure in another historic tale of the violent hero. He's everywhere. At
Disney World, Frontierland eases the guns into the background,
and only leaves the tropes of the Wild West: mesquite trees and Je-
rusalem thorns. The characters are goofy, absurd, foolish. We laugh
at them. But it's really the same thing. And even though *Song of
the South*, Disney's lost-cause-of-the-Confederacy film that is of-
fensively racist in the extreme in its depiction of Uncle Remus, has
been pulled from screens, last time I was there, when my children
were small, you could still buy *Song of the South* memorabilia. I
wonder, remembering that at some point I did see *Song of the South*
in a childhood rife with offensive imagery at every turn (it was the
'70s after all), about the errors of interpretation. We laugh inappro-
priately at all kinds of tragic moments. Maybe I shouldn't giggle at
Frontierland or about how off the wall it is that Disney World still
sells *Song of the South* souvenirs. It is laughing to keep from cry-
ing, sometimes. Other times, it is laughing at the woeful absurdity.
Other times still, it is at the strangeness of humanity. Was this the
misunderstanding? Perhaps I have a poor ear for laughter. Laughter
need not be joyful. Hilarity is also an assessment. I wonder if we
will ever tell the truth about the taste for cruel humor. Laughter
does the same thing beauty does: allows for us to believe we can
digest the indigestible. It's all fun and games until somebody ends
up dead.

Yet the people still come. Florida has become home to repeated waves of immigrants and migrants from farther south and
the North. Retirees, soldiers, migrant laborers, exiles, refugees, and
more. There is also a significant Indigenous population. Zimmerman killed Trayvon Martin in Seminole County, which was cut out
of the northern part of Orange County in 1913 and named for the
Seminole, an Indigenous nation composed of the descendants of
Muscogee Creeks who originally lived in the areas now known as
Georgia and Alabama. Their name means "runaway" because they

refused to submit to the settler colonial powers. (A quiet refrain, "like Trayvon," rings in my ears.) A significant number of Seminoles live in Oklahoma now, as a consequence of the Indian Removal Act. But several hundred stayed in Florida and their number grew over the generations. They constituted themselves a Maroon colony that, in fighting to maintain their land, would earn the distinction of becoming the longest-standing military defense against the United States waged by an African or Indian group.

Black Seminoles were racially distinguished from other Seminoles, at first. They fled slavery and became Seminole citizens. Though they lived separately, the two groups provided each other with mutual aid. In the First Seminole War, Andrew Jackson began by attacking the "Negro Fort" of the Black Seminole, attempting to recapture those who had been enslaved. Jackson's destruction of Seminole settlements and capture of Spanish towns enraged Great Britain and Spain, but eventually Florida was won by the United States in 1821. Thereafter, by treaty, the Seminole were pushed into the peninsula. Still, they survived, and some thrived.

Lieutenant George McCall visited a Black Seminole community in 1826 and said:

> We found these negroes in possession of large fields of the finest land, producing large crops of corn, beans, melons, pumpkins, and other esculent vegetables . . . I saw, while riding along the borders of the ponds, fine rice growing; and in the village large corn-cribs were filled, while the houses were larger and more comfortable than those of the Native Americans themselves.

The Seminole would join forces for the Second Seminole War, only to be separated again. The second war was precipitated by the Indian Removal Act. Black and Indigenous Seminoles fought back. Their forces included fugitives from slavery who were enlisted to join the tribe. The Seminole destroyed twenty-one White-owned sugar plantations, beginning on Christmas in 1835. And they remained in Florida. However, the dynamic between Indigenous and Black Seminoles changed when the Seminole were eventually pushed into Creek territory. The Creek allowed slavery. The Black Seminole weren't safe from capture into slavery, and found their community subject to raids. Some of them escaped to Coahuila, Mexico, across the border from Texas, where slavery had been abolished. There they were known as Mascogos. Some escaped to the Bahamas, where slavery had been abolished. Others made their way into Florida's wetlands.

In those wetlands, orchids grow wild, pink and white on tree limbs, feeding off of the landscape without being parasitic. They are more beautiful that way, lighting upon the sight line, in an environment that feels like it is weighting your limbs as you make your way through. There are alligators and water buffalo, and all manner of birds. Orchids are native to Florida, but you'd hardly know, as they've been rendered so exotic in our popular culture as to be wholly unfamiliar to us. The same often happens with Indigenous people, who are exoticized through the American refusal to witness them. But the struggles of indigenousness against colonialism that the Seminole sustained are not simply some long-past history. In the 1920s and '30s, they were displaced again by the conversion of wetlands to farmland. And then, in the '40s and '50s and '60s, there were cattle concerns and reservations, and treaties and overlapping claims and tribal reorganizations and the threat of losing legal recognition, and then, finally, though inadequately, in 1976, a monetary settlement was reached that granted the Seminole some security and stability.

Now the Seminole Tribe stands out as a leader in Indian gaming. They opened the first high-stakes bingo parlor in 1979 and participated in the major legal cases that ultimately recognized Indian nations' rights to operate casinos. In 2007, the Seminole purchased the Hard Rock Cafe brand, an international theme restaurant featuring rock music paraphernalia, and relocated the business to Florida, first to Orlando and then to Davie, just north of Miami.

The Seminole conduct annual historic reenactments of the Seminole Wars. They depict vulnerable and heroic times. At the Big Cypress Reservation, an historic shoot-out is acted out. Participants wear traditional attire and wield old-fashioned weapons as well as perform Seminole fighting methods. Visitors can buy crafts, eat Seminole food, and experience dancing, archery, alligator wrestling, and snake shows.

Although Hurston mocked Black people claiming Indian princesses in their family trees, I imagine she would have appreciated the way Black Seminoles participate in historic reenactments, too, in particular the Battle of the Loxahatchee. It was the largest battle of the Second Seminole War. The Seminole were outnumbered, 1500 to their 300. To save their own lives, they retreated into the swamp. But they survived.

In some ways the annual rehearsal of the Seminole Wars is analogous to the Confederate reenactments. In both, the population honors their foreparents who fought valiantly and lost but also won. Although the Seminole are an unconquered people, their land was stolen again and again. Their current economic victory hinges upon the sovereignty of Indian nations, and how they have been one of the few to find a lucrative way to sustain themselves. While the South lost the Civil War technically, White Southerners did not in fact lose the war substantively. After all, Jim Crow, convict labor, and lynching happened with near total impunity, and African Americans experienced decades of pernicious neglect from the federal courts and government. Exploitation ran amok. Inequality persists. And the nation turning a refusing eye, allowing the Southerners to work out their own business over the lives of Black people on the land of the Indigenous all across the region, gave the South their victory lap.

* * *

MIAMI IS THE MOST CARIBBEAN of American cities. But it is not just peopled with people from the Hispanophone Caribbean. It is a palimpsest of historic inequalities and a threshing of cultures where the heat radiates in waves off the concrete. Spanish explorers arrived in what is present-day Miami in 1513. But they struggled with forming a permanent colony until 1800, just a few years before the Louisiana Purchase. It was still nearly a hundred years before Miami was formally incorporated. And it's been changing ever since.

Black laborers built the infrastructure for settlement of the city, but were cast into the margins due to Jim Crow. Overtown was the first colored section of the city. It was peopled by folks who built the railroad and worked in the hotels. The early tourist industry was serviced by Black Southerners and Bahamians. Miami's proximity to Cuba made it an attractive tourist destination for elite European-descended Cubans who also sent their children to be educated in the United States. And over the course of the twentieth century, Overtown's demographics expanded to include the descendants of freedpeople from Trinidad, Jamaica, Barbados, and Haiti. In the late nineteenth century, Jim Crow had been established throughout the US South, and the US had gained a great deal of military control in the Caribbean as a result of the Spanish-American War, as well as economic control because tourist economies were heavily dependent upon White American visitors. As is often the case in imperial relations, this opened a flow of people and culture between nations, and a linked fate between different types of Black people.

There was also a community of Black Miamians in Liberty City, and one in Coconut Grove, though there, in the early twentieth century, Bahamian culture predominated. In the late 1920s, Zora Neale Hurston visited Miami and was delighted to witness a Bahamian dance. This prompted her to travel to the Bahamas, where she learned the dance, filmed dancers, and acquired a Bahamian gimbay drum. She also survived a hurricane during her visit, which had her contemplating her life's purpose. She continued her research, so it seemed that was her calling. Among Hurston's legacies is her extensive anthropological travel and narration of connections between the Caribbean and US South. In a sense she collected the common threads through culture, as historians had done through records of transport, sale, and shifting settler colonies. What is revealed repeatedly is that, even with variations when it came to the particulars, the color line persisted through the Deep South and Caribbean. It can even be called a single region if one tends to history more than borders. The impact of the Cuban Revolution on Miami tells this story.

After the Cuban Revolution, which promised racial equality and socialism, elite and White Cubans descended upon Miami. They settled in "Little Havana" and Hialeah. In 1963, Miami established the first modern bilingual school program in the United States. Though it raised the ire of some Anglos, the Jim Crow stratification of the city allowed Cubans to sit on top even with a separate program. By the 1980s, as the racial and phenotypic range of Cubans arriving from the island broadened, the national identity distinction softened in favor of a racial one. Black Cubans often found themselves in Miami's historic Black communities. And though ethnic distinctions were always noticed, increasingly race mattered most.

The middle-class African American enclave of Liberty City began to change earlier, in the 1960s, when I-95 was built right through Overtown, displacing residents. And as a result of changes wrought by the civil rights movement, middle-class Black people started to move into neighborhoods previously covered by racially restrictive covenants that had denied them access. The concentrated Black communities became poorer and more vulnerable. This suffering was made evident during the 1968 Republican National Convention and the ensuing conflict. In contrast to the 1968 Democratic National Convention, which has been the subject of numerous documentaries and films, and which is ensconced in national history, the upheaval during that year's RNC is all but completely disregarded.

A riot broke out in Liberty City on August 7. It started out as a civil rights rally that was supposed to focus on economic inequality, police misconduct, employment discrimination, and, in particular, preferential treatment for Cuban immigrants. Black Miamians had been all but excluded from even working at the convention, and they were alerted that the bridges to Miami Beach would be closed to prevent them access while the convention-goers were there. As people waited for the program to begin, a White reporter covering the rally was asked to leave. He wouldn't. Five police cars showed up in response to the crowd's effort to eject him. A White driver then drove through the neighborhood bearing signs on his car celebrating the Alabama segregationist presidential candidate George Wallace. The crowd, incensed, chased the driver and set his car on fire. This was four short months after Martin Luther King's assassination, after a summer of "burn, baby, burn" across the nation. Black communities everywhere were frustrated and grieving; the city was hot. Just a few miles but an entire world away, the Republican convention proceeded without them. And the neighborhood simply exploded. After two days, three people were dead, twenty-nine injured, and two hundred had been arrested. In the streets, the remains from looted grocery stores left a stink in the air. Fish, chicken, and beef smeared city blocks, covered in flies.

The uprising twelve years later was even more dramatic. In 1979, police officers chased thirty-three-year-old insurance salesman Arthur McDuffie on his motorcycle, claiming he'd made a vulgar gesture at them. When McDuffie toppled off the bike, police removed his helmet, beat him to death, and then replaced the helmet. My father used to have a copy of a poem about this event on his wall, titled "Who Killed McDuffie: A Definitive Question," written by Hakim Al Jamil, a prisoner at Leavenworth correctional facility in Kentucky. It begins:

> his brain was bashed
> cranium crashed
> skull fractured/broken
> all the way around
> but they said those who beat him didnt kill him
> so who killed mcduffie?

Al Jamil goes on to describe the litany of corporate and political entities that claim not to have killed McDuffie. Implicitly he indicts them all for fueling the kind of economic and social injustice that allowed such violence to flourish.

In the case of Arthur McDuffie's death, the officers who shattered his skull were charged with the crime. But a jury quickly returned a not guilty verdict and the city exploded on May 17 of 1980. This time 18 people died, 350 were injured, and 600 were arrested. The pattern continued.

In December of 1982, the Cuban-born Luis Alvarez, a Miami police officer, shot and killed Neville Johnson Jr., a young Black Caribbean American man, in an Overtown arcade as Johnson was playing a video game. The following conflagration left eighteen dead and shut down more than two hundred businesses. There was no conviction.

In 1989, on Martin Luther King Jr.'s birthday in Overtown, the Colombian-born police officer William Lozano crashed his car into a biker, Clement Lloyd, who was fleeing him. Another young Black man riding with Lloyd, Allan Blanchard, also died from the ensuing crash. Blanchard had just arrived in Miami from the Virgin

Islands. Three days of uprising, eight shot, one killed, 230 people arrested. At Lozano's trial, Colombian flags were waved by attendees in support of Lozano. Three stripes rather than stars and bars. And although he was convicted and sentenced to seven years, his sentence was overturned in 1991 by the Court of Appeals, on the argument that there ought to have been a change of venue.

Though the media covered these events as a sign of the local conflict between Latino and Black communities, something more complex was at work. Racial stratification of the sort that had existed throughout the South and the Caribbean was in operation. Racial stratification was the logic of slave societies long after slavery had ended, whether or not it fit the picture of White and Black Southerners. The concentration of political and economic power among high-status, politically conservative, and white-skinned Cuban Americans and others of Latin American origin was a factor in what transpired. These were the days of an intense national backlash against the civil rights movement. But it was also in the midst of Cold War politics. The US gave preference for Cubans who disdained Castro, a disdain that had to do not only with lost land and autonomy on the island, but with the loss of the plantation-based structure of Cuban society. In contrast, Black immigrants, from places over which the US exerted a lot of economic control, were treated with disdain.

Among the concerns of African American activists in the 1980s and 1990s was the dramatic difference in the way the United States government treated refugees coming from Cuba and Haiti. Jesse Jackson commented that the granting of citizenship to Cubans while requiring repatriation for most Haitians "reflect[ed] racism in the U.S. immigration policy that allows for preferential treatment for Cuban refugees but not for those with darker skin colors from Haiti and elsewhere." New York congressman Charles Rangel argued, "Immigration law and immigration policy [reflect] the confusions and dishonesty and racial attitudes and class attitudes we have in this country in other domestic areas, and I have found the same kind of irrational class-based, race-based kind of thinking existing in our immigration policies." In fact, though Black support for the Clinton administration is frequently touted, a number of prominent African Americans were outspoken both about how Bill Clinton advocated for welfare reform with an approach that deepened extreme poverty, and played into a culture of poverty myths about Black people, and at the same time embraced policies and practices that destabilized and dispossessed Haiti. Black politics in Miami were both local and hemispheric.

The most painful part is this: we mix and move and cross fates and link them. We are cast down and pushed aside in so many different ways, and yet so often we cling tightly to even the most fragile benefits of being located above the darkest of whichever plantation economy into which we were born. We don't have to do that. There are so many more of us who aren't of the planter class than those who are, of every race. And even those who are, you know you're wounded, too.

Miami is Southern because the South extends beyond the borders of the United States. It is the Global South and the American South as one. It took me some time to recognize this. It's like how I was with the floral plastic bottles of Florida Water that I first saw in New York City bodegas. Florida Water is an eau de cologne that is used throughout the Americas for various reasons. A blend of essential oils, citrus essence, and water, in various combinations, it scents freshly ironed clothes, is used for dressing candles, is part of ritual spiritual baths, and is good for cleaning. It is a precious and mundane artifact sitting in homes throughout the Caribbean, the US South, and in any location where migrants from those regions have aggregated. The most popular version is the one that has been sold by the New York–based company Murray & Lanman since 1808, but there are many other versions that can be found in old pharmaceutical formularies. Reportedly, its name is a reference to the Fountain of Youth that the Spanish sought. I initially assumed it was a part of the culture of the Spanish-speaking Caribbean. And it is. But not exclusively so. I misrecognized it as unfamiliar because it is part of a tradition I didn't know but to which I belonged. I, along with my friends from all over the diaspora, have it at home now. And there it also is in a 1931 ethnography of New Orleans hoodoo by Zora Neale Hurston, serving as a curative: ". . . in her bath she shall put of the waters of Verbena and the waters of perpetual youth called Florida Water, and a handful of the salt of the earth that she will be welcome in company of her kind." Florida is a world of its own. It is also our company in kind.

IMMOBILE WOMEN

Mobile

THERE IS A HIGHWAY THAT takes you out straight from Jacksonville to New Orleans, Houston, and eventually all the way to the Pacific Ocean in Santa Monica, where it is known as Rosa Parks freeway. I could make a joke here about all roads leading to Alabama. Anyway, before you hit New Orleans, you will pass through Mobile. Mildred Cram, in *Old Seaport Towns of the South*, wrote of this passage:

> Alabama was not Alabama until after the Louisiana Purchase, but it is as different from Florida on the one hand and Louisiana on the other as black is from white. I have never understood why the crossing of a surveyed line should take one from the racial and geographic characteristics of one state into those of another, why Connecticut is so unlike Rhode Island, why Vermont is so entirely different from New Hampshire and so on, ad infinitum. Florida is still Spanish and Louisiana is French, while Alabama, set exactly between the two and only separated from them by an imaginary line and a different colour on the map, is wholly

American. Alabama still belongs to a social past that was characteristically American in spite of, or perhaps because of its cosmopolitanism.

Cram was right. And yet it was people in Mobile who brought flambeaux, masquerades, and parades to New Orleans. Tourism has a strange way of codifying how we see culture and even how we live it. Like if you start from Jackson traveling along the Pearl River, which is 444 miles long, you would also end up at the Gulf of Mexico. Pearl is beautiful in the clearest way; on some stretches the water is blue-blue, and on either side the trees are bright and the sun sparkles, and it is so neat that even the wildness of the landscape looks like an amateur painting. At the tail end, the landscape turns from pastoral to tropical. But like Alabama, Mississippi is also often cut out of the Gulf Coast.

Along I-10 there are generalities. Rest stops and Waffle Houses for a long while. And along the Gulf Coast you can find one part of the country where mobile homes aggregate. Nobody is surprised about those being in Alabama or Mississippi.

The idea of building a home on a chassis is old. It goes back to the Conestoga wagon vintage *1717*. And in North Carolina, post-Reconstruction, horse-drawn homes were set up on the Outer Banks. But they became a different thing altogether after the automobile. There are a lot of reasons mobile homes have been popular in the US. For transient laborers, they allowed people to follow work. For working-class White people, they've given the allure of a homestead on a little bit of money, and mobile home parks sustained segregation long past 1968. To this day, many are all White, though they have increased popularity among African Americans and Latinos. For undocumented people, they provide an affordable place to live where they're mostly able to avoid the surveillance of immigration authorities. But the promise of freedom of movement and the appeal of the homestead have become a bit of a distorted seduction. Yes, owners own their mobile homes, but they rent the land on which they sit and the utilities they draw from while sitting there. That rent tends to be low, and mobile homes are the largest segment of nonsubsidized affordable housing. But when the landowners have an incentive to sell, which they increasingly do in temperate climes where condos and luxury homes can be put instead, they can easily dispose of the trailer residents by jacking up the rent.

And that's how we know the name is all wrong. The homes aren't mobile. Within a few years after purchase, many, if not most, are immovable, or essentially so because they fall apart when set on wheels to go. And so with the rent too high and the home stuck, the residents are forced to walk away from their investments and start all over.

This is an everyday thing. A less frequent but devastating occurrence is the ravage of storms. There are stories of mobile homes, so recalcitrant to being moved on wheels, getting swept up and turned over during hurricanes and tornados. They twist like paper planes in the air before crashing to the ground broken. Of course this is bound to happen more since climate change is being pursued full speed ahead by polluting American companies. I could tell an updated version of a "toast" about them, a rhyming ballad like the story of Shine and the *Titanic*, in which the fictional balladeer waxed poetic about Black folks having been excluded from the ship that sank. But the truth is, even as mobile home disaster is more likely to be a White folks' pain, Black people are charged more on average for mobile homes and suffer more from predatory lending when they own them. It's the changing same of racial inequality. And more significantly, the bad weather hits every single kind of vulnerable person. When the storms come, immobile mobile homes are uprooted, and in prisons the cells fill up with water as the cages remain locked. There is no evading the water. Bitter irony strikes those who longed for segregation. Uprooted trapped people and rooted trapping trees are a horror story.

When you're riding through Mobile along the Gulf Coast, the live oaks don't look so civilized. They are grabbing trees. They reach across the places they were planted to clutch at each other. It looks more like snatching than an embrace because of those vast tangling arms. And their skirts—because what else would you call a root that flies up so much that it cracks open the sidewalk?—flounce wide. Magnolias are the softer version of the same thing. They fly open, indiscreetly, revealing the easing turn from pink to brown flesh on the inside, or the other way around, lying on the dirt or pavement, plump, smashed, and fragrant. Maybe it is easy for some folks to ignore them, something you can just step on the ground and smear. But the oaks insist that you understand the power of nature.

Howell Raines told me, in an entertaining evening of Alabama anecdotes, about the town where Black and White cousins bear the same name and called each other family openly, about my neighborhood before it desegregated, and the most dramatic of all: that his son Ben, an environmental reporter, was the man who'd found the sunken slave ship the *Clotilda*, in Mobile.

The *Clotilda* arrived in Mobile Bay in July of 1860, fifty-two years after the slave trade was declared illegal. Slave traders broke the law by importing captured Black people, either from Africa or the Caribbean, and secretly depositing the cargo at hidden locations along the Gulf Coast. It was a lucrative game of cat and mouse. With the *Clotilda*, a man named Timothy Meaher made a bet that he could bring a ship full of Africans to Mobile without being caught. And that's how the *Clotilda* got here from Benin. Its captain burned the ship upon arrival to destroy evidence of the crime. The *Clotilda* sank underwater.

There had been false starts in the search to find the *Clotilda*. Other shipwrecks were unearthed. One a few years earlier had been surfaced by a bomb cyclone, but it was of the wrong size and composition, only pine, whereas the *Clotilda* was also composed of oak.

Gulf Coast family trees are more European than those of Black folk in the Black Belt, both literally and figuratively, having been places once claimed by France and Spain, cultures more amenable to racial admixture than the British. They are in other ways also more immediately African, being close to where the ships landed. New-world Africans became so there. As Robert Hayden, the epic poet of Black life, once said, they had voyaged through death to life on these shores.

In a photo taken by Ben Raines, the ship's remains look like a work of abstract art. Slashed pieces of wood are like brittle bird bones crisscrossed into star shapes on either side of a long ladder reaching to the water. Everything is stuck in the mud, crowded by pocking ulcers. This earth is the muddiest of mud colors. Not rich, not layered. Just dank, dark, and ashen. The *Clotilda*'s group of Africans lived on the margins of Mobile life during the first half of the 1860s. After the war ended, however, and they found they could not get back across the ocean to Benin, the Africans founded their own colony, Africatown, in a clearing in the middle of a pine forest just north of Mobile. Cudjo Lewis was one of the survivors of the *Clotilda*. Hurston took great pains to interview Lewis, failing initially to endear herself when she announced that she was an anthropologist who had come to research him. Later, she says, she played bootlegger in order to get on his good side. In her memoir, *Dust Tracks on a Road*, Zora briefly described her time with the old man in 1927. She wrote:

> I found him a cheerful, poetical old gentleman in his late nineties, who could tell a good story. His interpretation of the story of Jonah was marvelous. He was a good Christian and so he pretended to have forgotten all of his African religion. He turned me off with the statement that his Nigerian

religion was the same as Christianity. "We know it a God, you unner'stand, but we don't know He got a Son."

Hurston, a student of African retentions, was disappointed in Cudjo's adoption of Christianity. She was also heartbroken to learn he was sold to White people by other Africans. The title of her book on Cudjo's life, which was finally published in the United States in 2018, is *Barracoon*, named after the makeshift prisons on the coast of West Africa. The betrayal of Cudjo's fellow Africans brought Zora some philosophical perspective:

> Lack of power and opportunity passes off too often for virtue. If I were King, let us say, over the Western Hemisphere tomorrow, instead of who I am, what would I consider right and just? Would I put the cloak of Justice on my ambition and send her out a-whoring after conquests? It is something to ponder over with fear.

Although Hurston was much more interested in the African-ness of Black Southerners than someone like Albert Murray ever was, she *did* see a significant difference between the Africatown Africans and African Americans. The Africans never lost their homesickness. Hurston wrote of Cudjo, "After seventy-five years, he still had that tragic sense of loss. That yearning for blood and cultural ties. That sense of mutilation. It gave me something to feel about." Implicitly she showed that Africans in Alabama, who built their own world, Africatown, if not literally like the rest of us, were exactly who we were. I recall a college friend, an African American man, saying to me once that he kept being mistaken for Fulani on an exchange trip to West Africa. But, he noted, that was simply an accident, a body's false cognate. The combination of features happened to, in the phenotypic wheel of fortune, land on Fulani, but of course he was African in some much more general genealogical way. I thought about this when looking at the 23andMe results that named me 34 percent Nigerian, even though my ancestors were taken from West Africa long before Nigeria was even a concept for identification, much less declared a nation by Europeans.

Africatown is an apt name for a place in the South. "African" has a generality, a weaving of cultures that made Black people. "African" in a Creole sense—a blend of African peoples produced this Blackness even before one includes all the other cultural and genealogical parts of our family tree. Paul Theroux, in his book *Deep South*, mentions several times that Southern towns look like African villages. It reads somewhat disparagingly to me, but I prefer to note the simple truth rather than respond to a judgment-laden metaphor. Plenty of communities, houses, and bodies throughout the South are based upon a West African design.

You see shotgun houses everywhere in the Deep South, but they come from New Orleans via Haiti. They are economical. And the debates over the etymology of the name are revelatory. Some think it comes from a West Africa word: "shogun." Others think it comes from the fact that if you shoot through the house, it comes out the back in a clean shot. The rooms sit one after another. Shotguns flourished as a matter of practicality. They are efficient, suited to the weather and the constraints of space and money. Yes, these are African elements to the South. Some parts of the past are retained and remain with us, cherished. Other parts are buried, hidden, or simply forgotten. At moments of crisis, it always makes sense to return to the past to try to figure out if the arrangements of what is remembered and what is forgotten, or what is retained and what has been thrown away, are part of the problem. And, better yet, if a rearrangement offers a solution.

Wind and water threaten the shotgun houses just like the immobile mobile homes. They are efficient, but not always sturdy against increased environmental disaster. And a worsening circumstance doesn't mean that the fear is altogether new. In Southeastern folklore, people used to say that tie-snakes coming out of the water had immense strength and powerful poison. They caught humans and dragged them under with a spiritual power that could harness the water. Imagine barely escaping the slave trader and getting pulled down into the depth. Imagine, as the ancestors had, that you could see more than one life flash while drowning. That you could see what was before and what was above and also below.

Deep down in the water—and now I am speaking literally, but neither you nor I really know because we haven't been there—is an ancient cypress forest. When the shoreline was farther out, and the landmasses were higher, the glaciers held still, and the trees grew tall. Right at the edge of Alabama, deep in the Gulf, they remain and are far out of view. Sixty thousand years old, and that is a science-informed guess, the trees are still rooted. Over millennia, the waters rose around them and the mud packed them in. It is as if their connection to the earth's core held them safe from all the disasters of humans. And if you cut the bark, sap oozes out into the muddy water. There's always life, even on the underside. I wonder if any of the Africatown Africans, having converted to Christianity, thought these were the depths of hell.

I was tricked by a picture of home. It is of a girl and her aunt standing before a segregated movie theater with a neon red sign reading "Colored Entrance." A blue arrow pointed down some steps. It was taken by Gordon Parks in 1956 when he was in Alabama on assignment for *Life* magazine. The woman is dark and elegant, dressed in Tiffany blue with a slight patrician slouch and a falling strap of her pristine white slip. The girl is bright deep brown and attired in the classic Black Southern way: patent leather shoes, lace socks and bows. So many times I was dressed like that, dressed as self-regard, as civility, as grace. Because our bodies were prescribed for toil, used as repositories for rage, like rags for waste, we learned elegance as a way of loving.

When I first saw the photograph, I was sure it was taken not just in Alabama but in Birmingham, because it was so Southern *and* urbane. I soon took myself to be writing an essay about it and tried to verify the location. I called the Gordon Parks Foundation. I called art historians. No one could tell me for sure where it was. Although it was titled *Department Store*, I knew it was in front of a movie theater. Those were the only institutions that had neon Jim Crow signs. I pored over city maps and newspapers records to try to identify where the movie theaters were. When I told my mother what I was doing, she said with a sniff, "It's not Birmingham. We didn't have to go to segregated theaters. We had our own." I thought she was wrong, perhaps forgetting the full scope of Jim Crow in her youth. I posted on Facebook about my research trials. Then my aunt Cathy inboxed me, "The little girl in the picture is my soror. That's in Mobile."

Mobile smells differently from Birmingham, milder. But their voices are familiar. They drawl like us, to make Mildred Cram's point. They don't fill their mouths with a sphere of air like New Orleans folks, though it is nearer in geography. And there is the self-same self-conscious elegance, a conservativeness, like in north and central Alabama.

The South is so varying that it can seem endless. And yet you will still know "Southern" means something over and against other regions. I continue to marvel at how clearly Gordon Parks, a son of the Midwest, saw this. Since I first began researching it, images from Gordon Parks's photographic series *Segregation Story* have been printed and made available for purchase through art galleries in major cities. There is also a beautiful coffee table book. The photographs resonate because they show what we know of Jim Crow, vividly, but haven't often seen. When Parks arrived in Alabama in 1956, White folks in Birmingham were not eager to receive him. He was tailed around the city. As it turns out, the ominous presence was a member of *Life* magazine's local bureau who was moonlighting on behalf of the Klan. Having ways of navigating White supremacy that reached back into the antebellum period, the local Black political networks were able to warn Parks to get out of town just before the Klan planned to seriously injure him. Or worse.

Parks made his way farther south in Alabama with his assistant Sam Yette, who would later become well-known as a journalist who famously described White supremacist thinking as a form of genocide. Yette is the one who fielded a physical attack from a White man who jumped on the train to steal Parks's negatives. These details provide an important backstory. Parks wasn't just a witness. He lived it. In another one of the famous images from the series, small brown children stand with their fingers laced through the fence keeping them out of Funland. You have to imagine the smells of a carnival, the treats, and the sound of laughter. You have to see how carefully each child's hair has been groomed. You have to notice the delicacy of the stitches on each dress. And you have to know that the powers that be were ashamed for that ugliness to be exposed—denying itty-bitty children the joy of an amusement park—so they tried to slap the film out of Black hands.

The photographs taken in Black homes, bedrooms or porches, feature people who are a bit less carefully adorned but still well tended. A few hairs are out of place on the girls and women. The boys' overalls are frayed. But outside, whether it is leaning over the colored water fountain or walking along a city street, the circle skirts are pressed to perfection.

My favorite of the Parks photographs was taken in Shady Grove, Pike County, which was once upon a time a part of Florida. The wire grass in that part of the country stands up from the ground like a spreading golden afro. Longleaf pines, trees that look sparse even when they're old, once echoed with the clack-clack of woodpeckers, but that was before so much of the earth has been destroyed. We have to imagine.

There are two women at the center in blues. There are also two other women, and a man's sports coat sleeve, to the side and rear. They are all in front of church. It could have been a school, but the folks gathered off to the right, looking like Sunday, suggest otherwise. Each of the two central figures, who could be girls or young women, the picture doesn't tell, bows her head. They are both dark brown. They could be twins, but probably are not. On the right, her dress is a slightly lighter sky blue. Her face is framed with a lace sweetheart neckline and pearls. Whoever made this dress knew the particulars of pleating and darts, pulling into her waist precisely but without a bit of tightness. The dress is so strikingly perfect on her that the shoes, black with a thick heel, are fairly inconsequential. Her companion is, we might guess, either younger or from a more conservative family. Or simply had different taste. Her dress fits more loosely. It comes up high on her neck, with a long childlike bow at the throat in addition to vertical stripes that deaccentuate her body. The blue is closer to the summer sky than spring, but her shoes are white. She holds only her hands. It might have been her mother who pinned her curls back against her head.

I am always reminded of Toni Morrison's account of "Mobile women":

> These sugar brown Mobile girls move through the streets without a stir. They are as sweet and plain as buttercake. Slim ankles; long, narrow feet. They wash themselves with orange colored Lifebuoy soap, dust themselves with Cashmere bouquet talc, clean their teeth with salt on a piece of rag, soften their skin with Jergens lotion . . . They do not drink, smoke or swear, and they still call sex "nookey." They sing second Soprano in the choir, and although their voices are clear and steady, they are never picked to solo. They are in the second row, white blouses starched, blue skirts almost purple from ironing.

I resent this passage of Morrison's. It is a taunt that always seems to me unfeeling. And yet it is true, at least in part. I know it. I know how under the blue skirts and white blouses there are girdles. Before the waist trainers that are popular today, we wore panty girdles. They kept your flesh from jiggling and smoothed the line under your clothing. Like many forms of attire that were taken up for the sake of a lady's protection, they didn't protect, although they did signal. To the ones who couldn't see what they held inside, they were supposed to sign that you were lovely, ladylike. Inside they signaled that it was imperative, at least in public, to hold in the buoyancy of flesh and the fact of the body's fluids, its organic clefts and ripples. That secretive place, under the garment, held in sweat and desire, but also wounds and scars. It is a subtle thing, but the waist trainer of today, a modernized corset also like the girdle, is not quite the same matter. They are worn to tantalize, though still with artifice. They beg for the onlooker to wonder what is under the clothes. They create a burlesque of constraint, an illusion of fleshiness and abundance encased in doll-like form. They are enticement. The girdle is restraint.

These formulas are, for me, a source of grief. Not enough for me to refuse them, but because I know that whether based in drawing desire or thwarting it, there lives a terror about one's bumpy messiness hanging out. "Showing all your stuff," as we would call it, is dangerous. Without being tightly bound in, without restraint or constraint, it feels like every confusing humiliation, every wound to the body or because of the body in which you happen to be born, might just spill slick all over the ground around you. It might mortify you so much that you just can't bear to live with it a second more.

This is why Morrison's words on Mobile women make this hit dog holler. Underneath the nervous maintenance of a Black Southern good girl is an ocean of feeling. Always was. You have to listen and look for it. From a distance these two in this photo are like twin pieces of evidence. But what about the less explicit eruptions of history? Like the antebellum plantation owner who was recorded by a fabric merchant as saying that linsey cloth would only be acceptable to the slaves if it were blue. These slaves, with very little choice in life, chose the color of grace, of Mary, the hue of iron serenity for adornment in an ever-threatening life. How exactly ought we to read this legacy? Is it resistance, resignation, defiance, or just delight?

The church in this photo stands on stilts, a gamble against floodwaters. Faith, here, might claim that God provides, but that doesn't mean destruction isn't coming. It means God gave you some knowledge to hold on to, and you better use it. Designing a church knowing what will surely happen if you leave it touching the earth means you are not just concerned with heavenly matters. Trusting the lord is not the same as trusting his land.

The steeple is sharp. It looks like it would prick you. If, as a child, you were tasked with putting the pins in a piece of fabric to fasten the path the sewing machine would trace, the sensation comes to mind, as does the whirr of a Singer late into the night. When the foot eased up, the sound would stop. A scissor snip, a shifting gear, an untangle of the thread if the bobbin went awry. All of these are distinct sounds of the machine. Your ear learns the difference only by habit, and the quiet that surrounds them. Looking at these photographs, taken over a decade before my birth, I cannot tell you much about their particulars. But I can read them, trace their genealogies, tell you at least a little something about their provenance. I can tell you the sensorium of the world that made them.

Today, there are not a whole lot of seamstresses around in the South. Those who specialize in formal wear are the most frequently found. Prom season brings them out with coordinated cummerbunds and gowns, rhinestones, gelled updos and beauty queen smiles. The farther south you go, into the Caribbean, you find even more who are still making clothes with cotton. It breathes in the heat. Though we are clothed differently now than in the past, some things remain the same, like strictly matched outfits and perfectly laid hairdos. Shoelaces must be washed and bleached. Elders must be yes-ma'am'd with the sliding tongue. No matter the brand, the deodorant is so strong it might burn your skin. And the vulgarity of the blues juke joint on Saturday night has eased into the profanity of hip hop. And the same mouth that shouts at pussy popping and twerking calls on Jesus. A chosen few are always virtuous. More often there's a time and place for every tightening up and every release. Sterling Brown, long gone, is still right. The South, and Mobile women, both live and hold fast. They have to.

MAGNOLIA GRAVES AND EASTER LILIES

New Orleans

"I SAW YOUR MOTHER in the window at the convent, she had on the habit and everything. And she was so beautiful, I begged her to come down." My biological father grinned as he shared the story. She had been a brown-skinned afro-haired Rapunzel all in black except for the white fabric framing of her face. He beckoned.

When he stepped into the other room, my mother said, laughing, "None of that is true."

Theresa Perry spent several young adult years as a novice at the Sisters of the Holy Family convent in New Orleans, Louisiana. The order was founded in 1842 by Henriette Delille to provide a home for Black women with spiritual vocations. Theirs was the second order of Black nuns in the United States. The "Holy Familys" began as free women of color in the antebellum South who educated children, including those who were enslaved, and served the elderly, indigent, and infirm. Despite the decline in vocations, and repeated waves of racism and decay in New Orleans history, the order still stands.

My relationship to them was opaque as a child. They were part of my mother's life before me, obviously. New Orleans had shaped how she cooked; it was also the place where she was educated and she became a political organizer. That final commitment brought her out of the convent before she took her vows. So I suppose I can say I owe my very existence to the Southern freedom movement.

When I was growing up, we went to New Orleans annually. I do not remember which visit it was when she took me to the Bourbon Orleans Hotel. But I remember her finger, slender with heavy knuckles, like mine have become, pointing at the plaque "Former Site of Holy Family Sisters Convent."

The unmentioned historic purpose of the ballroom was that it served as a social center for the system of plaçage. Quadroons, octoroons, women of color of one-fourth African ancestry or so, or less, would meet White gentlemen there. A structured system of partnership often followed. The White gentlemen wouldn't marry the women—they'd usually have White wives—but they'd put the women of color up in houses, provide for their care and that of their children, including the provision of an inheritance. It was an arrangement that was less violent than plantation rape, but wholly predicated on White supremacy and patriarchy, so only somewhat less violent.

For the Holy Family nuns, the ballroom was a symbol of both domination and sin. They bought it in honor of the women who were sold in those rooms, not as slaves but nevertheless as possessions. Black women in US Southern history were once property who produced property. Their reproduction was a source of wealth. Their love for children, desperately nurturing them under a condition of dispossession and duress, had the perverse effect of sustaining slavery. Care kept the property intact. The bodies of Black women were also put to the tasks considered masculine: working in fields of cotton, tobacco, and sugarcane. Plaçage was a step above all that. But it was humiliating and unjust, and the Holy Familys provided an alternative to it, a refuge from the varying labors that Black women did underneath the structures of White supremacy and patriarchy. They controlled their labor and bodies in a property of their own. The nuns occupied the old Orleans Ballroom until 1964, when the convent was relocated to Chef Menteur Highway in New Orleans East.

Taking residence in the old Orleans Ballroom was something of a redemption. But of course, like everywhere else in New Orleans, the residue of the past remains present. One might even say it is active. The Bourbon Orleans Hotel is often said to be the home of ghosts who roam the hallways. Sometimes guests report seeing White men and sometimes golden-hued women.

As the story goes, Henriette Delille herself escaped a life of plaçage. Pale-skinned and straight-haired, she fled a pretty little "pigeon house," as they were called, and its owner. Though plaçage gave her a status that was recognized in varying degrees across the French empire, it was also a ritual form of humiliation. Henriette Delille chose a contemplative life instead, married to the Lord. What refuge could be better?

Because of my mother, I've always felt connected to New Orleans. Because of my biological father having been born to New Orleanians, a self-described prince to her Rapunzel, I've always assumed that I might one day run into a long-lost cousin on its streets. That's why, even though it is not my home, I nevertheless feel like a jealous guardian of its reputation. People alternately call it the most African and most European of American cities. There is a persistent fascination with its complex of cultural influences. Métissage! Between Black and White, ambiguous, tragic and beautiful, that's the fantasy of New Orleans. From a tourism lens, it is a form of exotica. But if we are to tell the truth about that history, we have to tell its tragedies as well as its miracles. That is where its mysticism lies, how the conflict sits up against itself, never fully releasing its tension even in the moments of revelry and bacchanal. New Orleans is the most Southern of American cities, and the evidence of this is right underneath the pleasure. Take an example: If you've been to New Orleans, you've seen the fleur-de-lis. It is a stencil version of a white and fragrant lily with baby skin soft petals. It is a signature feature of French heraldry. It makes the city pretty. And in the early eighteenth century, it had a particular purpose. If a runaway slave stayed away from his or her owner for over a month, their ears would be sliced off, and the fleur-de-lis permanently branded on one shoulder with a hot iron. Another infraction would require the runaway to be hamstrung, thus disabling them from ever running again, and the other shoulder would get the black lily burn as well.

In those years, the Company of the Indies, a French corporation that managed the empire's colonies, controlled the slave trade in the Gulf South. Over six thousand Africans, after enduring the Middle Passage, arrived in Mobile, Biloxi, and New Orleans. After Spain took control of Louisiana, in 1762, another four thousand odd Africans arrived. They were a multilingual and multiethnic people. Wolof, Mandigo, Yoruba, Igbo, Hausa, Ibibio, Bambara, and more. Then, in the early nineteenth century, after the Louisiana Purchase of 1804, two Americans came to dominate the slave trade in New Orleans. With a nation now twice the size, the prospect of land cultivation and wealth building provided a powerful enticement. Technology, specifically the cotton gin, further excited the capitalist imagination. Franklin and Armfield provided the means: more slaves.

Isaac Franklin and John Armfield began their business in Alexandria, Virginia, in what is now a DC suburb. John Armfield lived as well as worked in their headquarters. The main house included offices. A jail in the back held Black people. The captives spent their days outside in the courtyard. Imagine it like a contemporary prison yard.

Franklin and Armfield bought enslaved people for relatively low prices in the Upper South and sold them for high prices in the Deep South. Franklin set up the operation in New Orleans.

The Black people arrived in the city following a long march down through the Eastern United States, or a trip by paddleboat.

Slavery as an institution colonized New Orleans as much as any empire. There were auction blocks in parks and sometimes aboard the docked ships. A Black person suited for labor—skilled or manual, childbearing or sexual exploitation—could be bought at luxury hotels designed in Spanish or French styles. Slave pens were rapidly hammered up and filled with people. If in Maryland it is hard to specifically locate the sites of human trafficking, in New Orleans one can't avoid them. Auctioneers, brokers, and buyers gathered round everywhere. The traffic also flowed into a part of the city called Marigny. In the mid-nineteenth century, as it grew to be occupied by plaçage homes, the name came to have a secondary meaning, an adjective for lemon-vanilla-hued Black folks, pronounced like "Meriney." How they got that color wasn't a romantic story. Later, after economic decline, a section of it became known as "Little Angola," after the prison. Maybe that's why New Orleans is a place to drink oneself to distraction, to lean over the smell of rye, absinthe, and bitters, a grown musty scent to slip oneself into. Grief and pleasure are twins.

When the Haitian Revolution finally and completely ended in 1809, approximately ten thousand people left the island and came to New Orleans. This number included slaveholders, the enslaved, and free people of color (as they were called), those who were often mixed-race and of a higher status than their more African counterparts. Over the next few years some of the Haitian refugees who had gone to Cuba were expelled and made their way to New Orleans as well.

Everywhere there are remnants of the trade in human flesh and the transport of unfree Black people. And they are not just architectural. They are also sociological. Louisiana has the highest rate of incarceration in the world. The prison system is 66 percent Black, twice the state's Black population overall. It is a harrowing inheritance. When you watch the street dancer's masterful foot-work, hear the music in which wailing horns merge into up-tempo rhythms, it is evidence of a discipline exercised for human survival. You have to be able to work around the pain. Dancing is cathartic, and so is song. They sweat it out.

I would venture to guess that horror is also part of why New Or-leans food is so delicious. Food is the blues here. All the tragedies of the slave ports brought together on the tongue in slaughtered meats, flesh cooked to falling-off-the-bone tenderness and smothered in sauces. There is some improvisation, but there is also stringent tra-dition. Ask someone how they make their gumbo, and they will tell you both how and why it matters to do it that way.

About a mile away from the Orleans Ballroom, on St. Charles Avenue, stands the old headquarters of the United Fruit Com-pany. There they traded in bananas, shaped the history of Central America, and provided the template for the modern multinational corporation. The heyday of United Fruit can be traced to Sam-uel Zemurray. In 1877, he was born to a Jewish family in what is present-day Moldova. Zemurray immigrated to the United States as a teenager. He first moved to Selma, Alabama, where he already had family. But it is when he moved out of the Black Belt and into the Gulf Coast—first Mobile and then New Orleans—that he made his mark on history. Zemurray noticed that the local banana import-ers along the Gulf Coast were discarding overly ripe bananas. He created a business of selling the fruit, yellowing and blackened, at cut-rate prices. The business expanded along railroad lines, provid-ing more Americans with the popular fruit. In 1903, he joined his company, Cuyamel, to United Fruit, but over the next decades, the two businesses would sometimes be competitors and sometimes partners. In 1910, he bought five thousand acres in Honduras to grow bananas. His laborers were Jamaicans because their homeland was where bananas had first been cultivated. And it was Zemurray's business interest in Honduras that ultimately led him to use private military force to dominate the country.

Three days before Christmas, he, former president of Honduras Manuel Bonilla, private mercenary Lee Christmas, and New Orleans native and Boer War veteran Guy Molony went to a brothel in Storyville. Storyville was New Orleans's red-light district. Designed under a German model, it was a zoned location where jazz, liquor, and sex flourished. Blue books were produced as guides to the neighborhood, identifying each house by service and type, including the races of the sex workers. Black people were everywhere, but Black men could not purchase sex services from women of any race. Later Storyville would be cleared to establish Iberville public housing projects. But in 1910, it was a common location for moneyed men to seek entertainment.

This evening's venture, however, was a deception. The US government was planning to tax banana exports from Honduras, which would force Zemurray's prices to rise or his profits to shrink. He and his allies planned to support a coup that would reinstall Bonilla, who promised to advantage Zemurray once installed. Knowing they were being watched by the FBI, they all entered a brothel, but two of them—Molony and Christmas—snuck out and took a ship with a hundred mercenaries to Honduras. They cut phone lines between New Orleans and their destination. By the second week in January, Bonilla was back in charge of Honduras.

The designation of Central American nations as "banana republics" is not a term that belongs to the people, but rather to corporate elites, like Zemurray, for whom representation was always secondary to wealth. It was coined by the North Carolina–born writer O. Henry in his 1904 short story collection, *Cabbages and Kings*, which was based upon his six-month tenure living in Honduras while evading trial for bank embezzlement in the United States. He makes a relevant observation in the book:

There is a quaint old theory that man may have two souls—a peripheral one which serves ordinarily, and a central one which is stirred only at certain times, but then with activity and vigour. While under the domination of the former a man will shave, vote, pay taxes, give money to his family, buy subscription books and comport himself on the average plan.

But let the central soul suddenly become dominant, and he may, in the twinkling of an eye, turn upon the partner of his joys with furious execration; he may change his politics while you could snap your fingers; he may deal out deadly insult to his dearest friend.

The rival souls were essential to the hypocritical relationship between American democracy and its economic domination of other people, which stole their independence as well as autonomy, again and again. The United States began as a series of European imperial corporations, and even after the establishment of a republican form of government, the relationship between the United States and the Global South was profoundly shaped by that disposition and the second soul.

The other dominant banana company in New Orleans was founded by two Sicilian immigrants, the Vaccaro brothers, in 1899. They began with the importation of bananas from Honduras. They flourished because they bought up the city's ice factories in order to preserve the bananas. At the time, the company was known as Standard Fruit, and is now part of the Dole Food Company. United Fruit became, along with other companies, what is now Chiquita. When I was a kid, we all sang the Chiquita jingle along with the cartoon of an ambiguously brown tropical woman dancing. She could have been a resident of any part of the Caribbean, Central America, or the US South. She was, in fact, a product of them all.

The banana business was dominated by American businessmen, and the rights and demands of Central Americans for more than a subsistence wage were squashed due to the Americans' influence and power. The United Fruit Company, the most powerful company among them, came to be reviled by working-class people in Latin America generally. There was no better voice to describe their vulgarity than the Chilean poet Pablo Neruda. He wrote of it:

When the trumpet sounded everything was prepared on earth, and Jehovah gave the world to Coca-Cola Inc., Anaconda, Ford Motors, and other corporations. The United Fruit Company reserved for itself the most juicy piece, the central coast of my world, the delicate waist of America.

In 1932, Zemurray took over complete control of United Fruit, and the company's building in the French Quarter of New Orleans dates to that period. Zemurray worked with the CIA to facilitate the 1954 coup in Guatemala after President Jacobo Arbenz began to nationalize land owned by the company. It was just five weeks after the *Brown v. Board of Education* opinion had been published by the US Supreme Court. And in 1961, Zemurray provided ships to support the Bay of Pigs invasion of Cuba, three weeks before the civil rights movement Freedom Rides began. When one tells the history of the mid-twentieth-century South, it ought not simply be a story of the struggle for civil rights and its backlash. It is also a hemispheric economic history. And to the extent that the unfinished history of the movement includes persistent economic inequality that depended on the repression of labor movements, political domination, and extralegal violence, that is a history that sits within the region writ broadly. New Orleans is a crossroads.

Zemurray died on November 30, 1961. In his will, the mansion he owned in New Orleans was granted to Tulane University. It is now the university president's home. The process of contesting the exclusion of Black people from the student body of Tulane had begun in earnest in April of 1961 with the application of Black women graduate students. The litigants were armed by *Brown v. Board of Education* and also by a host of earlier state-based cases in which the court found that even according to *Plessy*, which held that separate must be equal, Black students ought to be admitted to public universities' graduate schools. Nevertheless, it would take two years before two Black women were finally allowed to enroll at Tulane. In 1961, Loyola University, in contrast, already did allow Black people to enroll. I know because my mother was there, with a smattering of other Black students, although most others were Creoles, with light skin and loosely curled hair. Like Zemurray, she'd come from Alabama and learned that although New Orleans was distinct, its order bore a lot in common with her home state.

The year 1961 is also the year in which the great Colombian novelist Gabriel García Márquez took a Greyhound trip through the South and found the region to be akin to his own:

> I saw a world very similar to my home town of Aracataca in Colombia. As a company town built by United Fruit, Aracataca has the same wooden shacks with roofs made of zinc and tin . . . There was the same kind of poverty contrasting with great wealth. In some ways, it seemed to me that Faulkner was also a writer of the Caribbean, because of the great influence the area has had on the Gulf of Mexico and on Mississippi.

The United Fruit building, with its permanent letters still engraved and prominent in the French Quarter, is an artifact of the relationship between the South, the Caribbean, and Latin America. García Márquez was expected to place himself on the colored side of things sometimes while in the US South. He had to use a colored water fountain, for example. That wouldn't have happened to him in Colombia. But I think it helped him to understand Colombia as much as the United States. The most passionately guarded hierarchies can sometimes be fickle, especially when someone challenges them.

I remember being surprised, when my mother took me to visit the Sisters of the Holy Family motherhouse in New Orleans East, about the number of elderly nuns who were from Latin America. And that the order had maintained a motherhouse in Belize as well. It was only in adulthood that I considered how the histories of slavery and capital built these connections. There were common roots, but also common routes, that shaped this network of women who, in every region of the Americas, were Black and female and therefore deemed inferior and routinely excluded from every opportunity. Against that backdrop, they built a home of their own, carved from inside the global power of the Roman Catholic Church.

When my mother belonged to the order, she was known as Sister Madeleva, a name taken from a medievalist scholar and poet. Once, when I asked one of her former housemates what my mother was like back then, Sister Martin de Porres said, "She was most brilliant and *most* holy." I imagine that her time spent in contemplation as a Holy Family, along with the sounds and sights of New Orleans, inspired her poems. The city has music and storytelling that is not only grand but mellifluous, a collage of influences. In the year she joined, along with three of her friends from Alabama, there were more novices from Honduras among the Holy Familys than from the United States. In unison, while their voices rose and fell in syncopation in prayer, glasses tinkled and horns screamed outside. But she hasn't ever told me that. She did tell me about the cruel Whiteness of power in 1960s New Orleans. She told me about how Black power took hold and straight-haired Creoles teased their hair in an imitation of nappiness, claiming Blackness more aggressively than their jealously protected genealogies ever said or believed they should.

My sense of belonging, genealogical and by means of personal history, in New Orleans was challenged by one of the most horrifying events of the twenty-first century, Hurricane Katrina. Like millions of others, I was devastated by it. But it also kept me away. I didn't return to the city for over a decade. I would have felt obligated, I believe, if I had really taken on the responsibility of being a daughter of the city. But I didn't. I was a distant, and negligent, cousin at best.

I cannot tell you the date when I first talked to my godmother, Sister Sylvia Thibodeaux, after the storm. I can only tell you it was fresh enough that both of our voices trembled. The Sisters were mostly elderly, even though they remained in active service to their community. When the evacuation order came, she told me, the Sisters were to be taken by bus to their property in Lafayette, Louisiana. Soon, however, she realized the man who was driving the bus to evacuate them was navigating them to the Superdome. That place, where the city's most vulnerable were deposited, would become known for the grotesque neglect of those who were stranded there after the storm.

Sister Sylvia, who was then the vicar superior and in charge of the order, walked to the front of the bus and started arguing with the driver. Their voices raised, she—steely, gray-eyed, nearly six feet tall—prevailed, and he took them to Lafayette, where they owned a building. A crisis was narrowly averted. The elderly nuns would likely not have survived in the Superdome. But another crisis was unavoidable.

The nursing home run by the Holy Familys, called Lafon, was in 2005 the oldest continuously running retirement home in the United States. It had been funded by Thomy Lafon, a prosperous Creole man. His mother had been in a plaçage relationship with a wealthy White man. Lafon took on his surname, even though his actual father was another White man from an earlier relationship. The Lafon name was influential, though, and worth capitalizing upon, even if informally. Before the storm, when I visited the Lafon nursing home, I remember it being quiet. A TV squawked in the background of the common room. We visited one of the older nuns in her room. She was infirm, a blue-black Mississippi woman with a gray afro and piercing blue eyes. Her longtime roommate sat next to her. She was gregarious, a Puerto Rican woman with an easy smile.

The contract between the Holy Familys and the families of the nursing home residents included the provision that in the case of natural disaster, the families would come gather their elders. But in the panic of the hurricane, many families did not come. As a result, twenty staff members, including six nuns, stayed on duty to tend to the hundred residents rather than leave to secure their own families.

They didn't move the residents because they believed that if they tried to transport them, many would die. As the storm grew and water poured inside, they took the patients from the first to the second floor. And still it rose. Food, water, and medicine went bad. After the generator failed, they were stuck in sweltering heat.

Day after day they tried to flag down emergency vehicles. But the need was so great and the conditions so devastating that by the time help came, nineteen people had died in the building. The Holy Familys were subject to an investigation into the deaths, which ultimately resulted in an affirmation of their innocence. Sister Sylvia sounded, when she told me this, as bereaved as she was relieved. Really the grief was thickest. And in the motherhouse, a number of historic documents of the early years of the order, a rare look into nineteenth-century New Orleans, had been destroyed by the water and the mud it carried inside on waves.

Katrina visited me in Philadelphia through stories. From family and friends in Birmingham and Houston as well as New Orleans. Of New Orleanians taking refuge across the South. They talked about the knives and guns in the Superdome. And of the gang-like rituals of self-preservation, with violence made sharper by trauma and rage and fear. Quelled because folks were already being treated like animals, at least in public, but the whispered stories haunted everybody. And the bodies were stacked upon each other. Death is where the chattel part of chattel slavery remains. The domestication of animals means that they are raised to be killed for our desires. During slavery, the enslaved were raised to survive, at least in the United States, and to satisfy desires. And then, after slavery, suddenly wanting Black people to stay alive to be worked *unto* death was less urgent. Being worked *to* death, for example in a convict camp, was more common than being worked to death as a slave. If you have a prisoner for ten years, you can work them much harder than if you are trying to keep a slave going for forty. The badges and incidents of slavery are not simply a matter of being treated like slaves. It is in the treatment of the Black person as fungible, as somebody who might be this or that based upon desire and immediacy of want, an absence of a presumption of care and value, a contingency of existence that might turn on a dime based upon the whims, fancies, and fears of whoever has control over you in that moment.

The stacked bodies were evidence that a decision had been made at the governmental level: these people were not worth the investment. The FEMA trailers, falling into rapid disrepair, carcinogenic, were evidence. The term "refugees" was more evidence. Here are people, it all said, who can be moved about or simply neglected, at the whim of the money-makers and money-havers. The powerful plunged the free and the freedom fighters into despair. And how hard was it really to push them over the border into being considered something less than citizens?

The event was singular, and yet it was also representative. New Orleans has a post-Katrina diaspora spread out elsewhere. Many have not been able to return home to neighborhoods that have been, at any rate, razed and gentrified. And New Orleans has always been a diaspora and a metropole itself. A space of dispersal and a space of gathering, a meeting place of the Atlantic world. Viet-namese people, also once colonized by France, have built a com-munity in the city since the Vietnam War. A familiar authority, a common Catholicism, and a fishing tradition facilitated their im-mersion. In recent years, they have been joined by those fleeing violence in both Central America and Syria, violence shaped by the long, albeit submerged, history of US imperialism and intervention. Yes, New Orleans was and is a place where the world's people meet. But New Orleans is Empire's graveyard. Katrina came through to us like a biblical story, but it was tragedy that took place on grounds that were already both sacred and damned.

When he was thirty-two years old, Thomy Lafon was listed in the 1842 city directory as a merchant. His mother was born a free woman in Haiti and had arrived with other migrants post-revolution. Lafon grew wealthy through real estate. The Holy Family nursing home was the result of one of many of his charitable donations made in service of Black people in New Orleans. He also provided financial support to the Underground Railroad. Lafon was known as the wealthiest Black man in Louisiana, and perhaps even the world. And in 1897, four years after Lafon died, and a year after the *Plessy v. Ferguson* opinion affirmed state-mandated segregation, a school for Black children was named in Lafon's honor.

Homer Plessy, a man who could pass for White, a Creole who occupied a higher status than the general Black public, cast his lot with Blackness by bringing a lawsuit disputing the Louisiana statute that required segregation. Like Lafon and Henriette Delille, Plessy had a skepticism towards the partial benefits of a half-caste status, and understood his linked fate with the undeniably African Black majority.

And like in Black communities throughout the South, the trag-edy of the *Plessy* decision did not quell aspiration in New Orleans. School building was one sign of hope and striving. The Thomy La-fon School was built in 1897 atop Cypress Grove African American

Cemetery no. 1. The burial ground had been neglected. It was a potter's field. Crawfish invaded the coffins, airing out death, animal excrement, and sea life in the neighborhood. The stench was terrible. And so the cemetery had to be filled to build the school at a cost of $15,000.

Three years later White people burned down the school as part of a routine of repression during Jim Crow. Nevertheless, the neighborhood grew. The school was rebuilt. In 1939, it became home to the famous Dew Drop Inn, the first desegregated nightclub in the city. Black and White folks drinking and dancing together was against state law. But still Dew Drop thrived with all the notable jazz, blues, and soul acts that came through to perform.

On the former cemetery land, two years later, in 1941, the city also situated the Magnolia Housing Projects. Wherever you are in the South, the accent of "Magnolia" is heavy on the first syllable. And in Louisiana, the ubiquitous hardwood trees produce flowers that are fragrant and leaves that are shiny and thick. Called by the nickname "'Nolia," the projects became well-known for producing popular New Orleans hip hop artists like Birdman, Juvenile, Jay Electronica, and Magnolia Shorty. It makes sense. It was adjacent to the Dew Drop Inn. And the closest park to the project, Shakespeare (which was formally renamed to A. L. Davis in 1979 for a local civil rights organizer) is a traditional staging ground for the Mardi Gras Indians: traditional carnival revelers who draw on both Indigenous and African roots in their pre-Lent rituals, like much of the Caribbean.

In 1954, a brand-new Thomy Lafon School was built in the middle of the Magnolia projects, and it was placed on raised piers in case of flooding. It was a beautiful example of modernist tropical architecture, rectangular and gleaming white with large windows. The school, which served New Orleans Black children largely from the projects, won the American Institute of Architects Honor Award.

This is the irony of a place of inequality and striving. Beautiful music, institutions, and culture grew alongside repeated deprivation. For example, Flint Goodridge Hospital, a Black-owned hospital, was a block away from the Magnolia projects. It had been established in 1896 by a group of Black women who belonged to the Phyllis Wheatley Club. It was first a nurses' training and pharmacy school. In 1915, it was converted into a fifty-bed hospital and a nurses' home. In 1963, a local historically Black university, Dillard, took control of the hospital operations. They were forced to close in 1983, however, as desegregation led to decreased use.

The hospital closed as death increased in the community. Beginning in the 1980s, crack became a scourge—leading to deaths from overdosing and the gun violence that goes along with the territorialism of drug trafficking. In 1990, a police substation was set up in the Magnolia in order to control the violence. Eight years later, with conditions unimproved, a plan for demolition was set for part of Magnolia. That year, on "Da Magnolia," Juvenile rhymed about dope deals gone bad, killings at second line funerals, and the kids who stepped outside of school and met violence. However, most of Magnolia was abandoned rather than demolished. But in 2005, Katrina destroyed much of the property. The Lafon School, with its superior construction on a raised platform, remained intact. Still it wasn't reopened. In 2011, a mixed-use, mixed-income apartment complex was put in the place of the projects under a cheery name, Harmony Oaks. The hospital is an apartment complex, too, but the old name, Flint Goodridge, remains.

The way private enterprise took over the grounds of public housing and Black life in New Orleans is consistent with the norms of late capitalism in the United States. Everything is subject to markets. Folkways have little power without capital. But there is a particularly sharp way gentrification cuts in the South, a region built by the people who were property. People who in freedom saw their perceived value plummet. It is worse than irony. It is devastation.

"Palimpsestic" is probably too gentle a word for the blood that soaks through the layers of history in the city's soil.

In 2018, I finally returned to New Orleans to participate in the IdeasCity Festival. The program was a culmination of a five-day residency for artists that took place in Treme, the neighborhood where Storyville once sat. I knew "recovery" was a word that had encroached on the city in the intervening years. I also knew it didn't fit what had happened. In the post-Katrina period, "theft" better captured what was happening to the place where Black people had built tradition. So I decided to do my lecture about Bras-Coupé. Bras-Coupé was an African king enslaved in New Orleans. He was, according to the stories, striking and heroic. He danced in Congo Square, with many other enslaved people, on weekends. And everyone, from all points on the color line, admired his grace and beauty. But once he fled the plantation, his captivating movement and dignified posture were deemed dangerous rather than entertaining. The fugitive was apprehended, and his arm was amputated. Hence his storied name: Bras-Coupé, "cut arm."

Bras-Coupé was real. His slave name was Squire. He was the property of William De Buys. But his story, as a historical artifact, was fictionalized. Sometimes fiction is the history, though. It tells you something about the nature of the place.

I was trying to make a point, in this lecture, about what it means to hold on after some fundamental part of your being had been stolen from you. That is what New Orleans people have done time and again, after the theft of family, body, and home. After my talk, I did a public conversation with the Philadelphia-native rapper Black Thought about the political undercurrent to all creative work. But before we talked, we'd had an invocation and a lesson. A group of Mardi Gras Indians had blessed the gathering with a performance.

The Mardi Gras Indians are Black people who have been parading for over a century. They honor the Indigenous people who assisted enslaved folks who ran to freedom, while participating in the rituals of European carnival merged with African cultural practices. I've been told that when the Plains Indians marched in Mardi Gras, Black New Orleanians were inspired to begin masking ritually according to social and civic groups. Over the generations, their attire has grown ever more elaborate. A single costume, hand-beaded, assiduously color coordinated, and feathered, can take a year to complete.

On this afternoon, I sang along, stood, and danced. We all swayed and clapped. One phrase stuck in my ear: "Pretty black panther with the purple heart." I loved the variety of associations. Black panthers, heroes of war, and oh so beautiful. There's that luscious boastfulness about New Orleans that makes it stand out and, as we say in the South to describe deliberately activating one's charisma, "show out." The lead singer's purple plumage was spectacular and sparkling, meticulously beaded with a geometric drama of repetition. The krewes of Indians often walk under the banner of a mythological Roman or Greek god. They arrange themselves according to the hierarchies of European royalty, and yet are undeniably African in tradition. All over New Orleans are places named for Africa and Asia: Algiers, Arabi, and Congo Square. All over New Orleans are places once framed and owned by Europe.

My friend Shantrelle, anthropologist, curator, Lucumi priest, hoodoo practitioner, and a creative in the broadest sense, had a voice that rose above the crowd singing with the Indians. She is a child of the city, generations back. After she gave the final presentation of the day, on her book about Black dandyism, a group of us went out to eat. We rode around the city, taking a long way to our destination. Shantrelle showed me places her family had lived, along with the signs of gentrification. Newly renovated homes stood where New Orleans natives had once lived for generations. I also asked her questions about her ancestors, who had come from Haiti, from Jamaica, from Philadelphia, and from West Africa to New Orleans. And yes, from Europe, too, though she doesn't dwell on that much. One of the reasons I love to talk to Shantrelle is that she refuses to code-switch. New Orleans, and specifically Black New Orleans, is always honored on her tongue, as though she carries her history not just as a form of knowledge but as a way of speaking herself into the world.

Usually I would go with my mother to Dooky Chase, the famous restaurant run by the late Leah Chase, which was a site of civil rights organizing. I longed to see it again, but I was more interested ultimately in being with friends and feeling inside the rhythm of New Orleans now. I wanted to hear details like the long-lost cousin I took myself to be. While riding along, we played phone tag with other folks from our group, trying to find a gathering place to meet. The first plan was to go to Neyow's, a local restaurant known for its oysters, but the line there was too long. So we happened upon another spot. I don't remember the name of the place, but it was good. Sitting at a big, long table, grubbing, were New Orleanians as well as West Indians, a Detroiter with roots in Alabama, a Boricua New Yorker, and me. We could have been, in ethnic composition, Holy Family nuns. The food was fresh cooked, as though made in a mother's kitchen. It was a day that felt like we were living in high cotton or, as my mother (whose lingo shows her New Orleans young adulthood) would say, as though we had "bookoo bucks," with an abundance of food and drink. Shucking and jiving in African American vernacular is a shameful act—stereotypical clowning for White entertainment—but vocal pleasure is not, and we laughed with abandon, for our own entertainment. Shucking an oyster, as I watched the others do, is a skill in which you open the animal's hinge in order to get to the good part. Once it's exposed, you slice off the residue but leave the briny underside. You can still taste the water when it slides down your throat.

Once darkness had fallen, Shantrelle and I made it to one of the places that is most familiar to me in New Orleans: Café Du Monde. It is a tourist's habitat, but also a local institution. Café

Du Monde has been on Decatur Steet in the Quarter since 1862. Back then it was part of the French Market. Despite that name, the French Market was initially an Indigenous trading post and is the oldest continuous open-air market in the country, as it began before the country and its colonies. Now Café Du Monde is a simple open-air restaurant where people drink chicory coffee and eat beignets.

The treats, a light pastry dusted with confectioners' sugar, as with many Southern delicacies, owe something to Black folks. Norbert Rillieux, cousin to painter Edgar Degas, an homme de couleur (man of color) offspring of a White planter, earned a place in history by creating what is termed the multiple-effect evaporator for sugarcane. Rillieux created a machine to harness steam from boiling cane syrup, putting it through three chambers. At the end of the process, he was left with refined sugar crystals. Rillieux's invention led to a sugar boom. Suddenly, sweetness was available everywhere. His methods were adopted in Cuba, Mexico, France, Egypt, and, of course, the US South in the 1830s. By the time Café Du Monde came along, sugar and confectionaries were flourishing.

However, Rillieux couldn't have eaten at Café Du Monde despite his prestige as one of the earliest chemical engineers and his distinguished lineage. Though the color line in New Orleans was perhaps more porous than in much of the South, it existed. Café Du Monde didn't knowingly serve Black patrons until July of 1964, in response to the passage of the Civil Rights Act. It's one of those stark reminders that New Orleans was and is very much the US South. If you look around, though there is always a wonderful motley of people in New Orleans, you can see the differences. Between Black and White, between tourists and locals. The locals are Blacker, often a bit rounder, frequently with tired eyes. The tourists drink the surroundings hungrily. The locals smile at them, but their faces blanch when the tourists turn away. I know I am supposed to decode here. What can I say? I was once reading an interview with James Baldwin, and he described a frustration he had with

Langston Hughes. He said when Hughes told you about a lynching, it was too realistic. That Hughes sounded like his daddy. Baldwin preferred Countee Cullen. He wanted the art, the suggestiveness, the distance to make it possible to digest horror. What made it art, instead of artifice like *Gone with the Wind* or *Song of the South*, is that it didn't falsify. It didn't pretend that everything was heaven or hell. But it was a composition. Composure with truthfulness. All of that is to say, I hate how many people who ought to be here in New Orleans are dead while the tourist theater continues. I hate the grief that rests all over this city. I hate that, post-Katrina, people couldn't come home. I hate that strangers come in and vomit on its streets and buy its wares and demand to be entertained, and the truth is nobody can just say "Fuck you" because when you are poor and the appeal is your smile, you have little choice. Before there were beignets, Black women hawked calas on the street. Warm and sugary. Or stage planks, flat gingerbread cookies that have now become covered in plastic and factory-produced. "Belles calas! Tout chauds!" All had disappeared by 1940. Maybe we're just witnessing another disappearance. Maybe Katrina wasn't an outlier, but just part of the dance.

Riding back to my hotel, full on beignets, Shantrelle and I passed a graveyard. I didn't know which it was, in the darkness: no. 1, 2, or 3. In St. Louis Cemetery no. 1, Homer Adolph Plessy is buried. This is also the burial site of Marie Laveau, the mythologized voodoo queen, who was such a shapeshifter that I can hardly imagine how to tell you a story about her that I know is true beyond the fact that she was once a real person. The first mayor of New Orleans, Jean Étienne Boré, is interred there as well. He is the man who first granulated sugar in the States, under the tutelage of two Cubans, meaning that every time you sprinkle it over your cereal or in your coffee, you might consider how he, like Rillieux, made the national addiction much more palatable.

I cannot help but think about sweetness born of the violence of slavery as a metaphor for New Orleans, which is a cradle holding together the South and its strands at the root. Like its native drink, a Sazerac, it's sweet and strong enough to knock you on your ass or knock you out. And of course, as often as people try to cut it off from the rest of the South, it functions like a phantom limb, one that we feel everywhere in the fabric of the country, even when we don't see it right there on us. The graves in New Orleans sit aboveground because of potential flooding. And so the dead are raised, and decorated with stunningly bright mausoleums and abundant flowers. The spirits hear the music and might be swaying, too. New Orleans choreography often feels like a dance at the Kongo crossroads.

During the pandemic some New Orleanians were arrested for having a second line, a ritual moving jazz band with accompanying dancers that is commonly used to celebrate the departed. I felt softer towards them than the Mardi Gras revelers who were visiting from all over the country despite COVID, who had decided their voyeuristic pleasure was more important than the coming disaster. The second liners were people who clung to the ways of grief in a grieving time, though it was against better judgment. Another mourning group, more cautious but no less soulful, posted a dirge on Instagram. And when the city lost one of New Orleans's most precious elders, Ellis Marsalis, the patriarch of one of the greatest music families in American history, like a chorus people wrote on social media: "He cannot even have a second line," "No second line," "Lord, no second line." Each sentence had volumes of grief. It was all of our grief in a sense. We were touching death shared in solitude rather than ritual. That's what the pandemic wrought: people who were shipwrecked in sadness.

South of I-10, there is a road from New Orleans to Baton Rouge that is beautiful. Along the way, the road rises from below sea level to aboveground. At present, the road is interspersed with grand plantations as well as industrial plants. It is called River Road, although the river views are obscured by the levees. And it seems strangely fitting that River Road is now, in addition to its old designation, Plantation Alley, also called Cancer Alley. Toxicity curls around its live oak trees and people. Along the route is the Nottoway House, the largest surviving antebellum plantation house. It is three stories tall with sixty-four rooms and has been named a triple-A four-diamond resort. Guests get to sleep in four-poster beds and have their pictures taken in the glory of the antebellum South. It survived the Civil War and the civil rights movement, and is pristine in its glorification, poisoned air or not. Throughout the South, it is worth mentioning, one can still find plantation homes advertised as such. "Farm" or "estate" would be just as good. The appeal of "plantation" as a word is rooted in slavery. These plantation homes boast acres and acres of the finest land, sometimes for hunting, sometimes farming, sometimes for replaying history, but with shiny new appliances. New Orleans, with its congestion and ornate metalwork, can make you forget that right outside the metropole are history's graveyards. So much remains untended.

In 2018, there was a public reckoning about former slave plantations. So many people want to live in their fantasies, especially for weddings, with little regard for the ghosts of slavery. The plantation has been evacuated of its sins, in the minds of celebrants at least, and affirms so many desires for a glorious celebration. Critics called the habit disgusting. But when piecemeal additions were made on plantation tours or placards, additions intended to tell the truth about the history of slavery, guests began to leave disgruntled messages. They surely didn't want to hear that the plantation wasn't all mint juleps and "I do declare," that they were sites of death and rape, violence and theft—of children, names, life, and personal autonomy.

Since that time, now and again, I hear that a plantation wedding is like holding a wedding in a concentration camp. But despite how distasteful it is, that's not a good analogy at all. Concentration camps were not intended to be glamourous. They were not meant to feed the fantasy of being a master or mistress who is gloriously indulged by their chattel. They were brutish. But the strange, cruel beauty of the plantation, its gothic horror, is a holdover from the past, intoxicating witnesses with the scent of honeysuckle and fried chicken along with the smell of blood-soaked soil.

There are some places that tell the ugly beauty overtly, not by innuendo or loud silence. Like the Whitney Plantation, also along the Great River Road, which has been restored as a way to tell the history of slavery. It retains all of its beauty and its horror. In 1811, the largest slave revolt in the US South took place there. About five hundred enslaved Africans rose up. When they were defeated, dozens of the enslaved were executed and beheaded. Their heads were planted on poles as warnings. Now, in a memorial to the insurrectionists, sixty-three heads are set before a white picket fence with twisting vines. Each face is rendered distinctly and permanently in ceramic. And yet I am unsettled about this permanent image of violence, as authentic as it is. I'd rather see them armed.

My Louisiana genealogical ancestry lies somewhere between the Mississippi and Amite Rivers in a part of Louisiana that used to be part of the Republic of West Florida. These ancestors are not listed by name in plantation records, only by age and gender. But they emerged from an obscuring history. I know where two of my paternal great-grandparents lived in Uptown New Orleans, at the bottom of the city's crescent. What I don't know is how my people got from one place to the other. But I've also grown to recognize the absence, the unmarked graves and the unrecorded names, as a storytelling mechanism. It is as valuable to speculate as it is to attempt to restore. It helps you remember that out of disregard, the people imagined freedom. Again and again. Our imaginative speculation is part of the tradition.

Shadows and ghosts are essential to this story. Frozen images, if we are honest about what they do tell and all that they cannot, are not verité but a fleeting taste. Underneath them are the layers that make you know that something that was here is gone. So we conjure them back up. That's not the thing itself, though. Rather, it's the definition of being haunted. Or history.

When I called Sister Sylvia, during COVID quarantine, I learned she had become a resident of Lafon. Each person was sequestered in her room. As we spoke, she was cooking for two women from Belize in the room across the hall. She connected behind a closed door to people all over the building. And then she ministered to me. She told me not to blame God for this tragedy. Human doings could not be blamed on Him. His gift of grace was our refuge from them. Her voice has a natural vibrato, and so I felt it in my throat when she said that I must remember, that it was important to know that though I dwell here, this earthly cruel and sinful place is not my home.

PARAÍSO

The Bahamas and Havana

THOMAS MORE CAME UP WITH the word "Utopia." He was inspired by Plato's fictional stories of Atlantis. Plato described Atlantis as a virtuous place, with people who were advanced and cultured. But Atlanteans became unethical and voracious after conquering Africa and making their way into Europe. Earthquakes and floods hit them, a spiritual punishment. And the island sank into the sea, creating an impenetrable blockade deep in the waters that was impossible to pass through.

Atlantis shaped how More envisioned a Utopia. He was also intrigued by European travelogues about the Americas, a place ripe for conquest and creation. So he made up an ideal society and called it, and his 1516 book about it, Utopia. Utopia was self-contained, abundant, and without private property. It had no social class at all, no crime, no greed for gold, no warmongering or capital punishment. And its majesty was made possible, according to More's story-making, because General Utopus killed all the "savages" who dwelled there before starting up.

Unsurprisingly, I immediately feel disaffection for, and the irony of, More's utopian aspiration, but the imagery of Atlantis still does captivate me a little. Not because the decadence is appealing, but because in the Gulf and the Atlantic, there are slave ships—once floating societies, theaters of horror, vulgar, filthy cruel places struck by rocks and storms and now sunk to the ocean's bottom like Atlantis. Other slave ships became ships that weren't slavers. Their names were changed, they were put to different purposes, or they were dismantled, plank by plank, and purposed for new architectures.

I went to places "Souther," as Toni Morrison put it, to catch a better likeness of the region and the nation: through contrast and comparison. Morrison criticized Albert Murray's 1971 book *South to a Very Old Place* because he refused to think about the larger landscape of Blackness beyond the borders of the nation. And though Murray's book is the most direct influence upon my own, I take her criticism seriously. Still, including Paradise Island of the Bahamas and Havana might seem unusual choices. To look at the scope of the South beyond its geographic boundaries, one could go to Chicago or Detroit. You could go to Liberia, a settler colony established for Black Americans. I could have gone to Nigeria or Scotland—as a genealogical venture. Better yet Haiti or Barbados—places that housed people who would later be enslaved in Louisiana and South Carolina. Or Trinidad, where formerly enslaved folks fled after the War of 1812. And what about Bermuda, the place of the shipwreck, while the crew was en route to Virginia, that Shakespeare fictionalized in *The Tempest*? Of course there are lots of places to go. Because the Southern region of the United States has both shaped the world and been filled by it.

So why these two? The arc is one answer. Look at a map of the South—follow the arch surrounding the Gulf of Mexico, cradle-like—and include these two island nations, the Bahamas and Cuba. If you trace it, it looks like the path to completing a circle. And both hold extremes and an array: a tax shelter and a socialist state; Anglophone, Francophone (a critical mass of Bahamians are of Haitian origin), and Hispanophone; an archipelago and a single-island nation; two places distinct from, independent of, yet deeply familiar and bound to the United States.

The term "Global South" is a metaphor of sorts. The man who coined it, Carl Oglesby, was born to Southern parents, from South Carolina and Alabama, and raised in Akron, Ohio. Idiosyncratic, Oglesby was a 1960s radical, a president of Students for a Democratic Society, who eventually became a rather conservative libertarian. He used the relationship between the Northern region of the United States and the South as an analogy to the one between rich nations and poor. The wealthy nations were at once parasitic and dependent, controlling and greedy. They begged loyalty from the small elites wielding control over their people, and who were controlled by the even more powerful. These are how regions of the so-called Global South are characterized, and they're literally very close to what we mean when we say "the South." For example, Bimini, part of the Bahamas, is just fifty miles east of Miami. In the nineteenth century, it was a way station for fugitives from the powerful, a home for pirates, a wrecking spot. Later it was known for alcohol smuggling and as the playground of that quintessential figure of American masculinist national literature: Ernest Hemingway. In fact, in his travels, he left a trail from the Florida islands through the Bahamas to Cuba, rendering broken utopian dreams of American machismo with a native backdrop. Maybe if I could reach for Atlantis, I thought, I might tell a better story in content, if not in composition. Maybe I could narrate the connection from different points along the underside, underfoot the American masculine hero, boss of us all.

June Jordan's essay "Report from the Bahamas" includes the following observation:

There's that white report card on the bureau. "Dear Guests:" It says under the name "Olive," "I am your maid for the day.

Please rate me: Excellent. Good. Average Poor. Thank you."
I tuck this memento from the Sheraton British Colonial into my notebook. How would "Olive" rate *me*?

It is a version of the question I ask myself every time I stay in a hotel in the tropics. Or bring American dollars to a place where they count for more than they do here.

Leisure culture bloomed in the 1980s, and I was a kid who longed for what was advertised. Islands filled with people who looked like me, feeding an American fantasy that didn't contemplate the actual me. Everyone said the little girl in the "Make It Jamaica" ad was my twin. I liked that association, and I wasn't knowledgeable enough to work it all out. I just wanted to go to paradise.

Atlantis, expensive as all get-out, was my fantasy because I'd heard it was like a massive playground. I finally went as an adult, even though by then it made less sense for me. I was well into my thirties. I'd grown to like museums and community centers in travel more than resorts. But the kids, I thought, they will like Atlantis. The truth is, I did, too. That was on my third trip to the Bahamas. It is one of those places that, like Disney World, is endlessly dreamy as long as you don't attend too closely to the seams. Look there and you might feel some unease, even nausea.

The Bahamas took a distinctly different course in relationship to the history of money-making than much of the region. African Americans who fought for the British in the Revolutionary War settled there to be free. Many of them came from the Low Country. In 1818, Great Britain declared that all enslaved Africans who set foot in the Bahamas would be manumitted. This fact attracted Black people from across the Atlantic world. In 1841, there was a revolt on a slave ship called the *Creole*, which was transporting people from Virginia to be sold in New Orleans. The insurgent Africans ordered the ship sailed to Nassau.

And yet, during the Civil War, Nassau served as a port for blockade runners making their way to and from ports along the Southern Atlantic coast, allowing for continued trade with the Confederacy. This may seem unusual for a nation that was populated by Black freedpeople. But it was also a proto–Jim Crow nation, ruled by Great Britain. Refusing to countenance slavery within their own borders didn't mean they wouldn't make money from it. The nation also profited during Prohibition in the United States, sneaking rum to the nearby US coast. Being so close, yet outside the purview of American law, has been a source of Bahamian prosperity in one way or another for generations, particularly for those seeking to protect profit from taxation. The Bahamas are well-known as a tax shelter. The bulk of banking on the islands is offshore, meaning that the accounts are held by noncitizens and nonresidents, and even in other currencies. The tellers don't see the account holders. The account holders don't see the land or people. It is an invisible transactionalism, but one that, along with tourism, provides the economic backbone for the Bahamas, and scaffolds the finances of wealthy Americans.

In addition to sitting in a vortex of the United States and Great Britain, the Bahamas are in the Caribbean and shaped by the forces in that geopolitical region. Over the course of the twentieth century, Haitians, escaping poverty and unrest, sought refuge in the Bahamas as well. It was and remains a deeply stratified place, sitting at a crossroads, with the global elites and their tax havens at the top and poor Haitians living in shanties at the bottom. It is one of the tragic ironies of global history that Haitians, the people of the first independent Black republic, the nation that inspired the Black world to fight for freedom, are so frequently treated as belonging at the bottom of social hierarchies in American nations. But it is precisely because Haiti has always been made to pay for being free. Their national debt, and recurrent economic suffering, began in the demand that they repay France for its loss of a profitable slave society. They were punished with military occupation and dominion that impoverished Haiti and Haitians. They are punished by disdain when they seek refuge in other nations. This reality became extremely clear in 2019 after Hurricane Dorian ravaged so much of the island nation. On Great Abaco Island, the shack-like dwellings populated by Haitian Bahamians were left in ruins. Pushed to the margins, they are nevertheless an integral part of Bahamian history and culture, by some estimates making up a third of the genealogy of the people here.

Another third come from the Southern United States. And that is why you can get grits for breakfast all over the islands. There's a repose, a version of the slow smile, that is deeply familiar to me as an Alabaman. The square builds, deep brown faces, and slight stomach paunch of many of the men is a body I know. But of course there are things that are different. The first time I went to the Bahamas, I ate conch fritters because they reminded me of hush puppies. My friend Michéle asked me, "You know you're allergic to shellfish, why did you eat that?" Who knows why—aesthetics took over, I guess—but the Benadryl haze that followed was not auspicious for our first day.

We—she Haitian, I Southern—were very "American" in the US sense in the Bahamas. We were tourists, lingering poolside and visiting nice restaurants. In many other places we'd been together, we blended into the general public. This wasn't as easy in the Bahamas. Local life isn't just outside of resorts. We went on tours for time-shares. The vendors tried to charm us in that insultingly saccharine way that seduces so many fat-wallet people from the States. Michele immediately cuts through the bullshit in those moments. I smile and nod many times before saying "Absolutely not" to a suggestion I buy a time-share. This is our good-cop, bad-cop routine that we take all over the world. I go back to those sites, in my mind, because standing in a shiny high-rise condo, mid-construction, and looking out onto the sea from the sky, and placing that trip alongside the detritus and heartache of Abaco is precisely why going here has to be part of the Southern story. This operation, of some having and some not having, of killing the land for those who have and giving the disaster to those who don't—that is the core of what has happened. And you can't see it all if you stop at the borders to where the United States ends today.

When June Jordan, the Jamaican American poet, wrote about her own trip to the Bahamas in "Report from the Bahamas," she was honest about the vexations of her tourism. She chose a multi-national American hotel because she imagined it would be and feel safer for her as a single Black woman. She saw the gulf that existed between her and the workers, as a matter of the immediate cir-cumstance, and wondered if an intimacy might exist at a different turn in their lives. The borders are porous and shifting. Reflecting on the cleaning woman, called Olive on the little hotel room report card, Jordan wrote "[E]ven though both 'Olive' and 'I' live inside a conflict neither one of us created, and even though both of us therefore hurt inside that conflict, I may be one of the monsters she needs to eliminate from her universe and, in a sense, she may be one of the monsters in mine." And she was right. I felt like that, too. It is an uncomfortable feeling. Being an African American, even an upper-middle-class African American, often insulates you from the guilt of empire. After all, "we," in any collective sense, have never been the ruling class. "We" have stood on the moral side of things, dominated and marginalized, often searching for solidarity with colonized and dominated people elsewhere. But the truth is that relaxing in a multinational hotel makes me part of the problem that women like Olive have to manage, and for too small a com-pensation. I become her monster, and she is mine, though she is blameless. Because just a generation ago, my people were her. I've laid claim to a heritage that includes women situated just as she is, yet here I am, now one of her exploiters. If that didn't provoke a moral crisis of sorts, I would wonder about my own ethics. Large tips don't exactly ease my conscience. But I suppose it's better than nothing. I don't imagine the housekeeper feels any particular gratitude because she shouldn't. I expect she rolls her eyes at some of the disorder I've left about, and I hope she sighs with a bit of relief because the cash is enough to cover a necessity or two.

There is the matter of wealth and the matter of sovereignty, and they both are part of the way citizenship sets us apart from our cousins in the Bahamas. It is strange how intense borders are when it comes to bodies, given how freely money moves today. Money respects no edges of land, even as land is deputized to sort out who belongs and who doesn't. Michéle draws my attention to borders when we travel. The signs of US dominion will sometimes announce themselves at customs, even before we have boarded planes returning home, saying that we have entered the jurisdiction of the United States. They remind everyone to govern themselves accordingly, i.e., that the empire is watching. Yet all of the American cruise ship companies that register in the Bahamas, colloquially known as floating tax shelters, are given free pass after free pass. They pollute the waters for American pleasure. They serve Americans who would rather not sleep in the places they want to peer at, quickly, with brief visits ashore. Trust me, I am not absolving myself just because I am afraid of cruises. My fear is not principled. It is simply because I had a period in my life where I read a lot of stories about people falling overboard and never being rescued. That's why I missed the best vacations my extended family ever took, fear not principle.

Ethically speaking, the resorts seem not much better and maybe worse. There are throngs of Americans running around in a playground, lots of drawls everywhere, and only a few Bahamians standing at the perimeter. At the very least, tourism in the Bahamas requires some grappling with the fact of our history. Here there are water slides instead of history. Even the sharks are kept in a tank, so you can look but they can't touch. Maybe that is grappling with history, or at least exposing it, if you think about it.

I went to the place they call "fish fry" with the American Southern idea in my head. For Southerners, a fish fry is a party featuring
cornmeal-battered fish. My assumption was a mistake. This was not
a social gathering. It is a constructed tourist location, to partake in
local cuisine, and a setup of sorts. The food is good but made very
mild for tourist palates. There are Black people there, Bahamians,
in much larger numbers than on the resort. So there's a proximity
to the "folk," but it also feels harder to crack through the wall of the
economy. I couldn't help but think of the most famous Bahamians
among Americans: Esther Rolle, who played Florida on *Good Times*,
and Sidney Poitier, who played a dignified Black everyman again
and again. Their polish when outraged on stage and film was always
recognizable. They always reminded me of my people, played us
well. But also, at once, at that precise moment, their voices would
lilt in distinctly Bahamian fashion. More songlike, more lifted at
sentence end. A shifted grace note.

It was harder for me to connect in the Bahamas than anywhere
else in the Black world I've been, in fact. But it was my inability to
find the register of fast friend that made it feel most Southern of
all. Everyone was gracious, yes, but there was an earned skepticism
that our common color is not enough to push aside. Skepticism is
an undercurrent of the proverbial "Southern hospitality." You're supposed to be kind to everyone, but that doesn't mean you trust or are
trusted. People have to know your angle before they let down their
guard. I felt that in the Bahamas, just like I have been trained to
conduct myself that way by my own people. I do not open my door
to any stranger who stops by. The Bahamians knew I was there to
shop and sun, even if I hoped for something more substantive.
Let's not pretend. It is like Jamaica Kincaid said:

> That the native does not like the tourist is not hard to ex-
> plain. For every native of every place is a potential tour-
> ist, and every tourist is a native of somewhere. Every native

everywhere lives a life of overwhelming and crushing banality and boredom and desperation and depression, and every deed, good and bad, is an attempt to forget this. Every native would like to find a way out, every native would like a rest, every native would like a tour. But some natives—most natives in the world—cannot go anywhere.

The Atlantis resort advertises its wonderful water slides. They are fun. My children and I traveled down them again and again. The shark-tank slide tube is so thick you can barely see the sharks. I was embarrassed by the clownish theater of "risk." If I were a native there, I would have laughed at me. She, I would think, knows nothing about what it means to risk, or seek a way to escape.

I wonder what it was like when Martin Luther King Jr. was here. Was he a tourist or something more? He loved conch fritters on Bahamian mornings. He was first encouraged to visit Bimini by Adam Clayton Powell Jr., the son of Black Appalachians who became a political player in New York, and stayed at the Big Game Club, cottage 3. It was a popular spot, frequented by Ernest Hemingway, among other famous people, as well. As the story goes, King wrote his mountaintop speech in the Bahamas, the last one he delivered at the Memphis sanitation workers' strike, the one he probably rehearsed at that little pine house in the Black Belt of Alabama.

Did he look at the azure sky as he wrote, which is brighter in Bimini than Memphis? Did he see the promised land up there, or perhaps in the glowing brown-black flesh of Bahamians, so close to our own? Tour guide Ansil Saunders remembers taking King to the "holy grounds" where mockingbirds, vireos, and sugarbirds flew above and snappers surrounded them in the water. King stated his belief in God as he considered that view.

Did it give him hope at his desk in his bungalow? Perhaps he had grits with his fritters that morning and imagined the striking workers also having that poor man's hearty breakfast, an armor in the fight for dignity. Maybe he visited the Slavery Wall, made of limestone and conch by Black hands once upon a time, now crawling with giant white crabs. I don't know, but I do feel fairly confident that King would gaze at Bimini today and see the stricken and ravaged dwellings of Haitians post–Hurricane Dorian and be reminded of why he had shifted gears in his last months to focus his organizing on poverty, economic exploitation, and neocolonialism. In two places in Bimini, a bust of him emerges from a shell: in Alice Town and amid the mangroves near the Healing Hole. I think that King would shift his eyes between Paradise Island and Bimini, and also between the tourist-friendly gentrified areas of Memphis, Beale Street and Parkway Village, places of dashed dreams and marketed pleasure, and see a real family resemblance. Yes, there is a shared genealogy, but there is also shared circumstance.

In the Bahamas, Junkanoo is celebrated from December 26 to January 1. I will not venture a guess into origins because the debates aren't even close to being settled. But it is a New Year's carnival. The costuming is at once extraordinary and competitive, like Mardi Gras and Carnival in Louisiana, Alabama, and across the Caribbean and Europe. An eclectic palette is accompanied by music and dance. The first time I read *Incidents in the Life of a Slave Girl*, the 1846 narrative written by Harriet Jacobs, a woman who had been enslaved in North Carolina, I was surprised to see her mention the festival with its drums and fancy dress. The historian Stephen Nissenbaum has described the celebration in Jacobs's native North Carolina: "Essentially, it involved a band of black men—generally young—who dressed themselves in ornate and often bizarre costumes. Each band was led by a man who was variously dressed in animal horns, elaborate rags, female disguise, whiteface (and wearing a gentleman's wig!), or simply his 'Sunday-go-to-meeting-suit.' Accompanied by music, the band marched along the roads from plantation to plantation, town to town, accosting whites along the way and sometimes even entering their houses. In the process the men performed elaborate and (to white observers) grotesque dances that were probably of African origin. And in return for this performance they always demanded money (the leader generally carried 'a small bowl or tin cup' for this purpose), though whiskey was an acceptable substitute . . ." Junkanoo was a brief moment when the racial hierarchy was supplanted, a time of releasing pent-up frustration and worry. Immediately afterwards, the racial order would be back.

Now Junkanoo is a tourism boon for the Bahamas, and has all but disappeared in the United States. In the Bahamas, Junkanoo is a way to make some money while still reveling in having survived and kept some of the language, dance, and old ways. That hustle is in the US, too. Some of it is found in the sober genre of civil rights tourism; some of it is in the bacchanal of hip hop or the beads of Mardi Gras. Cultural tourism is often charged with being inauthentic. Sometimes it is. But sometimes it is very authentic, even if only because it makes plain the negotiation between native and tourist. In either instance, when it comes to long-standing inequalities, the "hustle" is a necessary choreography of redistribution. The monied folks want an experience; the locals want to make a living. Everyone pretends that there's an earnest, friendly meeting of cultures, but the power differential, and efforts to renegotiate it, are apparent to everyone. I wouldn't call the interactions dishonest, but they are theatrical. Sometimes they don't even require any in-person contact. Songs and albums can take you on a whole cultural tourist journey, giving you an insider's view of an unfamiliar landscape. For the trip to be pleasurable means there must be some melodrama, some excitement, something fantastical. The tourist knows what they're in for, in part. That's why they take the ride. But the local must also provide something unexpected to make the experience special and vivid enough for the conjure to work.

* * *

FOR 102 YEARS, THE REMAINS of Columbus were housed in Havana. They were placed at the Havana Cathedral in 1796, when France took over Hispaniola. In 1898, when Cuba freed itself of Spanish dominion, they sent his ashes with them. In the Bahamas, Discovery Day, in honor of Columbus, was celebrated until 2012, when it was replaced by National Heroes Day. It was a rather restrained disengagement with celebrating the beginning of imperial histories in the Americas. Nowadays the way each country, including the United States, lives with Columbus is a story in itself. All roads must lead back to him, but whether he is deemed heroic, demonic, or neither has a lot to do with the national identity. In many Latin American nations, Columbus Day is the Day of the Race, or more precisely a day dedicated to the idea of mestizaje—the mixture of Indigeneity and Spanish ancestry, rendered gloriously. That is not the case in Cuba. Socialist and largely African, Cuba has at least formally abandoned romantic stories of empire, but the glory of the revolution has its own comparable mythos.

I went to Cuba alone, and somewhat spontaneously, while my children were on vacation with their father. It was one of those trips that I'd been expecting to take my whole life. But I never had. And I was worried about whether the relaxed prohibitions on travel that President Obama had introduced would be slammed shut by Trump. There was something emotional about my visit, too. When my father had told me stories of his trip to Cuba, he cried. Though a less sentimental and far less sanguine leftist than he was, I hadn't shed all of that romanticism, so I thought the tears would come when I saw Che and Fidel's faces on buildings and walls. They didn't. I knew too much, I guess. I'd learned that the revolution hadn't in fact created the racially egalitarian society that was intended. Nor has stratification all been eradicated, despite how much Cuba has achieved against odds.

Gabriel García Márquez wrote a concise, florid, and intriguing book about the nation pre- and post-revolution titled *Images of*

Cuba. In it, he describes the initial jubilee of Cuban Jim Crow top-pling, and then the chilling revelation that Cuba had, as of yet, no plan to be self-sustaining. Throughout the 1950s, Havana served as "a hedonistic playground for the world's elite," filled with gambling joints, jazz, and brothels, moneyed by the mob, politicians, and aristocrats. The playwright Arthur Miller described Batista's Cuba in *The Nation* as "hopelessly corrupt, a Mafia playground, [and] a bordello for Americans and other foreigners." In a manner that an-tagonized the Cuban people, the US government used its influence to advance the interests of and increase the profits of the private American companies that "dominated the island's economy." As García Márquez's work attests, Americans ran Cuba back then. They owned 90 percent of the mines and mineral concessions, 80 percent of public utilities, half of the railroad companies, and two-fifths of its sugar plantations. The US supplied two-thirds of the imports. A friend of Castro's, García Márquez tried neverthe-less to be frank about what the revolution didn't plan for and didn't make happen, at least by the time he wrote. Batista started out as leftist, but found himself negotiating with and then controlled by US interests, until Castro and Che and the revolution came along. They reclaimed the wealth and incensed the United States govern-ment. In the years since, we have lived with a barrier between the two countries, one erected by a trade embargo, Cold War policies, and steep ideological cleavages.

At first, I saw my own ugly Americanism. I was disappointed by my hotel. The disrepair did not go along with the price, I thought. If I had been a better planner, I would have rented a casa particular, which is the preferred accommodation for the sophisticated traveler to Cuba. In this great big building was a lot of carpet. If you have traveled to the Caribbean, you have probably noticed that there isn't a lot of carpet in most places. The tropical climate creates a mustiness in carpets. They swell and smell. The furnishings were once elegant and earth-toned, but now they were just dated. The drapes were polyester. But out of my window, the sea was visible. That, I loved.

Tourists love the cars in Havana, the carefully maintained "máquinas." Seeing them and riding in them, they say, transports you to a vintage scene. You can in fact delude yourself into believing you are back inside the time of Jim Crow Cuba, or the United States. The best cars, for a soft-focus nostalgia, are the American ones. I looked at them and imagined the migrants from Alabama up to Detroit who had built them for Ford. I thought about how they escaped from working the land to working the assembly line. How Northern Jim Crow wasn't segregated bus cars but racially restricted neighborhoods. How the Motor City changed the sound of gospel to the sound of doo-wop, but the kids were sent home down South for summers, and to sanctified churches on weekends, so they never quite forgot the root sounds. Did you know that Diana Ross went back to Bessemer for years in her childhood? Her ladylike restraint, even when her hair blows wild and she sings, "I was swept away with you," I think can be attributed to that.

Black hands made many of those cars. Black hands drive many of them still. In Havana, and in my home city, and really all across the South. Classic cars are maintained out of both respect and necessity. In the US South, you can see men in the yards leaning over them, working on engines, wiping the wetness off their foreheads with a rag. Or hand-washing with the hose from around the back, then a polish and wax. For a while my cousin Jabari even had his ride as his social media handle: 76Cutlass. Listen: you can stunt (as in dazzle onlookers) with a diamond grill caressing your teeth, a classic whip, a crisp white tee, and some restored kicks. Wealth isn't required. Sustainability has always been a practice of the poor and almost poor, and even for those of us who have money, an appreciation for keeping the old looking brand-new is baked in. But in Cuba the cars look even better than in the US South. Our paint tends to be a bit faded, while theirs glows. Standing in a row, in downtown

Havana, the cars and men shine. Teal, cherry, even canary. Gold, mahogany, ebony. Their drivers preen a bit, men in guayaberas and slacks whose bodies range from ivory to the sheeniest black, though most aggregate somewhere between caramel and mahogany. Even the seats are pristine. Of course there is a strategy there. It seduces the tourist. And they stunt, refusing the assumption that having to conserve is having nothing.

Cuba is Black. And everywhere I was assumed to be Cuban. Despite the fact that John Muir, the conservationist who trekked down the Appalachian train to the Gulf Coast and finally stopped at Cuba, said that Cuba had the ugliest and physically strongest Negroes he had ever seen (signaling his own ugly ways), I found little physical distinction between the people of Cuba and the Black folks in the South beyond sartorial style. Black Americans often dress wearing traditional tourist styles (big shorts, boxy tops, fanny packs, visors, etc.) when abroad, I've noticed, perhaps because we are deeply American, and perhaps to signal that Americanness. It is supposed to provide some protection. We know that Blackness marks us as unsafe in many quarters of the world, and so we often wield imperial citizenship as a safeguard. At least we try. But I prefer to see what I get to see by blending in.

At breakfast, the staff spoke to me. My Spanish, though inadequate, was taken to be a sign of having been Americanized rather than American at first. I think this has something to do with my time in Puerto Rico (the cadence of my Spanish, weak as it is, is Caribbean) and perhaps because Black people who speak Spanish are rarely taken to be anything but of the Caribbean. Plus, I was in a hotel that was not "American." The other guests were Italian, Argentinean, Colombian, not from the US except for three women, also Black, who were Caribbean American. They weren't eager to strike up conversation, but each morning I chatted with an older woman who worked in the dining room. She told me about her son who had moved to Houston. She'd stayed with him for a whole two months a year prior, which was especially wonderful because she got to take care of her granddaughter. The little girl, in a sleeveless pink top and banana-curled ponytail that hung from the top of her head, was snaggletoothed in her school picture. I cooed over how precious she was. I was also embarrassed that I was surprised she had a son in Houston, and that she visited him. As much as I thought myself savvy about the diaspora, I came with Cold War assumptions of Cubans being shut off from the world. It was a good thing to have my hubris dressed down. I needed to behave as though I was as ignorant as I actually was if I wanted to learn anything.

I was walking to downtown Havana, and a young man was speaking to me. I was behind him, his back was to me, but we were having a conversation. I revealed myself by telling him that he was speaking too quickly. "Por favor, chico, hable más lentamente." He looked around, furrowed his brows. I told him, "Soy de los Estados Unidos." "Pero pareces cien por ciento cubana." This was said with gusto and appreciation. Laughter, the Southerner's grace and currency, came right behind. What might have begun as a flirtation in his mind was soon shifted. I explained that I was his mother's age, and with that information he graciously became my guide instead. I understood that this generosity on his part was also a negotiation. In places where people struggle economically, the informal tourist guide economy must be respected. He was a college student, with a baby, but in a relationship that was on the rocks because his girlfriend had moved to a rural area and it was simply too difficult to visit them frequently. He was training to be a teacher but was hopeful that he might be able to get a formal job as a tour guide. That work is more lucrative than education, engineering, or the practice of medicine.

We walked and talked for hours. We visited his uncle, a cigar maker, and friends who were taxi drivers. He showed me the surveillance cameras on the street and the underground economy. I chatted with his aunt's friend, and we laughed about not looking our age "porque somos negras." I was tired, and about to return to my hotel, but we figured we would visit the bar, La Bodeguita del Medio, where Hemingway famously hung out. I walked in first; the bouncer put his hand out. It was a clear no. Luis protested. We were told this was for tourists. The claim that I was a tourist held no sway. I have Hemingway-esque outfits in my closet, smaller-sized, tapered-waist guayaberas that I match with gray tailored slacks and brogues, but when I am in the Caribbean, I wear cotton shift dresses, usually light or bright in color, with simple brown sandals. Dresses like the ones my mother used to make for us when I was small, dresses like women of my grandmother's generation wore across the South, good for the heat and ladylike, dresses like women in tropical places often still wear in an everyday way because they are both cool and elegant.

"Vamo'," I said. The sense of injustice on Luis's face was, of course, not so much about me being misrecognized. It was about race, it was about status, it was about the thing that has stayed even over a hundred years since slavery ended. It was about our brown faces that mark us as not belonging to places we enter all over the Americas. It was the same thing that had happened to me at a hotel in Salvador da Bahia (guests only), at Saks in Philadelphia ("Are you actually looking for something or . . . ?"), and on and on. When Langston Hughes traveled to Cuba, he'd been kicked off a beach in the Dominican Republic, like I had. Hughes had a local politician intervene on his behalf. But despite the fact that my friend and I had paid $20 US to visit the beach, and protested in English, we were treated rudely and ultimately disbelieved. People make a big to-do about the fact that there are gradations of race throughout the Americas, as though the one-drop rule in the United States is somehow crueler. But one thing I know is that the residues of empire, colonialism, and the transatlantic slave trade mean that no matter where you are, the Blacker you are, the lower your status, and any sort of Blackness at all can sometimes serve as a reason to kick you out, as the light-caramel wavy-haired Langston Hughes was an example of. Mulatto as he might have been in the Cuban racial order, he was too Black for that beach.

Mind you, in all of the places I named, plenty of Black American women visit without incident. That's the thing. Color lines aren't absolute in most places anymore. Bodies are read not just for race but alongside assessments of where one fits in the hierarchy of the world. Those assessments shape how the body is responded to. In fact, I have a photo I took from outside of La Bodeguita del Medio that night. There are two Black women inside the bar. I think they are Cuban, but I'm not certain. Perhaps they were there with tourists. Perhaps they were high-status locals. Perhaps they were known to staff. Maybe it wasn't even *me* who was being prohibited. It could have been Luis. Maybe the judgment of him, a poor skinny college student who looked fifteen years old, was the source of our dismissal. The truth is, I do not know.

Toni Morrison wrote critically about Ernest Hemingway's racial politics in his novel *To Have and Have Not*. She argued:

> These tourists in Havana meet a native of that city and have a privileged status because they are white. But to assure us that this status is both deserved and, by implication, potently generative, they encounter a molesting, physically inferior black male (his inferiority is designated by the fact that Harry does not use his fists but slaps him) who represents the outlaw sexuality that, by comparison, spurs the narrative to contemplation of a superior, legal white counterpart.

Hemingway, for his part, distinguished between Cubans and "niggers." The latter status was permanent. It crossed national borders, a sort of permanent inferiority that he asserted in Florida, the Bahamas, and Cuba. This is what I mean when I talk about a form of Jim Crow that crossed borders. Jim Crow ways weren't identical, but the color line was structured everywhere. And some kind of solidarity comes out of that, at least on the wrong side of the line. I filed the bar exclusion away as an instructive story. But it hurt this young man who could have been my son. "Let's eat," I said. We went to a Cuban restaurant, where cats prowled around our feet begging for red snapper, and I listened to his hopes. I prayed for them, silently. Hoped he would be rejoined with his girlfriend and baby, and get the lucrative job in the tourist industry he wanted.

The next morning, I walked along the Malecón, made a right on Avenida 23, kept going past Parque Martin Luther King Jr., where his face is embossed in a large flat tablet surrounded by palms and benches, made a right on Calle L, found a babalawo, a religious priest in a Cuban iteration of the Yoruba spiritual tradition, Santeria. My approach to spirituality is always at once ecumenical and Emersonian. I like to soak it all up. This man was as white-skinned as Fidel, with stick-straight hair. His neck bore elekes, strands of devotion. He held cowry shells and coral. Black, I imagine, of the sort that lies deep in Gulf Coast waters. The coral name "black" does not refer to its color, which varies—pink, yellow, brown—but to its skeleton underneath. He was my height and I suspect of my generation, but he carried himself as an elder in the way priests of certain traditions always do, regardless of age.

The babalawo told me that the orisha were uncertain of my intentions because the circumstances of my life were different than when I had seen a Mae Do Santos, a woman Candomblé priestess, in Bahia, Brazil. He described the personal changes I'd undergone with a remarkable precision, especially given that I hadn't told him anything about myself beyond my first name. I mean, I hadn't told him I'd ever even been in Brazil. As he editorialized about the limitations of the Brazilian Yoruba practice, his friend, a woman sitting with us, argued, "It's the same thing!" He rolled his eyes and went on. I don't pretend to know how spiritualists know these things or to argue that they all should be believed. I just know that time and again people know a great deal about me without me saying a word. Maybe the ancestors told him.

Langston Hughes was more skeptical than I. When he and Zora Neale Hurston visited a conjure man in the woods of Georgia, Hughes described his ritual in detail. "The conjur-man picked up his huge apocryphal Bible and began to read from it. He then rose and darkened the room after having laid out various chalks and powders on a nearby table . . . He sprinkled water and mumbled an incantation. Then he gave us each a small stone to hold. He strick a match and put it to the stones and each stone began to blaze . . . After the stones had burned a while he spoke in tongues, performed other simple rites behind our backs, and then raised the curtains and opened the doors and charged us seventy-five cents . . ." Hughes reported that Hurston, who had visited lots of conjurers, said this one wasn't very good. And neither understood his reported popularity. Hughes concluded ironically, "Yet I guess if you really believe in a burning sulphur stone dripping a cross, it might perhaps be good for what ails you."

Whatever the case, visiting holy people soothes my spirit. I won't share the details of what he told me; just know that it was all true and useful. And if there is a dramatic difference, besides language, between there and here, it is that the Cubans, no matter how white their skin, do not deny the fundamental Africanness of who they *are* the way Southern White people do, *assiduously.* Visiting this babalawo helped me think about that fact. What exhaustion must be required to passionately deny that which has shaped so much of who you are? Maybe this is part of the White evangelical discipline of prayer. To absolve the self-denial. To drown it in catharsis. White Cubans have no need. But I do not think that is a mark of virtue as much as it is a marker of nationalisms. Countries get accorded races, no matter how multiracial they are. And Cuba is Blackish brown. The US is White; we (Black people) are its built-in other.

In the Yoruba tradition, you only need the name of an ancestor to venerate them. Ibaye. I called the names of all of the ancestors I could recall at the babalawo's direction. You do not need to have a census document or a surname, or the year of their birth. The tradition allows received knowledge in the absence of Western systems of recording. And perhaps most importantly it is a faith that centers around character rather than status. All of this seems to me to be part of why it has lived in the diaspora and also why so many of my friends, people I have mentioned throughout this book, people born into Catholicism, Protestantism, and agnosticism, have found themselves drawn to Yoruba practices. And when I call the name of my ancestor named Pink, or the two named General or Queene, or Easter and Esther, both names twice in my family tree, the boldness of their appellations tells me something about how I am supposed to hold them in high regard. That alone makes the action divine.

And at the same time, I understand why, for African Americans in the United States, the Kongo faith has been more resilient, even if we often aren't aware of it. The way we think of conversion, a journey to standing at the crossroads between life and death that strikes us down and rebirths us, the way we operate in spiritual practice as though we stand between divinity and the ordinary, the way we walk in circles when we dance, and wear crosses about our necks, and invite spirit possession, and have permanent diagrams drawn on our bodies in homage to the ancestors? That all comes, primarily, from the Kongo root. But still we blend.

I walked back and forth across the Malecón along the sea, over and over again, for miles. I ate snow cones and watched the fishermen who kept buckets of fish that I would have thought necessary to throw back for being too small. There was a familiar toughness that differed from how people told me it would be. I'd been sold a fantasy, akin to how people describe New Orleans. Havana was not a nonstop party of continuous celebration. Folks talked shit and hung out, sang and made do. A young West African woman, who'd been raised in the US and had recently moved to Cuba, complained to me, "This is not socialism. This is state capitalism. The cops still harass Black people. The rich white people still live in their fancy apartments." She was twenty years my junior, and she sounded like the revolutionaries I grew up with, twenty-plus years my senior.

I can tell you a story of how and why this is. How wealthy White Cubans fled the revolution and were re-baptized White in the US and have fed inequality on the island by sending money to their relatives. Meanwhile others have to make do with resources that are limited because of the endless embargo, the ongoing fallout of the end of the Soviet Union, and the steady global erosion of socialist possibility. Even if a nation isn't capitalist, the global marketplace is. There's really no avoiding it now. The heartbreak of a stymied revolution, and the failure of a nation to eradicate the badges of servitude and the legacy of slavery, is what it is two times over. The difference, this young woman reminded me, is that sometimes *something* is actually done about racism in Cuba. Unlike, she opined, in the US.

Julia de Burgos wrote in her poem "Presencia de amor in the isla" (Presence of love in the island) the following words about Cuba:

I remember that once the stars talked to me
From a buried corner, without a glance and without a
    voyage
Something like a world detained in its history
Like a trill astray, like a wing without a bird . . .

Even in the most virtuous of moments, the legacy of the twentieth century and its promises careens between bittersweet and bile.

I ran out of money. And this mattered because there was no straightforward way for me to get money in Cuba as an American.

The staff of the US embassy had been moved out of Havana. American bank cards don't work there because of US policy. I know, I should have known this. I mean, not only had I studied Cold War history, Cuban culture, and music, I'd spent my whole life around people who traveled to Cuba when it wasn't legal to do so. What can I say? Impulse weakens judgment. Anyway, because of the relations between Cuba and the United States, I couldn't get cash from any bank, or use my credit card. So I had to find someone back in the states who knew a Cuban citizen and could get money to them, to get for me. And I did that. More details, as with Frederick Douglass's recounting of the Underground Railroad, are impolitic or even dangerous to offer. Maybe at a later date.

The point of even telling you this is that my arrogant error let me see another side of Cuban life. Finding my way to friends of friends who helped me, I saw the lines at Western Union; the empty shelves in supermarkets that were, merely a decade ago, stocked; the bodies, which are Southern and Caribbean bodies, which are the bodies of a tangle of Africa and Europe and Indigenous, in housedresses, rollers in the head, chanclas or strapped sandals, babies sleeping slung over softened bellies, people stopping and telling stories, and most of all waiting to be attended to, waiting for an influx of dollars. I saw elders and smiled at babies and heard more stories of lives than I had anticipated.

And I did something else that mattered a lot, for me. I visited a woman in exile, a Black American woman. And it was not Assata Shakur. It is worth mentioning for the purposes of this book that most of the Black revolutionaries from the 1960s who fled to Cuba were from the Deep South. William Lee Brent, from Louisiana; Eldridge Cleaver, originally from Arkansas; Lorenzo Kom'boa Ervin, from Chattanooga; Huey P. Newton, originally from Monroe, Louisiana; Robert F. Williams, from Monroe, North Carolina; and Assata Shakur, who grew up, in part, in Wilmington, North Carolina—these were people whose connection to the land in places with large

Black populations made Black nationalism a much more distinctive reality. I would say that many of them could imagine creating independent Black nations and new political economies precisely because they had lived up close to the history of slavery, in the US South. And that was a colonial-like condition in many ways. And so the revolutionary ideal of Cuba wasn't so far afield. They stood in the tradition of Martin Delany, the West Virginian Black nationalist Union soldier who wrote *Blake*. They could visualize insurrection and revolution on the land where the Civil War had been fought and beyond it, too. In fact, among the rumors about Assata over the years includes the claim that she returned to the States covertly in order to claim title to her ancestral land in North Carolina. Property, land, and freedom are all intertwined for us.

But this woman I visited was not, in fact, Southern. She was a Northerner through and through.

My taxi driver did not want to stay to see if I got into her house. She sped off the moment I stepped out of the car. I walked up to the complex and shouted. I said who I was looking for, "Estoy buscando . . ." "Sube!" a man told me to come up. I walked up five flights, following the bass-heavy voice. On the third landing, a small man stood and pointed up. It was my first feeling of trepidation since I'd been in Cuba. And it wasn't him. Cuba felt as safe to me as people had told me it was. I was nervous because of the relationship between my nation and hers, nervous about surveillance and systems of power and how they might be wielded in the lives of two Black American women.

Inside her hearth was a slice of Black life that was distinctly US and diasporic at once. We moved between Spanish and English. And we talked shit along the way. Music, politics, homesickness, all of it came up. We traded thoughts on Malcolm X. "He was the first one to really embrace Fidel," she said. I told her I had been sitting in Birmingham's airport with my sons when we heard Fidel had died. It was announced on the television screens showing old footage, and along the wall, cat-a-corner from the television screen, there was a video montage of Black protestors in Birmingham civil rights–era protests. The same period was reflected back simultaneously, one with acclaim, one with derision, both with the idea of freedom.

We also talked books. She asked about the ones I'd written and was preparing to write. And then we got to the topic of Jackson, Mississippi, and the election of Chokwe Antar Lumumba as its mayor.

"That was a victory."

"Yes, it was."

It brought tears to our eyes. I suspect just as it was not the first time for me, it wasn't the first for her either. You take the victories. You cherish them. Because there is so much to still endure. My friend—and she became that in a matter of minutes—had built a life here, but she'd missed so much of her life there, in the US, because of her version of revolutionary dreams. She told me that she still considered herself a "New Afrikan," though her children were "African Americans." She accepted their choice, but loved her own. She saw herself not simply as an exiled citizen of the United States but as a daughter of this whole region, as a figure in the history of this conquest, this slavery, this theft, whose life purpose is to undo it all.

I gave her some money. I slid it to her in a medicine bottle, and she laughed. "See, nobody's ready for how slick us Black people from the US are. Cubans think they slick, but they ain't got nothing on us!" She laughed a drinker's raspy laugh and told me a story about a visit from one of her good friends, decades prior. They'd gone out to a club, and at the end of the night, the taxi driver didn't want to take them all the way back to her apartment. Her friend, a Black American woman, insisted. The driver refused. They argued, and then he pulled out a machete. Her friend was unfazed. "Motherfucker, I said take us home!" And she told me, she guessed he'd figured "these Black women are crazy if they ain't scared of a machete. I better take them home." So he did. We laughed again, to tears.

She got tired. Standing was hard; walking was harder. Illness had worn her body down. A melancholy settled, and the light streaming through the living room window waned. She looked at me, in a way that older Black women reserve for younger Black women, and told me, "You are so beautiful." I will not have that look always. I am approaching being an elder myself, and my job will be to look upon younger Black women and say "You are so beautiful" and mean it. History will make it my turn to return that favor. And I will do so because it has been one of the most sustaining gifts of my life, that look of love that is a witness to everything we have endured and everything we have held onto despite it all. We do not go gently into the night; we spend the final years and days imparting everything we have learned to make this thing survivable. We teach people how to live with the daily heartbreak on your chest, and still laugh and find the pleasure in cursing out somebody who deserves it. We teach you how to remember the moments of humiliation sliding down your face while not killing anybody or yourself too much, to hear the snatch of fabric or the snicker, the feel of blood stuck on you, the shoving, and still push up your chin. As an elder, you have to look for the ones who are told they are wrong, find them, and reassure them, even at the very end, when more than anything you just want to rest and watch TV and escape because you have been disregarded and thrown away. It is an honor nonetheless.

I came home. She died.

CONCLUSION

I PLANNED FROM THE BEGINNING to end by going home. But I couldn't go home. COVID-19 hit, so 2020 was the first year of my life in which I didn't spend a single day in Alabama. Or anywhere below the Mason-Dixon Line. We were relegated indoors, fearful of a killer virus. Frontline workers faced a horror that the rest of us witnessed on television, or else in the privacy of our homes as we, or our loved ones, were laid low. In cities we heard the ambulances. On social media we heard rumors more often than information. It was a terrifying time filled with more grief than we could have imagined. In May we all learned about George Floyd, the latest in what seemed to be an endless parade of deaths of unarmed Black people at the hands of police officers. He'd survived COVID but not cops. Nine minutes and twenty-nine seconds with police officer Derek Chauvin's knee on his chest. Too long and so short to suffocate a life.

He yelled, "Mama."

I could hear he was from down South.

This time the protests were global, stretching far beyond Minneapolis. We had been inside. Contemplating. And feeling, and fearful. And the wail that rose up reached into the depths of our grief, and our outrage about a world that seems to be ordered in a way that refuses to prioritize care, love, or even decency was unleashed.

As is part of the standard choreography, news stations rushed to find any infraction Floyd had committed. I do not understand this impulse. At best it is a bizarre effort at evenhandedness, as though execution is a casual punishment. At worst it is the same old American way of declaring Black people unworthy. Theft and incarceration were featured. Blazoned on screen and paper: Floyd was incarcerated nine times on charges ranging from drug possession and theft to armed robbery. Some commentators noted his later religious devotion, trying to be fair. He was one of a group of men who left Houston for Minneapolis, seeking opportunity.

A year later, we were still inside. Still grieving. And the officer who killed him, Derek Chauvin, was tried and then convicted of his murder. Rare. Remarkable. Five other police killings became national news the same week. Unremarkable. Common.

Floyd was a year younger than me. For all the digging into Floyd's past, relatively scant attention was paid to his membership in the Screwed Up Click as a rapper named Big Floyd. Like many, he was a follower of the late DJ Screw, a trained musician who fell in love with deejaying. Screw slowed down and restructured classic songs, laying them over each other and mixing in the voices of local artists. Originator of Houston's signature hip hop sound, Screw died from its celebrated intoxicant: lean, purple drank, syrup. These are various recipes of liquid narcotic that blend the sugary beverages first made by Southern pharmacists with the often emergency-room-prescribed codeine syrup. Like Screw, Floyd struggled with addiction. He tried to start over in Minneapolis. He struggled still. He caught COVID. He survived. Then he was murdered.

Context has its place.

Floyd's home was Houston. It's yet another Southern place

through which one can tell the story of the nation. I want to share a bit about Houston. It's just a fragment and a reminder that I have left out so many stories of the South, so many places, themes, and dynamics. But this is a good place to meet the end of the book. Because our mobility—trains, planes, and automobiles—owes so much to Houston. And mobility is what we missed in COVID, and also what, I guess, we ought to fear in America. Because going to Minneapolis didn't really allow Floyd to escape the trap. It set the stage.

By the 1890s, Texas was settled into the fabric of the nation, or mostly anyway. A Jim Crow industrialist class ruled. Texas wealth was concentrated in the port city of Galveston. But in 1900, Galveston suffered the deadliest natural disaster in US history, a hurricane that left somewhere between 6,000 and 12,000 people dead, a fourth of the people homeless, and the entire city in shambles. The storm started as a wave off the coast of West Africa. It traveled through the Windward Islands, over the Dominican Republic, skirted Cuba, and then strengthened in the Gulf of Mexico before landing upon Galveston, the jewel of Texas, and razing it. By now you know, such rising and falling of status is not uncommon in Southern history.

Galveston sank. Houston rose. Less than a year later, in January of 1901, the gusher came. On Spindletop Hill, oil shot out of the ground. The soil in most of Houston is black gumbo, dark heavy clay. When it gets wet, it stays wet. And it's hard to work for farming. But something farther below yielded more. Eons ago, living beings—algae, plankton, and plants—died. Their remains cascaded down to the bottom of bodies of waters. Held there, over millions of years, under the pressure of earth piling on top, their carcasses turned into a viscous mass that eked its way through rock pores. The ground is like a hardened sponge; if you drill it, oil pushes its way out. At Spindletop, it took nine days to harness the force of what would be called "black gold" and make Houston, Texas, rich.

There were millions of barrels in the first two years. Global companies you know, like Texaco, Gulf, and Mobil, began with the stunning abundance of that first gush. Oil has an energy density ten times that of dynamite. So we've built our society and shaped our world around its power. People even started driving around in the new technology, cars, in the early twentieth century because they had the fuel to do so. Abundance created desire.

Houston both had this remarkable new abundance and sustained and built upon some old ways of making money. For example, in 1916, the American Cotton company, the world's largest cotton exchange, was founded here. While prominent people wielded power locally as well as internationally, working-class people sought their fortunes in Houston. Black people from rural areas migrated to the city during the Great Migration, making it the Southern city with the largest Black population, larger than that of Atlanta or New Orleans, by 1940. Its two HBCUs—Prairie View, a land grant university founded in 1876 just outside of Houston, and Texas Southern, founded in 1927 in Houston's Third Ward, a middle-class Black enclave—also made it a hub of Black aspiration.

Houston's prosperity as a result of the oil industry guaranteed its prominence. It also created desires that would become desperation. We are an enormously oil-dependent nation. And our foreign policy, developed over the course of the twentieth century, reflected and reflects this. The oil-rich regions of the Middle East were eyed greedily by American and European oil companies in the early twentieth century. A consistent anxiety, when it comes to US foreign policy, has been how to sustain access to that oil, and the possibility that governmental actors in the Middle East would control oil prices, particularly in the Cold War years and whenever Middle Eastern nations considered nationalizing their resources. These anxieties led to an American habit of regional military interference, of supporting fundamentalists and dictators, of funding insurgents, and of dissuading socialism by any means necessary. The Iran-Contra scandal pivoted around these fears and interests.

When the Reagan administration illegally sold arms to Iran, betraying an embargo initiated by President Carter because Iran had taken fifty-two Americans hostage in 1979, they did so to provide weapons to Iran for Iran's planned invasion of Iraq. With the proceeds of the arms sale, the US government covertly flooded Nicaragua with financial support for military juntas that resisted the rise of the Sandinistas, a socialist movement in Nicaragua. Though Oliver North, a Texan and member of Reagan's National Security Council, took the fall for the administration, over the years the tangle of corruption has been revealed to have included Bush family oil interests, cocaine trafficking between Colombia and Nicaragua that was aided by the CIA, and the funneling of crack into Black neighborhoods in the United States. We've never stopped living the complications caused by oil dependence. We are embroiled, seemingly forever, in political choices motivated by the control of oil, a word that we laypeople say with little thought to the consequences of how it binds us.

In this hemisphere, the shifting borders of Texas, and the interests of its power brokers, make Mexicans, Central Americans, and Indigenous people part of both the history and present of Texas. But the numbers of Mexicans and Central Americans living inside of Houston increased dramatically during the labor shortages caused by the World Wars. The historic Mexican community in Houston began in the Second Ward and eventually moved into the First and Sixth as well. In the 1970s, around the time when my uncle settled there, large numbers of Mexicans and Tejanos from other parts of the state were moving to Houston as well, along with African Americans from Louisiana and Arkansas. There was a lot of work to be found, particularly in the oil business, at least until the bust of the 1980s. The vectors of modern Houston had been settled. There were the poor; there were the extremely wealthy; there was the professional class, many of whom served the industry that built the city's wealth and influence and guided its political moves.

Today Houston is one of the most diverse and cosmopolitan US cities. Anglos, White people who are not Latino make up 24.6 percent of the population. African Americans make up 22.5 percent, and the Latino population is 44.8 percent of the city. Asian Americans make up nearly 7 percent of the population, and Houston has the largest Nigerian population in the United States. Nigerians have aggregated there due to two economic sectors: oil, which is also the source of much Nigerian wealth, and health care. Due to the US system of immigration's preferences, Nigerian Americans, the most highly educated demographic in the United States, are admitted into this country on the basis of their educational attainment and class status before arriving. Thus, the Nigerian community is quite prosperous among communities of color.

Houston may be a shining city. But George Floyd had to leave Houston to get his life together. After the tragedy in Minnesota, elegies came from down home: Tobe Nwigwe, a rapper who has garnered a large following on Instagram, sang his outrage. "Try Jesus, not me. 'Cause I throw hands." Along with his partner, Ivory, known as Fat, and producer LaNell Grant, they provide in the square frames of Instagram a theological service under the hashtag #gettwistedsundays. It is profane, socially critical, gospel-inflected, and unapologetic hip hop.

Their forty-four-second song, "I need you to," was one of the plethora dedicated to Breonna Taylor. And it, too, resonated with the spiritual anguish, rage, and steeliness of the moment when we stepped out of the house, facing the virus to protest.

Nwigwe, Fat, and Nell's seafoam-green Instagram palette dazzled in the 2020 BET cypher. It was an all-virtual show, and their performance was a standout. Dressed in a full-length coat adorned with the images of Breonna Taylor, George Floyd, and Elijah McClain, tall and dark-skinned Tobe stood alongside Jabari Johnson playing the electric guitar and singing. Johnson, whose first name means "brave" in Arabic, has served as lead guitarist for the choir at Bishop T. D. Jakes Potter's House evangelical megachurch in Dallas. But this performance, while sanctified, was far from pious. Tobe rapped, providing a concise portrait of aspiration and childhood adversity in Houston. But it was this part that was the fever pitch: "Shout out to those who told me Tobe was a pet name." It took your mind right to that moment in Alex Haley's *Roots*, when his African ancestor Kunta was brutalized into submission with the name Toby. When asked, "What's your name?" he kept on answering back "Kunta," defiantly, until the whip became too much. He submitted quietly to "Toby," blood pouring.

Responding to the call "What's your name?" Nwigwe answers back: "TOBECHUKWU DUBEM NWIGWE is my correct name. Praise God for follies of my colleagues who embody everything that I overcame . . ." It was an African turn and return. Literally. Tobe is Nigerian American, with a full-on Houston hood drawl, sparkling teeth, and athlete's gait. Even his dental grills are sometimes emerald along with diamond and gold. The women in their chorus chanted and supplemented the action, wearing tiered skirts in chiffon. Their choreography veered off-kilter and then back in unison. Fat led them in, giddily celebrating that Beyoncé had acknowledged their gifts. Tobe spoke of his aspiration to get on a track with Atlanta hip hop legend André 3000. It was earnest and hopeful.

Isn't that what we want, that irrepressible hope? Maybe it isn't just an American mythos. Maybe it's an American wonder. After all, from the bottom, from the depths, from the fields, from the ashes, hope just keeps on rising and radiating off sweat-glowing skin in Southern heat.

A nation is an imagined community. The shared narrative and common mythos of countrypeople produce fellow feeling and common identities. In the United States, our heterogeneity, our size, our federalism, and our ever-present conflicts have always splintered some of these myths. We intuitively know the claims to singularity are platitudes.

I needed to witness Floyd and Nwigwe in 2020, in the first of my forty-nine years without setting foot in Alabama. After all, Imani, you returned, ravenous, repeatedly, year after year. It is your anchor. But you have learned that the anchor doesn't just belong to you. Nor does it belong to the ever more perfect union. It belongs to possibility. It belongs to the ones breathing dirty air. It belongs to the bombed. It belongs to the children wearing lace socks and charred flesh. It belongs to the untended graves. It belongs to George Floyd's baby, and Breonna Taylor's mama. And your responsibility to history hasn't receded, no matter how far from it you travel.

You scan your neighborhood, Ensley, in your mind: its soft pale-colored houses, its small yards, gray block pavement, and peeping blades of green. You can see it from here. You can learn it all over. Sun Ra, that eccentric jazz master who walked the same blocks, once told us what he wanted to do with the Du Boisian veil, that persistently pitch-perfect metaphor of the color line, the divider not just of the nation but, in Du Bois's estimation, of the world. He wanted to pull aside the veil, to reach to a deeper truth, to see it not as a dividing line but as a portal into something new.

Dreaming isn't dead. It can't be. We can do it anew. Me and you, both of us are required. I believe writing can be a moral instrument if it asks you to do more than read. Do you? How many times will you witness people being starved or worked to death, driven out of their homelands, the land blasted and lives destroyed, and be only quietly horrified? When will you finally be repulsed enough to throw a wrench in the works? When will you allow curiosity and integrity to tip over into urgency? I'm asking you. I'm asking myself to dig deep enough for the truth to flood in. Let's sing those blues.

Like Murray said:

The objective of the blues musician is to get rid of the blues; is to stomp the blues and of course you stomp the blues not with utmost violence but with elegance. The more elegant you can be, the more effective you'll be at getting rid of the blues. Because it's a matter of having the blues on the one hand; that is, feeling despondent, feeling sad, feeling melancholy, feeling defeated, feeling out of it. That's having the blues, that's having the blues as such. Whereas blues music has to do with playing the blues. It's the right word for music because music is an art form. You can't get to art in any reenactment—you have a ritual, you can have religious reenactment and so forth, but when you get to the playful reenactment, you're on your way to fine art, and that's the most effective way . . .

Art is nothing more and nothing less than the human application of skill and imagination to creation. Homesick and lonely, I still had art at hand. I danced before my Instagram feed and bedroom mirror. I was snatched back into memory. I wondered what my dead were doing. I wondered if I would live. I cried a lot. I worried more. I tried to understand. I wrote and rewrote these words. I held on.

If America is to be salvific, it can only be so because underneath our skyscrapers lie the people who have tasted the red clay, the loamy soil. Lashed, hidden, running, captured. Crucified for gain, bloodying the soil. If their dreams can become "we" dreams, hope will spring. "Greatness" is such an egotistical and dangerous word. But in the land of big dreams and bigger lies, we love greatness anyway. And if we want it, if we aren't afraid to grab it, we have to look South, to America.

ACKNOWLEDGMENTS

WITH ABUNDANT GRATITUDE FOR Tanya McKinnon and the McKinnon literary team, and for my Ecco publishing community, especially Sara Birmingham, a truly extraordinary editor; TJ Calhoun, for helping the book cohere; Mary Beth Constant, who did so much more than copyedit; as well as Dan Halpern and Denise Oswald, who brought me into the fold. My loved ones, including everyone in the Perry family, were integral to this project. I am especially grateful for those of you who in one way or another had a direct hand in this book. That includes: every single person who has ever spent the night at 2345; my Princeton AAS students, especially those from the South and Midwest, who heard and responded to all of these ideas with sharp critical thinking and warmth; and loved-one interlocutors Michéle Alexandre, Mayor Richard Arrington, Yaba Blay, Regina Bradley, Sarah Monique Broom, Adrienne Marie Brown, Tarana Burke, Judge and Mrs. U. W. Clemon, Michelle Clemon, Johnny Coley, Angela Davis, Dave Dennis Jr. (and his parents, by proxy), Gina Dent, Dr. Walter O. Evans and Linda Evans, Tom Gardner, Eddie S. Glaude Jr., Gail and Marshall Goldberg, Reena Goldthree, Farah Jasmine Griffin, DaMaris

Hill, André Holland, Assata Lake, Carolyn Lake, Kiese Laymon, Shantrelle Lewis, Mitch McEwen, Adam McNeil, Dwayne Miller, Linda Mizell, Freida Outlaw, my brother Chris Craig Patterson, Marva Perry, Thelma Perry, who is an educator and historian in everything she does, Jacki Perry, a healer of bodies and spirits, the brilliant Theresa Perry, who fed me every book imaginable and just as many stories, Darien Pollock, Melynda Pryce, my soul sister Jillian Robinson, Karl Schaffer, Keeanga-Yamahtta Taylor, and my father by rearing Steven Whitman—especially because from the time I understood language until the time he passed, he never stopped telling me what a gift it was for me to be from Birmingham. One of the last things he said to me was that he hoped I would eventually return home.

My grandmother Neida Garner Perry remains my muse. There are not enough words of thanksgiving to capture the depth of the inheritance she left me.

My sons for each having the kind of beauty, intellect, and integrity that drives me to become better with every effort. Wholly unique and yet both soul-nurturing forces in the world. I listen to your every critique because I know it always comes from love and wisdom. Thank you, Freeman Diallo Perry Rabb and Issa Garner Rabb.

Finally, my ancestral tree is stripped and even bare in places. At least that is the case according to the rules of the West. But according to the traditions of my people(s), I have a lineage that is abundant beyond measure. I choose us. Ibaye, I bow my head in humility and appreciation from this side of the crossroads.

INDEX